Praise for *Pawpaw: In Search of America's Forgotten Fruit*

"With *Pawpaw*, Andrew Moore walks firmly in the steps of the great literary journalists John McPhee and Mark Kurlansky. Stories deftly told, research deeply done, this book is an engaging ride through the haunts of a fruit many Easterners quietly — secretly, even — gorge themselves on each autumn. A ripe pawpaw is as illicit as Persephone's pomegranate, and Moore captures that passion well."

— **HANK SHAW**, 2013 James Beard Award winner, Best Food Blog, and author of *Hunt, Gather, Cook: Finding the Forgotten Feast* and *Duck, Duck, Goose: Recipes and Techniques for Cooking Ducks and Geese*

"This book is a love song singing the praises of a unique, delicious, and once-abundant fruit that has been sadly neglected. Andrew Moore takes us on a very personal journey investigating how and why North America's largest indigenous fruit largely disappeared and documenting efforts to revive it. *Pawpaw* is a pleasure to read, and if you do, you'll probably find yourself searching for and loving these delectable fruits."

— **SANDOR ELLIX KATZ**, author of *The Art of Fermentation*

"*Pawpaw: In Search of America's Forgotten Fruit* is a fun and well-researched, informative romp through the culture and horticulture of this uncommon fruit. Uncommon, yes, but who would have imagined that there were and are quite a few other pawpaw nuts out there? If you don't know pawpaws, you should, and you will."

— **LEE REICH**, PhD, author of *Uncommon Fruits for Every Garden*

"Like a gumshoe detective, Andrew Moore tracks down a mystery at once horticultural and culinary: Why is the pawpaw, America's largest indigenous fruit, so little known? The answer, like the fruit's beguiling taste, proves multi-layered and slippery, and after reading Moore's engaging account, I'm ready to light out for pawpaw country myself in search of this homegrown original."

— **LANGDON COOK**, author of *The Mushroom Hunters: On the Trail of an Underground America*

"Tropical growers have many shade crops to choose from, like cacao and coffee. Here in eastern North America we have our own luscious fruit for shady places — the pawpaw. Andrew Moore's *Pawpaw* tells the story of this fruit and the people working to bring it to our gardens, markets, and restaurants. It's the story of an eastern native fruit on its way to domestication, finally earning the place in our hearts and our cuisine that it deserves."

— **ERIC TOENSMEIER**, author of *Paradise Lot* and *Perennial Vegetables*

"This book took me on an enchanting and engaging ride through the history, folklore, and science of a neglected but magical food plant. Andrew Moore shows us, in delightful prose and a wealth of fascinating stories, the role that the under-appreciated pawpaw has played in North American culture. I was constantly surprised to learn of the quiet influence the pawpaw has had on the people and environment around it, and like the author, am hopeful that it can find its rightful place among the better-known fruits that we all love."

— **TOBY HEMENWAY**, author of *Gaia's Garden*
and *The Permaculture City*

"America, get ready for pawpaw mania! Andrew Moore's book tells the definitive story of the wild fruit that is part of our nation's heritage, and in the process the author joins the ranks of food-preservationist heroes. Prepare to be overwhelmed with longing for the sweet scent and taste of the pawpaw."

— **POPPY TOOKER**, host of *Louisiana Eats!*

"Andrew Moore has done an amazing job demystifying one of America's most misunderstood and neglected fruits. *Pawpaw* deftly navigates between his own personal journey and the facts and history of the fruit, leaving readers — including chefs interested in heritage and tradition — with a true sense of how important it is to embrace this indigenous treasure."

— **TRAVIS MILTON**, chef and co-owner of
Shovel and Pick, Richmond, Virginia

"Here is proof that culinary odysseys don't always need to involve globetrotting or the pursuit of rare, exotic foodstuffs. But, then again, in his pursuit of the lowly American pawpaw, Andrew Moore reminds us that America was once considered an exotic destiny on its own, and has always had more than its fair share of culinary rarities."

— **DAMON LEE FOWLER**, author of *Essentials of Southern Cooking*
and *Beans, Greens & Sweet Georgia Peaches*

"I was fortunate to have experienced early in life, from my Monacan Indian and Black community friends, the joy of the pawpaw, as well as maypops, chinquapins, mushrooms, and huckleberries. Andy's book is one of the road maps to the resurrection of another rooted American food commodity. *Pawpaw* will generate enthusiasm for this unsung fruit and hopefully engender passion in a few."

— **TOM BURFORD**, author of *Apples of North America:
Exceptional Varieties for Growers, Gardeners, and Cooks*

PAWPAW

PAWPAW

IN SEARCH OF AMERICA'S FORGOTTEN FRUIT

ANDREW MOORE

FOREWORD BY MICHAEL W. TWITTY

CHELSEA GREEN PUBLISHING
WHITE RIVER JUNCTION, VERMONT

Project Manager: Bill Bokermann
Developmental Editor: Michael Metivier
Copy Editor: Laura Jorstad
Proofreader: Helen Walden
Indexer: Peggy Holloway
Designer: Melissa Jacobson

Printed in the United States of America.
First printing July, 2015
10 9 8 7 6 5 4 3 2 1   15 16 17 18 19

Our Commitment to Green Publishing
Chelsea Green sees publishing as a tool for cultural change and ecological stewardship. We strive to align our book manufacturing practices with our editorial mission and to reduce the impact of our business enterprise on the environment. We print our books and catalogs on chlorine-free recycled paper, using vegetable-based inks whenever possible. This book may cost slightly more because it was printed on paper that contains recycled fiber, and we hope you'll agree that it's worth it. Chelsea Green is a member of the Green Press Initiative (www.greenpressinitiative.org), a nonprofit coalition of publishers, manufacturers, and authors working to protect the world's endangered forests and conserve natural resources. *Pawpaw* was printed on paper supplied by Maple Press that contains 100% postconsumer recycled fiber.

Library of Congress Cataloging-in-Publication Data
Moore, Andrew, 1985- author.
Pawpaw : in search of America's forgotten fruit / Andrew Moore.
   pages cm
Includes bibliographical references and index.
ISBN 978-1-60358-596-5 (hardcover) -- ISBN 978-1-60358-597-2 (ebook)
1. Pawpaw--United States. 2. Pawpaw--United States--History. I.
Title.

QK495.A6M66 2015
583'.22--dc23

                    2015012301

Chelsea Green Publishing
85 North Main Street, Suite 120
White River Junction, VT 05001
(802) 295-6300
www.chelseagreen.com

FOR ERIKA

CONTENTS

Foreword   xi

Prologue   xiii

PART I

PAWPAWS IN HISTORY

1: What's a Pawpaw?   1

2: A Brief History of Pawpaws in America   9

3: Toward Domestication   23

4: A Tale of Two Fruits   29

PART II

PAWPAWS TO THE PEOPLE

5: Johnny Pawpawseed   37

6: Hunting the Lost Ketter Fruit   47

7: Peterson's Gambit   61

8: In the Orchard   69

9: The Ohio Pawpaw Festival   85

10: Tobacco, Acetogenins, and Ice Cream   99

11: The Ohio Pawpaw Growers Association   113

12: Into the Woods: A New Orchard   127

PART III

WAY DOWN YONDER: TRAVELS IN THE PAWPAW BELT

13: St. Louis   139

14: Historic Virginia   143

15: North Carolina   149

16: Down South   165

17: Appalachia   205

18: Cherokee   221

19: North and Midwest   227

Epilogue   241

Acknowledgments   247

APPENDIX 1: Pawpaw Ice Cream   249

APPENDIX 2: A Selection of Pawpaw Nurseries   251

APPENDIX 3: Cultivar Profiles and Impressions   255

Notes   265

Index   281

WAY DOWN YONDER IN THE PAWPAW PATCH

Where, oh, where is little Susie?
Where, oh, where is little Susie?
Where, oh, where is little Susie?
Way down yonder in the pawpaw patch.

Come on boys, let's go find her
Come on boys, let's go find her
Come on boys, let's go find her
Way down yonder in the pawpaw patch.

Pickin' up pawpaws, puttin' 'em in a basket
Pickin' up pawpaws, puttin' 'em in a basket
Pickin' up pawpaws, puttin' 'em in a basket
Way down yonder in the pawpaw patch

— TRADITIONAL AMERICAN FOLK SONG

FOREWORD

The past twenty years have witnessed an upsurge and return to wild foods not seen since the 1970s. For many, the exploration of the indigenous American landscape as a source of rediscovered food has become a passion on both vernacular and professional levels. At the very least it is a call to conserve our heritage ecosystems while utilizing them sustainably and responsibly. In my own work aiming to restore the culinary heritage of African Americans before the Civil War, the call to return to the land is a search for redemption. In many ways, all American food cultures suffer from a legacy as damaged by cultural amnesia as much as they are by ecological ignorance and irresponsibility.

Thus enters the pawpaw, *Asimina triloba,* which I first learned about in the Foxfire series and then traced through a dozen odd guides to edible plants. Irregularly shaped, suggestively rather than definitively flavored, the pawpaw is an anomaly in so many ways. It's a tropical tree in a temperate landscape that thrives in the understory rather than transitional zones on the forest edge or in open fields. It's a triple threat — it gives food, thrives in shade, and provides shade. It's a slow food that we wish came faster, but unlike the rest of the plant kingdom, it stubbornly demands its devotees retain their patience and sense of seasonal novelty.

In my own work I saw pawpaws described in early America as fit only for "Negroes and Indians." As I explored the landscapes left by Black communities, I saw these treasure trees growing outside of the dwellings of enslaved people and clustering close to their settlements. It was the pawpaw, cognate to species known to their ancestors in West Africa, that along with the persimmon, honey locust, and others gave them diversity in a diet built on nutritional monotony, and enabled them to nourish themselves on trails North to freedom.

In a food tradition that documents itself with seeds left in the ground, whispers of folk songs and random tidbits from scattered narratives, the pawpaw was at best for me a pleasantly exotic footnote. I didn't know it had any life beyond the past. How could I reconstruct a part of the cuisine that nobody seemed to eat anymore? Then I met a fellow young seeker named Andy Moore, and I never looked at this fruit the same way again.

In a time when finding the next hot indigenous wild, heirloom, or heritage food is often a self-aggrandizing exercise in staking territory in the edible past, Andy Moore gives to us a pure mission in this tidy, heartfelt work. This is not a pat on the back. Pawpaw is at once a prayer for our willingness to preserve nature, history, memory and taste, and a poem — an ode to the ancestors, the conservationists, and the cooks in kitchens humble and high who want to keep this remarkable "poor man's banana," a centerpiece of truly American food.

Andy has undertaken a true odyssey. His interdisciplinary approach necessarily incorporates biology, folklore, anthropology, culinary technique, and the hidden histories of pioneer, African American, and Native American foodways. The greatest benefit to the reader is that it is not a tome based on other tomes. It is an actual journey, a book written in pawpaw seeds and footprints across eastern America. You can walk where Andy walked, and if you do, you will discover, as he did, the bewildering narratives that such a stunning food can engender. This is more than a celebration of an American food; it is equally in awe of the everyday people who incorporate it into their identities.

No fruit has captured the imagination of the forager community in the past twenty years like the pawpaw. I get asked about pawpaw like no other wild fruit in creation. With this at once serious and joyful account of the resurrection of an odd and storied fruit, Andy has given its seekers both a guide and a mandate. He invites us to live interdependently with *Asimina triloba,* making us a part of its future even as it challenges the imagination of the new American plate.

— MICHAEL W. TWITTY, culinary historian
April, 2015

PROLOGUE

On my first pawpaw hunt, I had no idea what to look for. I'd been told that the pawpaw was the largest of all edible fruits native to the United States, but had never tasted or even seen one. I hoped this day would be the day.

Yellow blooms of goldenrod lit the field leading to the edge of the woods. A path wound beneath the canopy of oak and hickory — a lush, green, late-summer forest. I dodged mud puddles, poison ivy, clouds of lazy gnats hovering at eye level. Leaves and twigs crunched under my steps. Then, after just a few minutes, I saw the distinct, symmetrical leaves of a pawpaw tree, exactly as a friend had described them; I'd made it to a sprawling grove. More than a foot long and a deep, vibrant green, the leaves are also among the largest in the eastern forest. From where I stood, the trees seemed to be the only thing in the understory. As far as I could see: nothing but pawpaw.

I smelled the fruit — a sweet, tropical aroma — before I could see it. None of the pawpaw trees were very big. Some were ten feet tall, their trunks smooth and gray, but still no thicker than five inches in diameter. My hand easily wrapped around the first tree I shook, feeling for the weight of fruit. I looked up, and through the jungle-like canopy a single pawpaw was lit by the sun. I reached for where it clung to the end of a skinny branch, and at my touch the fruit fell neatly into my hand as if it had been waiting for the slightest movement to come along and release it. A gust of wind might have done the same. I had no other fruit on hand to compare and declare the pawpaw the largest in the United States but it definitely had heft — it was no berry, no wispy puff of sugar. It looked like an expensive import on a grocery store shelf, not something you could pick for free. I looked down and noticed there were two more on the ground. At the base of an oak tree, a third. Scooping them up felt like I was getting away with something, like I'd just discovered someone's secret stash of goods. I couldn't have realized it then, but in just those brief few moments I became hooked on pawpaws. And I hadn't even eaten one.

The pawpaws still in the trees were green, reminding me of unripe mangoes. On the ground, the bruised fruit was purple and gray, and quite soft. With the push of my finger their skins broke. Some were shaped like eggs, others like overstuffed peanuts. While many were as big as peaches and apples, others were smaller, teardrop-like runts, no bigger than figs. I placed my hat, which was filled with fruit, on the ground and relieved myself of my shirt-turned-basket as well. It was time to eat.

Not knowing the right method, I tore one in half, which was easy despite the large seeds in the center. The pulp-filled, sticky interior was colored a soft orange, like cantaloupe. I wasn't expecting such vibrancy, which seemed out of place in the Ohio woods. Squeezing some pulp into my mouth, I sensed first the texture — like custard, smooth, and delicate — then the flavor, which was truly tropical, with hints of vanilla, caramel, and mango. Then I ate another, which tasted like melon. Both were unlike anything I'd eaten before, certainly unlike anything I'd ever pulled from the northern woods. I went for yet another, whose large, black, lima-bean-sized seeds were packed in its center, wrapped in pulp. I sucked on each one for every morsel, which seemed sweeter around the seeds, before spitting them out onto the forest floor.

I enjoyed my first pawpaws, but I was shocked that I had not heard about the fruit until recently, and was only now seeing and tasting it. Had someone kept it a secret all this time? Who else knew about it? I'm a gardener, I camp, I hike, and I even pride myself on knowing the names of quite a few trees. How had I not heard of pawpaws before? I began to wonder, what was this strange fruit — which looked as if it'd be more at home in Central America — doing in these temperate woods, in a forest that would soon turn a riot of reds and yellows before growing increasingly cold and covered in snow? Surely the pawpaw wasn't hardy enough to survive. These small trees, like ornamental hibiscus, would wilt and die soon, right?

But the answer was no. Rather than wilting and dying, these same pawpaws would continue to thrive and grow, and for several years I would return each September to pick their fruit.

Shortly after that first trip to the Ohio woods I learned that the pawpaw's lineage does originate farther south. In fact, it's the only member of the custard apple family, Annonaceae, that's not confined to the tropics. But that just led me to ask how it got up here, and again, *really*, how had I and most other Americans — including my friends and family — never heard anything about it before?

More questions followed. But first, I ate another pawpaw. And another. Soon my feet were encircled by a ring of seeds, in the middle of a seemingly endless pawpaw forest.

છે

Those initial questions I had about pawpaws, both before and after my trip — what do they taste like, where do they grow, how did they get here, and why have I never heard of them — are more or less the same for anyone who's first introduced to the fruit. Partly because of this mystique, they've engendered a great passion in some people, including myself, who've become enamored, obsessed even, with pawpaws — many of whom I would later meet at festivals, farms, and gardens throughout the Midwest, South, and mid-Atlantic.

"It is said that no habit gets a stronger hold on a man than the pawpaw habit," wrote one garden magazine in the 1920s.[1] But at the beginning of my journey, I had no idea that such aficionados existed, and besides that one Ohio patch, I had no idea where pawpaws grew. After my earliest bit of cursory research, I was thrilled to learn that my adopted home of Pittsburgh, Pennsylvania, rested at the edge of the pawpaw's native range. I'd ramble up hillsides, into roadside woodlots, searching. When I did chance upon a patch of fruit, whether on the banks of the Youghiogheny or along city streets, I shared them with friends, extolling their many virtues, and made pawpaw ice cream, pawpaw smoothies, pawpaw cream pies, and pawpaw bread. As a gardener, I saved seeds and even began to grow my own trees in five-gallon buckets. When the trees sprouted I gave them to friends, to community gardens, and eventually planted a pair in my own small yard. I knew it could take up to eight years before they would produce fruit, but that was okay. I was prepared to put in the time. I couldn't get enough.

In my quest to find more trees and more fruit, and to learn as much as I could about them, I began to travel farther and farther from home.

And I started to realize that while the culture at large had forgotten about this unique fruit's existence, I was meeting people who remembered eating pawpaws — and many who still did — more often than I would have thought. After I learned to identify them, the trees that had once been so elusive seemed to be everywhere I went. In the following pages I offer a history of pawpaws, chronicle the efforts of growers and plant breeders to increase their popularity and marketability, and recount my travels in the American Pawpaw Belt. And if you've never tasted one before, I hope this book inspires you to find your nearest pawpaw patch.

PART I

PAWPAWS
IN HISTORY

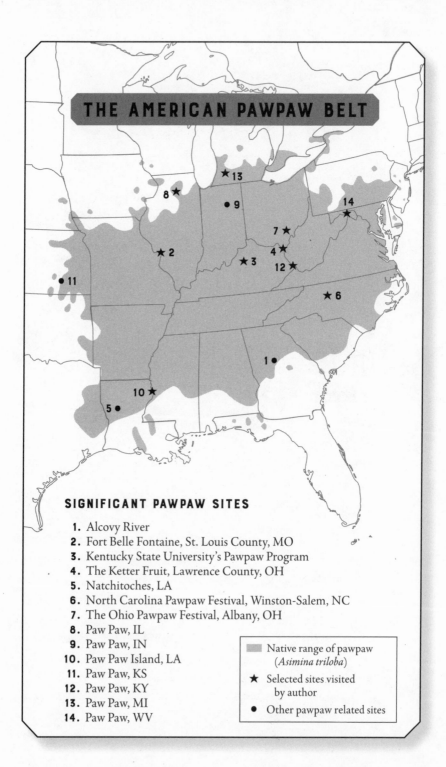

THE AMERICAN PAWPAW BELT

13
8
9
14
7
2
4
3
12
11
6
1
10
5

SIGNIFICANT PAWPAW SITES

1. Alcovy River
2. Fort Belle Fontaine, St. Louis County, MO
3. Kentucky State University's Pawpaw Program
4. The Ketter Fruit, Lawrence County, OH
5. Natchitoches, LA
6. North Carolina Pawpaw Festival, Winston-Salem, NC
7. The Ohio Pawpaw Festival, Albany, OH
8. Paw Paw, IL
9. Paw Paw, IN
10. Paw Paw Island, LA
11. Paw Paw, KS
12. Paw Paw, KY
13. Paw Paw, MI
14. Paw Paw, WV

Native range of pawpaw
(*Asimina triloba*)

★ Selected sites visited
by author

● Other pawpaw related sites

CHAPTER ONE

WHAT'S A PAWPAW?

Throughout the years it's gone by a lot of names — frost banana, Indiana banana, fetid-bush, bandango, custard apple, prairie banana, poor man's banana — but most of the time it's just been called pawpaw. At first glance, both the fruit and the tree seem out of place in North America. A cluster of young pawpaws hanging from its branch resembles a miniature hand of bananas. And those clusters are tucked behind the tree's lush foliage, shaded by leaves often a foot in length, larger and broader than those of avocado or mango. Wild pawpaws often appear kidney-shaped, two to six inches long, and one to three inches wide; they typically weigh from just a few ounces to half a pound. But under cultivation — and yes, there are pawpaw breeders and growers — fruits that weigh more than a pound and a half are not uncommon.

American landscapes are filled with berries, plums, persimmons, grapes, and all sorts of other edible fruits. But there is no native fruit as large as pawpaw. To walk into a wild grove is unlike any other American foraging experience. Rock-hard when underripe, the pawpaw eventually turns as delicate and fragile as a raspberry, and only at this stage of extreme vulnerability is it ready to be picked. If unpicked by human hands, ripe fruit will fall to the ground (hence the chorus of the American folk song: "Picking up pawpaws / Put 'em in a basket / Way down yonder in the pawpaw patch") and can then be eaten. Or, if you don't want to wait for them to fall on their own accord, a shake of the tree's trunk will release any fruits that are ready. But you must be gentle: Any unripe fruits shaken down too early will fail to ripen at all. A prematurely picked pawpaw will turn black and rot, yet never sweeten to its potential.

In the Deep South, pawpaws usually begin to ripen in late July or early August; in the mid-Atlantic and Ohio River Valley, early September; and in the fruit's northernmost range, with fruit ripening in mid- to late September, pawpaws can be picked as late as the middle of October. Each tree produces ripe fruit for about thirty days. But, as with everything else in nature, the timetables depend on fluctuations in weather. I've begun to associate pawpaw with goldenrod: When the fields are yellow with the latter's bloom, it's time to check the pawpaw patch.

Pawpaws vary greatly from tree to tree, but even fruit from a single tree will differ in taste considerably depending on its ripeness, the amount of sunlight it receives, and a host of other factors. There is a stage in the ripe fruit's development when its flavor is perfect, but this, of course, is subjective. Regardless, after it's picked, the pawpaw's skin will begin to blacken in just three days, and its sweetness will intensify until caramel is the overwhelming flavor and scent. Alabamian Dale Brooks once told me you can judge a good pawpaw the same way you judge a Cajun gumbo. "If after you eat it and a minute later you start to talk and your lips stick together — that's a good one."

Many old-timers who grew up with the fruit as children would never eat a "green" pawpaw. "If you let them fall off, lay them up on the windowsill, and let them get real black — oh *man*, they're real good!" For them, the only ripe pawpaw is purple-black, shriveled, and incredibly sweet. "My favorite pawpaw is one that's black and starting to ferment just a little bit," another man told me in eastern Kentucky. "It tastes like wine, pawpaw wine." Others, however, prefer a pawpaw just a couple of days after it's picked, when the flesh is still firm and bright, its flavor sweet and mild.

The pawpaw's flavor is most often described as a cross between banana and mango, hence "bandango." But again, they vary greatly. Wynn Dinnsen, a pawpaw grower in Pittsboro, North Carolina, keeps a log describing the fruits of more than two hundred unique trees he has raised from seed, including notes on their weight, seed-to-pulp ratio, and flavor. In the pages of his notebook, slightly stained from pawpaw pulp, he has recorded flavors ranging from melon and pineapple to cotton candy and anise. A "Hoosier lad" once told author Euell Gibbons, "They taste like mixed bananers and pears, and feel like sweet pertaters in your mouth."[1] Jerry Dedon, a grower in Louisiana, says there are just two basic flavor types: banana or mango. Still others will state plainly, "Pawpaw tastes like pawpaw."

❧

Pawpaws are a river fruit. They grow under many conditions and in many climates, but they're most abundant and reliably found growing in the deep alluvial soil of American bottomlands, along creeks, streams, and great rivers from the mighty Mississippi to the Wabash, Susquehanna, Missouri, and Potomac. In the wild, pawpaw trees grow in the understory, beneath the forest sentinels, the towering oaks, hickories, tulip poplars, and black walnuts. In such company, trees can grow to between fifteen and thirty feet tall, but are usually much shorter. The pawpaw is content, has thrived as such for millennia, in the shadows of dark hollers and thick woods. It has never needed to stand out. And so each year as the fruit ripens, most Americans are unaware of the edible abundance in the nearby woods, and the pawpaws fall to become a mash of green and orange, a syrupy sweetness amongst the leaves and twigs, berries and nuts, returning once again to the soil.

The wild pawpaw is also a reluctant fruit tree. Because of its tendency to sucker — to send up sprouts or runners from its roots — the pawpaw often forms colonies, or dense patches of trees. And because it is able to multiply quite successfully in this way, the production of seed-laden fruit is only a secondary measure for ensuring survival. As a result, wild patches of pawpaw often bear little to no fruit at all. That first patch I stumbled into, with its intoxicating abundance, was not typical. There may be good years when pawpaw patches are loaded with fruit, both on the ground and in the trees, but just as often there is no fruit to be found. There are a few reasons for this. When a single pawpaw tree has been highly successful at sending up suckers, it has surrounded itself with clones; the DNA of every tree in that pawpaw grove will be identical. Typically, for fruit to set, a pawpaw tree needs to cross-pollinate with a tree that is genetically different. The more vigorously a wild pawpaw suckers, the less likely it is to find a successful partner for reproduction. But again, because of its ability to sucker, this reluctance to set fruit doesn't stop the pawpaw from reproducing. In fact, due to its tenacity some foresters consider the tree a problem, a fierce competitor unwilling to share space in the understory. "I have been growing papaws for seventy-five years, not willingly, but because I could not help it," a gardener once wrote. "It is claimed there is no way to kill a papaw except to transplant it and try to make it grow."[2] Indeed, I was told in Rock Cave,

West Virginia, "Around here pawpaw used to grow like goldenrod—just everywhere, like a weed."

Second, pawpaws aren't pollinated by bees. Rather, their maroon flowers are visited by carrion flies and beetles—the same insects attracted to decomposing animals and similarly colored and scented flowers. These pollinators are less efficient than bees, however, and their annual presence and performance are highly variable.

Perhaps they're not as picturesque as the honeybees and bumblebees of other orchards, but the pawpaw does have its own unique love affair with insects. Its leaves are the only larval host for caterpillars of the zebra swallowtail, *Protographium marcellus*. Without pawpaws this large, black-and-white-striped butterfly would not exist.

Each spring pawpaw flowers appear in the forest like bouquets of miniature roses. The small flowers—whose color is thought to approximate flesh, at least to pollinators—are perfect, meaning they have both male and female reproductive units. Because these flowers are pollinated by carrion flies and beetles, some growers have taken to hanging such pungent baits as roadkill and chicken skins in their pawpaw trees. Corwin Davis, the late Michigan plantsman who spent more than thirty years working with pawpaws, reported that placing dead animals in and under in his trees at blossom time worked quite well. "The only objection is your neighbors might not enjoy the idea very much," he wrote.[3] Others have used manure, strategically placed trash cans, and oyster shells; still others, having no need, do nothing at all.

Finally, as an understory tree, pawpaws receive less light than those in the forest canopy. Despite this being the tree's natural niche in the ecosystem, the conditions are not optimal for fruit: The less light a pawpaw receives the less fruit it produces. In recent years, growers have taken to planting pawpaws in full sun, which has resulted in more and larger fruit.

✣

Although they can seem weirdly out of place when first stumbled upon—as they did to me—pawpaws have been in North America for hundreds of thousands of years, long before any humans arrived. According to one theory, a group of Annonaceous trees evolving near the border of present-day United States and Mexico likely included an early ancestor of *Asimina triloba,* our common pawpaw.[4] Since then, pawpaws have survived, or more precisely *evolved,* along with the advances and retreats of at least two glacial coverings of the continent. When one ice sheet receded around 130,000 years ago, the tree marched slowly northward, aided in its dispersal by the epoch's megafauna. Other Annonaceae either failed to make the trip or perished in the colder weather, while through some genetic disposition or mutation, the proto–*Asimina triloba* did not. When the most recent ice sheet advanced eighty-five thousand years ago, the ancient *Asimina* population was pushed south again to Mexico, and east, to present-day Florida. Today there are at least seven other *Asimina* species, six of which are found only in Florida or southernmost Georgia (while *A. parviflora,* or dwarf pawpaw, occurs as far north as Virginia and west into Texas). "Through the ages [*A. triloba*] has wandered away like the proverbial prodigal son," wrote the late horticulturalist George A. Zimmerman. "It has never gotten back into the fold."[5]

Perhaps owing to its equatorial heritage, the common pawpaw is one of the last eastern trees to leaf out in the spring. Some observers have posited that this trait might have been an evolutionary defense mechanism. Rather than let its foliage emerge early and risk a late frost, the pawpaw learned to stay longer in its dormant, protective state. April can be too cold for the pawpaw, so instead its leaf buds stay tightly wrapped late into spring.

The pawpaw was a pioneer, the only tree in a vast family of more than two thousand species hardy enough for the temperate North. Even much of what we consider the sweltering, subtropical climate of Florida would not suit certain tropical Annonaceae for long, the occasional frost and freeze wilting their tender leaves and twigs. Not so the pawpaw, which though a member of the tropical custard apple family is strong enough to survive temperatures of twenty degrees Fahrenheit below zero on the banks of a frozen river, as well as near the ice-capped shores of the Great Lakes. Indeed, though it thrives in the Deep South, the pawpaw still requires winter and a certain number of hours of dormancy each year. Even much of peninsular Florida is too far south, too warm for this peculiar "tropical" fruit.

❧

Historically, pawpaws were one of the many fruits Native Americans culled from the forest. To the earliest European settlers, the fruit was both a curiosity and at times an important food source. At least two founding fathers were interested in pawpaws: Thomas Jefferson sent seeds to contacts in Europe, and George Washington planted them at Mount Vernon. Various species of pawpaw were described in *Bartram's Travels* — written by the famed naturalist William Bartram — accompanied by sketches of leaves, flowers, and fruit. Decades earlier, William's father, botanist John Bartram, was among the first Americans to send pawpaw seeds to Europe, in 1736. John James Audubon painted ripe, yellowing pawpaws and leaves in his portrait of the yellow-billed cuckoo as part of his seminal work, *Birds of America*. And pawpaws have been celebrated in poetic verse — from the works of James Whitcomb Riley and Kentuckian Jesse Stuart, to Walt Whitman. Pawpaws even kept the Lewis and Clark expedition fed — and contentedly so — during a stretch when their provisions were reduced to just one biscuit per man. One of their last journal entries reads, "Our party entirely out of provisions subsisting on poppaws . . . [but] the party appear perfectly contented and tell us they can live very well on the pappaws."

Towns named Paw Paw exist today in Illinois, Indiana, Kentucky, West Virginia, Michigan, and Kansas. Then there's Paw Paw Island, situated in the Mississippi River; Paw Paw Cove in the Chesapeake Bay; Paw Paw Cemetery in Ohio; and Pawpaw Plains, Tennessee; not to mention hundreds of Paw Paw Roads, Streets, and Avenues. Considering that each of these places was named for the locale's abundance of pawpaws, it's strange to think that the pawpaw went from something town founders couldn't help but notice and marvel at, to being nearly forgotten. Considering this, I wondered, why didn't the pawpaw become as American as apple pie?

Of course, it's not really true that *no* Americans today are familiar with the pawpaw. Naturalists, woodsmen, hunters, fishermen, and rare fruit and nut enthusiasts have remained acquainted with it throughout the years, though more so in some regions than in others. And in my conversations with older Americans, from West Virginia and southern Ohio to Arkansas and Missouri, I've been regaled with fond and colorful pawpaw pickin' memories. One woman recalled that, as children, "starting about the middle of August, every kid was expected to walk the creek bottoms coming home from school and pick up pawpaws for dessert." But at some point in the twentieth century — as many of the same old-timers have concurred — it appears that pawpaws disappeared from common knowledge.

Although pawpaws were once widely sold at local markets, and regional newspapers even reported on the quality of the wild crop, the fruit was never brought into domestic cultivation. The most common explanation for this has been that pawpaws have too short a shelf life, and are too fragile to meet market demands. And with the rise of a global food system, the ease of shipping tropical fruits — bananas, pineapples, and more recently mangoes and avocados — had diminished the need for the poor man's banana. But as I began my research, I suspected that this wasn't the whole story.

In the few years since I first tasted a pawpaw, the fruit has experienced a modest comeback. Organic gardeners have become interested in it because, unlike so many fruit trees, pawpaws are virtually unaffected by pests and are easily grown organically. Native-plant and butterfly gardeners appreciate the tree both as a larval host and for its important niche in forest ecosystems. And because pawpaws are highly nutritious, they're gaining the interest of health-conscious eaters. Scientists have even shown that certain compounds found within the tree — Annonaceous acetogenins — are among the most potent cancer-fighting substances yet discovered. Still, despite this history and this potential, those in the know remain a distinct minority.

To get the whole story of the pawpaw's importance — and later unimportance — to human cultures, I started at the beginning, traveling forty miles from Pittsburgh to the Meadowcroft Rockshelter. Meadowcroft is the earliest known site of human presence in North America, with the longest sequence of continuous use — at least sixteen thousand years. Among the fossils that have been discovered here are those of pawpaw seeds. When I visited several years ago, at least a dozen pawpaw trees were growing along Cross Creek, a tributary of the Ohio. I was humbled to see that pawpaws, trees that provided food for the continent's earliest inhabitants nearly twenty thousand years ago, were still there, still flowering each spring, still producing fruit each fall. And yet despite such a long history, how many people today know they can eat those Cross Creek fruits, or the millions of others produced along similar creeks and streams throughout the Ohio Valley? Meadowcroft is a reminder that before we can talk about the pawpaw making a comeback, we need to look at where the story of pawpaws and people begins.

CHAPTER TWO

A BRIEF HISTORY OF PAWPAWS IN AMERICA

North America circa fifty-six million years ago was quite different from the land we know today. Palm trees thrived from the continent's center to present-day Alaska, and crocodiles lurked in waters as far north as the Arctic Circle. There were also giant ground sloths, woolly mammoths, saber-toothed tigers, various hooved mammals, active volcanoes, ancient ferns . . . and pawpaws. Archaeological evidence, which includes fossilized fruits and other remains from sites as diverse as Mississippi and New Jersey, indicates that pawpaws grew in North America as early as fifty-six million years ago.[1] Those prehistoric megafauna were the primary dispersal agents of the fruit, enabling the ancient pawpaw tree to spread into various latitudes as the climate warmed and cooled. The large, fleshy, sweet fruit, with its numerous large seeds, emerged, evolved, and developed for a specific purpose: to be noticed, desired, eaten, and eventually planted elsewhere via the digestive systems of the continent's massive herbivores and omnivores.

Other mammals including bears, opossums, raccoons, and foxes also ate and dispersed pawpaws, albeit with considerably less efficiency. When after centuries of biological and climatic change humans finally arrived in North America, they too began eating pawpaws in great quantities. Pawpaw seeds and other remnants have been found at archaeological sites of the earliest Native Americans, and in large, concentrated amounts, which suggests seasonal feasts of the fruit. Whether at Meadowcroft or the rugged hills of Arkansas, the earliest Americans put pawpaws to great use.

Native Americans are thought to have expanded the pawpaw's range in North America — in effect picking up the work of the recently extinct megafauna. Literature suggests that native peoples brought the fruit far west of the Mississippi River, into present-day Kansas, Nebraska, and eastern Oklahoma, as well as Ontario, Canada, and western New York. These Native American horticulturists, carrying seeds in satchels rather than their stomachs, were effective stand-ins for the sloths and mammoths that had disappeared.[2]

As they cultivated pawpaws, Native Americans may have selected for characteristics that were most desirable — taste and size, for example. They likely did not plant orchards in straight rows, isolated from other forest species, but would have certainly tended and selected trees. A pawpaw patch of superior-tasting wild fruit discovered today may in fact be a remnant of an orchard abandoned long ago.

To extend the pawpaw harvest, the fruit was often dried and later cooked into stews and sauces. The Iroquois, for example, who called the fruit *hadi'ot*,[3] dried and mixed them in sauces, as well as cooking them into corn cakes.[4] Since corn is low in digestible niacin, Iroquoian cuisine demonstrates a beneficial pairing: Pawpaws are incredibly high in this particular nutrient. Other breads, cakes, sauces, and relishes were also made from fresh and dried pawpaws.

"It is surprising to see the great variety of dishes they make out of wild flesh, corn, beans, peas, potatoes, pompions, dried fruits, herbs and roots," James Adair wrote of the southeastern tribes in 1775. His descriptions are among the most detailed of the few that exist of American Indian foodways from this era. "They can diversify their courses, as much as the English, or perhaps the French cooks: and in either of the ways they dress their food, it is grateful to a wholesome stomach."[5] Pawpaws were most often dried, treated with lye or ash, and cooked into breads or rehydrated in soups or stews. They were also likely incorporated into drinks, as other pulpy fruits were, pounded and mixed with parched corn flour, creating a smoothie-like beverage.[6]

Today several reports indicate that eating pawpaw fruit leather, or dried pawpaw, leads to brief bouts of illness. Food scientists don't yet know the cause. However, the Iroquois and other Native Americans were able to eat it dried. Perhaps the addition of lye or ash made dried pawpaw palatable, but we don't know for certain, a reminder of the great loss of cultural knowledge that followed conquest by the Europeans.

❧

There remains much to learn about the importance of pawpaws to Native American foodways, but the historic citations are few. The modern map, however, offers some clues. In Louisiana, for instance, the town of Natchitoches translates to "the pawpaw eaters," and is derived from the place-name given by the Caddo, who called pawpaw *nashitosh*.[7] In Georgia, various places bear the name Alcovy, including Alcovy Mountain, the Alcovy River, and two separate towns. Alcovy is derived from *Ulco-fau*, part of the Creek place-name *Ulco-fau-hatchee*, meaning "pawpaw thicket river." These examples illustrate that pawpaws were often so abundant, and useful, that places and even people were named for them.[8]

Pawpaw trees also represented more than food. The Cherokee used the tree's fibrous inner bark to make strong rope and string.[9] Since pawpaw trees were common along the rivers and streams of the Cherokee's southern Appalachian homelands, they would have been a readily available material. American fishermen in the Ohio Valley took notice and continued to string fish with pawpaw ropes even through the end of the nineteenth century.[10] Anywhere pawpaws grew, from Iroquois lands to Chickasaw country, American Indians would have used pawpaw fibers. Clothes were mended and baskets woven with the tree's inner bark; and as medicine, it is reported that pawpaw seeds were crushed into powder and applied to the scalp to treat head lice. The pawpaw's uses — from food to fiber to medicine — spanned millennia, and were as diverse as the words used to name it.

❧

On May 8, 1541, Spanish conquistador Hernando de Soto and his small army reached the Mississippi River just south of present-day Memphis, Tennessee. Searching for gold and glory, the four-hundred-man expedition had made quick enemies of the Indians while marching through subtropical forests, pine savannas, and here, the Mississippi Delta, a bottomland of tangled hardwoods. Nearer to the river, where the water was lined with cottonwoods and willows, wild pawpaws grew on bluffs, between oxbows and atop high banks.

For decades, it has been written in books and countless articles that the De Soto expedition reported Native Americans growing pawpaws in orchard-like settings, somewhere in north Alabama or Georgia. But this assertion is not easy to prove. The primary text, *Narratives of the Career of Hernando de Soto in the Conquest of Florida*, credited to "the gentleman from Elvas," includes accounts of foods eaten by the army, some cooked and grown by natives, and some taken from the woods. The fruit they called *ameixas* appears most often in the text, eaten green, fresh, dried in large quantities, and cooked into loaves. But that fruit was the American persimmon. There were also clear descriptions of chestnuts, mulberries, walnuts, and other edibles. Yet there is one description that might fit pawpaw: "There is everywhere in the country a fruit, the produce of a plant like ligoacam, that is propagated by the Indians, having the appearance of the royal pear, with an agreeable smell and taste."[11] One historian has noted that the "ligoacam," to which the fruit's tree is compared, was likely a species of lignum. Lignum trees belong to a tropical genus, *Guaiacum*, which consists of five plants native to the tropical and subtropical Americas. Since the common pawpaw does not greatly resemble any *Guaiacum* species I have seen, perhaps the author meant that the pawpaw looked "tropical"; or maybe the fruit in question was an endemic Florida *Asimina*, which would more closely resemble *Guaiacum*; or perhaps it was *Annona glabra*, the edible pond apple native to the Everglades. We don't really know. Editors of a 1993 edition of *The De Soto Chronicles* wrote: "From the description of the fruit, it is probable that this was the alligator pear or avocado (Spanish, 'aguacate')."[12] But the gentleman from Elvas was speaking of a fruit in Florida — a land to which the avocado had not yet been introduced. Avocados are also virtually scentless, lacking then the noted "agreeable smell."

Pawpaw, on the other hand, could fit the "royal pear" description — green skin fading to yellow. It is also famous for, if nothing else, its fragrance. I can certainly attest to this — when I collect pawpaws each September, my entire home takes on their sweet, floral aroma, which borders on overwhelming and can last for weeks. Even as I write this in midwinter, I can still conjure the smell, which I agree is agreeable. So perhaps it's true that De Soto and his expedition did encounter groves of pawpaw throughout the country, propagated by the Indians.

Regardless, the Spanish were certainly thankful for wild foods — whether pawpaws, persimmons, deer, or rabbit — whatever names they might have attached to them. "Fruit is common for all, because it grows abundantly in the woods, without any necessity of setting out trees or pruning them," the gentleman from Elvas observed. But the expedition didn't rely on foraging alone. De Soto's army also helped themselves to whatever food they could take by force from various villages and towns, often setting fire to cornfields once they had gotten their fill.

Additionally, the Spanish brought Old World crops and livestock to the "new" continent. In Florida, oranges, cattle, and pigs were all introduced, though soon abandoned (the scrub cattle were eventually wrangled by subsequent settlers, but the feral hogs persist). Other fruits, including watermelon and peaches, were introduced and would spread through the American South like wildfire — the pawpaw would now have a hemisphere's worth of new fruits competing for people's palates.

⚬₩⚬

Almost seventy years after De Soto first landed on the coast of Florida, the English arrived on Virginia's Eastern Shore in 1607. But whereas De Soto's group had come to explore, the Jamestown settlers intended to stay. Two weeks after landing, they planted European wheat,[13] and they eventually grew many types of Old World grains, fruits, and vegetables.

The settlers brought not only seeds but also agricultural traditions with them from the Old World. In addition to finding familiar foods comforting in an unfamiliar place, they likely wouldn't have thought to try growing anything other than what they'd always known, in the manner that had always worked. But the realities of the Virginia climate soon forced them to adapt, and in just two years they planted, and came to rely on, corn, beans, and squash — and a great many wild foods as well.

The Jamestown settlement was located within the greater Powhatan chiefdom, specifically in a territory of the Paspahegh tribe. The Powhatans ate a combination of wild and domesticated foods, and many groups cultivated tree crops, including crab apples, persimmons, hickories, black walnuts, and pawpaws. Pawpaws abounded on the Virginia coast of the Chesapeake Bay; the humid climate of Jamestown has helped it remain to this day one of the most productive locales for the fruit in the country. I've explored this peninsula between the York and James Rivers and found groves of pawpaws spanning miles. The Jamestown settlement was carved out of the edge of America's vast eastern pawpaw thickets.

Among the English settlers was a man named George Percy, who was tasked with exploring beyond Jamestown. In his journal, Percy wrote of encountering "wild beasts unknown," as well as "strawberries, mulberries, raspberries, and fruits unknown."[14] Of course, the entire landscape would have been largely "unknown." If Percy discovered a ripe pawpaw in the forest, he might have taken special notice of its unique flavor and texture, but then he also would have tasted persimmons and muscadines, seen the stunning flower and fruit of the wild passion vine, or maypop, plump blueberries in the pine savannas, blankets of strawberries, the glossy leaves and creamy blooms of *Magnolia grandiflora*, the bandit-masked raccoon, the white-faced opossum, the deep-red flash of a passing cardinal, and, as the colony pushed westward, herds of buffalo. There was a whole world of new plants and animals to experiment with foraging, growing, and hunting. Pawpaws were just one more new thing.

It wasn't long, however, before the pawpaw was noted, in print, by the English. Jamestown colonist William Strachey wrote in 1612 of the "assessemin" — from the Powhatan word *Assimin* — which he translated as "wheat plum."[15] There is no doubt then that the English encountered the fruits, and likely ate them in late August and September each year. What's not clear is whether the colonists began to experiment with pawpaws or add them to early colonial orchards. And at least part of that obscurity is due to language; the names given to this peculiar new fruit were often muddled.

❦

The English explored the Caribbean and Atlantic coasts for decades before the settlement of Jamestown, where they encountered a variety of new tropical fruits, including one called papaw. But in those cases the word was referring not to the fruit of *Asimina triloba*, but to the papaya. Papaya (*Carica papaya*) is a melon-like fruit native to southern Mexico, and a now-common item in modern US supermarkets. The indigenous Arawak or Taino word for the fruit, as recorded by the Spanish in the Caribbean in the sixteenth century, was *papáia*, and that word eventually became our *papaya*. How *Asimina triloba* also came to be known as pawpaw is less clear. Some say that Spanish explorers called our *Asimina* papaya because it reminded them of the Caribbean fruit. Another theory traces the word from England. As early as 1598 the English wrote of papaws — likely an English corruption of *papaya* — and in 1624, Captain John Smith celebrated the "most delicate Pine-apples, Plantans, Papawes" from Bermuda.[16] By 1704 the words *papaw-bush*, *papaw-thicket*, and *papaw-tree* were attached to fruits being sold in Europe — but again, those advertisements, and the writings of John Smith, referred to papaya.[17] Then, however it happened, by the first decade of the 1700s *pawpaw* (or a variation on that spelling) was used in print to describe *Asimina triloba*. Though I've never seen historical texts referring to our North American *Asimina* as papaya, naturalist Stephen Lyn Bales blames the transition to pawpaw on "generations of lackadaisical tongues."[18] To this day, pawpaw (or papaw) is also used as the common name for *Carica papaya* in many English-speaking countries, including parts of West Africa, the Caribbean, and Australia. The confusion between the two very different species began at least three hundred years ago, and it's not likely to be a settled matter in the popular mind anytime soon.

꿔

As colonial land surveyors pushed westward, they were often accompanied by Native American guides who pointed out to those explorers what wild foods were safe for eating.

One such traveler was Englishman John Lawson. An entry in *A New Voyage to Carolina*, his 1709 account of his travels in the Carolinas including descriptions of the plants, animals, and peoples of the region, appears to be the first time a variation on the word *pawpaw* was used to describe *Asimina triloba*. The "papau," he wrote, was "as sweet, as any thing can be . . . The Papau is not a large Tree. I think, I never saw one a Foot through; but has the broadest Leaf of any Tree in the Woods, and bears an Apple about the bigness of a Hen's Egg, yellow, soft . . . The Apple contains a large stone." In addition to eating the fruit raw, Lawson noted, "they make rare Puddings of this Fruit." It's not clear to whom "they" refers, however, because Lawson references alternately the practices of the natives as well as the colonists and enslaved Africans.

Through the hospitality of the Santee Indians, among others, Lawson ate new items such as barbecued venison and peaches, chinquapin nuts, roasted acorn, sweet corn, corn beer ("sweet like the Sugar Cane"), and a venison-opossum ragoo. In the woods, he ate wild grapes, persimmons, raspberries, huckleberries, and also pawpaws. But the cultivated crops of the Old World were already growing exceptionally well in the Carolina climate. "All peaches with us are standing," he wrote. "We have a great many sorts of this fruit, which all thrive to admiration, peach trees coming to perfection with us as easily as the weeds."[19] There were also pears, quinces, fig, currants, cherries, and walnuts from England and France. English colonists had only been in America one hundred years at the time of Lawson's travels yet had already established great quantities of their familiar trees, fruits, and vegetables in this hospitable new soil.

In just two centuries, what began haphazardly with De Soto — the scattered introductions of various plants and animals — had coalesced into the beginnings of a new American agriculture. By this time pawpaws were known by the colonists of Carolina, and yet like other wild foods, they did not make the transition out of the woods and into the colonial orchard.

cℋ⌒

French explorers of the late seventeenth century pushed deeper into the continent's interior before other European groups. Forts and trading posts were established as far west as present-day Montreal and Detroit, and as far south on the Mississippi River as Louisiana.

At this time, there was no single name for *Asimina triloba*. To give just a few examples, the Choctaw — a Muskogean linguistic group — called pawpaw *umbi*;[20] the Koasati, also Muskogean, said *ombó*.[21] The Ofo of Louisiana said *ephu*;[22] the Osage, *htóžɑke*;[23] and the Atakapa called pawpaw *ol'*, for "sweet."[24] Although none of these words would transition into the new American lexicon, another Native American word would in fact be used to name the plant's botanical genus.

While the pawpaw's common name appears to have come from the South (via papaya), its Linnaean or botanical name comes from the North, via the French explorers of the seventeenth and eighteenth centuries. Louis Joliet — a companion of René-Robert Cavelier, Sieur de La Salle — was the first European to map the Mississippi, and described the fruit in his journals as *"des assons, qui sont des petits fruits qui ne sont point en Europe,"* or "some *assons*, which are little fruits which do not occur at all in Europe."[25] Around 1699, explorer Julien Binneteau wrote that the Illinois — a group of approximately thirteen tribes in the Upper Mississippi Valley — called a fruit *asimines* (though later historians and linguists state the word would have been properly spelled *rassimina*).[26] Writing in 1744, Pierre-François-Xavier de Charlevoix included "les Aciminiers"[27] as one of the three "most remarkable . . . fruit-trees, peculiar to this country."[28] And the Swedish-born plant explorer Pehr Kalm noted that the French of Canada called them *acimine.*[29] Finally, in 1763 naturalist Michel Adanson named the genus *Asimina*, which endures.[30]

༂༚

As the American frontier pushed westward, settlers crossed a wooded Appalachian landscape filled with wild foods — pawpaws among them — that became tools for survival. Daniel Boone, the quintessential American folk hero of the trans-Appalachian frontier, is often said to have enjoyed pawpaws. He likely encountered the fruit as a boy, hunting and exploring in the woods of Pennsylvania, and later in the Yadkin Valley of North Carolina.

Kentucky, of course, was the landscape of Boone's famous adventures, and Kentucky rests at the heart of the American Pawpaw Belt. Of that country Boone wrote in his autobiography, *The Adventures of Colonel Daniel Boon*, "Nature here was a series of wonders, and a fund of delight. Here she displayed her ingenuity and industry in a variety of flowers and fruits, beautifully colored, elegantly shaped, and charmingly flavored . . ."[31] Surely as part of this sweeping description Boone could have also been thinking of pawpaws. The idea of him slurping down their custardy pulp in the Kentucky wilderness is certainly more probable than, say, his defeating an attacking bear in hand-to-hand combat armed only with a hunting knife.

Timothy Flint's biography of Boone, *Biographical Memoir of Daniel Boone, the First Settler of Kentucky, Interspersed with Incidents in the Early Annals of the Country*, gives clearer indication of Boone's familiarity with pawpaws: "When a social band . . . planted their feet on the virgin soil, the first object was to fix on a spot, central to the most fertile tract of land that could be found, combining the advantages usually sought by the first settlers. Among these was that the station should be on the summit of a gentle swell where pawpaw, cane and wild clover, marked exuberant fertility . . . The virgin soil, as yet friable, untrodden and not cursed with the blight of politics, party, and feud, yielded, with little other cultivation than planting from eighty to a hundred bushels of maize to the acre and all other edibles suited to the soil and climate in proportion."[32] Although

Flint demonstrates the settler's familiarity with pawpaws, corn was clearly the more valuable crop. It's not clear that Boone or his contemporaries would have spared any of those identified pawpaw trees from the ax. The pioneer cleared several acres for corn and vegetables, and at the edge of these fields, pawpaws would have been among the foraged foods a pioneer family could gather and put on the table. The woods would have seemed immense and endless — to plant and cultivate, or even conserve wild stands of pawpaws (or any other wild fruit), would have seemed unnecessary, an unfathomable notion.

Boone's autobiography was originally published in 1784 as part of John Filson's *The Discovery, Settlement and Present State of Kentucke* (Filson is also credited with co-writing Boone's autobiography). Filson moved to Kentucky in the early 1780s, and his writings cataloged and described the native flora and fauna, which Americans were still discovering. Like the newly opened Kentucky territory itself, the plants were mysterious: some full of dangers, others of potential. Filson writes of honey locust beer and the "good coffee" of the Kentucky coffee tree, of the rich highlands and the bushels of corn it produced. "The fields are covered with abundance of wild herbage not common to other countries: the Shawanese sallad, wild lettuce, and pepper grass, and many more, as yet unknown to the inhabitants, but which, no doubt, have excellent virtues," he extolled. One of the trees he found virtuous: "The pappa tree does not grow to a great size, is a soft wood, bears a fine fruit much like a cucumber in shape and size and tastes sweet."[33]

Filson's writings — and the many about Boone — celebrated the frontier. Other voices from that period were more sober, revealing a time of rapid, often violent change. In September 1786, at the outset of the Northwest Indian War, twenty-year-old William Sudduth volunteered for a campaign to attack several Indian towns at the head of the Great Miami River, at the present border of Kentucky and Ohio. Sudduth, a contemporary of Boone's, would later write about his life, including the ensuing battle, in an autobiography. After one battle near Elliott's Town, a call for volunteers was given to take the Wapotomica town, four miles away. "The town stood in the edge of a beautiful prairie," Sudduth wrote. "When we discovered it, [we] went through the town to the edge of the woods; where we saw some baskets of paw-paws thrown."[34] Soon thereafter, the army reached the town, and Wapotomica was set on fire.

It might seem an insignificant though oddly specific detail to present, but the sentence provides a description of how a group of Shawnee gathered pawpaws — by the basketful, in a patch on the edge of town. The baskets would have been brought back and distributed, eaten in a great feast, or perhaps even dried and stored for later use. But Colonel Logan's attack destroyed the town, and the pawpaws were never eaten.

During these frontier wars, any trip through the woods became extremely dangerous. In November 1780, seven-year-old Sarah Graham moved with her family to Kentucky, a time when "there was not at that time a hewed log house in Kentucky."[35] Because of the hostilities, she was forbidden to wander from her fortified town of McGary's Station. In an interview later in life, she recalled sneaking off with a group of children to gather wild cherries and "paw-paws," eventually finding a spring to drink from. The boys she was with saw the tracks of Indians, and warned them to "fly for our lives." Despite the dangers, the promise of a sweet treat, free from the woods, was too great a temptation for the young Graham. Pawpaws may not have become prized by orchardists of the day, but for the youth of Appalachia, hunting pawpaws was a tradition that would stick.

༄

For enslaved African Americans, pawpaws were among the wild foods that supplemented meager provisions — that is, of course, if they were afforded the liberty to forage or hunt at all. Often, these activities occurred at night, when pawpaws offered a second advantage — the sweet fruit baited raccoons, opossums, and other small, nocturnal animals that wound up in frying pans and stews. Culinary historian Michael W. Twitty has noted that a former slave cabin standing today in southern Maryland remains surrounded by a grove of pawpaws.

The flavor, texture, and aroma of pawpaw fruit would also have seemed familiar to any Africans with memories of the Old World. Pawpaws are related to many fruits eaten in Africa; there are at least 400 Annonaceae species native to the tropical regions of that continent. Among them, *Annona senegalensis*, or wild custard apple, is native to West, East, and southern Africa, as well as Madagascar and the Comoros and Cape Verde Islands. Its white pulp has been described as having a pleasing, pineapple-like taste, and as "the best indigenous fruit in most parts of tropical Africa."[36] This wild custard apple grows along rivers and swampy coasts, behaving and tasting much like its transatlantic cousin the pawpaw.

Pawpaws were also part of the folk medicine practiced by slaves. In some communities, seeds from the fruit were worn around necks and believed to prevent various diseases.[37] In Charleston, South Carolina, slaves even played a dice game called *papaw*, though its connection to the fruit may only be a coincidence (the game was also played in Boston, and Paw Paw was also a common name used for Africans from the port of Popo).[38] Or perhaps not: In 1887, the publication *Drugs and Medicines of North America* suggested that the very name pawpaw, as used for *Asimina triloba*, was likely brought into usage "by negro slaves brought from the West Indies."[39] As mentioned earlier, the first time pawpaw appeared in print referring to *Asimina triloba* was in John Lawson's description of the fruit in Carolina in 1700, during the period in which the English began importing large numbers of slaves from the Caribbean to the Carolina coast. This forced migration and cultural adaptation could certainly have been one of routes by which the Arawak *papáia* became our pawpaw. And perhaps the "African dice game" had a forgotten connection to pawpaws too.

For an escaped slave, finding a pawpaw patch could have meant the difference between life and death. Guides along the Underground Railroad instructed on not only which routes to take and where to find welcoming homes, but also what wild fruits and berries were safe to eat, and where to find them. This information was essential to survival. According to one estimate, as many as one hundred thousand slaves escaped to freedom between the years 1810 and 1850 alone, on routes that cut directly through pawpaw habitat.

⁂

As frontiers were settled, as towns and trade networks grew, wild foods diminished in importance. But through the middle of the twentieth century, Americans would return to these foods during times of economic and social hardship, whether the country was at war or in the midst of the Great Depression.

During the Civil War, both Union and Confederate troops ate pawpaws, often for a lack of other rations. When Robert E. Lee wrote to the Confederate secretary of war, he said the main cause of desertions was "the insufficiency of food, and non-payment of troops. There is a suffering for want of food."[40] According to one historian, "replenishing scant larders," meant soldiers took fruit and vegetables from gardens and homesteads, in addition to "foraging" for "nuts, berries and pawpaws."[41] But even when other foods were available, pawpaws were still a welcomed treat. While encamped on Sicily Island in Louisiana, one Confederate soldier wrote, "Whilst wandering through the woods one day, I found myself in the midst of a pawpaw grove and for the first time in 14 years tasted of that fruit that I had so often run over the hills in search of in my youthful days."[42]

In September 1862 Union forces, then stationed in the Cumberland Gap — a mountain pass at the junction of Kentucky, Tennessee, and Virginia — were ordered to evacuate toward the Ohio River. The gap was part of the Wilderness Road, an ancient route originally used by Native Americans and, more recently, by settlers of the Kentucky frontier. This particular march was through the rugged eastern Kentucky mountains. "As the army advanced, the difficulties increased a thousand fold by the rough nature of the ground," wrote John Randolph McBride, a veteran of that campaign. "The supply of rations continued to diminish as the army advanced, [farms] yielding only an occasional patch of corn, isolated instances of 'stunted' cattle, and a limited number of 'razor-backed' hogs sometimes called 'elm-peelers.' The succulent pawpaw, however, was generally in abundance all along the route, and gave some nourishment to the hungry men."[43]

CHAPTER THREE

TOWARD DOMESTICATION

Pawpaws were not exclusive to frontiersmen and rural peoples; nor were they eaten solely as a survival food. As the colonies of the eighteenth century transformed into the United States of the nineteenth, pawpaws often ended up at city markets. In 1867, pawpaws were included in *The Market Assistant*, a book "containing a brief description of every article of human food sold in the public markets of the cities of New York, Boston, Philadelphia, and Brooklyn." Author Thomas Farrington De Voe wrote that "[pawpaw] is found plentiful in the Southern and Western States, and appears somewhat, in form and color, like a small cucumber when ripe."[1]

In 1886, the *Drugs and Medicines of North America* quarterly reported, "In cities like Cincinnati, where the shrub grows, the fruit . . . is sold quite largely in the market, but is not shipped to other cities to any great extent."[2] An 1890 article on wild fruits noted, "The small quantities brought to the markets of some of the eastern cities, mainly by negroes, are usually sold to persons of their own race, or to others who buy it as a curiosity; there are some who eagerly seek for it as a delicacy."[3]

Whether in large or small quantities, the pawpaws likely did not come from orchards, but rather were the work of foragers gathering in the woods, or the enterprising farmer who, upon observing overburdened pawpaw trees at the edges of his fields, went to gather baskets of fruit (or sent his children to pick them up). The bounty of the forest was not wasted. Pawpaws were sold at markets everywhere from Kentucky and Indiana to Kansas and Missouri, and all points in between. As late as 1918, a box of pawpaws sold for twelve cents at markets in Harrisburg, Pennsylvania,[4] and in Ohio for fifty cents a bushel.[5]

At the same time, pawpaws occasionally found themselves in the hands of experimental agronomists. By the nineteenth century, horticultural publications in the Northeast and Midwest — the fruit was mentioned as early as 1830 in the *New York Farmer and Horticultural Repository* — were publishing discussions of the fruit's merit. If pawpaws were to become domesticated, to become more than a wild fruit, then someone within these societies of farmers and scientists would be the one to do it.

After the Civil War, more serious attention was given to pawpaws with regard to domestication and commercial development, and horticulturalists were curious as to what breeding might accomplish. In 1888, the American Horticultural Society, headquartered in Greencastle, Indiana, published a report of its annual meeting held in San Jose, California. They wrote:

> *There is probably no native fruit of greater real value and more promising in its character as likely to yield readily to the domesticating influences of horticulture than the papaw, which yet remains wholly unimproved. It combines a natural disposition to vary greatly in size, quality, season of ripening, fruitfulness, etc., all pointing to the ease with which it may be trained to sport into varieties combining points of excellence adapted to the tastes of the experimenter.*[6]

More than 125 years ago, then, the pawpaw was identified by an American horticultural society as the native fruit of the highest potential, with predictions that the domestication process would be easily achieved. Plant breeders and others would continue to make claims on the pawpaws' destiny for commercial agriculture, but for various reasons it was not an easy course.

Others were beginning to champion the pawpaw not for its fruit, but for its ornamental beauty. In 1904, J. Horace McFarland, perhaps best known as a leader of the City Beautiful Movement, wrote of pawpaws, among other trees, in an essay titled "Some American Trees," celebrating their architecture and the beauty of their flowers. He described the fruits as being "all too luscious and sweet, when fully ripe in the fall, for most tastes, but appealing strongly to the omnivorous small boy. I suppose most of my readers know its banana-like green fruits . . . [but] it is the very handsome and distinct little tree, with its decidedly odd flowers, that I would celebrate, rather than the fruits." McFarland argued that the tree was "not nearly so well known or so highly esteemed as it ought to be," and deserved to be planted for its "spreading richness of foliage."[7]

Whether because of their fruit or their visual beauty, similar pleas were made over and over throughout the years, for pawpaws to be granted greater attention and appreciation. And it remains so to this day. With each season the case is made in newspapers, magazines, and blogs, with predictions that pawpaw will be the next "exotic" superfruit.

 confe

In 1905, the *Country Gentleman*, "the oldest agricultural paper in the world," included a dispatch from the Indiana Horticultural Society reporting the following: "James A. Little of Cartersburg, the 'original pawpaw man,' was on hand with a collection of the fruit that has helped to make the Hoosier State famous. Mr. Little has an orchard of trees at Cartersburg. He has prepared a treatise on the pawpaw, which says this fruit is often called 'the Hoosier banana.'"[8] But as revered as the fruit may have been in Indiana, Little's pawpaw story began in Kansas.

In 1860, one of the worst droughts on record hit the Kansas Territory, and would last eighteen months. James A. Little, who was living in the southern part of the territory, reported that the Neosho River dried up and no farm products could be raised. Settlers were confronted with starvation and many were forced to leave the area. "Providentially there was one of the greatest pawpaw and nut crops ever known in the Neosho bottoms," Little later wrote. In the fall, many people subsisted partly on pawpaws and pecans. "Some of us spent a good deal of our time out in the woods with our hammers cracking nuts and eating pawpaws . . . We may never realize what great a blessing the pawpaw was to the first settlers while they were clearing the great natural forest and beginning to build cabins." Many of the settlers, from northern and eastern states, had never seen or heard of pawpaws, but Little noted that the Indians were frequently in camp on the river and were great lovers of the pawpaw. "Nature seems to have been generous in producing the Indians with one of the most delicious fruits," he wrote. Forty-five years after this record drought, Little published the first ever substantial work on pawpaws, a twenty-two-page treatise titled *The Pawpaw* (Asimina triloba), *A Native Fruit of Great Excellence*.

Little said no other fruit received less attention than the pawpaw during his forty-plus years as a member of the Indiana Horticultural Society. He knew of only three other individuals in the nation studying pawpaw: Benjamin Buckman, of Farmingdale, Illinois (a name we will return to), propagating and experimenting; Geo. Remsbury, of Oak Mills, Kansas, writing a paper; and Professor M. A. Barber of Kansas State University, conducting a study of pawpaw. Little was among the earliest to sound the modern refrain: "It is particularly strange that a fruit of so great excellence as the pawpaw should be so little known or receive so little attention."

Little, like many today, believed perishability was why pawpaws were not commonly found in markets. He recognized the fruit's benefits as a native tree, which was then thought to have no insect or fungal pests, and therefore wouldn't need to be sprayed with chemicals. No livestock was thought to browse the tree or fruit. "So we have one fruit that is immune from the ravages of blight, insect, and fungus troubles and that means a great deal to the fruit grower."

Unlike the earlier writers predicting the pawpaw's great future, however, Little wanted to have a hand in shaping it, and so on his Indiana property he conducted a pawpaw-breeding experiment. Little looked for the best varieties in the country and collected their seeds. He wrote that these trees produced "fruit that are hard to excel." From these experiments Little produced one variety he believed superior to all others. He named this cultivar Uncle Tom, and it is regarded as the first named pawpaw variety (whether the name was inspired by Harriet Beecher Stowe's novel, or by a relative of Little's, is unknown). The Uncle Tom was as large as any pawpaw in its day, and its tree produced for an entire month. It produced so well that Little needed to support its burdened limbs, some of which inevitably broke. At nine years old it stood fifteen feet tall.

Little also claimed to have planted the first "regularly laid out pawpaw orchard" in the United States. It was planted in October 1895 for Judge Hadley, of Danville, Indiana, who was a great lover of the fruit. At ten years of age its trees, which stood fifteen feet tall, bore more than fifty bushels of pawpaws.

❧

Little believed, as do I and many others, that the primary use of the pawpaw is to eat from hand, though he allowed that it does make a splendid pie, and that "there is no finer dessert than pawpaw eaten with cream and sugar." According to Little, Colonel Benjamin Goss, who plotted Neosho Falls (and who was present during the drought of 1860), was the first to put these ingredients together, which, with milk, are all that is required in the best pawpaw ice cream recipe I have come across. Little also said a pawpaw could be used to make beer, the same as with persimmon, by putting it in a jar, mashing it, adding water, and letting it stand until it fermented. "It is also said that brandy, equal to peach brandy, is made of pawpaws," he wrote. What Little's list of products demonstrates is that at the turn of the twentieth century, pawpaws were fairly well known and used in a variety of ways. This native American fruit had become part of the fabric of the rural heartland. Now Little wanted to take it to the mainstream.

More than a century before I was introduced to pawpaws, and was flooded with my own questions about the fruit, Little attempted to address one question folks commonly struggle with today: If they have so much potential, why haven't pawpaws been cultivated? "It is because it has always grown so plentiful in a state of nature that anyone could go out to the woods, pastures, and get all they could carry home," Little wrote, "so there was no need of cultivating trees."

For someone who enjoyed pawpaws, the fruit in the woods would have tasted good enough, and there were plenty of them. But Little claimed he was living at a time when the fruit's wild abundance was in decline. He said that farmers and other landowners had once been forgiving of foragers seeking fruit on private property, but as timber disappeared, and as land was converted from woods into fields of corn, tobacco, and so on, pawpaws were becoming scarce. Over time, those forgiving farmers began to object to the pawpaw hunters, especially when fruit wound up for sale at markets.

Since Little's time, a century of clear-cut landscapes, surface mining, housing developments, and strip malls have accelerated what the author observed in 1905. In many of the remaining green spaces, invasive plants compete and crowd the pawpaw's habitat. Even where pawpaws persist, American interest has waned; those former foragers and farmland interlopers now live in cities and suburbs. Fewer and fewer Americans turn to the woods for fruit, nuts, greens, and meat, and fewer Americans grow gardens.

Little concluded that in response to this situation, "It is very evident that the pawpaw will receive attention and be brought under cultivation for home and market purposes." Echoing the statement made by the American Horticultural Society almost two decades prior, he wrote, "I feel confident that no fruit is more susceptible of improvement than the pawpaw . . . I intend to devote a portion of my time to developing it and then someone else will continue its cultivation."[9]

His prediction, however, was premature. Not only did wild stands of pawpaws — and the ease of access to them — begin to disappear from many landscapes, but the fruit was not taken under cultivation either. To whatever extent it was ever known or cherished in American culture, in a few more decades it would further fade and be forgotten.

— CHAPTER FOUR —
A TALE OF TWO FRUITS

In 1916, the American Genetics Association announced a contest to find the best pawpaws in America. The purpose of the contest was to collect genes of superior wild pawpaws, from which a serious, scientific breeding experiment could then be conducted. Writing in their publication the *Journal of Heredity*, they asserted that the pawpaw's "drawbacks [could] probably be removed by intelligent breeding." Not only was it exactly what Little had advocated for a decade earlier, but the contest was to be conducted on a national stage. Members of the association had studied and experimented with uncommon fruit from Europe and the tropics, including dates and figs, and they now turned their attention to their country's indigenous flora. This signaled a turning point in the pawpaw's story; American scientists were laying the groundwork for developing a global, commercial crop. Nothing like it had ever been attempted with pawpaw.

The association offered two rewards: "Fifty dollars will be paid for the largest individual tree, and $50 for the tree, regardless of size, which bears the best fruit." Contestants were required to send a photo of the tree and a statement about its growing conditions. Additionally, for the excellence of fruit award, contestants had to send at least six fruits by parcel post to the association's office in Washington, DC. "The award will be made on the excellence of flavor, small number and size of seeds, but more particularly on the condition in which the fruits reach this office," they wrote.[1] With these criteria, the association was selecting for genetic characteristics that would allow pawpaw to be shipped greater distances — or simply at all — a feat determined necessary for the pawpaw to meet market demands. Six fruits arriving in good condition is a tall order even with today's modern advances in speed and packaging. Again, picked too early and the fruit won't ripen; picked too late, and the package arrives rank, sticky, and full of flies. Nevertheless, it was accomplished. The association received reports from more than 230 different sites, and fruit from seventy-five trees (which, if directions were followed, meant at least 450 individual pawpaws). Entries came from "almost the whole of the recognized range of the species," including Alabama, Mississippi, Louisiana, North Carolina, Delaware, Pennsylvania, Tennessee, Kentucky, West Virginia, Ohio, Indiana, Michigan, Wisconsin, Illinois, Kansas, Missouri, Arkansas, east Texas, and as far west as the Texas panhandle. However, the top seven fruits came from just five states: three from Ohio, two from Indiana, and one apiece from Pennsylvania, Maryland, and a lone western representative, Kansas. Interestingly, no more than 2.27 degrees of latitude separated any of the top seven locations.

The prizewinning fruit, submitted by Mrs. Frank Ketter, was picked from the hills of Lawrence County, Ohio, in the southernmost part of the state. It arrived in perfect condition, the association reported. "The flesh is medium yellow in color, mild but very rich in flavor, neither insipid nor cloying. The amount and quality of the flesh, together with the good shipping and ripening qualities of the fruit, make this an extremely desirable variety."[2]

Suddenly, the best of America's pawpaw folk knowledge, and the best pawpaws themselves, were in the hands of scientists. With a little time and research the fruit appeared poised to break out. Like the cranberry, the pecan, and other native American crops, it would surely soon be domesticated and brought into agriculture. Alas, it did not. On the heels of this contest came no radical change in the pawpaw's standing. Nothing much happened at all.

❦

Today blueberries are one of the most common fruits eaten and grown in America, and in much of the temperate world. In 2012, Americans harvested more than 564 million pounds of wild and cultivated blueberries for an industry valued at approximately $780 million.[3] The fruit has long been harvested, from Maine to Florida, but as a cultivated, commercial crop, blueberries are still young. It has been only one hundred years since plantsmen successfully domesticated the plant. At the time of the 1916 pawpaw contest, blueberries and pawpaws occupied essentially the same place in food culture: wild foods that Americans gathered and ate. Then all of a sudden both were being given serious attention by scientists, and for the blueberry, the right man entered at the right time.

Frederick Vernon Coville was a career botanist with the US Department of Agriculture, where he served as chief botanist. In 1910, Coville published *Experiments in Blueberry Culture* (USDA Bulletin 193), in which he wrote that blueberries must be grown in moist, highly acidic soil. A simple enough statement. Indeed, this is common knowledge to anyone growing blueberries today, on a farm or in their backyard. But at the time it was revolutionary. Whereas most cultivated, edible plants want soil with neutral pH of 7, blueberry thrives only at pH 4.5 to 4.8. And Coville made a second discovery: that blueberries are not self-fertile, but require cross-pollination. "Soon after, he made the first successful crosses designed to improve important traits, such as berry size and flavor," J. Kim Kaplan wrote in *Agricultural Research* magazine. "The blueberry was tamed."[4]

With the science determined, Coville collaborated with New Jersey farmer Elizabeth White — who had also been working with the fruit — to develop a commercial variety of blueberry. The two were successful, and in 1916 — the same year as the *Journal of Heredity*'s pawpaw contest — the first domestic blueberry was released. So while blueberries entered the domesticated commercial world of agriculture, pawpaws did not. Robert Brannan, a pawpaw researcher at Ohio University, puts it this way: "Pawpaw lost, blueberry won."

Pawpaw development did continue, however, just at a much slower pace than blueberries. Between 1900 and 1960 at least fifty-six pawpaw cultivars appeared, chosen and named because they were believed to have special merit, though fewer than twenty of those are still available today.[5] For comparison, a 1905 publication listed seventeen thousand apple cultivars referred to in American publications between 1804 and 1904.[6] Organizations like the Northern Nut Growers Association, comprising both professional and amateur plantsmen, became important networks for pawpaw enthusiasts to share information on growing conditions and requirements, and for sharing cultivated material.

In California, legendary plant breeder Luther Burbank grew pawpaws, and wrote of his belief that cultivated varieties "[are] superior to that of any other fruit, and as they can be still further improved, the Pawpaw will soon become a grand standard fruit in America, and will be cultivated like other fruits."[7] Celebrated horticulturist David Fairchild, who introduced soybeans, pistachios, mangoes, dates, bamboos, and certain cultivars of wheat and rice to the United States, was also drawn to work with pawpaw. At his home in Chevy Chase, Maryland, Fairchild grew a tree from seeds of the prize-winning Ketter pawpaw, which produced fruit he considered superior even to the parent. He named this tree for himself, and it became yet another cultivar. Although Fairchild was more interested in true tropical plants, and would move full-time to his home in Coconut Grove, Florida, he did encourage another northern plantsman, George A. Zimmerman, to continue working with pawpaw. Zimmerman undertook an ambitious eighteen-year pawpaw-breeding project that included more than sixty named and unnamed varieties — likely every known cultivar of the era — that he'd begun collecting in 1923.[8] But despite the potential he clearly saw in the fruit, Zimmerman reported that it was difficult to convince farmers or scientists to give the pawpaw serious attention. "The fruit men won't even condescend to look at it," he wrote in 1938.[9] Luckily, there were a few others, true believers in the pawpaw, who didn't need convincing.

Every fall, Ernest Downing and his father explored the Ohio woods on horseback, searching for exceptional fruit. At least two cultivars — Middletown, selected in 1915, and Mason-WLW, in 1938 — were discovered on these Sunday excursions, and propagated at their fruit farm outside New Madison, Ohio. Homer Jacobs, of the Holden Arboretum in Kirtland, Ohio, grew seedlings from fruit collected in West Virginia. A superior-producing tree Jacobs selected in 1945 was subsequently named Sweet Alice. Both Middletown and Sweet Alice have remained in the fruit trade to this day.[10] And between 1925 and 1958, Pennsylvania nurseryman John W. Hershey offered cultivated trees for sale, including crosses of Fairchild and other varieties at Zimmerman's orchard, via a mail-order catalog. In the late 1950s, Corwin Davis began exploring the woods of Michigan; he would over the next thirty years select and name at least five cultivars that are still among the best.

Yet Zimmerman was the foremost expert on pawpaws in his time, the man whose work was most likely to bring the fruit to the greater American public. But his work ended abruptly in 1941. "Dr. Zimmerman's early death was a horticultural tragedy," Fairchild wrote.[11] Between 1950 and

1985, outstanding wild fruit and crosses of superior fruit continued to be selected — notably by Davis, Gibson, Ward, and Glaser — but with few exceptions these horticulturalists did not experiment with Zimmerman's material. It was as if his breeding work, his collection of sixty named varieties as well as the germplasm gathered from the 1916 contest, never occurred. The knowledge he accrued, and the plants themselves, were vanishing.

It's unfair to put the burden of an entire fruit's development on one man's shoulders, but I have to wonder, if Zimmerman had lived, where might pawpaws be today. Surely this is what Fairchild had considered when he wrote those words. But in the early twentieth century, there was no breakthrough moment for pawpaw. Blueberry had a champion in Frederick Coville. For that crop, it came down to one man at the right moment making the right discoveries. For the pawpaw, that champion had yet to arrive.

PART II

PAWPAWS TO THE PEOPLE

— CHAPTER FIVE —

JOHNNY PAWPAWSEED

There's a photo of Neal Peterson easily found on the Internet — the first image I see of him — that captures the essence of the man we might call Johnny Pawpawseed. He's in a thick patch of trees, with his head positioned next to an unusually large cluster of pawpaws, one of the biggest I've ever seen, containing at least nine large fruits. He's wearing a collared, button-down white shirt, sleeves rolled, and a salmon-colored headband. He appears young, with kind eyes, sporting a thick brown mustache and tousled hair. I guess that it was taken in the late 1980s. He looks every bit the mad scientist out in the field, deep in a lush jungle. This grove of pawpaws and others like it have, in fact, been his laboratory for decades.

I'm meeting Neal for lunch at the Country Cafe in Harpers Ferry, West Virginia, where he has lived since retiring from the USDA's Economic Research Service. I spent this cold, sunny, early-December morning exploring the town — much of which is a national historic park — and saw the sights: where John Brown raided the armory; the Appalachian Trail, which leads through the center of town; rapids at the confluence of the Shenandoah and Potomac Rivers. I popped into tourist shops, bookstores, art galleries, historic buildings dating to the early nineteenth century, and asked folks about pawpaws. I figured that since it was the home of the pawpaw's long-time champion, the fruit would be well known. But like so often, it wasn't.

When Peterson enters the café, he looks much the same as he did in the photograph, with a few exceptions: his mustache is now gray, and there is a ball cap in place of the headband. He has always known pawpaws. As a child in St. Albans, West Virginia, he tells me, they were abundant, but had only one primary use: for throwing at other kids. In summer, they're hard as rocks; toward fall, they explode, splattering into a gross, sticky mess. Neal had no idea you could actually eat these things. "I'd known them from the time I was a child, but I'd never eaten the fruit because no one had ever told me that I could do that," he says with formal elocution. "I never ate a pawpaw, but I knew them very well. They were around, growing in the woods behind our house. And how do you miss them with those big, long leaves?"

Now, though, Neal knows more about these things than just about anybody else who has ever lived. Certainly he has been working with pawpaws longer than any other person. Yet Neal is modest, even a bit hesitant to broadcast the news of his work. What he lacks in bombast, though, Neal makes up for with the quirkiness of a true "pawpaw nut" (his own preferred expression for those of our ilk). For example, on his website, the following instructions are given for contacting him: "By Foot: Follow the Appalachian trail to Harpers Ferry and then inquire with the Town Office or with Laura at 'The Outfitters at Harpers Ferry.'" Or, "Follow the C & O Canal trail to Harpers Ferry and then inquire, as above, with the Town Office or with Laura." Neal says at least one person — a true devotee no doubt — has followed those instructions to the letter. Others have hitchhiked to meet him. I drove and called ahead.

It might seem strange that someone would go to such lengths to talk with him. But consider the following: It's safe to say that without Neal, even fewer people would have any clue about pawpaws. He has bred the fruit for the past three decades, and is responsible for six of the best cultivars that exist, which are sold through licensed nurseries throughout the country. He has been a tireless promoter and teacher, earning the nicknames Johnny Pawpawseed, Papa Pawpaw, and Mahatma Pawpaw. And three decades later, he's still at it, still growing from seed, still hand-pollinating, still grafting and breeding pawpaws. More succinctly, as his colleague Robert Brannan once put it, "Without Neal, pawpaws are still in the woods."

To be sure, pawpaws are far from being an important agricultural crop. But if the fruit continues to climb in popularity, Peterson will likely be regarded — as Frederick V. Coville and Elizabeth White are with blueberries — as the one who brought pawpaws out of the wilderness and onto the table.

❧

Peterson's love affair with gardening began with the common blue violet. At the age of twelve his mother gave him free rein in the woods. Their home was just a quarter mile from the edge of town, but the backyard blended into a wide expanse of woods where the neighborhood's children could wander and explore. Worn paths formed by foot traffic crisscrossed the woods. With his parents' encouragement, Neal transplanted trees, shrubs, and flowers, and rearranged them to his liking in the woods at home.

Because he was working in the shaded forest, Neal gardened almost exclusively with native plants and wildflowers. "I loved tramping through the woods," he says. "It became a pastime and a passion to learn the flowers, to get books on this, learn to identify all the trees." Nature became a comfort during the malaise of his teenage years. He shared a bedroom with his brother, but, "I can go off to the woods, and I'm alone," he recalls. "And it's beautiful to boot. I feel really at home."

Colleen Anderson, a friend of forty years, met Neal while both were in their early twenties, a few years before his pawpaw conversion moment. What began with violets had by this time bloomed into a broad love of the natural world. Anderson remembers the charming young Neal as an avid outdoorsman. "One of the things I loved about Neal was he knew everything about plants," she says. "So going for a walk with him you learned a lot." And when he wasn't in the woods, Neal developed a love for theater, classical music, and poetry.

Neal spent three and a half years at the University of Chicago, but finished his undergraduate degree in agriculture at West Virginia University. But it was while working on a master's in plant genetics at WVU that Neal's life would be set on a new course.

ↄ⟊ↄ

The year was 1975. Neal was in the floodplain of the Monongahela River in Morgantown. It was September, and he was a lab instructor for an ecology class, teaching students how to estimate the size of animal populations. There were pawpaw trees throughout the woods and, it being September, the fruit was ripe. The forest was fragrant. A friend, who had recently completed hiking the Appalachian Trail, was staying with Neal at that time. The friend returned with an enthusiasm for foraging. Further, a broader wild edibles movement, sparked by Euell Gibbons's book *Stalking the Wild*

Asparagus, had put pawpaws back on Neal's radar as something that could be eaten, and not just thrown. He recalls that "the scent was in the air." But surrounded by his students, he felt he shouldn't be eating wild fruit. It wouldn't have been professional. When he returned later that week, though, the singular experience would change his life.

The ripest fruit were already on the ground. Neal picked one up and broke it apart. "I ate it, and it was just an epiphany, a revelation." He thought of the wild edibles in Gibbons's book — like jack-in-the-pulpit, which, if not boiled repeatedly, can kill you — as merely survival food. "[Pawpaws] just didn't compare," he says. Pawpaws weren't the fare of last resort; they were a luscious dessert.

As a scientist, Neal immediately began to wonder: What were the earliest wild oranges like, or peaches in the forests of China — were those fruits even half this promising? They must have been good, or else the ancient plantsmen wouldn't have bothered. But for comparison, a wild peach is a tiny bit of flesh surrounding a large pit. And wild apples are just a fraction of the size of our cultivated fruits. With thousands of years of breeding, look what they've become. But the wild pawpaw Neal had just eaten was already large and filled with sweet, edible pulp. "What if pawpaw, instead of being in the wild today, had three thousand years ago the same sort of breeding?" Neal says. If this is the beginning for pawpaw, he wonders, where can it lead? "Just blows your mind," he says.

Neal was taken, to say the least. Colleen Anderson says she can't remember the first time Neal told her about his discovery, and that she probably didn't take it too seriously at the time. "But of course, one of the things you know about him," she says, "is that he didn't stop talking about pawpaws."

After that day along the Monongahela, Neal was left with an endless list of questions. Was anyone growing and breeding pawpaws? He couldn't recall ever seeing varieties offered in catalogs. None of his acquaintances — beyond the pages of Euell Gibbons — had any information on pawpaws. Had they ever been selected and bred? As a young student, Neal's teachers inculcated in him that all research starts at the library. And so if he wasn't completely hooked on pawpaws that day in the bottoms, his commitment would soon be sealed with a little time in the stacks.

One of the first items he came across was the *Journal of Heredity*'s 1916 contest, which occurred at a time "when America was still close to the woods and the wild," Neal says. "People had been in the woods for centuries, and since pawpaws are long-lived, particularly as a patch, the reputation spreads and locally people tell one another, and a certain patch is well known as being really good. Even in some cases I think knowledge would have been transmitted from Indians, because that was part of their whole livelihood." He then adds, "When there were good relations." All of this, to Neal's mind, meant that the fruit from the 1916 contest contained centuries' worth of exceptional genetic material. It was as exciting as the fruit itself.

While at WVU, Neal bought a small farmstead in Webster County, a remote place in the middle of the Mountain State. He was inspired by the back-to-the-land movement and by his love for nature and agriculture. The farm was beautiful, he admits, but not practical. He could practice subsistence farming there but would likely live in poverty. The property demonstrated to Neal, as much as his education, the reality of farming in Appalachia and the difficulties of making a robust living. "By the end of my senior year I'm thinking, What could I do to be of assistance to Appalachia, my home state? It was my upbringing in both my family and the nature of my town that one contributes, and doesn't just live for oneself alone," Neal says. "There's a lot of poverty in this region of Appalachia. And it becomes more and more clear that it's not essentially a physical, technological problem in the region; it has more to do with economics and the relationship with people to the land." So Neal decided to do further graduate work at Michigan State University, in agricultural economics. Perhaps he could solve problems at a macro level, he thought. Meanwhile, his interest in pawpaws did not abate. In the back of his mind, he believed that pawpaws could also benefit small farmers in Appalachia, that the forgotten tree, native to West Virginia's hillsides and hollers, could be a high-value crop. Its potential not just as a natural specimen, but as a fruit of economic value to people, was waiting to be tapped.

"I was interested in what could I do with my life that would be useful," Neal says. "Not that everyone would agree to domesticate the pawpaw is a need — of course they wouldn't — but I looked at it and said it's a species with incredible potential, therefore it should be utilized. There was a certain pathos to it, I thought, that the naturally occurring resources of North America have not been exploited — in a good way, to a good purpose — in the way that the resources of Asia, Europe, Africa, and South America have been. But there's nobody there to take up the cause and make it happen."

What Neal envisioned was a large scientific breeding experiment, as advocated by James A. Little in 1905, and the *Journal of Heredity* in 1916. "I know my own abilities," Neal recalls, "I said, 'I can do this.'" Despite not having the land (he had by this time sold his property in Pendleton County) — and lacking backing from any university or private firm — Neal decided to attempt what had so far eluded other American plantsmen: to breed the wild pawpaw.

The logical first step was to gather the best pawpaws available. "But you look and find that after 1950 or so, it's just gone," Neal says. *It* meaning many things: the folk knowledge of particularly good patches, as well as the patches themselves, with land having increasingly been cleared and developed. Also, interest. There were at least forty named cultivars available in the first half of the twentieth century, but only two of those had survived. Corwin Davis held a contest in 1950, yet few discoveries were made (he and a few others had, however, selected quality fruit from the wild over the years, and many of those cultivars are still highly regarded). In general, pawpaws seemed to have been left behind, as much a relic of the old county life as gristmills and muscadine wine. If the wild patches were largely forgotten, it seemed futile then to conduct yet another contest. Neal did some exploration of the woods, but how many pawpaw trees, in how many counties, in how many states, could one man explore?

Neal returned to the library. He pored through publications of the Northern Nut Growers Association, the California Rare Fruit Growers, and the North American Fruit Explorers, searching for the identities of the last century's pawpaw growers, and the locations where collections might still exist. The task was clear: travel to Illinois, Pennsylvania, and Virginia, and track down the lost cultivars of the 1916 contest.

೩೪

Benjamin Buckman was an important horticulturalist who, between 1900 and 1920, approximately, collected and experimented with pawpaws, among other fruits and nuts, in Farmingdale, Illinois. His orchard contained 1,743 varieties of more than twenty species of plants, and he is noted for introducing the Farmingdale pear rootstock. Working independently of the 1916 contest, he collected twelve named varieties of pawpaw, receiving fruit and seed from Arkansas, Indiana, West Virginia, Ohio, and his home state, Illinois. No one else had a collection like this.[1]

When Neal arrived at the former Buckman estate in 1981, which was surrounded by miles upon miles of corn and soybean fields, there were no orchards. In a small patch of woods beyond the home and its adjacent yard, though, he found a number of pawpaw trees. Neal hoped these trees would have been the offspring, or root suckers even, of material Buckman had collected. But the fruit was disappointing — in size, in flavor, in all respects. Not that Neal was yet a pawpaw connoisseur, but Buckman's collection was supposed to have been exceptional, and nothing here was better than the typical, wild fruit Neal had already tasted.

Buckman's farm once held a collection of some of the world's best apples and pears, peaches, plums, pecans, hickories, pawpaws, and persimmons, but they were all gone. In their place, more soybeans, more corn.

Still, George A. Zimmerman's Fernwood held more promise. To find the home, Neal first went to the courthouse in Harrisburg, Pennsylvania, and after several hours found a copy of Zimmerman's deed, and eventually its place on the map. Near Piketown, Pennsylvania, Zimmerman's former estate was set back along a private drive, far from the road and nestled among rhododendron and pawpaws, under a shady canopy of oaks and maples. The home, built from Pennsylvania's indigenous limestone and surrounded by nature, appeared frozen in time. Throughout these grounds Zimmerman had propagated and collected more than sixty named varieties. He experimented with hybridizing pawpaw with *Annona squamosa* and *A. atemoya* — two of the pawpaw's tropical cousins — though was ultimately unsuccessful. He was, however, the first horticulturalist to successfully cross *Asimina triloba* with four of the subspecies found in Florida: *obovata*, *reticulata*, *longifolia*, and *incana*. As a member of the Northern Nut Growers Association — an organization that had been studying and reporting on pawpaws since 1911 — his piece of land was, as a successor to Buckman's, the era's greatest repository of pawpaw information. Neal was hoping even a glimmer of that potential had survived.[2]

Zimmerman wrote that a dozen or so of his collected varieties were of special merit, and some of his finest specimens came from Buckman's collection. The standout pawpaws Neal hoped to find included Fairchild, Ketter (the contest winner), Hope's August, Long John, Taylor, Osborne,

Buckman, and Martin. But there were no labeled trees on the property, and none of the fruit was impressive. Yet one fruit, picked from a tree across the road, in the pigpen of a neighbor's yard, did stand out. "[It] had one of the most complex, intriguing flavors I've ever tasted," Neal recalls. "It sparkled almost." Neal collected seeds from this tree to be planted as part of his breeding program. But nothing else at the Fernwood seemed special. Zimmerman's collection appeared gone.

Fortunately, however, in 1941[3] Zimmerman's widow donated to the Blandy Experimental Farm in Virginia a portion of the pawpaw collection, including four controlled crosses of Ketter, Buckman, and Taylor.[4] It was Neal's last chance to reach 1916.

❧

On another sunny winter morning, Neal and I walk the grounds of the former Blandy Experimental Farm — now the State Arboretum of Virginia — as he tells me the story of his final efforts to recover Zimmerman's collection. Though it's cold, and most trees leafless, the plants appear to come to life when Neal speaks of their pedigrees, of mothers and daughters, parents and offspring.

In 1980, when Neal arrived at the Blandy office, he inquired about the pawpaw collection. Yes, he was told, there were some trees right beyond the offices along a short stone wall. Orland White, Blandy's director from 1926 to 1955, was interested in pawpaws from the beginning. It's why Zimmerman's collection was brought here. Behind the office then Neal found five trees. The oldest, Neal later learned, was Fairchild No. 2, a daughter of the Fairchild cultivar planted by White in 1926. It drew a line all the way back to Ketter, the prizewinning fruit. Had he known then, Neal would have collected fruit or taken cuttings (however, the diminutive tree he shows me this day is not Fairchild No. 2 but a root sucker of some other tree).

But five trees was not a collection. By 1980, several decades after Orland White's departure, Blandy's staff had no great interest in pawpaws; apparently that had died with White. Neal pushed them for more information. Was there more? Yes, they replied, perhaps in the backwoods there were some pawpaws, planted years ago for some kind of experiment.

Neal walked down a gravel lane, past oaks, maples, and ginkgos. When he came to the backwoods, he saw small pawpaws in the understory, below the eighty-foot oaks and other hardwoods. Most were small and skinny. But he was not after wild fruit. Avoiding poison ivy, trying to make sense of the woods, he noticed English ivy. As a non-native, it indicated the presence of people. He noticed a thick, tall pawpaw tree. And then another. And another. He took another step, and the tallest trees came into order, forming a straight line. Though they were towered over by oaks and encroached upon by suckers, they clearly stood out. "Humans planted this. This is a collection now," Neal said. Thirty feet farther in, a second, parallel row appeared. He hadn't yet tasted the fruit but was certain: This planting was a collection, and possibly contained the lost Zimmerman material, a repository dating back to Benjamin Buckman, back to the 1916 contest and the turn of the century.

Neal returned to Blandy in September to analyze and collect fruit. There was no guarantee that the quality would be any better than what he'd found in Farmingdale or Piketown, but he was not let down. The material here was truly exceptional. Ever meticulous and organized, Neal put labels on every tree believed to have belonged to the collection (on our December visit, we find one metal tag, its identifier barely legible, nailed to the tree he'd selected more than twenty years ago). He took notes on each tree's fruit. One tree in particular, BEF-53, really impressed Neal. Not only was its fruit the biggest he'd ever encountered, but it was very round and fleshy. "Which is, of course, what I already knew that I was going to be breeding for."

Neal thought the collection was not grafted, but rather a seedling repository. Which was a blessing, because grafted material would have likely succumbed from the neglect and passage of time, as it had at Buckman's and the Fernwood. But there was no risk of this with seedlings, trees growing on their own roots whose suckers would be replicas of the original.

Neal was disappointed in Blandy's organization: files, particularly those relating to pawpaws, were amassed in a closet with no apparent order. He wished to have known the origin of each seedling — in addition to Zimmerman's collection, White received material from states including Alabama, Indiana, Maryland, New York, and Tennessee — but the records didn't indicate where any particular acquisition was planted. "As scientists [the plantings] must have been material that they thought was superior," Neal says. "In its own right it was some sort of a breeding experiment." Which, frustrations aside, is precisely what Neal had been looking for:

superior pawpaw genes, alive in this oak understory, waiting for several decades. His job now was to get them out of the woods.

In 1980 Neal took a job with the USDA's Economic Research Service, in Washington, DC. "Part of my interest in going to DC for work," he says, laughing at the memory, "was that it would be close to this previous pawpaw activity": the Blandy Experimental Farm, the Fernwood, and David Fairchild's former home in Chevy Chase, Maryland. Like the earliest Americans centuries ago, Neal was co-evolving with the pawpaw.

Neal didn't waste time. He had already begun growing seedling pawpaws in a greenhouse, and in April 1981 his first eight-hundred-tree pawpaw orchard was in the ground. They were grown from seeds Neal collected at Blandy, Zimmerman's Fernwood, a wild patch in Paint Branch, Maryland, and from seeds shared by the previous generation of pawpaw experimenters, including Corwin Davis. In taste and appearance, this material comprised the best pawpaws known to the nation.

That Neal would make even this much headway with an experimental orchard was never a sure bet, especially considering two key factors: He was not a plant breeder by profession, and he didn't own land. This first orchard was planted at the University of Maryland Wye Research and Education Center under the auspices of Professor Harry Schwartz, who allowed Neal to use a portion of the Wye's unused land for his pawpaw breeding.

"Neal is a very charming person," says Colleen Anderson. She, herself, was convinced to join Neal's PawPaw Foundation a few years later and served on its board. "He's the kind of person that you will go out of your way to be around." And evidently, the type of person you would loan land to. Neal has managed to do this time and again, beginning at the Wye, later in Keedysville, Maryland; on the farm of Bill Mackintosh, in Virginia; and most recently at the West Virginia University's Kearneysville Tree Fruit Research and Education Center. His borrowing of land is more fodder for Johnny Appleseed comparisons: Wherever Neal could acquire land, a pawpaw orchard would sprout.

With the first eight hundred trees planted, there was only one thing left to do: wait eight long years.

CHAPTER SIX

HUNTING THE LOST KETTER FRUIT

Between South Portsmouth and Vanceburg: In the summer, back from the river a short distance, the wild strawberry shines like red tufts on a new green carpet; the wild blackberry grows in great, thorny tangles; the pawpaw is plentiful in hillside thickets; and the persimmon bears fruit for the coon and 'possum, which boys hunt at night.

— KENTUCKY: A GUIDE TO THE BLUEGRASS STATE (1939)[1]

At the Lawrence County Courthouse in Ironton, Ohio — a handsome Greek Revival structure built during the town's industrial twilight — I find Mrs. Ketter's name (which had been printed in the *Journal of Heredity* only as Mrs. Frank Ketter), her tax records, and the deed to her Fayette Township property, where the fruit was picked.

I've come here to find the lost Ketter tree, the winning cultivar from the 1916 contest that had eluded Neal Peterson. Through the collection at Blandy, Neal presumed he found links to the other prizewinning fruits, but not the top fruit itself. Estella M. Ketter's fruit grew on a tree somewhere in Lawrence County, Ohio. Almost a century later I'm here to find that tree.

If I find it — not even the original, but a sucker from that same patch — then that tree's genetic information could be used by today's breeders and growers to develop a pawpaw of the highest quality. Or it could simply be propagated as is, a new cultivar for backyards and orchards. And frankly, the Ketter fruit holds sentimental value. It was once deemed the best in the country. Why not try to celebrate it once more? I've imagined calling Neal Peterson to report the discovery, bringing him to the site. After all, he'd once told the *Washington Post*, "Anybody wandering in the woods is just as likely as a scientist to find a more perfect pawpaw. The treasure hunt is far from over."

The deed is vague: "Being known as the eastern half of the southwest quarter of the northwest quarter of section 33 . . . 22 acres, more or less." So I head wherever I perceive "there" to be. In her letter to the *Journal of Heredity*, Mrs. Ketter wrote that the pawpaw grew wild on her Fayette Township property, received no attention whatsoever, and was surrounded by a thicket of mulberry and locust. I have two days to find it, and this is as good as my intel will likely get.

On the map I see only two roads in section 33. The first branches into a holler where on either side are well-kept homes, some set back near the rising ridge, others close to the road. Judging from the architectural styles, all appear to have been built sometime in the middle of the twentieth century — fifty years after Mrs. Ketter described her pawpaw patch for the journal.

I meet a woman and her teenage son, who are following several unleashed dogs into a field of tall grass. The woman is friendly and says it will probably be fine for me to walk in the woods and look for pawpaws. There's a pond farther up where neighborhood kids often gather, but she doesn't know who owns the property.

The road ends ahead, however, and I ought to just turn around there and not proceed up the last driveway, she says. I might get a gun pulled on me, she then adds with a smile, petting one of her dogs. But when I do come to the end, I push on through the NO TRESPASSING/PRIVATE PROPERTY signs nailed to a wooden post. I'm on a mission, shotgun be damned.

At the base of the hill an old log home sits in the clearing, painted black and white, by far the oldest structure in the holler. Maybe the Ketters built it, a retreat from their home in Ironton, "Little Chicago," and its once booming factories and smokestacks. Perhaps it was the family's weekend hunting lodge.

The house appears uninhabited, and though I find it beautiful, parts of the roof are falling down. On the other side of a circular gravel drive is a patchwork quilt of a mobile home — looking less mobile and more of-the-woods. A woman stands on the porch with a can of soda, watching me approach. I stammer something about pawpaws-and-research-and-hello-how-are-you, still heeding the gun warning. Then Mary Williams and her husband, Clyde Williams, welcome me to their porch step, and proceed to graciously answer all of my questions with stories of life in Appalachian Ohio.

Years ago Clyde "worked away" as a mechanic. But, he says, "Industrial revolution, when it was phasing itself out in the '70s, and times got . . ." then trails off. "You had to go back to the farm. And that's what I did, go back to the farm. Started living most of it off the land." He and Mary both laugh at the memory. "Like my grandpa and grandmother and everybody else did." Clyde and Mary once raised their own produce, kept chickens, goats, hogs, cattle, and as many as 250 rabbits — but they also turned to the woods. They'd snack on pawpaws and persimmons, make sassafras tea and herbal tinctures. One Christmas, since the hills were without pine trees, Mary dug out and decorated a little sassafras tree with fruit and candy.

Then Clyde tells me about Catfish, Man of the Woods, the late mountain-man herb doctor, born Clarence Gray. Catfish practiced and promoted herbal remedies and folk medicine from his home, over the river in Glenwood, West Virginia. When Clyde was younger he took an inter-est in the folk remedies, bitters, and other concoctions Catfish promoted and sold. Just the previous week, in fact, he and Mary dusted off an old recipe and made a bottle of Catfish's famous cure-all. Clyde brings up "the Catfish" because I want to know about pawpaws. To Clyde, pawpaws belong to a particular way of life — one that includes sassafras tea, butcher-ing hogs, and log cabins — and to a time of self-sufficiency and knowledge that is disappearing. "Young people don't know anything about it," he says. "Everything's dying away."

Clyde was born over the river in Kentucky, but grew up here, and in nearby Sunrise Holler. The log cabin was built by Williams's father and himself, as a boy, with poplar and oak taken from these hills. I eventually get around to asking about the Ketters, but they haven't heard of anyone by that name. However, both Clyde and Mary do have fond memories of paw-paws. Clyde remembers as a boy having to drive the cattle in from pasture at night. "I used to go up and bring the cattle in, and there was pawpaw, little pawpaw bushes and trees and stuff all over the tops of them hills up in there," he says. "I'd go up there and eat pawpaws with them, me and the cattle. I'd get me a pawpaw, maybe stick me a couple in my pockets" — he laughs — "and bring them home with me, you know." I ask if his family ever cooked with pawpaws. "We just ate them is all we did," he says. "Back then, my mom and dad, everybody, they all ate pawpaws and stuff, when they was plentiful. All over the pasture fields there were pawpaw bushes everywhere." He repeats himself to underscore the point: "You found them everywhere."

Clyde says there used to be pawpaw trees in this holler — once known as Bear Meat Holler — when he'd first moved here, but they all died out. "I don't know whether it was that ethanol plant that put out all that chemicals, but there's just not any around here anymore," he says. And beneath power lines and along gas lines, companies began spraying with chemical herbicides. "They're all gone now."

After talking with the Williamses I drive back to the open field where I spoke to the woman with her dogs. I continue beyond the pond to a small, forested ridge and hike for thirty minutes, thinking I might find a patch Clyde had missed. When I first left the courthouse, deed in hand, I thought I might find the Ketter fruit easily, in the woods where Estella reported picking it. But all I find is a single seedling no more than a foot tall. None of the timber is very large, the vast majority of trees no older than fifty years. In fact, it's clear the landscape has been altered a good deal since the Ketters were last here — trees cut, trees regrown, new roads and a few more houses built. Or perhaps their patch of land was elsewhere; the documents, unfortunately, aren't explicit. Regardless, a good amount of bushwhacking awaits.

More than twenty years have passed since Clyde Williams ate his last pawpaw. The lapse is fairly common. Many older Appalachians have told me they remember eating it as a kid — either loving the flavor or despising the taste and smell — but somewhere along the line, for various reasons, they stopped eating pawpaws, or encountering the fruit at all. Some, like Clyde, say the trees are harder to find in their part of the woods. Or as they got older, they spent less time wandering, were less eager to poke their faces through spiderwebs or risk poison ivy, less able to descend steep hillsides. Perhaps you get to a certain age and you begin to fear that trespassing, even in the relatively innocent pursuit of pawpaws, will result in the fabled shotgun greeting.

As Clyde and Mary told me, pawpaws were once part of the rural life in southern Ohio. In her 1955 novel *Squaw Winter: A Love Story Based on the Indian Folklore of Highland County*, Violet Morgan wrote:

Hanging from the rafters in the cabin were bunches of sassafras, bags of herbs, peppermint, catnip, and dried apples and peaches; fat bags of chestnuts, walnuts, hickory nuts, and butternuts. On the shelf in a corner were pots and glass jars filled with persimmons, berries, pickle beans, tomatoes, apple and paw-paw butter, tree molasses, and sweet bee honey; and wines full of the glint of the wild flavor of the Ohio hills. Buried deep behind their cabin was their store of potatoes, turnips, and cabbages.[2]

Although shelves stocked with pawpaw butter may be a rarer sight today, collecting fruit is not by any means over. A few miles upriver, in Chesapeake, Ohio, I meet eighty-eight-year-old Ruth Austin, who spends her weekends selling homegrown vegetables at the flea market, and when they're in season, pawpaws too.

Ruth's daughter, Ann, grew up with pawpaws. As a young girl, Ann would mimic her grandfather, and on hunting trips they'd stop and eat fresh pawpaws — but only the black, extremely ripe ones. "It was part of the farm life," Ann says. "Everybody ate them. A lot of people liked them. I grew up with them too, but I didn't eat them. I just wiped them off of my hands." Ann shakes her head in disgust at the memory. "That's not my kind of fruit."

Yet it was Ann — who during our conversation repeatedly declares her hatred for the rotten-smelling fruit — who recently began putting pawpaws into the hands of friends, family, and strangers. Years ago, she began collecting unwanted fruit from friends' yards — plums, pears, and spare apples that would otherwise have rotted in the grass. And in one backyard, in Ashland, Kentucky, a friend had two pawpaw trees (unlike Ann, this friend was fond of the fruit). Ann originally brought them home to her mother, knowing they'd be a treat. When it was clear there was still an abundance, Ruth began selling them at market. Now, to meet the demand at the market, Ann collects fruit from the woods on her mother's farm.

Her pawpaws are the first taste many have had in decades, offering a sweet memory of the old days. One man for whom a friend was caretaking, and who was ninety-five years old and ill, had been talking about pawpaws nonstop, how badly he wanted one. But the caretaker had no idea how to find one. When the story was finally relayed to Ann, she sent as many as she could. "The old guy was so tickled to get pawpaws," she says.

Unlike her daughter, Ruth loves pawpaws. Since she lives alone on her farm, selling produce at the market — which is just over the bridge from Huntington, West Virginia — is her main way to socialize. The same is true for many of the vendors. If there are any leftover tomatoes or peppers at the end of the day, it's all given away. It's mostly older folks who buy pawpaws from Ruth, people of her own generation. On the farm, Ruth still raises a large vegetable garden, shells piles of stubborn black walnuts, cans food, and even hunts with her grandsons. "She's quite a deer hunter," Ann says. "And she's a crack shot."

Ann says roadside pawpaws are harder to find, and like Clyde Williams also cites spraying. But her mother says they're still to be found along cricks, near springs, and especially abundant in Gallia County, where it just so happens another of the seven exceptional fruits of the 1916 contest originated (and where, in the eighteenth century, the Scioto Land Company once told French colonists, "French custard, ready for serving, hung from the trees.")[3] But as to whether there are now more or fewer pawpaws growing in an area, I've often noticed such discrepancies in reports. Even within the same family, some people say the pawpaw is abundant, while others claim it's disappearing. Perhaps it's a game of memory: The fruit seemed more abundant in the past, when it was more appreciated, and when, from a child's perspective, the woods seemed endless, giving, and filled with more of the sticky, too-sweet fruit than any one person could eat.

❧

I got the tip to check the Chesapeake flea market one afternoon while pulled over on a back road somewhere in Lawrence County. I was looking at my oversized county map when a man in a small pickup truck drove up and asked, "Are you looking for me?" No, I wasn't, I told him. He let on that he was waiting for someone, so then I explained what I was up to. I'd been driving around all day, on ridgetop roads and along streambanks, looking for pawpaw trees. I'd found some wild ones — a few small patches, but none bearing fruit. The man knew where a tree was, he said, and offered to drive me there. I followed him a short distance to the property. The trees were far back in a woman's backyard, and were small, recent plantings. I then asked the man about the Ketter family. He said he knew where some Ketters once lived, grandchildren perhaps, on another dead-end road that I had already been down, and where I had found nothing.

At the end of another holler in section 33 I stop to speak with a man out on the lawn with his German shepherd. He walks me out to the woods behind his home to show me a large pawpaw tree. I ask if I can explore the woods a bit more. He says sure, and my new friend, the dog, leads the way. We jump over streams, crouch under prickly vines, but make no discoveries.

The man grew up east of Charleston, West Virginia, along the Kanawha River. "You could go into the hills and get anything," he says when I return, and of course there were pawpaws, and walnuts, persimmons, hickory nuts, and whatever else was in season and abundance. He bought this property in 1968. The previous owners — not the Ketters — had farmed cattle on seventy acres. There was an old farmhouse and barn back then, but now the buildings are gone.

The Ketters I am so desperate to find weren't cattle people of course, but fruit people. In the early 1900s, the family operated an orchard in nearby South Point called Spring Hill Orchard.[4] But Frank Ketter's exposure to fruit began even earlier. At a young age he worked for the C. H. Ketter Grocery Company. Later he and his brother ran the Ketter Produce Co. (The Ketters were prominent Irontonians: A relative operated the Ketter Buggy Co.; others, early auto mechanics, operated the Ketter Garage.) Looking through microfiche at the Briggs Lawrence County Public Library I find advertisements in the *Ironton Evening Tribune* listing the Ketter Produce Co.'s available Christmas fruits: oranges, grapefruit, lemons, apples, pears, grapes, raisins, figs, and dates; nuts: walnuts, almonds, filberts, Brazil nuts, pecans, coconuts; and vegetables: Irish and sweet potatoes, cabbage, carrots, beets, celery, and lettuce. Quite the offering. But of course, December was not pawpaw season. Unfortunately, I find no advertisements in September issues of the *Evening Tribune*.

But it was Estella, not Frank, who mailed the box of pawpaws to Washington, DC. "Mrs. Ketter was a beloved resident, one whose life was associated with the cultural development of the community and one whose days were filled with intimate contact with the city's leaders," her obituary reads. She was a member of the First Presbyterian Church, Daughters of the American Revolution, the Tourist Club, Ladies Association of the Presbyterian Church, and the Music Club, among others. Although the *Evening Tribune* republished the *Journal of Heredity* article proclaiming Mrs.

Ketter's fruit the best in the country ("Lawrence County to the Front in Pawpaw Culture"), her obituary in May 1939 made no reference to her success with pawpaws. I'm aided at the Briggs Library by Marta Ramey, director of the local history department. Ramey, who knows more about Lawrence County history than most others, has never heard of Mrs. Ketter and her pawpaw fruit. Judging by the obituary, its noteworthiness appears to have faded even before Mrs. Ketter's passing.[5]

In Burlington, Ohio, I pull over to a roadside produce stand where an older gentleman sits in a chair, boxes of tomatoes and apples at his feet. He has a second empty seat in the shade of a tree. He says he had a feeling someone might want to stop and talk awhile. And so I do.

In most parts of the county, ask a vendor about pawpaws and you'll get a predictable response: a confused look, and the return question: "What's a pawpaw?" But not Mr. Cox. He coolly replies, "Not today, but I can get you some." Over on Greasy Ridge — named for bear grease, he says — there's lots of pawpaws, and he knows a man that could gather some.

Stewart Cox, I learn through our conversation, is the great-grandson of Nelson Cox, a pioneer in American apple production who established orchards in this region in the mid-1800s. The Encee (or NC) cultivar is named for him. Stewart spent his younger years on Greasy Ridge, where his family continued the tradition of apple growing, and still does to this day. But I'm interested in a different fruit.

"Pawpaws are a peculiar kind of fruit," Cox says. "You have to have a certain kind of taste to appreciate them." His family gathered and sold them, *of course* (Cox's emphasis), but they'd also eat them. "And Dad always bragged on them, loved them. But the rest of us didn't care that much for them." Cox laughs. "I'd rather have an apple."

Stewart's grandfather was influential in establishing the state fair and state market. But fruit was also trucked to the large markets in Columbus, and nearer, to Huntington. "And of course they'd have pawpaws on the trucks — in season — when there was a crop," he says, "but as a wild tree there wasn't always a good crop, or any at all." The current year attests to that. "They were not as well loved as you think, probably," Cox says. "They were the poor man's banana."

℘

In the mid-1800s, steamboat pilot Jacob Anchutz plied the Ohio River between Pittsburgh and Cincinnati. In southern Ohio — between those two cities and not too far from the sites on this trip — he maintained a half-acre orchard of large apple trees, and "quite a number" of pawpaw trees. In 1844, Anchutz, who was also a schoolteacher, invited his students to the orchard for a lesson in fruit trees. Writing for the Wisconsin State Horticultural Society, former pupil C. Hirschinger recalls, "The Papaws were ripe and the children and teacher were soon engaged eating them, and those acquainted with a good, ripe Papaw will imagine how we relished those." But of the apples, Hirschinger said, "[We] only found one variety that was fit to eat, and that was a very small apple called the Lady Apple."[6]

But it was an important apple orchard nonetheless. According to Anschutz, it was planted by none other than John Chapman, better known as Johnny Appleseed.

Johnny Appleseed famously planted apple trees from Pennsylvania to Illinois, including large nurseries in Ohio, Indiana, and present-day West Virginia. He did not graft trees and propagate preferred cultivars; rather he planted random seedling "nurseries." The fruits from those seedlings were primarily used for cider making and not fresh consumption (indeed, it wasn't until Prohibition that Americans began eating apples in any great numbers). Which might explain the reason Chapman "would soon be welcome in every cabin in Ohio," as Michael Pollan writes in *The Botany of Desire*, "Johnny Appleseed was bringing the gift of alcohol to the frontier."[7]

And it just so happens that Johnny Appleseed's adventures, his barefoot tramping in a burlap sack and tin-bucket cap, occurred in the heart of the American Pawpaw Belt. His legend is properly set among the most fertile, bountiful pawpaw patches in the country. And as we learned from Hirschinger ("how we relished those [pawpaws]" as compared with apples unfit to eat), what is today's forgotten fruit was then better eating, more palatable and far sweeter than the common apple. Southern Ohio, and other states in Johnny Appleseed country, are in fact places where the culture of pawpaws persists the strongest. So I had to wonder, did the man who hiked and rowed canoes across states, with bushels upon bushels of apple seeds, ever dabble in other fruits? Specifically, did he plant or even eat pawpaw? Chapman knew the medicinal plants, herbs, and wildflowers of the Old World and New; he was intimate with the natural world like few others. It's not a stretch then to imagine Johnny Appleseed eating pawpaws in September, perhaps even as he stood at a cider press, working bitter apples into drink.

⤗

As the sun sets I decide it's time to call it a day, determining that poking around is best suited to the daylight hours. During my trip, I've spent my evenings several miles upriver in Huntington, West Virginia. In the renovated downtown historic district, people fill restaurants and bars, and the outdoor spaces at Pullman Square. Tonight I'm drawn into one restaurant by the smell of wood smoke. The restaurant's decor keeps to the theme, with tree trunks serving as pillars in the dining room, and handcrafted tables and bars made of reclaimed wood. I have a draft beer and a smoked tuna steak appetizer. I wonder, momentarily, whether pawpaw wood is good for cooking, but cringe at the idea of chopping down any large trees for the experiment.

But others have had no such qualms. In the early 1800s, one of Lawrence County's earliest settlers, a doctor, built his entire cabin home of pawpaw trees.[8] This would have been a grove to see — numerous trees large enough for timber! And the doctor, knowingly or not, may have been on to something: A chemical in pawpaw twigs and leaves repels many native insects. It's the same reason why deer and livestock are reluctant to browse the plants, and why pawpaws can be grown organically. Perhaps the pawpaw cabin, like an oversized chest of cedar, was able to ward off the bite of mosquitoes in the humid Ohio bottomlands.

In my initial research on Huntington, I found two important culinary leads: first, that hot dogs are extremely popular — the annual West Virginia Hot Dog Festival is held here each July — and second, that Jim's Steak and Spaghetti House is a beloved institution not to be missed. Since 1938, generations of local families, visitors, and celebrities have dined here. After an earlier day of pawpaw hunting it seemed like the right place for me, and I took a seat at the counter.

When I told a waitress it was my first visit to the restaurant and to Huntington in general, I got a big welcome, and the staff bloomed when I mentioned pawpaws as the reason for my visit. Then it happened.

When I mentioned pawpaws, the woman who had been operating the griddle dropped her spatula, turned, and looked into my eyes. She was extremely well dressed for her task — a white lace top, immaculate hair. I couldn't tell if it was joy or anger in her eyes. Had I done something wrong? A waitress — wearing a white uniform dress, like all the others — went on to tell me about several trees her grandfather had planted near Marshall University. Meanwhile, the cook kept moving toward me. Then, with her spatula-turned-metronome, she began to sing: "Pickin' up pawpaws, put 'em your pocket; Pickin' up pawpaws, put 'em in your pocket . . ." She knew. The woman was Jimmie — named for her father, Jim — and the current proprietress of the restaurant. The griddle wasn't her normal station, but she could stand in where needed.

With pawpaws on the figurative table, smiles were bigger, and everyone seemed to come to life. Now we really had something to talk about. One waitress remembered an uncle's favorite phrase ("I didn't just fall off the pawpaw tree"), while another waitress asked, to be sure she had the right fruit in mind: "They're a rotten-looking fruit, ain't they?"

Jim's serves homemade pies, made fresh daily. Today was banana pie day. I ate a great big slice, with coffee, and thought about how well fresh pawpaw could substitute in this recipe. I later tried it at home and it was delicious.

❧

A bar and restaurant near Marshall University have become my office. I come here to decompress, strategize over Google Maps, and fill up on good food.

Members of a traditional old-time band are regulars at the bar, and the three young men pass fiddle, banjo, and guitar freely among one another, taking turns on each. They're in their early twenties, and had come to Marshall University from Point Pleasant, another West Virginia town, situated upriver at the confluence of the Ohio and Kanawha. In high school they'd played blues and garage rock, some jazz, but over the past several years were drawn to the music of their home state. Indeed, most of the songs they perform tonight are West Virginia tunes. In due time I of course get around to asking about pawpaws. "I've eaten them before," the guitarist says. "Yeah, one of those things you grab whenever you're out hiking." The fiddle player adds, conclusively: "We've eaten some pawpaws in our time."

I tell the band why I'm here, about the 1916 contest. Pawpaws are well known in West Virginia; in Appalachia, perhaps more than any other region. Yet only a few contest entries came from the Mountain State, and West Virginia wasn't among the seven superior fruits, although its border states — Ohio, Pennsylvania, and Maryland — were. The band considers my conundrum, and the banjo player offers his thoughts: "We keep our secrets pretty close to us around here."

It would be a poor excuse to the scientific community (and I'm sure there were other more sound reasons), but to the modern pawpaw enthusiast it doesn't seem that far-fetched.

ↄ৮৹

The next day I drive to Huntington's Old Central City. Oversized quilt patterns are affixed to the sides of several buildings, like those I've seen hoisted onto barns along the region's highways. The neighborhood reminds me of pioneer towns in old western movies. Flat, one-story wooden facades resemble those of old taverns or frontier general stores. To round out the scene, kids cruise the streets on bicycles, carrying water guns. Otherwise, it's quiet; tumbleweed would not be out of place.

The farmers market in Central City is located in an old train depot. I arrive on what is an off day for most vendors, but a small, permanent stand is still open. I buy a bag of Rome Beauty apples, a variety selected over the river in Rome, Ohio, and then ask the market manager, Lori, about pawpaws.

"They're a kind of popular thing around here," she says. One particular vendor — who is absent but whom I'd have met on market day — brings pawpaws each September. "People see them and they get excited. They'll say, 'I haven't seen one since I was a kid!'" They're most popular among older folks who ate the fruit years ago under different circumstances, she guesses. "People were poor and they'd go into the woods and gather pawpaws and different things."

But if I want pawpaws today, all is not lost. A man down the road in a tan house — she points to it — has trees and sells to the public.

The sidewalk in front of Finley Pauley's house is a market stand in its own right — Concord grapes, tomatoes (both red and green), butternut squash, and apples are piled in crates and baskets, all of it grown in his own backyard. He sells other things too: bicycles, including a vintage folding model, compact fluorescent light bulbs, VHS tapes, a wide assortment of goods. The short path to his front door is lined in rosebushes and grape arbors.

And, yes, he sells pawpaws. But the trees are all done. It has been a strange and early season, weather warm and dry.

I ask Finley when he first became interested in pawpaws. "Well, when I was a boy that's all we did. We ate pawpaws, pawpaws, and pawpaws to survive and this and that," he says with a chuckle. "When I was a kid we ate so many pawpaws that I just don't care for them now." He hadn't even planted the trees in his yard. They just came up, he says. Someone — maybe Finley, maybe not — spat out some seeds once, he supposes, and well, here they are. Folks come to Finley year after year. "I don't even advertise," he says. "I sell every one I get."

༡

At the Briggs Library I learned that the Ketters had an orchard in South Point. Poring over a map of the town I find a road called Orchard Lane, and wonder what relics I might find here. It's a dead-end road, surrounded by large open parcels on either side. I wonder if this was the site of the Ketters' orchard, and set off one more time to find a trace of Estella's fruit. Although I don't believe it was grown commercially in their orchard, perhaps with pride they had brought a single graft of the prizewinning fruit out of the woods. The road begins at a grid of newer housing, and then climbs a large hill where the houses are fewer and widely spaced. At the very top, the view opens up to the Ohio River; parts of Kentucky, West Virginia, and Ohio are all visible.

It must have been a most beautiful orchard when it was in production, whoever it belonged to. But there is no trace of it today, just private lawns and a few second-growth woodlots — no thickets of pawpaws, no scraggly apple trees, no unkempt peach trees.

Back in town, though, as I drive along the river road I spot the unmistakable teardrop leaves. Those unfamiliar with the tree might mistake it for an ornamental exotic. "Welcome to tropical southern Ohio," I have been told. It is only mid-September, but several leaves are already yellowing, a sign of stress perhaps. It has been a hot and early spring and summer.

A vegetable patch grows adjacent to the pawpaw tree. Inside rows of tomatoes staked five feet high, a ninety-year-old man is hoeing weeds and harvesting kale. He wears a white beard, jeans, and a long-sleeved shirt. He grew up eating pawpaws, and still enjoys them, he says. Unfortunately, a much larger tree that had borne well had to be cut down because it was in the power lines. I assume he is eager to finish his work and get out of the heat, and so I say good-bye and thank him for his time.

As I drive back to Huntington I accept that I am unlikely to find the Ketter fruit. But what I have found, and perhaps this is more valuable, is a living pawpaw culture. Here, at least, the pawpaw is not a forgotten fruit.

✿

In the morning, after a biscuit and fried apple breakfast, I decide to look for the trees planted by the uncle of my waitress at Jim's. Since the Ketter fruit has thus far eluded me, it would be a boost to my sleuthing esteem to at least track down something.

I find them, a massive pair, each thirty or forty feet tall, reaching above the power lines, and more or less right where she said they would be, their leaves a deep green fading to yellow at the top of each pyramidal shape. They've managed to make a Bradford pear and black walnut look small in comparison.

I stand in the grass taking photos when a neighbor calls out to me from her porch across the road. "Some people want to cut those trees down," she says. I ask why, and who. Just some neighbors on the block, she says. "They just want them gone. Don't want them anymore." I tell her I don't see any sense in that, that they are good trees. "Tell me about it!" she says. I'm confused by all of it. But at least it offers some explanation as to why some things disappear: whims of the obstinate.

Taking my time back to Pittsburgh I drive north through beautiful hill country. Often the only car on two-lane byways, I wind around the edges of farms, through crossroads towns and shaded hollers, over tiny creeks. Time after time I spot telltale leaves at the woods' edge, and the quiet and lack of traffic make it too easy to just pull over, walk through fields of goldenrod and, listening to the sound of crickets, on into the woods again to hunt down that lost, best pawpaw. If Ketter's tree is indeed gone, maybe there is another waiting to be found. Soon I come to Athens County, and the original patch where I had my first pawpaw. Just before the sun sets, I find a medium-sized tree, small enough to shake, with one good, visible cluster of fruit. One piece falls, ripe. It's delicious: notes of caramel without any bitterness, a bit melony. Perhaps not the next best cultivar, but it will do for now.

— CHAPTER SEVEN —

PETERSON'S GAMBIT

In 1988, Neal Peterson's Wye orchard produced its first substantial crop. He had waited eight years for his trees to mature, and now he could see what they were made of. It was an incredibly exciting period for Neal; he was about to literally taste the fruits of his labor.

Neal had long considered the seediness of pawpaws to be the main impediment to commercial development, a trait to be bred out. So for each seedling he determined the seed-to-pulp ratios by separating seeds and pulp, and weighing each. As he expected, there was a consistency to each tree. Neal collected every bit of data possible: He recorded the weight of fruit from each tree, the flavor profiles of each seedling, as well as overall visual beauty, color, texture, and more. The data went into tables. He determined averages and standard deviations, and later performed statistical analysis.

In the second year of production, Neal was surprised to find that not a single tree he'd identified the year prior as outstanding now ranked in the current crop's top tier. It was highly unexpected. Reflecting on this, Neal tells me, in an email: "Trees are incredibly complex, sophisticated organisms. We must admire them. Even on a single tree, fruit can vary in flavor from branch to branch. And certainly flavor varies from year to year. And flavor is but one dimension of tree quality." Tree selection takes time.

Neal kept at it for two more years, narrowing the field for the very best. He wanted trees with a large yield, and whose fruit tasted great, was large, and contained relatively few seeds. Fleshiness, as Neal terms it — the seed-to-pulp ratio. Three future cultivars — trees he would later release to the public — were discovered in those first three years: the Shenandoah, Susquehanna, and Rappahannock.

At the end of three years Neal selected nine trees, the best according to the data, and cut the rest to stumps. "It was pretty ruthless," he says. The following spring, he grafted those best varieties (as well as cultivars he'd received from other hobbyists), which accounted for little more than 1 percent of the original orchard, onto the stumps of the former trees. He was following standard scientific protocol — and those nine trees (or genotypes) would now need to be evaluated by other scientists in other locations.

A few years after planting the Wye orchard, Neal arranged to plant a second orchard in Keedysville, at UMD's Western Maryland Research & Education Center. In Keedysville, he conducted the same trials of observation — data collection and taste testing — with another unique batch of six hundred additional trees.

In September there was time for nothing but pawpaws. Neal stayed with friends on the Eastern Shore and each morning he would arrive at the orchard, pick all day, measure data, eat dinner, sleep, and repeat. His vacation allotment from the USDA was consumed each harvest season, and he would need to take additional unpaid leave to complete the work.

At its peak, Neal's program included fifteen hundred trees in two orchards. "Ten thousand would have been ideal," he says, "But to evaluate ten thousand trees, you need a staff. It's beyond one person." Still, the effort was unprecedented: Previous breeding efforts from Buckman to Zimmerman to Davis never exceeded thirty or forty trees. Further, Neal believes that had he been affiliated with a university, his work would not have been supported. Grant-funded research requires a quick turnaround; most funding agencies or university administrators do not have the patience to wait the decades needed to conduct a proper breeding program. And grants tend to operate on two-to-three-year cycles, not twenty-year intervals.

Neal did not have a staff, a salary, or any compensation for his work. But he did have friends. The first year at the Wye, Neal did everything himself — taste testing, evaluation, seed cleaning, and so on — and he had had enough. In Septembers of subsequent years, Neal was joined by the friends he could convince and, through correspondence, whatever willing pawpaw nuts that were able to travel.

Jim Gilbert, renowned plant explorer and operator of One Green World, an Oregon-based nursery, remembers his first meeting with Neal at the

Wye orchard. "He's a very magnetic guy," Gilbert says of Neal. "He'd get all these guys to come out and help do things." Those tasks included picking and hauling fruit, tasting, recording observations, and perhaps the most dreadful of all pawpaw jobs, seed cleaning and processing. Neal had borrowed a seed-cleaning machine, so it wasn't quite done by hand, as many do today, but it still required handling and sorting pawpaws in various stages of rot and fermentation. The uniform for the job included rubber boots and yellow rain suits.

John Popenoe, a former director of the Fairchild Botanical Garden (1963–89) and former horticulturalist for the Federal Agricultural Marketing Service, was another of the volunteers (Popenoe happened to be the son of Paul Popenoe, and nephew to Wilson Popenoe, plant explorers and scientists who were colleagues of David Fairchild's). Ray Jones, who in 1991 began publishing the *The Pawpaw Tracker* newsletter in California, even traveled cross-country to assist Neal in his experiments. There were others, including Zhanibek Suleimenov, Stevik Kretzmann, and Lorraine Gardner, devoted friends and volunteers, helping to pick fruit, conduct taste tests, and clean seed.

In 1988, Neal formed the PawPaw Foundation, a nonprofit with the goal "of contributing to a pawpaw revival by promoting scientific research in the areas of pawpaw breeding, growing, managing, harvesting, fruit quality, and use." Also in the early 1990s, Brett Callaway was in the process of establishing the Kentucky State University Pawpaw Program; by 1994, KSU became the USDA National Clonal Germplasm Repository (or gene bank) for *Asimina triloba*. A small but dedicated force of pawpaw enthusiasts, both amateur and professional, was beginning to coalesce, and Neal was very much at the heart of the movement.

"I think it will take about another 25 years to get the strengths and weaknesses of various varieties sorted out and to get breeding programs going," Neal told the *Washington Post*'s Hank Burchard in 1999. "But it's going to be fun all the way; we can have our fruit and eat it, too."[1]

❧

Around this time, Neal knew of a few farmers planting large, commercial pawpaw orchards. With his advanced selections emerging, he was ready for the same. In 1998 he bought property in Pendleton County, West Virginia.

After nearly two decades of work, he would finally have his own orchard on his own land. The project required more than a quarter million dollars. He retired from the USDA and, to finance the orchard, cashed in his pension early. He gambled everything.

Pendleton is a thinly populated, remote county in West Virginia, located at the headwaters of the Potomac River. Here, Neal planted a ten-acre farm of three thousand grafted seedlings that were all a year and a half old. Unfortunately, 1999 – the year his trees arrived – would record the worst drought in seventy-five years. Pendleton County hadn't been this dry since the Great Depression; even the region's corn crop failed. The young transplants never stood a chance.

Neal had been on a tight schedule, he says. He retired in 1998, and the grafted trees arrived the next spring. He had no way of knowing what that summer would bring. If the trees arrived just one year later there would have been no drought, and the trees would have been older and stronger. Perhaps Neal would today be the owner of a successful commercial pawpaw orchard. Instead, he lost the farm. "Maybe there's a bit of an American tradition to go all out and place everything you've got on the bet," Neal says, "and, well, that's what I did. Including my pension." He invested everything, his entire retirement from the USDA, on pawpaws, and he lost. "You can say, 'Pawpaws or bust,' and I went bust."

As devastating as the experience in Pendleton County was, his second-round crosses at the Wye orchard were beginning to produce. Neal had studied, analyzed, crossed, grafted, and regrown the superior varieties. And now the pawpaws were going to market.

❧

Neal had data; he knew what impressed his friends and colleagues; he'd partnered in Regional Variety Trials with a number of universities in half a dozen states; and KSU's pawpaw research program was now nine years old. For a short while Neal would cold-call chefs at DC restaurants, dropping off boxes of fruit to get feedback and stimulate interest. But there was a still a big, nagging question. "What do people think of these things?" To find out, Neal decided to bring pawpaws to market in the nation's capital.

"We need to select superior varieties that are good enough and might be the basis of a farming commodity, that could take their place along with other fruits," Neal says. At that time, so few people were growing them — typically just one or two trees in a yard because of a regional interest in Appalachia, Ohio, and Indiana. "Pawpaw deserves more than that," he says. "That's why we started selling at the farmers market" — to bring pawpaws to the people.

The Dupont Circle FreshFarm market was established in 1997. At its peak each summer the market features forty farmers offering fruits and vegetables, meat, fish, cheeses, pies, breads, fresh pasta, cut flowers, and soaps and herbal products. The historic neighborhood — gentrified, educated, and with disposable income — was an ideal proving ground for the pawpaw as a high-value commodity. The fruit was labor-intensive and wouldn't be cheap. Despite Neal's faith, and his decades of work, it was still unknown whether anyone would actually want to buy and eat them.

Every Saturday Neal made the hour-and-a-half drive from the Eastern Shore to DC. The fruit was picked Monday through Friday, and the next morning it was ready to go. By midday, market work could be as exhausting as the orchard: rise early, drive, unload, stand on concrete, and attempt to explain to first-time customers, briefly, what these strange-looking fruits were.

On September 17, the Friday before market day, the *Washington Post* ran a three-page spread about pawpaws, with color photos, recipes, and a summary of Neal's work. "Science has discovered a tree that bears delicious fruit, kills bugs and fights cancer," Hank Burchard wrote. You couldn't buy this kind of hype. He went on: "Ripe fruit can be hard to find, unless you have your own secret pawpaw patch. Happily, this Sunday fresh pawpaws from one of Neal Peterson's research groves will be offered at the Dupont Circle farmers' market." The story would prove to be an incredible break.[2]

Before the market's opening bell had rung, a line had formed thirty people deep, all intent on buying pawpaws. They had come from across the region, as far as Baltimore, people who hadn't eaten one since childhood. "And that of course is a very significant event for pawpaw eaters," Neal says. "'I haven't had one since I was a boy!' 'I haven't had one since I was a girl,' they'll say. 'I remember loving them so much!'" There was a mystery to pawpaws. In these people's minds, pawpaws had vanished, and all of a sudden they'd reappeared on Neal Peterson's market table.

Other vendors looked on with amazement; Neal was sure they were wishing for that kind of attention, buy-in, and devotion. Buyers were filled with child-like wonder. *What are these things and why haven't I heard of them?* People wanted entire boxes, which held twenty-three pieces. "Five dollars a pound, and people didn't flinch," Neal says. Customers were rationed to two pawpaws. "Can you imagine that?" Neal laughs. They had brought all the pawpaws they could pick and sold out in two hours. There wasn't a moment's pause in the selling. Subsequent weeks and years weren't equal to that, he said, but, "With rare exception, we always sold out."

⁂

Apples have Golden Delicious, Arkansas Black, Granny Smith, Pink Lady, Sundance, and Pumpkin Sweet. Tomatoes: Black from Tula, Cherokee Purple, Jubilee, Yellow Pear, Pritchard's Scarlet Topper, and Pink Accordion. And pears: Bon Rouge, Elektra, Harvest Queen, Moonglow, and Luscious. Clearly, pawpaws would need great names too. But giving out names requires discretion. "You only give a name to it when you have that certainty, and you're going to release it to the public," Neal says, "pretty much like naming a child." For a few years Neal stuck to numbers as identifiers. Some customers at the DuPont Circle market even came to know which particular fruits they liked, 2-9 or 1-7-1, for example, and would ask for them each week. But 1-7-1, as a named variety, isn't too friendly. It isn't warm and inviting. It certainly doesn't tell a story. "It's like a Social Security number rather than a name," Neal says.

Consumers at the market identified 1-7-1 as a fabulous fruit, which didn't surprise Neal. "I'd been growing these things since they were seeds," he says. "I watched them grow up and flower and start to fruit. But it wasn't a surprise to me, a shock, that this was a good tree, a good fruit." Neal recalls his friend Stevik, who taste tested, picked, and sold fruit at the DC market, asking him, "Why do we bother with any of those other varieties? This is the very best." But that wasn't Neal's philosophy. He wanted a diverse selection for genetics, but also because different people have different tastes.

Nurserymen acquainted with Neal's work encouraged him to release his varieties to the public. Jim Gilbert recalls how frustratingly careful and meticulous Neal was, not wanting to release any inferior, untested cultivars. "We kept telling him, 'Let them out, let people grow these!'" he laughs.

Neal eventually chose to name his cultivars for American rivers with Indian names, a tribute to the pawpaw's native habitat and to its original horticulturalists. And so 1-7-1, this exceptional fruit, became Shenandoah.

After three years at Dupont Circle, Neal's market experiment was finished. In 2003 his company, Peterson Pawpaws, began online sales of his trademarked, patented varieties: Allegheny, Susquehanna, Shenandoah, Wabash, Potomac, and Rappahannock. The world's best pawpaws were now available to anyone who wanted them. Kentucky State University's Kirk Pomper says, "For a plant breeder to come up with even one great, or two great varieties in their lifetime is an achievement. You think, Neal came up with maybe five — that's the lifetime achievement award in plant breeding right there as far as I'm concerned."

⁊

In the early 1990s, an opportunity arose that could have been a monumental breakthrough. A product development specialist from Ocean Spray wanted to experiment with pawpaws. Neal was ecstatic. This was it! And all he had to do was ship one ton of pawpaw pulp to Ocean Spray's facilities in Massachusetts. But a ton was impossible. Neal was only producing a couple hundred pounds. Even combined with other growers of high-quality fruit, it still wouldn't be enough. It couldn't be done.

If Neal had been able to supply Ocean Spray, and if they had developed a marketable product, it clearly would have been a game changer for pawpaw as a crop. But this wasn't the case. And the inability for anyone to supply Ocean Spray with enough pawpaws was a red flag for the problem of developing pawpaws: If consumer interest grows, will there be enough fruit to go around?

Pawpaws needed to be broadly marketed — something that an Ocean Spray juice would have absolutely accomplished — but there was a risk that demand, or nascent, budding interest, would outpace supply. It wasn't hard to imagine interest growing exponentially. Just look at kiwi and pomegranate, even açaí and other so-called superfruits that seemingly overnight were added to all manner of juices and products. But it wouldn't amount to anything if there wasn't enough fruit.

It's one thing for a traditional farmer to add a patch of heirloom, organic tomatoes; to add a few apple trees in an established peach orchard. Apples and tomatoes have a reliable, proven market. But to plant a pawpaw or-chard, a tree fruit for which there isn't really any demand, a tree fruit that needs six years of waiting before it produces — a period filled with a good amount of anxiety over who is going to buy these strange things if they ever do produce — is a far different thing. Neal had lost his farm in Pendleton County. Who else was willing to take the risk? Who would come along and plant an entire pawpaw orchard?

CHAPTER EIGHT

IN THE ORCHARD

In rural Carroll County, Maryland, two-lane roads pass woodlots, hunt clubs, and small farmsteads. It is quaint, unassuming, well-kept country. But turn right onto a narrow, one-lane drive, climb a small hill shaded by thick woods of hickory and oak, and you'll see something rather unusual. The very top of the hill is treeless, cut open to the sky, making the landscape look like the smooth dome of a friar's tonsure. After a bit of grass and wildflowers the compact, orderly rows of Deep Run Orchard appear, where Jim and Donna Davis operate the largest commercial pawpaw orchard in the country: more than a thousand trees on five acres.

Even if there were hundreds of pawpaw orchards, theirs would stand out as exceptional. The Davises pick and ship two to three tons of fruit — up to six thousand pounds — each year. Every pawpaw person in the know speaks of Deep Run with reverence. So I've come to the Davises' orchard this September to help pick and pack fruit, to learn firsthand what a first-rate commercial pawpaw orchard should look like.

When Jim bought the land in 1996, it was fallow, a former cornfield. Since then, he and Donna have built a beautiful home just a few yards from the orchard and are two decades into reforesting the rest of the property, planting sweetbay and umbrella magnolias, red maples, oaks, and other native trees. Jim raised and released bobwhite quail and ruffed grouse, the first young fowl to browse this hilltop in decades. Ensconced by nature, the two are at home; Donna is a forester for the state of Maryland, and though he is an indoor landscaper by profession, Jim too is an outdoorsman and naturalist at heart. The interior of their home is decorated with Jim's collection of Indian arrowheads, many collected on Youghiogheny River canoe trips. Among their artwork is a print of Audubon's colored engraving of the now-extinct Carolina parakeet.

In addition to reforesting and reintroducing wildlife, Jim also wanted an active farm project. Carroll County extension agent Tom Ford introduced Jim to Neal Peterson in the early 1990s. Neal was then looking for a site in Maryland for one of his Regional Variety Trials. Jim had eaten wild pawpaws in the past, but Neal's cultivars really impressed him. The two became fast friends. Once, I asked Neal what he was most proud of looking back on his career. His friendship with Jim Davis ranked at the top.

Jim is soft-spoken and kind, but beneath his easygoing demeanor is a stubborn experimentalist. "I don't like people telling me I can't do something," he says.

Most people he talked to said it just wouldn't work, that there's simply no market for pawpaws. "That's what intrigued me in the beginning, the challenge of trying to introduce this fruit to the market," Jim says. "And in the beginning, I really had no idea if this was going to work or not."

"I think a challenge and a difficult pursuit motivates him," Neal Peterson says. "And he obviously has ambition. He didn't just plant a couple trees in the backyard." Indeed, Jim's orchard has grown steadily from one acre to five. He has invested in irrigation, cold storage, and a barn's worth of farm equipment — all things a commercial orchard needs — not to mention countless hours of hard work. And, like Neal's attempt in Pendleton, it was all a gamble.

The majority of Jim's fruit is shipped overnight to high-end customers through marketers and distributors like Heritage Foods and Earthy Delights. Last year, retail customers paid a hundred dollars for a ten-pound box of pawpaws. A majority of that cost is in shipping; boxes are overnighted to customers from a facility in Westminster. If you've ever eaten pawpaw in New York City, in a restaurant's dish or from a specialty grocer, chances are the fruit came from Deep Run.

Like most pawpaw growers, and plenty other farmers, the Davises have careers outside the orchard. Throughout the year, pawpaws demand a certain amount of attention — watering, fertilization, pruning, pollination, and so on. But when the fruit is dropping there's time for nothing else. "Sunrise to sunset," Jim says. Donna took vacation days to be in the orchard this week; Jim somehow makes it work.

Jim was happy to show me the ropes, but most years he doesn't hire outside help. Picking pawpaws, especially for Davis's high-end customers, must be done carefully. It's certainly not as intuitive as gathering nuts, nor as forgiving as harvesting apples, pears, or bananas. The treatment of oranges, piled atop one another and left to rest for days under the hot Florida sun in the back of a tractor trailer, would be an unthinkable way to handle pawpaws.

Unfortunately, there's little in the way of color change or color break to guide a pawpaw picker. Most pawpaws won't turn from green to yellow while on the tree. Rather, it's all in the touch. Each pawpaw must be given a gentle squeeze between forefinger and thumb, feeling for the slightest bit of give. This means Jim and Donna test each pawpaw, multiple times, before harvesting. More than six thousand pounds are handled this way — that's three tons of fruit checked, rechecked, and finally handpicked.

If a pawpaw is picked too early, it never ripens; if you wait too long, it falls. I know of at least one other grower who pads the ground with beds of straw. Foragers, meanwhile, are able to gather fruit from the forest floor and still make sales at markets. But due to food safety regulations, Jim won't sell those that hit the ground. And he's had a few bad experiences, including helpers picking fruit too early (a waste), and fruit handled too roughly, which then bruises and discolors. "I'm getting a little older now," Jim says, though you wouldn't know it by looking at him, "so occasionally we have a few family members come in, but it's just mainly my wife and myself."

We spend most of the first day hauling fruit. Our first stop is to Macbride & Gill Falcon Ridge Farm. Stanton Gill, who runs the farm with his wife and kids, buys ninety pounds of pawpaw. He will resell the fruit — along with his own Asian pears, cherries, apples, grapes, blueberries, figs, and currants, depending on the season — at farmers markets, but also takes fruits to restaurants, another important aspect of the business that Jim just doesn't have time for. "They're looking for local-grown fruit that you can't get other places, and looking for unusual," Stanton says. "And this fits right under the bill for them." Not far from Deep Run, in Westminster, Bud's at Silver Run recently served flambéed pawpaw ice cream for one of their wine dinners. The ice cream was made by South Mountain Creamery, a dairy in nearby Middletown. Jim hopes a local winery or brewery will also become interested in pawpaws.

Central Marylanders aren't as traditionally familiar with pawpaws as those in the western, Appalachian part of the state. But Stanton's family makes an effort to educate their customers. They offer samples, have printed materials and signs on hand, and are able to answer the typical questions that arise.

In 2011, Allison Aubrey produced an in-depth radio story on pawpaws for NPR, which created a huge buzz for the fruit. Growers and promoters were ecstatic. Stanton had typically been able to sell fifty pounds of pawpaws a day. After Aubrey's story, this doubled. "It was just because everybody heard about it," he says. The pawpaws, of course, came from Jim's orchard. "It's fallen back this year because now it's back to people don't recognize this fruit," Stanton says. "You have to explain it." But Stanton has another tactic. He simply lets the pawpaw freaks do their thing.

"They create customers for us," Stanton says. "Because they get in and they tend to get glowing on the thing, and talking about it. If someone's going, 'Wow, I love this, I'm putting it on my yogurt,' I'll see [other customers] looking at the fruit and next thing they're picking up two or three. They go, 'I guess I better get one.'" Donna Davis once told a reporter, rather diplomatically, "The people who like them are passionate about them, I suppose because it takes so much to grow them, and they have that delicate flavor."[1] But then she added something probably closer to the truth. "It's kind of a cult thing." Stanton has one customer in particular who comes each week to sing the praises of pawpaw. He encourages other marketgoers to buy them, lists their benefits, describes their unique flavor. He can't help himself, he's been bitten by the bug. "The thing is," Stanton says, "he's learned to grow them himself."

An organic farm in Rappahannock County, Virginia, picks wild pawpaws from the woods surrounding its fields, which sell for twelve dollars a pound at its urban markets. And in cities from Atlanta to Chicago there's a growing demand for the fruit. Oriana Kruszewski, a pawpaw grower in northern Illinois, says, "We can't produce enough to meet the demand in Chicago." Like Stanton's pawpaw freak, the fruit's admirers are growing numerous, but they're often disconnected from the sites of production. To be clear, these demands are strong among a handful of individuals, but still account for a small slice of the buying public — there are no picketers outside supermarkets demanding greater pawpaw importation.

Perhaps the pawpaw's unfamiliarity to central Marylanders, Chicagoans, and Atlantans is what helps engender the desire for pawpaws, the paradoxically exotic native, the fruit that Americans should have been eating all along but haven't. As long as it remains new and curious they're willing to pay a premium for the fruit. But are those high prices sustainable? In eastern Kentucky you'd be hard pressed to sell pawpaws for twelve bucks a pound (in Pikeville, I witnessed a gentleman buy a bag of wild fruit for just a dollar). Neal Peterson remembers what he was told in (of all places) Paw Paw, West Virginia, when he attempted to sell his cultivars at a town fair. "Why should I pay four dollars a pound when I can go into the woods, and they're free?" Improved cultivars, though far and away larger and reliably better tasting, are harder to sell in places where pawpaw culture has remained the strongest.

❧

At a gas station on the outskirts of Gettysburg, Pennsylvania, we meet Bill Mackintosh. Since 2007, Mackintosh Farms has sold Jim's pawpaws at their home market stand, and at the farmers market in Berryville, Virginia. We're meeting to replenish their stock. "You better be calling Jim," Bill's wife, Lori, had said. "They're gone."

"I think people are starting to think about us in September as having pawpaws, now, thanks to Jim," Bill says. The farm's high earners are peaches, tomatoes, and apples. "But all these little things are just more that we can do to maybe draw some other folk in."

In the past the Mackintoshes hand-processed their pulp. "It's several days in a row, somebody that's sitting there working on it," Bill says. Jim laughs, and adds in agreement, "It gets old pretty quick." In the back of Jim's truck is a box of pawpaw rejects, fruit that is either (or both) bruised or undersized. Bill has found someone who wants to experiment with a machine processor. "A big part of the problem is that there hasn't been an easy way to get all the seeds out, and get the skin off," Bill says. It's not for a lack of trying on Jim's part. For four years he drove to Cornell University in Ithaca, New York, with a four-hundred-pound truckload of fresh pawpaws. "I'd put them in coolers, or just boxes, and pray that the weather was cool and that everything would get there okay," Jim says. One of Cornell's specialties is food science and processing; their labs discovered a fibrous subdural layer atop the flesh that also contains polyphenolic compounds that give the fruit an off-putting bitter taste. So it's not just the skins that contain those compounds, which might make processing pawpaws that much more difficult. The trips were educational, but Jim didn't walk away with an economical method or miracle machine that made processing pawpaws as automated as pressing truckloads of oranges into juice.

"But if somebody made it easy for them to take that next step, that may open up several markets that we couldn't even supply enough for," Bill says. "I'm hoping it goes through the roof."

Back at Deep Run the sun begins to set. We do just a little picking and prep work for tomorrow. I grab a few of the fallen pawpaws, lying in the grass — one for the morning's breakfast — and stash them in a mini fridge, which is already stocked, generously, with snacks and water for my visit. The workday is over.

We settle in for pizza and beer. Donna tells me about first meeting Jim. While they were dating he'd given her a pair of pawpaw seedlings to plant in her backyard — a romantic gesture of togetherness between the future orchardist and forester.

Jim walks upstairs from the basement, where he's been talking on the landline to a buyer in New York City. The buyer was haggling about price. "Can't you put the fruit in a different [read: cheaper] box?" Jim's been through this before — through costly (and sticky) trial and error they'd found these boxes and wrapping to be the best solutions.

The fruit is spoken for before Jim picks it. He commits several hundred pounds to each of his online buyers at the beginning of each season. But apparently this other New York buyer had made his own promises — of pawpaws to chefs throughout the city — and needed more than Jim could spare. In the end though, three hundred pounds is what Jim had, and it's what the New York buyer would get.

❧

The next day, I rise early and eat breakfast outside in a lawn chair. My meal consists of chilled pawpaw, and black coffee I've brewed in the camper. The fruit is so large — fleshy, as Neal Peterson would say — that I'm able to lazily pick around the seeds; unlike wild pawpaws, this one fruit is enough to fill me up. I have also found that the seeds — notorious for clinging to the flesh — seem to pop out with ease from a refrigerated pawpaw.

After a little while I hear Jim walking up the short gravel drive, his T-shirt tucked neatly into his jeans, ready for another day in the orchard.

Our equipment consists of four tools: clippers to snip the fruit from the peduncle (or fruit stem), plastic tubs and foam padding for storage, a John Deere cart, and our hands. In the orchard, trees are spaced eight feet apart in-row, and between rows, twelve feet. Jim determines which row we will start with, and we go up to the first tree, and look and feel. Many that we pick are already marked by faint fingerprints; Jim checked for ripeness just yesterday. They were rock-hard then, but now they're ready. Jim tells me to give it a try. The fruit gives slightly to the pressure of my fingers, telling me it's ripe enough. I snip the fruit from the peduncle, careful not to let any other fruit from the cluster drop. If any of the peduncle remains on the fruit, the stiff, twiggy attachment will cause the fruit to bruise while resting in storage. The fruit I pick, still nearly completely pale green, is firm and heavy.

Occasionally fragrance can be a guide. If there's a fruity aroma to the pawpaw — the one I'm holding has it — it's a sure sign of ripeness. "It may not be ready for the table, but in a day or so on the counter, it's ready to go," Jim says. Which is exactly how we want to time our harvest: The fruit will sit in cold storage for a minimal amount of time; in a day or so it will be processed for shipping, and then finally arrive overnight on someone's doorstep, fragrant and ready to eat.

In the first years of production, Jim lugged a stepladder around on his back. He quickly saw the benefits of pruning. Not only did it wear out his back, but climbing up and down a ladder just to check for ripeness was too time consuming. And also dangerous: Pawpaw wood is weak and flexible, and wouldn't hold the weight of a man on a ladder. The trees today, though stout and mature, are on average no taller than seven feet.

Jim typically begins combing rows for ripe fruit in late August. As the season progresses, he recalls which cultivars ripen when (PA-Golden is first, then the Alleghenies and the Shenandoahs), which rows have been checked that week, and when to return. "If everything works out, it's a good year, we might have fruit into the first week of October, which is usually Susquehannas." Each row is labeled by cultivar. Yesterday, he picked all of the remaining Alleghenies. As an earlier-ripening variety, they were done for the season.

We repeat this harvesting program for several hours, filling each plastic container only one-layer deep. I cut down a cluster of three pawpaws. Two are respectable in size, as big as mangoes, but the third is an obvious runt, maybe just four inches around. "Drop the peewee," Jim says. I toss it under the tree's drip line and give it a little kick toward the trunk. We do the same with anything of similar size, anything too small for a mail-order customer to receive. Any fruit that even suggests more seed than pulp is frustrating to a consumer, especially considering the ten-dollars-a-pound price tag. And since Jim doesn't yet have a system for processing the small, bruised, or otherwise disfigured pawpaws, under the tree they go.

But it's not a total loss. With such heavy fruit production the orchard trees are bound to have problems with nutrient deficiency — and a few rows are already showing signs of dried, blackened leaves and, in general, a fatigued, drained look. The hilltop's non-alluvial soil — a loamy clay-type mica schist — is not ideal for pawpaws. The topsoil eroded when the fields were full of corn. "It's weathered soil," Jim says. So then a few (but just a few, since too many could lead to fungal problems) decomposing pawpaws will aid, if only to a small degree, in giving back to the taxed soil.

Jim fertilizes in late fall or early spring. Last fall he put down a standard 20-20-20 general-purpose fertilizer of nitrogen, phosphorus, and potassium. Through soil tests he learned that the trees, in the artificial orchard setting, use a lot of magnesium, potassium, and nitrogen. And even from tree to tree, requirements can differ. "I couldn't quite figure out what was wrong with all the Alleghenies," he says. "Then I did the test run, and yep, they were low on nitrogen. But all the other trees were okay."

Spring came very early this year. Temperatures reached the high eighties in early March, and other than a few frost scares remained unusually warm through the summer. "If it is stinking hot, everything will start maturing rapidly, and if there's a drought, the trees start stressing," Jim says. We've taken the John Deere cart down to a small wooden shed that houses his water pumps. "To eliminate that problem we now have a drip system on here. So we shouldn't have any more drought issues here."

But it's September now and the heat has yet to abate. Under these conditions no amount of irrigation will stop fruit from ripening prematurely.

"You can see like this row here," Jim says, pointing to a straight line of Taytwos. "The problem is that when we went through this row, we would check the fruit and it was still hard. Thirty-six hours later when we're rotating back through the orchard, there's all this fruit on the ground. It just dropped, just like that." The line between under- and overripe, between profit and loss, is incredibly thin.

I've never handled this many pawpaws, and my hands have taken on a light, chalky coating. Pawpaws develop a barely noticeable dusting on their skin, but after handling several hundred my fingertips are white. It easily brushes off on my jeans, but it's a reminder that growing and harvesting pawpaws in a monoculture, in mass plantings like the Davises, is still new territory. These early orchards will continue to reveal new ways of understanding the fruit. Jim says the Shenandoahs, especially, give off the chalky residue. "Usually, when it's ripening, it'll have that on there." It's another tactile marker to guide the harvesting.

The wild pawpaw is thought to have few pests (if you even count the zebra swallowtail as a pest), but we're still finding out what happens when you grow several hundred, if not thousands, on a hilltop, out of the woods and removed from native plant communities. Growers do know of a few serious problems: the pawpaw webworm (*Omphalocera munroei*), which spin web-like nets around the limbs, and can (though not usually) defoliate entire trees; the pawpaw peduncle borer, which true to its name, bores into flowers causing them to drop; and the *Phyllosticta* genus of fungus. *Phyllosticta*, which appears in brown spots and scales on leaves and fruit, is most problematic as it can cause fruit to crack, and split fruit is useless at Deep Run. So far, Jim has been lucky in that pests haven't ravaged his orchard.

☙

I've seen large pawpaws, but these are ridiculous. Here, fruit weighing over a pound is routine. Many clusters grow behind leaf cover, closer to the tree's central trunk and out of direct sunlight, which is exactly where Jim would prefer they'd all grow. Anything on the outer limbs risks sun scald, cracking, and discoloration. Those on the inside are protected and able to grow and ripen relatively stress-free. And after Jim's thinning, they'll receive an even greater stream of nutrients once a few competitors have been removed. It's in here, behind the tree's mass of leaves, that I find what

I swear must be the largest pawpaw ever grown. I hold it out for Jim to see. "It's as big as a coconut!" I call out. But Jim is unfazed. At Deep Run, they're routinely this big.

These cultivars — mostly Peterson Pawpaws; Allegheny, Shenandoah, and Susquehanna, among others — are the result of just twenty years of breeding. The kidney-shaped, often bitter fruits of the wild seem like a different species compared with the Susquehanna I'm now holding in my hands, until I remember it's just two generations removed from the woods. As great as these fruits are, they're just the beginning.

In addition to the improved genes of these pawpaws, Davis's skills as an orchardist contribute to the size and quality of each fruit. In June, Davis conducts the first round of fruit thinning, reducing the miniature banana-like hands from five to seven in a cluster, to three or four, by pinching off the excess fruit. "That's a very tedious process," Jim says, "But if you want high-quality fruit, I don't want any more than about ten to fifteen pounds of fruit on these trees." Throughout the season he continues to monitor the fruit, removing anything damaged by disease or insects. It would be difficult for most pawpaw lovers to discard those young fruits, prized as they are from Atlanta to Chicago, but the benefits are proven.

❧

When our plastic tubs are filled we cart the pawpaws back to the outbuilding. Inside, Donna, with help from Jim's sister, Allison, is putting together stiff cardboard boxes for shipping. They lay a piece of bubble wrap in each box, cut from a large spool to the right of the worktable. The process is standardized and efficient. But the first shipments out of Deep Run weren't so successful. Early attempts using thinner boxes meant fruits arrived crushed, bruised, and if not inedible then definitely far from appetizing. Eventually they found a winner in the current shipping boxes, which are made of inch-thick cardboard and cost a dollar each. After Donna has built a box and filled it with padding, it's stacked with other empty boxes on a shelf against the wall. It won't be long until every one of them is filled with pawpaws.

Each plastic container is labeled by cultivar, dated, and deposited in the walk-in cooler, which is kept at a very chilly thirty-five degrees Fahrenheit. Jim has found they can be stored like this for several weeks until shipping day. When an order is placed, Jim drives to a pickup facility for FedEx and

UPS in Westminster, where he occasionally gives fruit to the employees. "They all get real excited about that," he says.

The cooler is enclosed by a large outbuilding, where today Donna is prepping shipping boxes. It's the most efficient, convenient pawpaw weigh, package, and storage station that currently exists. Just a few feet from the building's rolling doors, on the other side of a gravel driveway, is the orchard.

Jim's fruit has two main distribution streams. The first is through Earthy Delights, a specialty foods distributor based in Okemos, Michigan, that allows chefs and other home consumers to purchase an order of pawpaws Jim then mails direct. The second is through New York City's Heritage Foods via a similar process. Neal Peterson introduced Jim to Earthy Delights, and to Heritage Foods through the Slow Food USA movement, which had recently inducted pawpaw to its Ark of Taste (a catalog of heirloom foods facing extinction).

Pawpaws are considered too fragile, too perishable to ship, one of the main excuses given as to why they've never been brought under wider cultivation. But Jim and Donna are doing it. Sure, the process might be expensive for both producers and consumers, but several tons of fruit each year are packaged here and delivered to wholesalers and front doors throughout the country. The pawpaws arrive ripe, fragrant, and unbruised. Down the line, there might be breakthroughs in processing, or in value-added products that might help the Davises, but shipping is not a problem. In fact, it's working quite well.

৶

Last year, hurricanes wiped out nearly all of Jim's fruit. "That's the problem with this fruit," he says. "If you get bad storms, even a thunderstorm with a strong downdraft, wind shear, it can destroy your crop just like that." The hurricane tore entire limbs off trees, especially those burdened with heavy fruit. "Some trees were just not salvageable," he continues. "It was a real mess."

"It was terrible," Donna adds, with a laugh (I suppose humor helps in dealing with forces out of your control). "If you have apples or peaches, and they're starting to ripen and you know something is coming on, you can run out and pick them when they're not [ripe], and then just let them ripen themselves in the cooler. You just can't do that with [pawpaws]. We've tried it."

Donna has a small portable radio set up in the shed. There's warnings of severe thunderstorm, a double line, rolling through central Maryland. It's a good thing much of the harvest has been picked, and that the season came early. But there are still many pawpaws on the trees, and hard winds and rains are coming. "Even though you know that storm is coming, you can't pick the underripe fruit," Jim says. "You know you're going to lose — especially the large ones — sometimes a good number of them, and sometimes just a few. It all depends upon the severity of the storm."

Around midday, two visitors arrive, a woman named McKenzie and her friend Jordan. McKenzie and her husband are new part-time farmers, raising alpacas, twelve sheep, chickens, bees, and growing a host of vegetables. Jordan is a foraging enthusiast. They're both here to learn more about pawpaws, and to see what a commercial orchard looks like.

Since Jim doesn't use any fruit that drops, Jordan, McKenzie, and I eagerly gather fruit from below the trees. Both of their shirts are stretched into makeshift baskets and filled to capacity, and even though I've spent two days in an orchard, I still think of each individual pawpaw as valuable. It's a bumper crop of fallen, discarded fruit. McKenzie is considering pawpaws for her farm. She and Jordan plan to save the seeds of this fruit and grow trees, the beginnings, possibly, of another central Maryland pawpaw orchard.

But all of that is the future. Now, we eat. Jordan breaks a particularly large fruit in half, squeezes the pulp out, and eats as much as he can, as neatly as can be expected. We all soon join him, except for Jim. He usually eats one or two a year, and that's it. He appreciates their flavor, but his interest is mainly about the challenge of growing them and pioneering a market. Donna enjoys a few more than Jim, usually just snacking while she's out in the field. Otherwise, all the pawpaws are sent away.

Jim and I haul our last load of pawpaws back to the shed where Allison and Donna have built up the last of the cardboard boxes. Allison talks again of the approaching storm warnings, which now include a tornado watch. It's important that we've picked all the ripe fruit, as the winds and rains will surely strip a good amount of fruit from the trees. The sky quickly changes to a black swirling mass of clouds. Heavy winds blow over the ridge, contrasting deep-green pawpaw foliage against a background of pure-black sky. As a precaution Jim and I cart a gas-powered generator to the shed — if the power goes out, the coolers will stay on. We finish just as a hard rain begins to fall and hustle to the house before we're totally soaked.

We picked 218 pounds of fruit today, most of it Shenandoah. Jim broke a one-day record earlier this year (which had previously been 450 pounds), with a grueling 700 pounds.

Each year, when the fruit has all been picked and the season is finally over, Jim and Donna breathe and relax a bit. But by midwinter, work begins anew. In February, Neal Peterson typically comes to the orchard to collect budwood (also known as scion wood) of his patented varieties, which he then sells to licensed nurseries. After Neal has finished, Jim prunes the orchard. There's a large deer herd in the area that causes a lot damage to the trees. "Any trees that are busted up because of that, or just don't look right and I know from the year before were sickly looking, I'll remove those," Jim says. Fertilization is done either in late fall or early spring. In mid-April, the orchard flowers. By a month or so after that, while the leaves are still small, any fruit that will develop has formed. "We have a lot of pollinators — flies, beetles, little tiny things that I'm not sure what they are," Jim says. He hopes one day Stanton will be able to study the unknown bugs working at Deep Run. "But, you know, it's just one of those things on the back of the list." In June, the trees are in full leaf, and in a short time the zebra swallowtails have emerged. "To walk those rows when everything is leafed out, and have these little apparitions floating around," Jim says, "it's quite spectacular."

Once the rains have gone, I collapse in the camper and sleep to the sound of a wet orchard: water dripping, cicadas, and crickets.

⁂

After leaving Westminster, I drive to the southwest corner of Greene County, Pennsylvania, a mile or so from the West Virginia border. I am meeting Jeanne and Llew Williams, owners of Red Barn Farm. I know I have arrived because I see their big red barn. Guinea hens peck in the road; goats meander on a pastured hillside. Beyond, the dirt road curves and disappears behind a billowy draping of green hills. Llew directs me into the house where I find Jeanne stirring a large pot of applesauce.

I'd learned about Red Barn by calling the Morgantown Farmers Market, where Red Barn is the only vendor offering the fruit. Jeanne and Llew Williams began collecting pawpaws by accident. Several years ago, a sixty-four-year-old woman named Dorothy Eckert wanted to hike the Warrior Trail in a week's time. The trail is a five-thousand-year-old Indian path that runs along sixty-seven miles of ridgelines ("Clean across Greene County"), and was once used by Native Americans for quick access to flint deposits, among other things. Llew, who is president of the Warrior Trail Association, drove Ms. Eckert to the trailhead and arranged to leave a car for her at the other end. Since he was going to be out, Llew brought his kayak and paddled a stretch of the Monongahela River. He stopped at a creekbed near an abandoned farm whose barn and farmhouse were both falling in. "I was eating lunch, and these things were laying on the ground," Llew says. "They smelled really good. So I had to try one, and I thought, *It's got to be a pawpaw.* I've heard of such a thing, but I've never actually seen one." So he peeled one back and ate his first.

Each year, Llew and Jeanne return to the grove, and in good years they gather several buckets of fruit. Llew says this particular grove is an unusual place. "There's pawpaws up and down that creek, but nothing like this. I've never seen a stand of them all in one place like this — and they're big, and they're mature. And you would go in there and the ground would just be littered with them. I mean we would pick as much as we thought we could safely carry in a canoe and not even put a dent in the pawpaws."

Once Jeanne has finished with the applesauce, she and Llew give me a tour of the farm. Jeanne raises upward of eighty goats, along with several hundred broiler chickens and laying hens; across the road they raise vegetables in a mobile high tunnel. We walk to a cold cellar built into the hillside, adorned by the stonework of a local artist. Jeanne kneels to show me handfuls of pawpaws they've gathered in the wild. They are small, like misshapen plums, browning with just a few specks of green. This year, the wild pawpaw crop wasn't great; it was too dry and too hot, and they were likely too late in arriving, but there were enough. The pawpaws are kept here, without electricity, until Jeanne can pulp the fruit to make muffins, butter, and jams, an assortment of goods she sells at the Morgantown market along with her staples of goat meat and organic produce.

Across the road, along a stream, they have planted a few young pawpaw trees, but not any particular cultivar. The weeds have grown high around the young trees, but we locate them and they're surviving. Eventually they might grow to produce good fruit. Jeanne's goats will browse nearby, as will the chickens and guinea hens. But Red Barn Farm is not establishing a pawpaw orchard. For Jeanne and Llew, pawpaws have just become a part of life in Greene County, and of the changing seasons. They're another reminder of why they love living in the country, raising livestock and produce. The hunt has become a ritual late-summer outing; they pack a canoe with sandwiches and water, and spend the day paddling, savoring the waning hours of warmth and light. The act is as much about getting outdoors, spending time together in nature, as it is about collecting pawpaws. Neither Jeanne nor Llew grew up eating pawpaws, but the fruit and the foraging are now part of a new culture they're nurturing, and an older culture they're reviving.

You could argue that pawpaws have earned their day in the orchard, that the fruit has potential as a cultivated crop. But perhaps there's equal room in American culture for rituals like the one Jeanne and Llew share: going out with a loved one, by boat, by foot, and indulging in nature. Perhaps there's room to reap the wild bounty as well.

༄

A few days after my visit to Deep Run, Lance Beard drives a small pickup truck from Columbia, Maryland, to the Davises' orchard. It's a ritual Beard has repeated for the past six years. He has assembled a makeshift storage unit, two-by-fours nailed into shelving units in the bed of the truck. With Jim and Donna's help he loads more than six hundred pounds of fresh fruit — pawpaws Jim and I picked together just days before — into the truck bed. Beard then drives through the night, through the hills of western Maryland, West Virginia, and into Appalachian Ohio. His destination: the Thirteenth Annual Ohio Pawpaw Festival. He will have three days to sell more than a quarter ton of pawpaws.

— CHAPTER NINE —

THE OHIO PAWPAW
FESTIVAL

Each September Lake Snowden is transformed by a hive of *Asimina* activity, its low hills and open fields swarmed by all manner of paw-paw lovers: farmers, chefs, back-to-the-landers, millennial permies, ag scientists, and many who have only recently learned of the fruit. They are by turns obsessed, curious, entrepreneurial, proselytic, and nostalgic. And more of them come out each year for this signature pawpaw event, the one-and-only Ohio Pawpaw Festival.

"Right here in southern Ohio we're blessed with literally millions of paw-paws," says the festival's founder, Chris Chmiel. In fact, thanks to Chmiel and this wild plenty, I have begun to think of Athens County, Ohio, as the capital of the American Pawpaw Belt, and Chmiel its mayor. He created the festival in 1999 to get folks to pay attention to this abundance, and it has worked. The festival has grown from a one-day event attended by a hand-ful of Chmiel's friends to a three-day extravaganza celebrating Ohio's state native fruit (an official designation as of 2009). It's now the biggest outdoor party in the county, which is saying a lot considering the reputation of Ohio University. The festival — imagine the love child of a tie-dyed jam fest and a 4-H exhibition at the county fair — now includes live music, expert speakers, and a host of demonstrations and activities, drawing as many as eight thou-sand visitors. Many come for the food, including pawpaw-stuffed crepes, pawpaw salsa, pawpaw ice cream sandwiches made with oatmeal-spicebush cookies, and pawpaw curries, while others go for the beer: wheats, saisons, and pale ales all brewed locally with Ohio-grown pawpaws. The festival is proof that if you build it — or bake it or brew it — they will come.

I arrive on a Friday afternoon and set up a tent in the camping area atop a gentle hill. The event has had near-perfect weather for more than a decade; sunny September days and cool nights. It appears this weekend will continue that trend. But this is not my first trip to Albany. In fact, my first exposure to pawpaws — the event that hooked me and inspired this book — occurred at this festival, in a patch of woods between the park and a farmer's pasture. I came out of the forest with a bag of fruit, baptized in pulp. I'm sure hundreds have had similar experiences. I see the familiar look on people's faces as they come out of the woods or walk away from a sampling table, that of puzzlement and wonder, wheels turning, grasping at the mystery and the possibilities.

I walk the dirt road to the festival entrance. A hand-painted wooden sign reads, WELCOME TO THE PAWPAW CAPITAL OF THE WORLD. Inside, vendor booths and large tented spaces form orderly avenues in a village-like setting. The sleepy morning slowly comes to life with vendors brewing coffee, and potatoes and eggs frying in cast-iron skillets. Under the main tent official swag — T-shirts, hats, pint glasses, and posters — is arranged on tables with designs from current and past festivals — slogans like "Pawpaws to the People"; a cartoon-like illustration of a guitar with a pawpaw body; artwork inspired by Cesar Chavez–era farmworker propaganda, others in the street-art style of Shepard Fairey; and this year, an intricate and timely Mayan-calendar-inspired riff on pawpaws. There are pamphlets explaining what a pawpaw is and how to grow one; information from the Ohio Pawpaw Growers Association; the Ohio Hill Country Heritage Area; and others. Elsewhere, nurseries offer pawpaw trees — both little year-old seedlings and mature, flowering trees of six feet — as well as tropical herbs and other native plants. There's art, jewelry, handmade leather goods, clothes, pottery and sculpture. Later in the day there will be workshops and discussions on a variety of topics, from yoga and bicycle maintenance to lye soap making and traditional scything.

Toward the lake an atlatl, or spear throwing, contest is under way. Aside from being an enjoyable challenge, the ancient hunting tool is part of the wider acknowledgment of the indigenous groups who originally ate pawpaws ("Ohio's First Fruit" was the slogan of the 2003 festival). There is a strong sense here that the pawpaw is ancient and belongs to an earlier culture. "There's something very mysterious and romantic about the idea that this used to be central to the food systems of people who lived here, and it just disappeared one hundred years ago," a pawpaw vendor said. Organic and natural growing systems are embraced, as are human-powered tools: several Athens-area farmers use the scythe, while a tortilla company grinds corn with a bicycle-powered mill. The East of the River Shawnee Tribe of Ohio is also represented, hosting workshops on flint knapping and survival skills, flute playing, and demonstrating Shawnee storytelling, drumming, dancing, and singing.

Soon, various drums are pounding throughout the grounds, percussion mingling with banjo, guitar, and a growing din of voices. By midday fields are covered in cars and the festival grounds are packed with people (there are pedicabs, a horse-drawn wagon, and shuttle buses between Ohio University and Lake Snowden). Festival attire ranges from T-shirts and overalls to polo shirts and hemp-thread ponchos. It's a diverse crowd mingling under a shared love for, or simply curiosity about, pawpaws.

A circus of characters materialize between the music stage and beer tent. While a country-folk group performs I look over my shoulder and see a man on stilts with a goat mask and hooved feet, hovering above the crowd like a pagan reveler in carnival season. A pawpaw mascot in an overstuffed pawpaw suit (split in half to reveal his seeds) bounces about, posing for pictures. And for some reason I will never learn, someone with an old-fashioned megaphone periodically calls out a booming, monotonous chant, "Paw, paw, paw, paw, paw, paw, paw, paw . . ." Long after the festival this chant will ring in my head.

Under the main tent, which is dubbed the Pawpaw Tent, a panel of local experts (a grower, a chef, and a professor, among others) taste and comment on submitted fruits, some of which are named cultivars, some wild, and some even nascent breeding efforts. After sampling each entry, the judges will select just one to be named the year's Best Pawpaw. A second award is given each year for the largest pawpaw, and a third to the winner of the pawpaw cook-off contest, which has seen the likes of pawpaw semifreddo, punjabi pockets with pawpaw chili sauce, and pawpaw mojitos.

Like any good fair, there's also an eating contest. When the band has finished, contestants — young and old, men and women — sit at a table near the stage, hands tied behind their backs. Chmiel, the event's MC, piles a bowlful of processed pawpaw pulp, seeds and all, in front of each contestant. Their task is to eat all of the pulp, clean every seed by mouth, and then spit them out. The victor will be declared when all fruit is eaten and all seeds have been spat, shiny and clean. Chmiel asks an audience member to keep time and begins the countdown. "On your mark, get set . . . pawpaw!" The dozen or so contestants dive face-first into the pulp, cheeks smeared in yellow goop (it's quite messy for one man with a particularly long beard). In just a few minutes a young woman wearing a Ron Paul T-shirt hoists her fists high above her head and is declared this year's winner.

Elsewhere, pawpaws are eaten with a bit more grace. At the booth marked by a large Peterson Pawpaws banner, paper plates labeled ALLEGHENY, SHENANDOAH, and SUSQUEHANNA offer generous samples of cultivated fruit. These are the pawpaws that Jim Davis and I picked several days earlier at Deep Run Orchard, packed with care by Jim, Donna, and Allison.

Peterson Pawpaws have been present at the Ohio festival since its inception, and Lance Beard began hauling pawpaws from Jim's farm to the festival in 2008 (Neal himself is absent from the festival for the first time this year; Jim and Donna have wanted to return for many years, but September is always "full throttle" at their orchard). As he is most years, Lance is joined by Ken Drabik, and this year also by Nate Orr, one of Neal's close friends from Harpers Ferry.

I jump in to help with sampling. By one o'clock work at the booth is non-stop. To keep the sample plates filled I'm opening stacked pawpaw boxes and gently squeezing the fruit, checking for ripe ones to slice. With a flick of the knife a chunk falls to the plate, and it's just as quickly scooped up. I imagine what it was like at the Dupont Circle farmers market on the day following the *Washington Post* feature. Here at the festival, though, it's even more intense; the fruit is on the shopping list of nearly everyone in sight. This is one of very few occasions in the world when people line up to buy pawpaws.

These Peterson Pawpaws are not cheap. But knowing the work that Jim Davis puts into each piece, knowing the quality — never mind the decades of breeding and analysis — I'm the first to defend the price tag. They're sold one or two at a time, but an occasional large purchase of an entire box is made; the line is long and sales are brisk.

Our booth offers many people their first taste of pawpaw. Jim Davis, Neal Peterson, and certainly everyone at this booth would rather have it that way; they recognize the importance of first impressions. "You can have a good pawpaw, and a real bad pawpaw," Davis told me in his orchard. "And that's why I caution people who collect in the wild. It's a roll of the dice. You don't know what you're going to get. And if you had a bad experience it'll probably turn you off for the rest of your life." Not only can a wild, bitter pawpaw taste terrible, but under- or overripe fruit can be emetic. At this booth, however, with the fruit sent away in paper bags and offered as samples, Ken, Lance, and Nate know exactly what kind of experience each customer will have. They can't guarantee everyone will appreciate the texture and flavor, but they can be confident in the quality of the product.

As a biologist, Ken Drabik is interested in pawpaws from a scientific perspective. "I'm really fascinated from the genetics point of view of it," he says. "Ultimately when the pawpaw genome is sequenced, I feel quite confident we're going to find some interesting genes, probably unique to fruit anywhere. Because even though they are part of the Annonaceae — which are indigenous to a very large area of South and Central America — they are very much removed from them as well."

But it's not just the science — he's caught up in the excitement just like I have been, like Neal was, and like Stanton Gill's pawpaw freak in central Maryland is. In fact, when Ken first drove to the festival straight from Chicago he soon went to work. "I didn't leave the booth for like three hours," he says. "I just stayed there and talked and talked — eating samples — and immediately I just jumped in and just helped him cutting fruit."

"It's very exciting to be a part of the rediscovery of the fruit, and trying to find a way for people to reintegrate pawpaws into their diets and into their lives, into American culture and into American commerce," Ken says. "You kind of feel like you found a lost treasure."

Ken, a backyard grower with about a dozen cultivars, drives the eight hours from Chicago each year. And several years ago, when the pawpaw crop from Maryland to Kentucky had been decimated by late frosts, he drove all the way to Deep Run, loaded what little fruit Jim could cobble together, then drove back to Ohio. "We were sold out within two hours," he says. About twenty minutes later a group of four elderly women arrived, who had arranged to be driven the four hours from their nursing home and were heartbroken. They'd not had pawpaws in decades, and would have to wait another year. "I was just so devastated by this," Ken says. "So I kind of feel a responsibility to come and have pawpaw." And no matter how trendy pawpaws have become, if Ken and Nate and Lance hadn't made this trip, and certainly if Jim Davis wasn't growing them, this cultivated fruit would not appear at the festival. The producers are still few.

But most years there's plenty of fruit to go around. And standing behind his booth Ken is often handing over pawpaw to men and women who haven't tasted it in thirty or even fifty years. "Sharing in that joy that people have, it's an experience you can't beat," he says. "There's a thread interwoven between so many concepts, and individuals and organizations, and it's just a nebulous and warm and wonderful energy."

Although these improved cultivars are considered to be the best that exist, and at least twice the size of most wild pawpaws, Lance Beard still says the best pawpaw he ever had was as a child in the Missouri Ozarks. Lance was interested in nature and wildlife from a young age, but had not yet seen a pawpaw when he visited his great-uncle, the first person he'd met who actually had. So they rode in a pickup truck down to the bank of a small river and loaded up a bucket's worth. Lance was told, "You just go set those on the windowsill till they start to smell really good, and that's when you want to eat them." None since — not even Deep Run Orchard's — have lived up to that first pawpaw. "It had an intense caramel flavor. I loved it," he says. "And I never saw a pawpaw again for twenty-five years. I thought they must only grow on that one riverbank in that one area in Ozark County, Missouri, and if I ever go visit there again and am lucky enough to go at the right time, maybe I'll find some." Years went by, and then the Internet came along. He read about the Ohio Pawpaw Festival and about Neal Peterson. Now he can't help but work the festival every year.

"I wouldn't say I prefer a wild pawpaw, because there's too much variability," Lance says. "But if you can get the pawpaw at the right time — which is generally when you're standing under the tree and they just fall, and either you eat it right then or you take it back and put it in a sunny window — it's just something different. Something different happens to the fruit."

Yet Lance also recognizes the need for an appealing commercial fruit. "It's hard to market something that you want to get wrinkly and brown and have an intense aroma of caramel that will fill up a room," he admits. "That's not what people are doing with these."

Some folks taste the Peterson fruits then walk to purchase the smaller, less expensive pawpaws found elsewhere. There are two other vendors selling pawpaw this year. The Herbal Sage Tea Company — a wildcrafting business based in Athens — is offering fruit gathered from the local woods. I was at their booth Saturday morning, drinking fresh-brewed coffee, as a team of hired foragers unloaded a burlap sack of recently gathered pawpaws. They were then arranged on shelves from small to large, priced low to high, and as cheap as a dollar apiece.

Chris Chmiel, of course, sells pawpaws grown at his fifty-acre Integration Acres farm, as well as fruit gathered by his network of foragers. He started this festival to create buyers for that wild abundance. When that interest peaked, he found ways to incorporate the fruit into all manner of products. So along with his fresh fruit are pawpaw Popsicles, pawpaw autumn harvest chutney, pawpaw green tomato relish, pawpaw-spiceberry jam, various goat cheeses (produced from the goats that graze beneath his pawpaw trees), frozen pawpaw pulp, ramp crackers and ramp pasta — a full line of an Appalachia Ohio terroir. But there's one item at the festival that draws the most attention: pawpaw beer.

Pawpaw growers love talking about pawpaw beer. Even the more reserved among them smile mischievously when conversation turns to the kegs at the Ohio Pawpaw Festival, as conversations of the festival invariably do. Under the beer tent, cash is traded for tickets, which are then given to festival volunteers (the most coveted volunteer task) who pour your choice of beverage. This year's offerings: Pawpaw Pale Ale from Zanesville's Weasel Boy Brewing Company; Pawpaw Wheat from Athens's Jackie O's Pub & Brewery; Pawpaw Saison from Akron's Thirsty Dog Brewing Co.; another pawpaw wheat from Cleveland's Buckeye Brewing Company; non-alcoholic pawpaw soda from Athens's Do It Yourself Shop; as well as your typical domestic drafts. But really, on this day, why would anyone choose to drink something *without* pawpaws?

You can taste the fruit in some of them, but for the most part it's just kind of fun to say you're drinking a pawpaw beer. And in keeping with Chmiel's ethos, since all these wild pawpaws are produced each year, allowing them to ferment and be added to beer means they'll at least get used. They'll ferment readily, in a brewery's tank or in the woods; you might as well control the process and create a quality beverage. Further, there's a limit to how many pawpaws you can, or should, eat. But having them in a pint glass allows the celebration to continue.

To recap: that's four pawpaw beers from four Ohio breweries. And all of the pulp used in making these brews is supplied by Chmiel. This is exactly Chmiel's success: He has found willing co-conspirators. Beyond brewers, there's Snowville Creamery, a local dairy that whips up pawpaw ice cream for the festival every year. In addition to farmers market sales, restaurants in downtown Athens feature pawpaw products (Fluff Bakery, for one, makes a rich pawpaw cheesecake). Pawpaw beers are on tap in local bars — Jackie O's and Casa Nueva in Athens — and elsewhere throughout the state. Chmiel now supplies pulp for an heirloom pawpaw curd producer in Chicago. And here at the festival, vendors are encouraged to make creative dishes with pawpaw — for which Chmiel also supplies the pulp.

This is a model that any pawpaw grower can follow. Find a local creamery or ice cream shop, find a brewery, find a willing, creative chef. If you've built these relationships before your first heavy crop comes in (even offering Chmiel's pulp for early experimentation), there will be a local stream for the fruit. Chmiel certainly markets his products, but so does everyone who walks away from a good cup of pawpaw ice cream or enjoys a pint of pawpaw pale ale. The word-of-mouth enthusiasm for pawpaws is driven by these products — ice cream and beer — which, unlike pawpaws, are familiar and loved, and without a doubt will be consumed. So just add pawpaws.

Chmiel was also the first to offer a commercial, branded, frozen pawpaw pulp. For nearly twenty years Integration Acres has been successfully pulping and freezing the fruit on a scale that has yet eluded every other producer. And perhaps most important, the product is available year-round. Unless there's a run on pawpaws, the pulp can be shipped anyplace, anytime.

Pawpaws do well in the freezer. Unlike other fruits, frozen pawpaw pulp keeps its bright yellow color and flavor for up to three years, though Integration Acres also adds ascorbic acid to its pulp, which helps. Integration Acres offers fourteen-ounce packs through its own website, and through distributors like Earthy Delights, for twelve dollars a pound. The bags are kept cool with ice packs and shipped overnight in Styrofoam coolers (the price per pound is not high, but the shipping rates cause the overall price to jump considerably). The availability of frozen pulp allows potential customers, from chefs and brewers to creameries and juice companies, to sample the product during any of the eleven non-pawpaw months. Even better, the unacquainted don't have to fuss with pulping, peeling, and de-seeding the fruit, a time-sensitive and somewhat intimidating process, not to mention the uncertainty of fresh fruit arriving in good condition. The fruit's short season has been a limiting factor to marketing over the decades, but Chmiel's pulp goes a long way toward ameliorating that.

Most other large-scale pawpaw growers lament that they have no time to pulp the fruit, bag it, label it, freeze it, and market it, while simultaneously tending their orchards and other late-summer and fall crops (and, for most, other full-time careers). I can't say for certain how Chmiel does it. When I first asked to tour his facility a few years ago, Chmiel was too busy with the festival, with the harvest, and with his campaign for county council (which he won). So this year, since Chmiel is giving a talk under the Pawpaw Tent, I take the opportunity to find out more about his process.

"At home, what we do is we wash them, and we take them in half, and we kind of *squoosh* them out." Chmiel quickly demonstrates on an imaginary pawpaw. "And then if you have an onion bag, or a mesh bag, that works really well. Put them in the bag and most of the seeds will stay in the bag. We use some machinery for the seeds because we're dealing with tons at a time sometimes, so there's a way to do that." I push for more clarification. "That's pretty much it," he says. "We wash them, we squoosh out the pulpy seeds, and then we take the seeds out, and then we freeze them."

Later, while sampling food from various vendors, I gain some further insight on processing pawpaws from another Athens County resident. Since 1988, Brenda and her husband, Nisar, have operated the Ali Baba's food carts in the Athens area. In 1994 the family bought a nearby home on six acres. While exploring the woods, her children found strange fruits growing along a stream. Brenda had no clue as to what they were. "They look kind of rotten," she says, "And I said, 'Oh, kids, don't touch this stuff.'" It wasn't until the first Ohio Pawpaw Festival — at which Ali Baba's was a vendor — that Brenda learned that those strange wild fruits were pawpaws. Ali Baba's has served its food at every festival, but recently Brenda began incorporating pawpaw into her homemade desserts: pawpaw fruit fudge, pawpaw spicebush cakes, and pawpaw marzipan. Brenda and her children harvest pawpaws growing on her property and bring them to the Appalachian Center for Economic Networks (ACEnet), a business incubator that, among other services, provides the commercial-grade kitchen facility required for most processed food products, such as jams, sauces, and pawpaw pulp. At

ACEnet, along with industrial ovens, choppers, coolers, and freezers, is a machine called a pulper finisher that can separate seeds, skins, and stems from any number of fruits, including pawpaws. "When they came up with the machine at ACEnet, I said, 'Oh, great, you guys take care of it,'" she says. "They can take out those seeds — because otherwise we're cutting them in half, I was peeling them, and basically just mushing it up with my hands and pulling out the seeds. It just took forever." ACEnet is another reason why Athens County is the pawpaw's capital (ACEnet is also where Chmiel first began processing pawpaws before building a commercial facility at his own farm); there's infrastructure that allows pawpaw growers and pickers to make efficient use of not only their fruit, but also their time.

❧

On one morning of the festival, I join for breakfast a young couple who are cooking pancakes on a cast-iron griddle in the common area between tents. They currently live and work on a farm in Johnstown, Ohio where the wheat and eggs in the pancakes, as well as the maple syrup, were produced, but they're looking for a homestead of their own, perhaps near Athens. One of their reasons for attending the festival is to investigate the local sustainable agriculture scene, a community that includes the likes of Snowville Creamery; innovators like Chris Chmiel; and Shagbark Seed & Mill, a new processing facility that produces, among other items, stone-ground heirloom corn and whole spelt flour. It's the type of community where small, creative farmers can find support and partnerships.

Many at the festival, like the couple from Johnstown, are interested in pawpaws as a component of permaculture. Short for "permanent agriculture," permaculture is a sustainable design system modeled on naturally occurring ecosystems. And the pawpaw, as a native plant resistant to the ravages of most pests, is the poster child for American permaculture. "A lot of these native plants, they're just efficient," Chmiel says. "You're not trying to reinvent the wheel here. These things have been growing here for a long time."

Chmiel's Integration Acres is a model of that system. "When I started this whole thing, I put an ad in the paper," he says. "I put a bounty on pawpaws." He drove around southern Ohio gathering pawpaws from various property owners. "I went to this one guy's house, he had a bunch of goats. And all he had left in his pasture were pawpaws." Although goats are known for eating just about anything from tree branches to trash, Chmiel says they don't eat pawpaws. Not the leaves, not the twigs, not the fruit. Like deer and various insects, they're repelled by the plant's Annonaceous acetogenins and other compounds. Chmiel confirms that pigs are also repelled by pawpaws. "I've raised hogs for years and have tried to feed them pawpaw skins and such ... no luck," he wrote in an email. "For whatever reason, I've never met a hog that liked a pawpaw."

Permaculture principles suggest that animals and crops don't need to be as segregated as they tend to be in conventional agriculture. "If you look at agriculture in general, most people are either plant people or they're animal people," Chmiel says. "I think if we can't think more interdisciplinary, maybe we're missing some opportunities to be more efficient."

So Chmiel decided to raise his goats in the pawpaw orchard. This arrangement — the dense grouping of livestock and fruit crop — is economical for several reasons. First, space is not wasted. But further, with the goats' manure spread throughout the pasture, Chmiel doesn't need to buy fertilizers. "I don't have to spend any time or energy," he says, "my goats are working for me." And the goats' manure not only provides nutrients to the soil, but attracts pollinators as well.

Chmiel has pawpaw orchards, but he also collects from the wild. He cultivates patches on his own property as well those of his neighbors (his bounty on pawpaws still stands). But he doesn't stop there. He will even plant trees on the edges of cow and horse pastures belonging to other property owners (a very Johnny Appleseed thing to do); fencerows are great locations for pawpaws.

When Chmiel started Integration Acres farm, he managed wild stands to make them even more productive. The first step was to remove canopy trees, the ashes and sycamores casting too much shade. Then he analyzed the fruit. Chmiel wrote notes directly onto the trunks of trees with a Sharpie marker on the quality of fruit, production load, whether it produced early or late season, and so on. Those with good qualities were kept; the poorer ones were removed. Thus an orchard was culled from the existing thickets. Rather than clear-cutting the land and replanting with grafted cultivars, he took what already grew and made it work better.

Chmiel also uses permaculture to address another concern: the handling of fallen fruit. He plants ground ivy, a wild mint, under his trees. "It has a lot of vines, and it builds this cushion," he says. "Your pawpaws, they fall into that, they don't even touch the ground. Then when you're out there picking them up, it's like finding Easter eggs."

Integration Acres finds value in another wild Ohio crop: It processes black walnuts by the tens of thousands. Although many species of plants are killed by the juglone chemical released by the tree's roots, twigs, and nuts, pawpaws aren't — the two trees are forest companions. After processing tons of walnuts each fall, Chmiel uses the hulled shells as mulch in his pawpaw orchards. The juglone released by the nut hulls does not affect the pawpaws, but it does keep other weeds from growing. Everything is integrated. Chmiel says it's "like turning trash into treasure."

Others have begun intercropping in similar ways. On his tree farm in southern Indiana, George Hale planted more than three hundred black walnut trees for future timber harvests. In the meantime, though, he wanted to increase the land's productivity, and so he decided to plant pawpaws, of which he is a great enthusiast, in between the rows of black walnut. The pawpaws were planted about ten years ago, and Hale says they are producing quite well. The presence of the pawpaws doesn't detract from the value of the lumber, and Hale is rewarded with one of his favorite fruits. Elsewhere, in the parts of maple syrup country that overlap with the Pawpaw Belt, the fruit could find a similar niche in the sugarbush.

⌘

Pawpaw lovers have begun traveling great distances to attend the Ohio festival. This year I meet Kim Bailey, who has traveled from Ducktown, Georgia. In her spare time, she works at Cane Creek Farm, a seventeen-acre farm producing fruits and vegetables, including muscadines, blueberries, figs, and pawpaws, for her weekly CSA. Kim has traveled a great distance today, but it's not the farthest she has traveled for nature, an honor that might belong to one of the seven trips she's taken to Michoacan, Mexico, to study monarch butterflies. Her first taste of pawpaws came when, while on business in Columbus, Ohio, she found the fruit at a local grocery store. "That's when my interest turned to full-out infatuation!" Kim recalls. The thought of "growing tropical crème brûlée on trees," while also attracting butterflies, has led her to plant a number of pawpaws at her home.

I ask Kim whether other Georgians, those who aren't rare-fruit growers, are as familiar with the fruit as are folks in southern Ohio. "I don't think hardly anybody I know knows too much about pawpaws unless their families go back," she says. But with her ear to the ground, Kim did meet a fellow gardener (and beekeeper) with pawpaw tips in Dahlonega, Georgia. "He told me about the pawpaw pickin' place on the Etowah River. I went up there, actually that same weekend, and I couldn't find any. I found the trees, but no pawpaws." I suppose it's another reason why she, and so many others, come to the festival: Fruit is sure to be found here.

I meet other folks from South Carolina, New York, Virginia, Illinois. Some years, the truly dedicated have even traveled from Europe (nurserymen and plant researchers, typically). And the enthusiasm is spreading. Pawpaw festivals are popping up elsewhere in the country, in North Carolina, Delaware, Maryland, and even Rhode Island, which is at the northeastern edge of the fruit's range. It's being embraced by all manner of plant-minded communities too: Pawpaws are part of the Washington Botanical Society's newest logo; they're included in habitat restoration plantings from North Carolina to Missouri; various local and national news outlets feature pawpaw write-ups each September; and chefs, breweries, bakeries, and creameries create unique pawpaw beers, wines, sauces, breads, and gelatos. I often wonder where it will all lead.

I once asked Neal Peterson if he thought pawpaws could replace bananas in the American market. At the festival, this is the kind of talk you'll hear: "Why are we importing these tropical fruits when we have our own native fruit growing right here?" When I told Neal of the vision (which I've sometimes shared) that pawpaws could reduce the amount of tropical imports, he responded, "And why would they want to do that?" Bananas are produced and consumed year-round, while pawpaws are limited to just one month. And despite the nicknames — poor man's banana, insert-your-state-here banana — they're quite different. If a person wants a banana or mango or avocado, a pawpaw simply won't cut it. But even if in practice the pawpaw can't be a stand-in for bananas, it still represents the goal of the local-food ethos, that this native fruit that produces a tropical-like custard apple in the temperate North should at least be given a chance to become a regular part of our diets, and be cultivated, wild-harvested, and eaten each September. It should at least be known. We can eat bananas, but we should eat pawpaws too. Looking back, pawpaw was never the "staple" in Native American diets that many supporters might claim it was. There wouldn't have been enough, and ripe fruit was available for such a brief period each year, that it couldn't have been. But they ate or dried or cooked as many pawpaws as was possible, and it was used to its fullest extent and value as a yearly, cherished treat.

But the locavore idea, and ideal, persists. And although much improvement has been made since the days of the Banana Republics, bananas are still a poster child for frustrations with agribusiness, often representing exploitation and corruption. Bananas can be found in every grocery store throughout the United States, but only with a heavy reliance on fossil fuels, pesticides, and fungicides. To many, pawpaws represent a way out of that global model. It is a symbol of a different, perhaps older way of feeding ourselves and our families.

Many interests are represented at this festival, including Chmiel's own business, environmental groups, and Ohio historians, but there is an overriding, genuine excitement that prevails above all else. The energy stems from this symbol of the pawpaw as an opportunity to start over, to get agriculture (or permaculture, or just plain *culture*) right. People are excited because through the lens of the pawpaw they're seeing their backyards, their home states, and their shared histories with fresh eyes. It's not just the flavor of pawpaw that makes the festival a success, it's this palpable energy, which even if you're not a dyed-in-the-wool believer you can recognize and appreciate for its earnestness, the notion that this wild fruit might in fact be the next big thing, and it's been growing in our backyards all along.

❧

The Peterson Pawpaws crew eventually sells every bit of their six hundred pounds from Deep Run. Meanwhile, Chmiel's seemingly endless stream of pawpaws continues. By all accounts it's another successful festival. But when the sun goes down Saturday night the party has just begun. Bands, including headliner and zydeco legend C. J. Chenier and his Red Hot Louisiana Band, play late into the night, there's dancing and laughing, and although fresh fruit consumption has largely ended at this point, pints of pawpaw beer continue to flow under the beer tent. When the stage is finally shut down, guitars and drums are played around the warmth of scattered campfires. I look up, and amid the bright stars, I recall that this waxing moon, called *a;si-mini-ki-sTwa* (*a? · ši mini-ki · šөwa*) by the Shawnee, is the Pawpaw Moon.[1]

— CHAPTER TEN —

TOBACCO, ACETOGENINS, AND ICE CREAM

Kentucky State University is the only American university with a dedicated pawpaw research program. I discovered this fact early on in my research, and as luck would have it this particular September the university is hosting an open house of sorts in the form of the Third International Pawpaw Conference. More than one hundred people, representing eighteen states and several countries, have traveled to attend.

The gathering is predictably more professional and scholarly than the Ohio Pawpaw Festival, but no less passionate. "You've got some very unique individuals interested in pawpaw," says Kirk Pomper, who heads the program at KSU. "I guess anything that's new, it tends to draw people who are risk takers, or a little out of the mainstream." Curious newcomers like myself are here, but so are the plant's great champions, like Neal Peterson; Indiana's persimmon and pawpaw expert, Jerry Lehman; Ontario's Dan Bissonnette, who is working to restore a vanishing pawpaw population in Essex County; a nurseryman from the Netherlands; scientists from Romania; novice fruit growers; others who have grown, bred, and propagated pawpaws for decades; the globe-trekking botanical explorer Joseph Simcox; Sean Spender, a Canadian living and working on a farm in South Africa; Robert Hamilton, "the Atlanta Fruit Man"; Ken Drabik; Woody Walker, who discovered and promoted the Kentucky Champion pawpaw tree (standing more than thirty feet tall); and two gentlemen from Plant City, Florida, who, despite their ability to grow many tropical fruits, can't shake their desire to grow and consume *Asimina triloba* as far south as possible. It's a gathering of the pawpaw's most capable and energetic supporters.

KSU's pawpaw program was started by horticulturalist Brett Callaway in 1990, who saw not just the potential of the fruit, but the possibility that pawpaws could help people. "All along, I've been interested in things that would benefit small farmers," Callaway told Colleen Anderson in 1998. "Crops like corn and wheat, [small farmers] can't compete. But specialty crops can help a farm stay alive."[1] Historically that specialty niche was filled by tobacco, a crop that by the early 1990s was no longer viable. It was part of the university's mission, as a land grant institution, to aid struggling farmers. Pawpaws, Brett thought, might fill the void left by tobacco. Brett looked to the Kentucky Nut Growers Association, the Northern Nut Growers Association, and other strong agricultural groups in the state, and collected pawpaw seeds from the Kentucky State Fair, from the forest, and from others' collections. This material formed the basis of the first KSU pawpaw orchard. But like Neal Peterson, Callaway had also read about the 1916 *Journal of Heredity* contest, and was inspired to conduct another national search. "*Organic Gardening* advertised it and published the results," he recalled. "I had well over four hundred entries. They came in any way you can imagine. First class mail in shoeboxes. One lady stuffed her pawpaws into a nylon stocking. I got little pawpaws, big pawpaws. I got some real nice ones." The entries were judged by a panel of eight, who saw only sliced fruit on a plate. "The winner weighed well over four hundred grams and scored high on the taste test."[2] That cultivar, named Wells, remains available.

When Callaway took a position elsewhere in 1993, Desmond Layne took over. Fresh out of grad school, Layne inherited a program that consisted of a few dozen trees in the ground and, through the results of Callaway's contest, a cache of thousands of seeds. "Desmond Layne is a great scientist, and he's also an excellent communicator," Pomper says. "He really took everything to another level." For one, Layne initiated the idea of the germplasm repository, that KSU would be the official USDA collection site for unique and exceptional pawpaw material. Germplasm, the material used to propagate a plant, can be stored in the form of DNA, seeds, cuttings, even tissue frozen in liquid nitrogen. In the case of KSU, the repository is the orchard itself. With the help of Kim Hummer, who ran the national germplasm repository at Corvallis, Oregon, Layne received a grant to collect pawpaw seed from throughout the country.

The purpose of the repository is to preserve the genes of special pawpaws. Specifically it's used for distributing unique material to other researchers, for use in breeding and evaluation for unique characteristics. "We may find some that store longer, we may find some that are resistant to disease," Pomper says. Some trees might also have characteristics that represent answers to problems or preferences yet to be identified.

Pomper came on in 1998, having previously worked with the physiology of strawberries and the breeding of hazelnuts. "When I came here I had a unique skill set where I've worked with some odd things, but also I'm kind of a jack-of-all-trades, which is exactly what pawpaw needed," he says. Pomper now directs the germplasm collection, and his research has focused on pests, organic production, anticancer and antioxidant properties, and the genetic diversity of wild pawpaws, among other areas. In addition to visiting pawpaw growers, answering emails, phone calls, and letters, teaching, and experimenting with blackberries and hazelnuts, Pomper has organized an annual pawpaw field day to showcase the orchard and introduce the crop to potential growers.

Many small farmers lack access to USDA-inspected processing facilities like ACEnet in Athens, Ohio, which are not common. In 2010, recognizing this lack as a barrier to pawpaw growers' ability to process and store pawpaws, Pomper secured a USDA-grant-funded mobile processing facility. The county's pawpaw growers and sorghum growers, among others, are now able to extend their harvests and their capabilities to develop value-added pawpaw products.

Pomper has also, with the help of Sheri Crabtree, Neal Peterson, Ron Powell, and others, brought us all here today. On the first day of the conference, folks share their experiences growing, processing, and selling pawpaws; a few pawpaw-related products are pitched and sampled, including pawpaw pretzels and a pawpaw-chipotle barbecue sauce; and just before lunch, our appetites piqued, we taste cultivars selected by the university as well as advanced selections from amateur breeding programs.

To a packed room, Pomper introduces the first cultivar to be released from the program: the KSU-Atwood. With its greenish-blue skin, yellow-orange flesh, and low amount of seeds, this pawpaw stands out. The tree produces a heavy crop of up to 150 fruits and ripens midseason. And although it's a superior selection — KSU wouldn't have released it otherwise — Pomper says

Atwood is just the very beginning. "What we have now is about another half dozen really good ones, which are high yielding and even larger fruit size than Atwood." One fruit has an attractive russet appearance, several are exceptionally large (larger than Atwood), and others have a strong coconut flavor, a trait that is uncommon in most cultivars. But like any respectable plant breeder, Pomper is not rushing to release them. He has several years of data on the original trees, and has young grafted trees to observe when they begin producing in a few more years. In addition to the plantings at KSU, the trees have been planted at two sites in Ohio. One early standout from the KSU orchard, a fruit unofficially referred to as Pina Colada, had an outstanding and unusual pineapple-coconut flavor. But the trees, when grafted and planted out in Ohio, quickly died. "And so until I know I can actually propagate and maintain that good fruit quality, and look at yield," Pomper says, "I don't want to release it."

Neal Peterson's fruit has great seed-to-pulp ratios, about 5 or 6 percent seed, and good flavor. "A flavor that wasn't too strong, or too sweet," Pomper says, "so you could actually eat more." But in addition to low seed-to-pulp ratios and good flavor, KSU is looking for fruit that stores longer, is attractive, and shows a distinct color break, as well as trees that have higher yields. "We're always looking for fruit that basically are more round," Pomper says. As Sheri Crabtree explains, "the seeds are in a row or two down the middle of the fruit, so a thinner and/or smaller fruit won't have as much pulp around the seeds as rounder fruit" — the greater the diameter, the greater the pulp.

Pomper also wants the germplasm collection to represent the genetic diversity of wild pawpaws. "We have a pretty good sampling of what's out there," he says, "but there are definitely unique selections that I'd like to get and bring in. We have yet to capture what's out there, totally." The collection contains genetically diverse selections from West Virginia, Kentucky, and Indiana, among other states, but lacks diversity from southern states, like Louisiana and Alabama, and northern regions like Ontario, Canada. "I'm sure that there could be bigger pawpaws out here, there could be rounder pawpaws out there," Pomper says, "And some of this is not always apparent in what we see, sometimes it's in the genes. And it's not until you grow out the seeds that you see that."

⚬₰

Pomper and his predecessors are not the only scientists working with paw-paws. In fact, retired Purdue researcher Jerry McLaughlin has been working with *Asimina triloba* for decades and is responsible for identifying the plant's Annonaceous acetogenins. McLaughlin has shown that these chemical compounds might be the strongest cancer-fighting tool yet discovered.

McLaughlin's first exposure to pawpaws came as a child in Michigan. "When I was about four years old my dad gave me some of these and said, 'Jerry, you can eat these, these are Indiana bananas,'" he recalled during a lecture in 2003. "And I was hungry for bananas, because in World War II you couldn't get bananas. I ate a whole bunch of them, and I threw up, and I threw up, and I never forgot this, and I had it in for this plant for a long, long time. I knew there was something in there, because if you throw up from eating something you know there's something biologically active there."

Young Jerry eventually grew up to be a distinguished pharmacognosist at Purdue University. In the mid-1970s, McLaughlin began analyzing more than thirty-five hundred unique species of plants, sourced from several continents, to locate bioactive components that might help in the fight against cancer. "My group went through all those plants, one by one, and guess which was the best one?" he asks. "Pawpaw, growing two miles from my office . . . the best thing I ran into to fight cancer. There are some relatives of pawpaw that are tropical that are equally potent, but by gosh, this one was right there, and we had plenty of it available locally." The discovery would become McLaughlin's life's work.

In this search, McLaughlin isolated approximately 350 new compounds that were cytotoxic, meaning toxic to cells. To discover these compounds is expensive, time-consuming work. "This is what I'm good at," he says. "I can do grind-and-find research: I can grind up a plant, find what's in there, and tell you if it's biologically active." And the Annonaceous acetogenins, the chemicals that pawpaw folks are so familiar with today, were the most important leads.

Lab work showed Annonaceous acetogenins to also be effective at killing insects: mosquito larvae at one part per million, and both blowfly larvae and *Caenorhabditis elegans*, a parasitic worm, at high potencies. So when McLaughlin decided to develop an herbal product from the compounds, it made sense to use it to attack bugs. "The best insects I could think of to kill that would help people were head lice," he says. There was historical precedence for this, too. Medical journals from the eighteenth and nineteenth centuries reported doing the same. So with extracts from pawpaw trees, Nature's Sunshine produced a shampoo. McLaughlin partnered with school nurses to administer the shampoo and reported 100 percent success. The next product to be developed was Paw Paw Para-Cleanse, used to remove intestinal parasites. Its ingredients include pawpaw, pumpkin seeds, black walnut hulls, *Cascara sagrada*, artemisia, elecampane, clove, and garlic, among others. Nature's Sunshine sells as many as five to six thousand bottles of the para-cleanse a month.

But McLaughlin felt the pawpaw's greatest potential was not in killing insects and parasites, but in the treatment of cancer. The plant's Annonaceous acetogenins work by depleting energy in cells — whether insect, worm, or cancer cells — through the inhibition of the cells' mitochondria. The acetogenins also work in the plasma membrane, preventing cancer cells from growing anaerobically, without oxygen. "So we knock out the cancer cell's energy production in two ways," McLaughlin said.

McLaughlin worked with Nature's Sunshine from 1999 to 2004 and was able to introduce the Paw Paw Cell-Reg, a gelcap supplement taken orally. A clinical study with ninety-four participants showed that the pawpaw extract, containing a mixture of more than fifty acetogenins, is beneficial in a diversity of cancer types. After just four days on pawpaw, a melanoma patient, with lung metastases, could breathe again without the previous "burning" sensation; strength had returned and the patient could ride a bike and walk. Two lipomas had decreased in size, and as an unexpected bonus, a toenail fungus of ten years was diminished. In a breast cancer patient, after seven months of chemo and pawpaw treatment, a tumor almost completely disappeared, and a biopsy after radical mastectomy showed no tumors in fourteen lymph nodes. The patient was cancer-free. In all, McLaughlin reported significant reductions in tumor sizes and tumor antigen levels, with added benefits for treating cold sores, shingles, multiple sclerosis, acne, athlete's foot, eczema, and psoriasis. The only reported side effect was vomiting — the same effect you would expect after eating too many pawpaws or swallowing a seed. McLaughlin says patients avoid this by reducing dosages.[3]

McLaughlin's research showed that the highest levels of Annonaceous acetogenins are present in the tree's twigs, though the components are also present, in varying amounts, in the tree's bark, roots, fruit, and, in the least amount, its leaves and wood. The twigs are harvested when they are the most biologically active, and the concentration of acetogenins is highest during the month of May. "The extract is standardized biologically using an invertebrate bioassay, and/or spectrometric instruments," McLaughlin says. "This is a renewable resource since the trees are not killed during the harvest, and new twigs soon regrow."

McLaughlin's work has allowed the plant's compounds to be harnessed in ways like never before. But pawpaw has been used medicinally for centuries. In 1787, German-born botanist, physician, and zoologist Johan David Schoepf reported, "A wine prepared from the unripe fruit is odorless and is highly useful in children's sore mouth." It's unclear what soreness Schoepf was treating, but McLaughlin also found pawpaws to be effective in treating cold sores. In 1850, medical researchers wrote that "the powdered seeds are used to destroy lice on the heads of children."[4]

In 1871, the *Journal of Materia Medica* published the following: "The fruit of the Popaw is large and fleshy, and after it has been treated with port, yellow, sweet and luscious, and from its taste compared to custard; hence its taste. It is edible and has laxative properties." The journal went on to say that, domestically, a "saturated tincture of the seeds may be employed for emetic purposes, in doses of a teaspoonful. The bark is a useful tonic in forms of cold infusion."[5] In the 1890s, the Eli Lilly Company actually sold a fluid extract of pawpaw seed as an emetic.[6] Anyone who has ever had the misfortune of swallowing even a tiny bit of the seed has an idea of how well this might have worked (for better or worse, I can verify that it works quite well). Describing the practices of those turn-of-the-century doctors, McLaughlin remarks, "The physicians would make you vomit and they would bleed you and they would purge you to get you well. Remember that you sweat just before you vomit. As you sweat you're sweating the toxins out of your body. And that's what they believed would help to make you get better — and probably does."

Other plants in the Annonaceae family are also used medicinally. Extracts of graviola (*Annona muricata*, also known as soursop, guanabana, and, lately, Brazilian pawpaw) are sold by several companies. A quick Google search reveals well over a dozen companies offering capsules and powdered products, each marketed for its ability to kill cancer cells

(McLaughlin says graviola extracts, however, are variously twenty-four to fifty-six times less potent than the pawpaw extracts). In Thailand, extracts of *Annona squamosa, A. muricata, A. cherimolia,* and *A. reticulata* are also used to treat head lice. The book *Biologically Active Natural Products: Pharmaceuticals* reports, "For this, 10 to 15 fresh leaves of *A. squamosa* L. are finely crushed and mixed with coconut oil, and the mixture is applied uniformly onto the head and washed off after 30 min."[7] A former colleague of McLaughlin's also reported using the ground seeds of *Annona squamosa* to treat head lice as a child in India. And yet another member of the Annonaceae family, ylang ylang (*Cananga odorata*), which is native to the Philippines and Indonesia, is used widely in cosmetics, and its essential oils are used in aromatherapy to address high blood pressure, among other conditions. Its floral scent is used in perfumes, most notably as the principal ingredient of Chanel No. 5.

✺

Pawpaws are also turning out to be highly nutritious. Studies have shown that pawpaws are high in antioxidants, but, as Robert Brannan, current president of the PawPaw Foundation, says, "Finding antioxidants in pawpaw is unremarkable, because they're a fruit. It's like saying people have hair." The question is not just the levels of antioxidants pawpaws possess, but how good they are, and what they do. "And that's a much tougher question to get at," he says.

In 1982, a landmark study was conducted on pawpaw nutrition by Neal Peterson, John Cherry, and Joseph Simmons. Because it is a wild fruit, no analysis had been done before. Unfortunately, that study was done not just on the fruit's pulp, but the skin as well. But we don't eat the skin, so although the analysis gives us an idea of pawpaw nutrition, it's not quite accurate. According to Brannan's research, pawpaw pulp without skin contains about five milligrams of vitamin C per one hundred grams of pulp, which is less than one-third of the value reported in the 1982 study. "So all those numbers that you see for the pawpaw, they're all wrong," Brannan says. The 1982 study included skin because the experiment otherwise would have been drastically more expensive. Brannan is planning to conduct a new analysis, but it won't be cheap. "It's going to cost upward of ten thousand dollars in order to get it right," he says, "I am actively working on it right now, but basically what I'm trying to do is get someone to give me a Porsche at a Pontiac price. It's been slow going."

Although flawed, the current nutritional data does offer insight as to how nutritious pawpaws might be. The 1982 data shows that pawpaw is high in niacin and protein, as well as several minerals — calcium, phosphorus, magnesium, iron, zinc, copper, and manganese — with amounts far exceeding those of apples, bananas, and oranges. And several essential amino acids were exceptionally high, again, far greater than values found in more popular fruit, including isoleucine, leucine, lysine, phenylalanine, tyrosine, threonine, and valine.[8]

According to Brannan's research, we also know that pawpaws are about 75 percent water ("unremarkable for a fruit"); are very low in fat ("I've never gotten a fat lipid value of pawpaw that's been higher than half a percent — basically the only fat that's in there is the fat that's needed in the cell membrane"); are low in protein but high in carbohydrates, most of which are sugar; contain a high pH, or acidity level; and are low in fiber. We also know that pawpaw, like red wine, red grapes, cranberries, and chocolate, contains "health-promoting phytochemicals" known as procyanidins. Researchers state that these chemicals have been shown to "have a positive correlation with reduction of coronary heart disease and mortality."[9]

However, some research also shows pawpaws could be bad for us. In 1999, researchers investigated a possible link between the consumption of *Annona cherimola* and *A. muricata* and an atypical form of Parkinson's disease (the disease was abnormally frequent in Guadeloupe, where Caparros-Lefebvre and Elbaz conducted the study). They reported that a higher proportion of patients with atypical parkinsonism consumed *A. muricata* (97 percent consumed the fruit, and 83 percent took an herbal tea made of its leaves) than patients with Parkinson's disease (fruit 59 percent; herbal tea 18 percent) or a control group with no Parkinson symptoms (fruit 60 percent; herbal tea 43 percent). It's significant that 60 percent of the control group ate *A. muricata* fruit and showed no symptoms, but still, the correlation was strong. Further, younger people who showed symptoms and then stopped consuming *Annona* products (fruit or tea) were able to reverse their symptoms.[10] Yet both fruits — cherimoya (*A. cherimola*) and soursop (*A. muricata*), as well as at least a dozen other *Annona* species — are important food products. "It's possible that these folks are an island group and they're just genetically predisposed to get this," Pomper says. "Because, anecdotally, I know a lot of people who have eaten a lot of pawpaw for years, and they don't have any symptoms." And globally, there's an even larger population that appears to have been safely consuming soursop and cherimoya for centuries.

A 2012 University of Louisville study identified Annonaceous acetogenins as toxic substances that inhibit "critical biological functions."[11] Although the fruit contains far less of these substances than the tree's twigs and bark, they're still present (with frozen pulp containing lesser amounts than fresh). At this point, the study's authors "suggest caution and more study to determine the effects of consumption of these compounds."

Neal Peterson, however, sees no reason to be alarmed. First, he says, since the toxicity was found in rats when scientists intravenously injected the compounds into them, "this doesn't prove that [pawpaw] is dangerous to eat, only that it is dangerous to inject as one would heroin." Neal's response to the toxicity of pawpaw continues:

> *For millions of years of evolution, the pawpaw clearly had its seed distributed by mammals that ingested the whole fruit and defecated the seed. We suspect that the primary co-evolved distributors were extinct megafauna (such as mastodons). Whatever species it was, the route of mitochondrial toxicity is so basic that all mammals should be susceptible. Also, more than one mammal species regularly eats pawpaw. Fox, raccoon, bear, and possum consume it. And then* Homo sapiens *after arriving in North America did so. It is not logical that a severely toxic fruit would be consistently consumed.*

Not all pawpaws contain the same amounts of acetogenins; analysis shows some with high levels and others low. "We're trying to select for low acetogenin too, just because it's not a good idea to eat something that would be an anticancer compound at a high level," Pomper says, "I'm selecting for low whenever I can." But toxicity in foods isn't unique to pawpaws. Broccoli and other brassicas, for example, contain goitrogens—substances that can suppress thyroid functions and interfere with iodine uptake—as do soybeans, pears, and peaches. Other toxins we commonly consume include lectins (found in grains, legumes, and the nightshade family), hydrazines (mushrooms), opioid peptides (milk, gluten, spinach), phytates and phytic acid (soybeans, wheat, nuts, blackberries, strawberries), and so on. A variety of toxins are filtered and destroyed in our liver and excreted through our kidneys – and this may also occur with acetogenins. But how our bodies react to these compounds is still largely unknown. "At this point, we don't know a lot about bio-availability [through the gastrointestinal tract], how quickly they're broken down in the bloodstream," Pomper says. The Food and Drug Administration, however, considers pawpaw to be safe. "I've talked to the FDA," he says, "and they consider pawpaw a safe food source to eat, and have written me accordingly."

❧

In a few tangible ways, the work at KSU has paid off. Much of what we know about pawpaws comes from the collaborations between Neal Peterson and KSU researchers – including Brett Callaway, Desmond Layne, Kirk Pomper, and Sheri Crabtree. For the past twenty years, these researchers have published several dozen scholarly articles and presentations on pawpaw – from genetic diversity and geographic differentiation, to seedling rootstock recommendations and behaviors of the pawpaw peduncle borer. Their findings have helped growers like Maryland's Jim Davis understand the culture of growing pawpaws, and the literature coming out of KSU undoubtedly contributes to his success (not to mention that of the countless others who have reached out for answers to basic questions, and requests for seed and trees). But closer to home, there's another testament to KSU's success, a more basic and visual marker. For any other fruit, this example would seem insignificant, but when considering the pawpaw, it is absolutely a big deal: in Lexington, Kentucky, a local farmer's pawpaws are sold at a grocery store.

When Ilze Sillers bought her Woodford County farm twenty years ago, she could have planted anything. "It had a tobacco base, but I knew I did not want to grow tobacco, for personal reasons, health reasons, and that tobacco was, as a crop, facing extinction," Ilze recalls. She attended a Third Thursday program at KSU, a monthly workshop used to showcase new or uncommon sustainable agricultural ventures. "I happened to go to the workshop on pawpaws, and I thought, this is absolutely perfect," she says. "They're native to the area, they don't require pesticides, there seems to be an interest in the market for them, no one's doing it, and so I just got very interested." So Ilze planted pawpaws — three hundred of them.

Ilze was not the only small farmer in Kentucky moving away from tobacco. As an economic analysis published by the University of Kentucky states, "As those living in rural Kentucky look forward to the 21st century, it is becoming increasingly clear that the economic environment will continue to change radically. The future of tobacco, long the leading cash crop for the farmers in the Commonwealth, looks increasingly bleak, as federal officials renew efforts to further regulate the sale and use of tobacco products."[12] No doubt, growing tobacco is a strong cultural tradition in Kentucky, and if it disappears part of the culture disappears. But tobacco is not the only tradition.

As I've mentioned, Kentucky's original inhabitants ate and cultivated pawpaws; they wove clothing and crafted tools and nets from the tree's inner bark. Daniel Boone and the region's other settlers ate them. In 1828, botanist Charles Wilkins Short wrote that portions of Kentucky were "once the paradise of papaws, where immense orchards of large trees were everywhere met with."[13] In the late nineteenth and early twentieth centuries, newspapers reported on the wild pawpaw crop: "Pawpaws plentiful," noted Louisville's *Courier-Journal* in 1882,[14] and the *Lancaster Central Record*, in 1901, said, "Pawpaws have appeared on the market, and are said to be plentiful."[15] Pawpaws were the subject of poems, and, serving another form of inspiration, made into beer. In 1896, the *Courier-Journal* remarked, "A pint of it will take the paint off a brick house and make a man forget he has a mother-in-law."[16] Children made hats from pawpaw leaves, and a pawpaw whistle, crafted from the tree's bark, was once a widespread novelty.

Later, when the fruit began to fade from the broader American consciousness, many folks in Kentucky just kept on harvesting and eating. So when KSU decided to introduce the fruit as a potential replacement for tobacco, it seemed like a logical fit. "Rather than introduce something from another country that may not do well in the climate," Desmond Layne recalls, "it was something that was already available in certain farmers markets, and people in rural areas were familiar with it."

Growing pawpaws would be more sustainable and better for the environment than tobacco. Historically, tobacco cultivation has relied on fumigating with pesticides and herbicides. The crop has also been plagued by viruses, and in general growing tobacco is a very intensive system requiring numerous inputs. "The nice thing about [a pawpaw] orchard is that once the trees are planted and they've come into production, they are perennial, they are there for as long as those trees live," Layne says. Further, growing a fruit versus a toxin offers peace of mind to the farmer. "It's one thing to provide people with food, it's another thing to provide them with something that can kill them," Layne says. "I'm not castigating people who grow tobacco, because it's been a part of the nation's history since Native Americans were growing tobacco and trading it with the explorers that were coming over from Europe. But certainly, if I have the choice to grow other things that are going to also provide me with profitable income, I would much rather be growing food."

When choosing pawpaws as her crop, Ilze Sillers agreed. KSU connected Ilze with Oregon's Northwoods Nursery for grafted cultivars, including selections from KSU's germplasm collection as well as Neal Peterson's advanced selections (a few years before they were named and released). When they started to produce fruit, "it just was gangbusters for several years," Ilze says. She sold at the county farmers market as well as to restaurants, and she developed a relationship with Lexington's Good Foods Co-op. Each year, Good Foods buys more than a thousand pounds of pawpaws, approximately half of Ilze's crop, and sells each and every piece of fruit. Last year, Ilze sold another thousand pounds of pawpaws to a second buyer, Wildside Winery. What started as an idea — that pawpaws might be a niche crop for Kentucky's small farmers — is now being tested by folks like Ilze Sillers. So far, with a bit of effort, ingenuity, and salesmanship, it seems to be working.

҂

There have been many great presentations during the conference, but when we're finally able to tour the orchard, it's what we've all been waiting for. The alpha orchard, growing to the right of the small road that leads to the orchard, is the original collection planted by Brett Callaway. Beyond it, a long orchard makes up the germplasm repository. This collection was started by Desmond Layne and continued through Pomper's work at KSU. Typically, visitors are asked to refrain from picking up fruit, since the program uses the pawpaw for ongoing research. But at this point in the season, they've collected their information, and we're given the green light.

One observer describes the scene as looking like "a group of children on an Easter egg hunt."[17] We break into the mango-sized fruits, perfectly ripe, and some of us fill bags to take home. But with the Pawpaw Extravaganza Dinner awaiting, we're careful not to eat too much.

I've come to the conference for many reasons, not the least of which is the advertised dinner, a five-course meal with each dish containing a bit of pawpaw, to be served at the research farm's state-of-the-art facility. KSU's Sheri Crabtree did most of the cooking (with a few desserts prepared by the University of Kentucky's Robert Perry, and Gary Gotenbusch of Servatii Pastries). Before dinner, we gather in the building's atrium for pawpaw smoothies and Kentucky freshwater prawn tails with pawpaw cocktail sauce. An acoustic trio plays folk tunes, including, of course, an enthusiastic rendition of *Way Down Yonder*. When we take our seats for dinner, the feast begins. We begin with curried pawpaw–butternut squash–sweet potato soup and hearts of romaine salad with pawpaw vinaigrette, then move on to various entrées and sides (I eat all of them): pork loin medallions with sweet pawpaw sauce, baked Kentucky tilapia with fresh pawpaw salsa, roasted new potatoes, and mixed fresh vegetables. And then, finally, dessert: a rich, caramel-like-pawpaw crème brûlée, with pawpaw ice cream and pawpaw cookies. The ice cream is thick, floral, brightly colored, and all-around wonderful. It's a good ending to the weekend.

Pomper believes that pawpaw ice cream is the fruit's best product, and where the crop might have a future. Chaney's Dairy Barn, in Bowling Green, currently makes pawpaw ice cream for KSU on a regular basis. Kirk and Sheri use it to introduce the flavor to groups who are unfamiliar with the fruit. "I think it really comes down to the flavor," Pomper says. "You show them what the potential is on a product like that, then hopefully you'll get more people to do it. If you show people the potential of pawpaw, they'll start believing in it."

CHAPTER ELEVEN

THE OHIO PAWPAW GROWERS ASSOCIATION

Ron Powell doesn't do the Boy Scout cut. Instead, he glides the grafting knife toward his hand, the blade's edge dangerously close to carving his callused thumb. Occasionally he does get cut. But this is the method that works for him, and he has become extremely good at it. He is seated on a five-gallon bucket in the grass at Ohio's Wilmington College, where at least fifty members of the Ohio Pawpaw Growers Association are gathered around him under a large shade tree. All eyes are on Ron, but he is not nervous. "I use this Band-Aid and put it around my thumb, and it's enough to catch the knife," Ron says. "And after your thumb gets toughened up, you don't cut it too bad anymore."

The demonstration is part of the group's annual member meeting. We're listening, asking questions — *Must you use a grafting knife? What about Kevlar tape? What's your success rate, Ron?* — as he gives a whip-and-tongue grafting tutorial. The knife slices down a thin branch of scion wood, a diagonal cut about two inches long, exposing a vibrant layer of green cambium. The cambium — a layer of meristematic plant tissue between the tree's inner bark and wood — is where new growth occurs; it is the growth ring. The DNA stored within this layer of a pawpaw twig can produce a clone of the original tree, which in this particular case is a cultivar named Quaker Delight. The young tree will eventually produce fruit identical to that of the original, which was found growing here at Wilmington College. It grew in the school's arboretum, and OPGA member Dick Glaser was the first to notice its favorable qualities: an early ripening date and lightly colored, creamy-textured pulp. Glaser was right to notice it: Quaker Delight won the

Ohio Pawpaw Festival's best pawpaw contest in 2003. And if it weren't for grafting, no one would be able to taste this celebrated fruit; the original tree died several years ago. It's one reason why Ron teaches the craft of grafting: so these named varieties — heirloom pawpaws like Quaker Delight — can go on living.

At Ron's property in southern Ohio — Fox Paw Farm — is a collection of nearly every named pawpaw cultivar known to exist. Which, with over 140 single varieties totaling more than four hundred trees, means a considerable amount of grafting. Each winter, Ron takes cuttings from his trees and stores them in a refrigerator. In late spring, he grafts the budwood onto common pawpaw rootstock — seedlings he and his wife, Terry, raise themselves, grown from seeds they also process, clean, and sort themselves. Like Neal Peterson, through correspondence and research Ron has tracked down heirloom pawpaw cultivars. In several instances, fading cultivars have been rescued from obscurity because of Ron's quest. "Part of my goal in my life is to collect all the remaining varieties I can," Ron says. It also helps that he is a skilled horticulturalist. As he prepares rootstock for grafting, he stores budwood in his mouth — which is cleaner than the ground. His grafts have exceptionally high success rates, causing one member of the gathering to joke, "I think there's something in his saliva." If anyone were to lead the effort of building a pawpaw industry, after years of collecting and growing, Ron Powell is well equipped.

Chris Chmiel founded the OPGA in 2000, and Ron — also a founding member — took over as president in 2005. According to the group's current mission statement, the OPGA is an "organization of pawpaw enthusiasts and commercial pawpaw growers, large and small, dedicated to educating and promoting the superior traits of the pawpaw, developing a pawpaw industry, marketing plan, and preserving and studying the wild pawpaw genetics." And while Powell is committed to the state of Ohio, he is also working to push the industry at the national and global level. OPGA's membership has for years included folks outside Ohio, and so in 2011 he formed the North American Pawpaw Growers Association, which now includes members in twenty-two states as well as Canada.

Integration Acres and Deep Run Orchard may be successful, but if interest continues to grow, Jim Davis and Chris Chmiel won't be able to meet even a fraction of the demand. Two farms is not an industry. As that interest grows, the OPGA is a statewide support system for experienced and novice growers, sharing tips on grafting, germination, orchard practices, and even how to sell and market the fruit. Pawpaw orchards are novel and their culture is unknown, they reason, and growers will need help.

While the market for fresh fruit is still in its infancy, OPGA members have begun selling thousands of seeds, many of them winding up overseas. "There are actually more pawpaws being grown around the world, and more research being done around the world, than what we are [doing] in the US, which is really unfortunate," Ron says. In 2012, the Natural Sciences and Engineering Research Council of Canada (NSERC) awarded a two-hundred-thousand-dollar grant to Bevo Agro Inc. and the University of British Columbia to develop a new pawpaw cultivar (Bevo Agro committed a matching amount to the initiative).[1] And when Ron sells seeds, although some stay in the United States, lately the majority have gone to South Korea. In fact, as part of just one recent pawpaw experiment, one million pawpaw trees were planted in South Korea, and another two million are scheduled to be planted next year. According to Robert Brannan, these Korean planters are interested in the tree's medicinal qualities, but in a few short years three million trees will produce an unprecedented number of pawpaws. A hypothetical juice company, which might need a ton of pulp for experimentation, could certainly put that amount of fruit to use. It's unknown whether there will be a market for fresh pawpaws in Korea, but with that many trees I imagine someone will give it a try. Cliff England, a Kentucky nurseryman with acres of pawpaws, persimmons, nuts, and other trees, says there are well over a hundred nurseries in Korea alone growing and selling pawpaws, where there is growing interest in the fruit. I spoke with him recently, and he had just shipped more than two hundred pounds of pawpaw seeds to Seoul, at a value of ten thousand dollars. England — who is fluent in Korean — says the fruit is valued abroad, in Korea but also throughout Europe, because it is exotic. Meanwhile, Ron and the OPGA would like America's great fruit to be successful at home, too. "The interest is there," Ron says; "the demand is growing."

❦

For an industry to develop, growers want a reliable and consistent fruit: in other words, cultivars with the pawpaw's best characteristics. "Sooner or later, if we're ever going to get this thing going, we're going to have to pick a variety or two or three, and say, 'We need people to plant this variety,'" says Robert Brannan. It's widely thought that too much diversity in a commodity, and too much variation in quality, will hinder the marketing of a fruit like pawpaw. Eventually, when that field has narrowed, these cultivars will need to be readily available to willing orchardists. Like most fruit trees, the cultivars aren't grown from seed; grafting is currently the only way to propagate pawpaw cultivars. For decades American scientist have tried and failed to reliably propagate pawpaws through tissue culture — the laboratory production of microscopic plantlets. However, at the 2011 International Pawpaw Conference, Romanian scientist Florin Stănică announced that scientists in Europe had succeeded in propagating pawpaw tissue culture. I was in the room when he gave that presentation; it was the biggest breakthrough of the weekend. The room was quiet, and every grower who had struggled with failed grafts, mislabeled scion wood, and unruly, unwanted suckers clearly saw the value of this discovery. These pawpaws plantlets, specific cultivars, would grow on their own roots, meaning all suckers, all regrowth, would be identical to the original. Neal Peterson collaborated with the project lead, Giuseppe Zuccherelli, sending budwood and other plant material to Europe. Yet that method is still proprietary. Neal is now partnering with a firm in Texas, and hopes the trials will be successful. But in the meantime, grafting is it.

For today's member meeting, Ron has brought everyone a young pawpaw tree, each around three years old, and at least two feet tall. I grab my treeling and comb through the cooler of scion wood, cuttings Ron has taken from his Ohio farm and is graciously sharing with us today. The budwood is taken in late winter through early spring, as Ron advises, when temperatures have been above freezing for twenty-four to forty-eight hours (which in Ohio means January to March). I know that the Overleese cultivar is an old-time favorite, so I select a pencil-sized twig from that bag. It's my turn to graft. "Just remember, you're doing surgery here," Ron says. "It has to be clean." I wash my hands with isopropyl alcohol, and then also the tools. Marc Stadler, another OPGA member and experienced horticulturalist, is my teacher. His preferred grafting knife is actually a simple penknife, so that's what I use. Ron demonstrated the whip-and-tongue method, but Marc teaches me the cleft graft. "The cleft graft meets two important criteria," he says. "First of all it's effective. And secondly, it's very easy." I'm sold.

"I always say, I grow pawpaws because I can't grow lemons and limes on my property," Marc says. "Everything about this tree is so tropical, except that it's adapted to our zone." Unlike many other temperate trees, pawpaws are grafted late in the season, when it's actively growing and leaves are on the trees — a trait that may hark back to its tropical origins. Pawpaws are more difficult to graft than a vigorous tree like apple, but compared with nut trees they're quite easy. With my knife, I cut down the center of the rootstock. If the blade is too dull, I risk a ragged cut, inviting infection and a poor graft. "You can't go to the dance in Kentucky without a good sharp knife," says one OPGA member. "I don't start using my knife until I can shave the hair off my arm," Ron adds. "Some years, I may spend twenty or thirty minutes sharpening my knife. It's that important." I make my cut. I slide the scion wood into place, carefully lining up the layers of green cambium. I tie a rubber band around the graft, wrap it tightly with grafting tape, and I'm done.

At the Ohio Pawpaw Festival, the OPGA offers a free seedling pawpaw to each person who signs up to become a member (and pays their dues, of course). Ron's logic is that the more people there are growing in diverse conditions, the more he can learn. "We need more data," he says. There are lots of cultivars, and they don't perform uniformly across the country. Rappahannock, for example, has always done poorly in the Midwest, but had a banner year recently in North Carolina. Derek Morris, a grower in Winston-Salem, reported medium to large fruits of great quality and low seed count on productive trees, and he reported Rappahannock kept well, undoubtedly a valuable trait to commercial producers. But again, positive Rappahannock reviews in Ohio are few. To sort this out, Ron wants data on everything: which pawpaws have good color break and turn yellow when they're ripe, as Rappahannock typically does; which are easier to process and peel, ripen sooner in the colder North, and have a longer shelf life; where and under what conditions these observations are made. Ron has his own collection, and he can observe trees at Fox Paw Farm, but information on a tree's performance in southern Ohio will hold less value to growers in such diverse climates as upstate New York and central Georgia.

In 1993, Kentucky State University's Desmond Layne and Neal Peterson, under the auspices of the PawPaw Foundation (PPF), began a similar effort to collect data on pawpaw cultivars. The joint venture sought to test ten existing pawpaw cultivars and eighteen advanced selections from Neal's experimental orchards. Between 1995 and 1999, the initiative expanded to twelve cooperators, primarily universities, in what would be called the Pawpaw Regional Variety Trials (PRVT). The objective was to evaluate those commercially available, named pawpaw varieties (such as Overleese, Sunflower, and PA-Golden, among others), as well as Neal's advanced selections — the future Peterson Pawpaws — within and outside the fruit's native range. Plantings were made in Princeton, Kentucky (at the University of Kentucky), Louisiana, North Carolina, Oregon, and South Carolina, with additional plantings at KSU, Indiana, Iowa, Michigan, Maryland, Nebraska, New York, and Ohio.[2]

There was a lack of funding to support the project, and some of the plantings failed to thrive. The majority of them, however, grew well, but without any staff dedicated to the pawpaw projects, there was no serious evaluation of the fruit and only minimal data. Still, the project confirmed that pawpaws could be grown and reliably fruit in a wide variety of climates, from lower Michigan to southern Louisiana.

∼

Ron wasn't always a pawpaw guru. As he approached retirement, he and Terry were looking for a plan for their farmland in southern Ohio, so on the suggestion of a friend they went to visit the orchard at KSU. "This is what I want to do with the farm," Terry recalls saying. "It was instantaneous." She'd known pawpaws as a child, "because I had a great mom that took us kids into the woods and told us what things were. And one time she picked up a pawpaw and let us try it, and I loved it." After she married Ron, he would occasionally bring home a sack of pawpaws if he chanced upon a tree, but often there wasn't much time — they both worked full-time — for pawpaw hunting. Which made the KSU orchard seem so enticing — that you could actually grow your own pawpaws was a novel idea. "We just were blown away when we saw the trees planted orchard-style, because we'd never seen that before," Terry says.

At the farm, Terry does most of the planting, as well as mulching, picking, processing, and eating (Ron and Terry both admit she's never come across a pawpaw she didn't like). "She was probably the biggest inspiration I had," Ron says. "If it wasn't for her, I wouldn't be this far along."

I ask Ron what drives him to do this work, to go to such lengths and efforts. "It's something I can wrap my hands around," he says. "I see it as a fledgling industry, and I see the potential in the fruit itself. It has a lot of historical significance. And I grew up in West Virginia, so you know, familiar with pawpaws," he says, matter-of-factly. "Now, my mom never ate it. She said, 'Oh, I didn't like it.' My grandmother liked it. But you know, Mom I remember would go out every spring and dig up "sassyfrass" and wash the roots and boil the roots down, and we drank sassafras tea. So even though she didn't do the pawpaw thing, she was in the woods." It's a meandering answer to a difficult question, and he may not have said it outright, but I believe Ron takes such an interest in pawpaw, at least in part, because it belongs to the folk culture in which he was raised. It's the neglected, native, West Virginia–Ohio–North American fruit. It's part of the history that he belongs to. And yes, it has potential.

Robert Brannan, who is the current president of the PawPaw Foundation and a food scientist at Ohio University, believes the "industry" should take a page from the pomegranate playbook. "We don't eat the pomegranate, but it's *in* everything," he says. "Because it's healthy, because somebody paid all this money to do the research. You put enough money into a fruit and you're going to find out that it's pretty healthy for you. So if any million-bazillionaires out there want to put money into the pawpaw, then we can put it in everything and no one will ever have to actually eat the fruit – but then we'll have a big industry. And I'm not being cynical. That's why the pomegranate exists." In fact, Brannan thinks something similar to the pomegranate story could develop out of the millions of pawpaws growing in Korea.

But rather than waiting for a big industry to develop – for pawpaw plantations on the scale of midwestern corn and soybean fields – the OPGA is concentrating on small farms. They have a partnership with the Ohio State University for research and outreach to small farmers about growing pawpaws.

Brad Bergefurd is an extension educator with the OSU's South Centers, in Piketon and Sciota Counties, and today's guest speaker at the OPGA meeting. "We try to find any economic opportunities for our growers that can make them money," Bergefurd says. "Those farms [in northern Ohio] can do pretty well with grain crops. But when you get down south, we have such small-acre farms that for generations tobacco was the highest-valued crop." The tobacco industry has changed, though, and it's no longer a viable earner for the small farmer. "My job is to identify economic income opportunities for these small farms," he says, "and it has to be on high-value crops – that's all we can do."

Bergefurd, Ron Powell, and many others believe pawpaw is one of those high-value crops. This is what Brett Callaway hoped the KSU pawpaw research program could accomplish, a notion that's still rippling through Ohio and this association. And right now, if you are connected to the right markets, where pawpaw can sell for up to ten dollars a pound, there's not enough fruit to go around. Ron, with his three-acre orchard, still can't produce enough seed to satisfy his buyers. In Cincinnati, select grocers can't keep the shelves stocked. The demand is there; the buyers exist. And many of these small-acre farmers already have pawpaws, albeit wild ones, in their surrounding woods. "Nobody really manages them," Bergefurd says. "The things fall to the ground."

There is a boutique demand, yes, but the future for a robust pawpaw industry is unclear, as is the question of how many Americans will want to eat them. There are a few modern examples of new fruits entering American markets and succeeding. Kiwi, for example. Significant imports of kiwifruit to the United States began only in the 1950s, when it was essentially unknown. An early description draws more parallels to pawpaw. "[The fruit's] external appearance is not particularly attractive, [but] the flesh is an attractive emerald green color and has numerous small, jet-black, edible seeds."[3] Americans quickly embraced kiwi. In the next few decades as demand exploded, the California kiwi industry grew 667 percent; nearly twenty-seven thousand tons of kiwis are grown domestically today (not to mention imports from Chile, New Zealand, and Italy).[4]

Of course, pawpaw's texture is more difficult than that of kiwifruit. It doesn't slice cleanly, and won't work well in a fruit salad (the primary way my mother prepared kiwi while I was growing up). Some are quick to point to the pawpaw's other flaws: Its shelf life is too short, it doesn't ship well, it's too full of seeds. An inside joke among breeders, "We're still working on the seedless pawpaw," is likely to never come true. But as more consumers develop a taste for pawpaw, I'm not convinced that seediness will actually be a problem.

Consider two of pawpaw's cousins: *Annona cherimola*, or cherimoya; and *Annona muricata*, known as soursop in English, *guanabana* in Spanish. Soursop, a prickly-skinned tropical fruit that's citrusy and gummy (it even tastes a bit like Juicy Fruit), can be incredibly seed-laden — large fruits contain from a few dozen seeds to as many as two hundred.[5] To eat the fruit you scoop out chunks and separate the pulp from the seed with your mouth — far more work than eating an apple or banana, but it's not considered a problem because of the simple fact that it tastes wonderful. It's eaten widely across the tropics as fresh fruit; it's found in sugary fruit drinks both in the regions where it grows and at ethnic markets throughout the United States. Frozen soursop pulp (often labeled only in Spanish, *guanabana*) is also widespread. Cherimoya's seed-to-pulp ratio and consistency aren't much different, and it too is cultivated widely in the tropics. I've even found fresh cherimoya, shipped from a great distance, at Asian food markets in Pittsburgh. And domestically there's already a burgeoning cherimoya industry in California.

Although we now have seedless watermelons, for centuries we never balked at black-specked slices of this delicious, red fruit. Rather than be intimidated, we held seed-spitting contests! Food doesn't always have to be easy. We like eating our sunflower seeds in their hulls, wresting steamed crabs from their shells, and so on. Granted, apples and bananas are much easier to eat and transport, and no amount of breeding is likely to change that for the pawpaw. "I wouldn't foresee it as a pawpaw-in-every-kid's-lunchbox kind of an industry," Brannan says. "It will have to be different than that." And that's okay. Ultimately, if Americans come to love the taste of pawpaw, perhaps its seediness — low compared to these other Annonaceae — won't actually be the problem that many believe it to be.

Processed pawpaws, for use in juice, ice cream, tea, soda, you name it, could hold even more potential. But in order for that to happen — and this has been said time and again — an efficient method for separating pulp from seed and skin will need to be developed.

Ron's modified Roma tomato processor sits prominently in the center of the auditorium. We spend time inspecting it, rotating the arm, and passing his tools around. At the suggestion of Kirk Pomper, Ron and Terry began using this particular food processor because an electric motor can be attached to it. Ron has also removed an inch and a half from the machine's spiral auger to allow seeds to pass through, and uses a salsa screen. This method is good for home use, but wouldn't be in a commercial setting, since Ron says the seeds must be passed through the processor twice to remove the majority of the pulp, and removing the skins is still done by hand. Because there's no industry standard processor yet, the DIY methods are many.

Marc Boone has traveled for today's meeting from Ann Arbor, Michigan. He describes his processing method, which includes a repurposed deep-fryer basket, to a small group of backyard growers. "I crack them right into a deep-fry basket," he says. "And I take my spatula and as fast as I can, I push that pulp through the grating, and then I've got a deep fryer full of seeds. I probably only get about 30 percent of the pulp when I do it that way. But it's the quickest way for me to do it, and being efficient with my pulp is not as important as being efficient with my time."

In 2009, Iowa State University's Patrick O'Malley began an experiment to determine how producers could commercially pulp and store pawpaws. Using the university's existing pulper, they demonstrated that skin and seed could be successfully removed by a mechanized pulper. But that process yielded only 53 percent skin- and seed-free pulp — 47 percent was wasted. And hand labor was still involved, as fruits needed to be halved lengthwise before entering the pulper. Further, O'Malley reported that the cost of the system, estimated at more than seven thousand dollars, may be well out of reach of the small grower. Integration Acres, the nation's largest pawpaw processor, uses a machine that would also likely be cost prohibitive for smaller growers (however, its Athens County neighbor, ACEnet, offers a cooperative model that may find success elsewhere). Meanwhile, O'Malley suggests exploring a Roma food strainer as a cheaper alternative.[6]

In terms of quality control of mechanized processing, Chris Chmiel is considering removing the seed sacks from his pulp, based on research showing that the same bitter flavor encountered near the fruit's skin is also present around the seeds, though he and others actually enjoy the flavor and eating of the seed sacks. Still, personal preference aside, he would like to keep bitterness out of the packaged pulp.

Although the processing problem hasn't yet been solved, Robert Brannan is already looking to the next step — fresh, processed pawpaw pulp in your grocer's refrigerator. Thanks to a recent breakthrough in high-pressure processing, fresh, ready-made guacamole is now available in grocery stores. It's a relatively new tool in food science; without it, the guacamole would turn black before it got off the assembly line. It could be used for pawpaws too. "It's like four thousand elephants standing on this thing," Brannan says. "It inactivates enzymes, and it can kill, pasteurize, pathogenic organisms." Although pawpaws freeze well, this would be another tool to expand their distribution and storage.

⚬⚬⚬

OSU is also experimenting with hops, and when Bergefurd mentions this during his presentation, Greg Hoertt shifts in his seat and asks several questions about the quality of Ohio-grown hops. He's a homebrewer. I speak to Greg after the grafting demonstration and learn he has pawpaw beer in his car. I'm eager to try it, but he decides not to crack it in the parking lot of the Quaker college, and instead invites me to his home.

At Greg's home orchard the ground is wet from the recent spring rains. We're just outside Xenia, where the Shawnee leader Tecumseh lived at the time of the American Revolution, and a few yards from Caesar Creek, named for the escaped slave who, according to the legend, later joined with the local Shawnee. Greg grew up nearby; as a child, he and his father would hike these storied woods and occasionally snack on pawpaws.

It's spring, and though his pawpaws are just beginning to leaf out, the trees have dozens of small pawpaw clusters. A few weeks ago, wanting to give his trees a boost, "I gave it a big drink of this concoction that I make of blood meal, and dung meal, and feather meal, and kelp concentrate," he explains. "The other thing that's good about using that concoction, I let that ferment and then, man, the flies are here within a half an hour." It's the flies, of course, that do the work of pollination.

Greg's great-grandmother was Miami Indian. Although many in his family have not been particularly interested in that heritage, Greg is, and part of his joy in cultivating pawpaws is this connection to his Native American roots. Greg is also equally interested in his Alsatian German heritage. His Kölsch-style pawpaw ale fermenting in copper kettles, and featuring pawpaw pulp spiced with European hops, represents a culinary bridge from the Miami River to the Rhine. And while planting pawpaw trees can't resuscitate the once great nations of the Ohio River Valley — it doesn't return land to the Shawnee and the Miami, or undo broken treaties — it can be a way of honoring their traditions and legacies by returning a once beloved fruit to its home in a new American culture. "Xenia is where Tecumseh lived," Greg says. "I'm on Native American land, growing a Native American fruit, I have Native American genes in me, and I just kind of like all that."

In developing a pawpaw industry, its history cannot be overlooked. Kiwi and pomegranate are wonderful, and they were once novel in the US, but pawpaw has always been here, and many an American's grandparents ate it and cherished it. "It has a story," Jim Gilbert has said. "I think people like the idea of something that's native, and part of the appeal of any crop is its story."

❧

Like the fruit itself, not all pawpaw beers are great. "The style of beer, the yeast, and then the pawpaw, all have an outcome on the final product," Greg says. And though he admits that the malt, hops, and style of beer will affect taste, Greg is looking for specific cultivars that are best suited for brewing. "I think I'm going to want sweeter, and I'm going to want more flavorful," he says. Greg doesn't put fresh fruit in his boil because it would lose too much flavor (rather, he waits for the secondary fermentation). A number of breweries in Ohio make a variety of terrific pawpaw beers, and nationwide pawpaw beers continue to debut everywhere from Indiana and Michigan to North Carolina and Missouri. These beers are seasonal, and often play on regional nostalgia for the fruit, as well as the appeal of local breweries using local ingredients. Fruit beers can divide an audience, but Magic Hat #9, brewed with apricots, is very popular. Maybe pawpaw is next.

Americans have experimented with fermenting pawpaws for centuries. In the early 1800s, François André Michaux wrote, "At Pittsburg, some persons have succeeded in making from it spirituous liquor;"[7] and before long pawpaw brandy was a fixture from the Ohio River Valley to Missouri. During the Civil War, Sandusky, Ohio, native John Beatty wrote of receiving "a box of catawba wine and pawpaw brandy from Colonel James G.

Jones, half of which I was requested to deliver to General Rosecrans, and the other half to keep to drink to the Colonel's health."[8] And in 1921, the *Sandusky Star-Journal* reported "Pawpaw beer, properly made, is said to have the hardest kick of any of the home brew drinks. It has become quite popular in some parts of Ohio since the coming of prohibition."[9]

Finally, and carefully, we open a bottle of Greg's pawpaw beer. Greg has made pawpaw porters, wheats, and sours, but this brew is the Kölsch mentioned above, with fruit pulp added during a secondary fermentation. It tastes great, one of the best pawpaw beers I've had. "Like I tell my niece," Greg says, "I don't make it because it sucks." In fact, Fifty West Brewing Company, located just outside Cincinnati, adapted one of Greg's pawpaw recipes for its Fox Paw, an English pale ale. Down the line, if enough growers can produce enough fruit, perhaps it could become a year-round ale. For now, it's a seasonal treat.

❧

I camp near Yellow Springs at John Bryan State Park, and in the morning hike down to the Little Miami River. I'm on the Clifton Gorge trail. On all sides of the path, much of the woods are overrun with Japanese honeysuckle. Before this plant's arrival, the area would have been prime pawpaw habitat. I've seen other forests like this, where pawpaws are abundant, extending for miles, but here the traditional understory has been supplanted. A cardinal passes by; crows caw. Finally, after a mile or so, I begin to see pawpaws with immature, early-spring leaves, their flowers dropping. The tallest stands at least thirty feet, skinny and straight.

One of the seven outstanding fruits of the 1916 contest came from Springfield, Ohio, just fifteen minutes north of Yellow Springs. The fruit was submitted by S. C. Martin, and mailed on September 19. It weighed ten to eleven ounces, with flesh "yellow and of superior quality, seeds not large, skin tough," according to the *Journal of Heredity*. "Fruit arrived in perfect condition and matured evenly."[10] The pawpaws in this country were exceptional then. And in nearby Adams County, where Ron Powell's farm is located, a geological surveyor reported in 1838 that the density of the stands "did not permit us to range on an average more than 130 feet at a time."[11] Those wild thickets – in Adams County and in Springfield, as elsewhere – are fewer now, supplanted by subdivisions and highways, plowed under for larger corn plantings, and often in the remaining wild places edged out by invasives. It's in this light that Ron Powell's work of saving cultivars, the best fruit of an earlier generation, seems even more important.

About a month later, at my home in Pittsburgh, my parafilm-wrapped graft has broken through its bandages — it's putting out new growth. The graft will grow about 10 inches this year — a success! In a few years I'll have a productive Overleese pawpaw tree, a cultivar selected from the wild in Indiana by W. B. Ward back in 1950. According to KSU, it ripens in early September in Kentucky, and the first week of October in Michigan. Its fruit size is large at KSU, with the average pawpaw weighing more than 170 grams, and the trees bearing around fifty-five fruits each. Hopefully all of the grafts that we did back in May will succeed, and in a few more years Ron will have useful data coming in. I hope to be able to report on my own Overleese in southwest Pennsylvania, and the others I'm growing. All the while Ron will be collecting data, assessing the culture of growing pawpaws in America.

– CHAPTER TWELVE –

INTO THE WOODS:
A NEW ORCHARD

I've forgotten to get rubber boots. Instead, I hold my ankle-high hiking boots in my arms, pants rolled above my knees, and prepare to ford Pierson Creek. Though it is now May, the temperature is still in the midfifties Fahrenheit and the water is quite cold. "I told you to bring your rubber boots," Steve says, again. It appears I'll be getting wet. We find the narrowest point, and cross.

Steve Corso is an amateur pawpaw researcher; we are in South Stebbins Forest, a tract of the three-thousand-acre woods of the Holden Arboretum in northeast Ohio. We're hunting wild pawpaws, but not for the fruit; if we find them, the trees will show only the earliest signs of leafing out. We search instead for a confetti of maroon blooms: pawpaw flowers. Today Steve is working on a study for the Geauga County Park District to learn how pawpaws influence the development of forests, including the mycorrhizal fungus around the trees' roots. In addition to our current trek, he will visit such colorfully named places as Big Creek, West Woods, Swine Creek, Frohring Meadow, Eldon Russell, Beartown Lakes, and Chickagami. But Steve is not a scientist by profession; a former teacher, he just happens to be very interested in pawpaws.

Between us we're carrying a diameter reader, a PVC pipe for carving out root and soil samples, ziplock bags for the collections, two apples, and a recently purchased iPad for GPS mapping. With pants rolled and boots in hand, I cross the river. The cold begins to sting, but our gear and my boots remain dry. We head into the woods.

With a full pack, Steve darts up the first hill with the energy and agility of a twenty-something. In fact, when I first met him, at the international pawpaw conference in Kentucky, I'd assumed he was around my own age. At forty-three, he sports a pointed goatee and mustache, a red flannel hunter's cap, and with his tools and knee-high rubber boots looks the part of quirky woodsman scientist. Steve is also a beginner farmer. In addition to various heirloom vegetables, he cultivates currants, persimmons, Russian seaberries, nut trees, and a sizable young pawpaw orchard. He grew up a short distance away in Mentor, Ohio, and went on to Ohio University in Athens. But he didn't catch pawpaw fever there. Oddly enough, he caught it in California.

Steve had moved west, to the San Francisco Bay Area, smitten with that region's landscape and culture, where he met his wife, Tatiana. But after a while, they got the urge to try their hands at farming. The couple, now with two children, envisioned life in rural California, but eventually it was Ohio, near where Steve grew up, that was the most practical choice. Before moving back east, though, he had a serendipitous encounter at a farmers market in Oakland, California. Arranged on a vendor's table were round green fruits, and though this was California, they weren't cherimoyas, smooth-skinned avocados, or even mangoes. Here, twenty-five hundred miles away from their native range, were fresh, farmers market pawpaws. If Steve needed a reason to be excited about moving back to Ohio, here it was: a fruit that was not only native to his home state, but would actually thrive better in the humid East than in the otherwise famously fertile valleys of California.

Steve and his family moved to Geauga County in June 2010, and by spring 2011 his pawpaws were planted. Steve ordered half a dozen grafted pawpaw trees and one hundred seedlings. He attended the International Pawpaw Conference in Frankfort, Kentucky, and the following year planted an additional sixty grafted cultivars and fifty more seedling trees. Steve saved seeds from both the wild and the cultivated fruit he ate, and raised them in containers. Not all of these seedlings would survive, but when I arrived earlier in the day, nearly two hundred were beginning to leaf out. The family's homestead had in just three years become a pawpaw headquarters in the making.

❧

Our hike is through the western edge of the Allegheny Plateau. A shaggy carpet of green ramps (*Allium triccocum*) covers the rolling hills, while canopies of beech, ash, tulip poplar, and stands of hemlock filter the spring sun. Mayapple emerges from beds of last year's fallen leaves like miniature woodland umbrellas, and in a few months it too will produce a unique edible fruit, whose flavor Steve likens to starfruit. In 1818, William P. C. Barton — surgeon in the US Navy and University of Pennsylvania professor of botany — wrote that mayapple was "one of the most important medicinal vegetables indigenous to our country."[1] Farther on, spicebush grows up to six feet tall, its leaves like pawpaws' but miniature. Spicebush too holds potential — its leaves for tea, and its berries for spice. Chris Chmiel has even launched a Spicebush Summer Solstice Festival, hoping to raise the profile of the "Appalachian Allspice." We've hiked only a short distance, but already there is ample evidence that the potential of the eastern forest is vast.

We push on. Steve is looking for familiar landmarks, including an equestrian trail that will lead us to the first pawpaw patch. Although he earned a master's degree at the University of Michigan in 1996, and published a study describing a new genus of woody vines found in Mexico and Central America, Steve hasn't done too much scientific work since. I ask him what made him want to do this work, and why now? The question seems to catch him off guard, and he turns it around. "Why are you writing this book?" He then gives an honest and straightforward answer. "Basically it's an excuse to get permits to go anywhere I want, and look for pawpaws," he says, laughing. "Hunt pawpaws, hunt mushrooms." It's a good answer; in many ways, it's my own.

In 1995, Steve traveled to Suriname, on the Caribbean coast of South America, and fell in love with the diversity of fruit there. But as he continued to travel he developed a love–hate relationship with the region. When he arrived in the tropics, he wanted to be home; when home, he longed to be away. "When I finally realized I was not going to move to the tropics, I think a pawpaw orchard became the perfect substitute," he wrote to me in an email. "The Eastern US is basically the tropics during summer and pawpaw would have fit perfectly among those fruits I first experienced on my visits to the tropics." *Tropical Appalachia.* In the summer we share the heat and humidity, the dense green forests, cicadas, mosquitoes; they have passionfruit, we have passion flower; they have allspice, we have spicebush; there, *guanabana*, here, pawpaw. Indeed, the pawpaw's exotic appearance has long been noted. In 1897, Wisconsin journalist Reuben Gold Thwaites floated a skiff down the length of the Ohio River; of one stretch, he wrote, "For the most part, these stony slopes are well wooded with elm, buckeye, maple, ash, oak, locust, hickory, sycamore, cotton-wood, a few cedars, and here and there a catalpa and a pawpaw giving a touch of tropical luxuriance to the hillside forest."[2] Occasionally such tropical-temperate analogies were made of the southern regions themselves. A 1913 Amazon River adventure novel finds several Americans in South American jungles, and among their new experiences they encounter the region's fresh fruit. "The natives call 'em chrimoya . . . See, it is a pie, already made . . . Inside was a delicious soft pulp, thickly sown with black seeds. It reminded the boys of the Indiana pawpaw."[3]

Growers and enthusiasts, or anyone who gets excited about the fruit, will often say, "It's a tropical fruit that grows right here," *right here* meaning some temperate place far from the Caribbean, or from south Florida. The farther north you go, the greater the annual snowfall and percentage of days with below-freezing temperatures, the greater the excitement. For those who travel, dream of traveling, or have moved to the United States from tropical regions, the pawpaw is a way to make the world a bit smaller, to bring faraway places to a backyard in Ohio, Indiana, or Michigan. And understanding the history of *Asimina triloba*, its evolution and relationship to other Annonaceae, does make the world seem more connected — and is a reminder of how much there is yet to know about the plants that surround us; the million-year journeys these plants have taken to get where they are, and to appear as they do. The pawpaw — flowering here in Stebbins Forest — is in fact a tropical plant that willed itself, over millennia, to thrive where it shouldn't.

☙

We arrive at the first patch, and after I clumsily slide down a steep bank to the creekbed, we start to collect data. The pawpaw flowers look like hundreds of cut red roses, nodding downward from leafless twigs. In addition to studying fungi, Steve is attempting to define what constitutes a patch — where one stops and another begins. In some places the divide is clear; in other forests, the "patch" never ends, continuing on and on. In his study, a patch "is defined as a group of pawpaw stems separated from other stems by at least three meters." According to one study, pawpaws have been able to increase in some forests by as much 724 percent in just a few decades.[4] That number is astounding, but, anecdotally at least, I've seen evidence of patch prowess. The previous summer I traveled to Lancaster County, Pennsylvania, to see a pawpaw grove described by locals as the "largest pawpaw patch north of the Mason-Dixon." It delivered. A walking trail, hugging a steep bluff overlooking the Susquehanna River, wound through a seemingly endless grove of pawpaws. But was it one massive patch, clonally replicated, or were there many unique trees among the thousands? Here in Stebbins, the patches are more manageable. We're able to identify one large thirty-foot tree, with smaller trees radiating out from its center. We record the diameter of flowering trees, collect soil samples, and march on.

How patches spread is still poorly understood. Recently, Kentucky State University researchers conducted a study to determine whether various patches of pawpaws were established by suckering, or water transport of seed. The difference would mean that a patch was either a group of clones, or made up of genetically distinct trees. Researchers selected three wild patches and determined through DNA fingerprinting that each was genetically distinct. One patch was entirely clonal; a single tree had multiplied itself through its root suckers. Another patch, however, contained greater genetic variation, and its location along a stream suggested the involvement of water transport, or animal transport of seed. The takeaway from the study was that pawpaw patches are predominantly made up of clones, but most do have genetically distinct seedlings interspersed throughout.[5]

✧

In late winter, pawpaw flower buds begin to swell. Alabama grower Dale Brooks calls these buds "little fuzzy BBs," a description I find fairly apt. Both leaf and flower buds are covered in a dark-brown, thick pubescence, which creates the fuzzy appearance. Then, in April or May, pawpaw flowers emerge. Desmond Layne observed that in the Ohio Valley and mid-Atlantic states flowers come on immediately after the peak of dogwood blooms. Once they have matured in size, the flowers will have outer and inner layers of three maroon-colored petals.[6]

It's often said that pawpaw flowers smell like rotting meat, and that this is in order to attract pollinators, the various blowflies and carrion beetles attracted to decomposition. But beyond being grotesque, that description might not be altogether accurate. Besides, we pawpaw lovers need a more pleasant analogy for the flower of our favorite fruit. Enter scent scientist Katherine Goodrich. "Until recently, the scientific study of scent was . . . relatively confined to the perfume or wine industries," Goodrich writes. But advances in scent sampling and analysis techniques have broadened the scope of scent study, and scientists "are increasingly interested in the role that plant scent compounds play in plant-animal interactions." In her research, Goodrich has found that the maroon-pigmented *Asimina* species "all share yeasty 'fermentation' floral odors," specifically compounds that give the flowers "a scent similar to red wine or rising bread dough." But flesh persists as well. Goodrich goes on to say, "The small maroon flowers with yeasty scents may represent mimics of food substrates or brood sites for pollinating beetles and/or flies. It is possible . . . that the odors produced generate a learned response from pollinating insects."[7]

The pawpaw flower is not alone in nature as a mimic of fermentation. The largest flower in the world belongs to a species known as *Rafflesia arnoldii*, or corpse flower, and is found in the rain forests of Indonesia. Measuring up to three feet long and weighing up to twenty-four pounds, this maroon-colored bloom emits an odor said to be horrible and repulsive, "similar to that of rotting meat." Another enormous tropical flower, *Amorphophallus titanum* — also colored burgundy red on the inside — is similarly scented, and is also known as the corpse or cadaver flower.[8] And in North America, among the deciduous forests' spring ephemerals is *Trillium erectum*, a small, nodding woodland wildflower that looks strikingly like the blooms of pawpaw. Its maroon flowers are, you guessed it, commonly described as smelling like a wet dog or rotting meat. Furthermore, each of the above examples is pollinated by flies and beetles.[9] But again, let's use red wine and rising bread dough when describing pawpaws, please.

Flies and beetles are listed as the primary pollinators of pawpaws, but they're not the only insects conducting business inside the flowers. The pawpaw peduncle borer (*Talponia plummeriana*), a moth larva, lays eggs within the flower and then consumes it. Although much scientific research remains to be done, Neal Peterson has closely observed these relationships for decades. "There seems to be a whole ecology in the flowers," he says, "between the insects coming in and the spiders that are there waiting to eat the insects." Occasionally, human beings are part of that ecology.

Botanically speaking, pawpaws are perfect, which means they have both male and female reproductive parts. Being protogynous, the female parts (the pistil) come to maturity before the male parts (the stamen). Yet despite having all the necessary equipment, pawpaws don't enjoy reproducing alone: They're self-incompatible and require a genetically different tree/flower for cross-pollination (however, the Sunflower cultivar is widely reported to be self-fertile). So for various reasons, pawpaw growers occasionally choose to get involved. "It's all very easy," Neal Peterson writes, "but — like human sex — it isn't necessarily obvious how to do it the first time."

Pawpaw flowers begin as females, and later become male, a fact that actually discourages self-pollination, since pollen is produced last, after the flower's receptive female parts have transitioned. In the first stage, petals are held tightly together, forcing flies and beetles visiting for nectar to brush against the stigmas. During this time, the petals turn from green to maroon, and once the flower has darkened, the fetid aroma — of red wine, rising dough, flesh — intensifies. The flower is now male. Anthers turn from green to brown and release their yellow pollen. An insect pollinator must then travel to a female flower of a different tree to create fruit. As human pollinators, we have a certain advantage: We can collect pollen one day and return another. Once pollen has been collected, the orchardist can use these visual cues to then pollinate the female flowers. "I find that I get the best results on a perfect spring day, when the sun is bright, the air is warm, the breezes gentle or not at all," Neal Peterson writes. "I don't do it in the early morning or late in the day. When in doubt about how to do it, think like a flower, think like a beetle."[10]

❧

Steve and I are lost. It's okay, he tells me, it happens every time. We have GPS, but after a few minutes we conclude that for whatever reason the maps Steve downloaded won't merge with the placemarks, so we're looking at free-floating pinpoints with no context. Steve discovered the patch we're looking for a year ago. It produced a good amount of fruit, even when other patches didn't during last year's hot, dry summer. The fruit wasn't too bitter either, he says, and neither vibrant orange nor stark white.

One theory that Steve is contemplating is that the pawpaw may affect surrounding forest composition chemically via its Annonaceous acetogenins.

Another factor might be leaf size: A dense patch of broad-leafed pawpaws could shade the forest floor to the exclusion of other species. In his Geauga County tramping, Steve notices that pawpaws overwhelmingly occur in the understory of beech, sugar maple, and black cherry. Kirk Pomper also suggests pawpaw might inhibit the spread of invasive exotics, such as Japanese honeysuckle. However, his research shows that only the largest, densest pawpaw colonies stand much of a chance in this fight.

We're now following blue blazes because at least we know they will lead us to some destination, though Steve isn't sure what that will be. We cross TRAIL CLOSED signs, ominous clouds hover above us (it has been raining for days), and a cool breeze blows, signaling more precipitation. Steve isn't worried. After about a mile we stumble upon the next pawpaw patch. I'm getting hungry and have already eaten my apple, so I munch on the greens of as many ramps as I can pick, though it seems I could pick for days without doing much harm. In this forest, I can anecdotally confirm that ramps grow quite well at the roots of pawpaws. We collect the last of the day's data and manage to beat the rain back to the stream and to the car.

We come out of the woods and return to Steve's orchard. In addition to the trees he has ordered, he is raising trees from seed. KSU recommends sowing seeds to a three-centimeter depth (about an inch and a quarter) in a "moist, well-drained soil or other medium that has good aeration." California grower Ray Jones observed that planting seeds one inch deep, with the small end up, and after a warm-water soak, worked best.[11] And experiments have shown that germination is hastened by ten days if the soil is heated to 29 to 32 degrees Celsius (or 84.2 to 89.6 degrees Fahrenheit) after sowing.[12] At least one OPGA member starts his seeds in containers in his basement, which are placed on heating pads. Taking things a step farther, Arkansas's Blossom Nursery pre-germinates all seeds before planting its nursery stock in containers (and offers excess germinated seed for sale online). Because of its long taproot, pawpaws should be grown in tree pots—four-by-fourteen-inch containers are commonly used. Other less orthodox methods include PVC pipe and, my own method, ten-and-a-half-inch repurposed milk and juice cartons.

According to pawpaw grower Barb Ernst, there are two rules basic rules to follow for the successful germination of pawpaw seeds. Rule number one:

"NEVER LET THE SEED DRY OUT." And rule number two: "NEVER LET THE SEED DRY OUT."[13]

They are good rules to follow. Once it has been cleaned, pawpaw can be stored in a moist medium, such as peat or sphagnum moss, and then sealed in a ziplock bag. Before they will germinate, pawpaw seeds need to overwinter. Luther Burbank once wrote that pawpaw "has a habit of 'thinking it over' six months in the greenhouse before it begins to sprout."[14] This overwintering process, called stratification, occurs naturally in the wild, but can be replicated with even more reliability in your refrigerator at around forty-one degrees Fahrenheit (but not your freezer — the deep freeze can kill the seeds) for approximately one hundred days. At his home, Steve stores seeds in old yogurt containers with a damp cellulose sponge that has been "soaked and wrung out mostly." "Another method is to plant them in the fall," Corwin Davis once advised. "Mice and squirrels will not bother them. If fall planted, mulch with leaves to prevent heaving."[15]

❧

Traveling and farming don't always go hand in hand, especially when you have vulnerable young pawpaw treelings planted in full sun. Last summer, Steve and family spent a couple of weeks in Russia, Tatiana's native country. Since he had young pawpaw trees to worry about, he installed a drip irrigation system, which was a good thing since northeast Ohio was hit with drought. It saved most of the trees from dying, but this spring they're hardly thriving, and many look miserable. Still, as the season progresses, only a few prove dead. Steve will plant fifty additional pawpaw trees later this year. When these mature, they won't require much upkeep, so once the orchard is established, trips to Russia, Suriname, or wherever the family wants to visit will be much easier.

Steve must wait several more years before he gets even one fruit from his young orchard. In the meantime, he sells vegetables and berries at local farmers markets. He has even sold foraged pawpaws to a local ice cream maker. He's making sales, which is obviously the farmer's goal, but he's also trying to get a head start on the marketing work he'll eventually be faced with when the cultivated fruit is ready. "What's a pawpaw?" customers will ask. "They grow *here*?"

PART III

WAY DOWN YONDER:

TRAVELS IN THE PAWPAW BELT

— CHAPTER THIRTEEN —

ST. LOUIS

In September 1806, Captain Meriwether Lewis and Lieutenant William Clark were six months along their return trip from the Pacific Ocean. President Thomas Jefferson had ordered the expedition to find "the most direct & practicable water communication across this continent for the purposes of commerce."[1] It had been more than two years since the Corps of Discovery set out, and back in Washington it was feared that Lewis and Clark and the others were long dead. Though far from it, mortality surely crossed their minds when food supplies started running low. The crew was eager to reach home, but they suddenly began anticipating something else as well, as evidenced by the last sentence of a journal entry dated September 11: "The papaws nearly ripe."

A few days later, near the entrance of the Kansas River along the Missouri, Lewis and Clark went ashore to gather "pappaws or the custard apple of which this country abounds, and the men are very fond of." The crew then shot an Elk, and "secured and divided" its flesh. They went forty-nine miles that day and encamped "a short distance Above Hay cabin creek." The weather was disagreeably warm, but steady winds broke the suffocating humidity. And they were now well fed on a feast of native foods, including elk meat and pawpaws. It must have been a good year to have such abundance.

In addition to enlisted men from the US Army, the corps comprised "backwoodsmen" from Kentucky and Indiana, "skilled in hunting and outdoor life and used to hardship," men who likely became "very fond of" pawpaw in their lives back home.[2] They would have picked pawpaws from the forest floor, and shaken trees to let ripe fruit drop. Some may have brought fruit back to their boats; others would have feasted in the woods, breaking the fruit apart, squeezing to release the pulp. Seeds and skin discarded, they would have reached for more.

Several days of slow going and warm weather followed. On Thursday, September 18, they met up with a team of hunters they had sent ahead, but who had killed nothing. "At 10 o'clock we came too and gathered pottows [pawpaws] to eate we having nothing but a fiew Buisquit to eat and are partly compelled to eate poppows which we find in great quantities on the Shores." The heat continued unabated, but the relatively cool, oak-filled bottomlands offered a measure of relief. They saw few deer, one bear, and just three turkeys, but were able to kill none.

"Our party entirely out of provisions subsisting on poppaws. We divided the busikit which amounted to one buisket per man, this in addition to the poppaws is to last us down to the Settlement's which is 150 miles . . . the party appear perfectly contented and tell us they can live very well on the pappaws."

They traveled fifty-two miles that day. The next morning they descended the Missouri with great velocity and only came ashore once, again, for the "purpose of gathering pappaws." Eager to reach the Illinois, they did not want to halt for hunting. And with pawpaws in such abundance, they didn't need to. Eventually, they came upon a French village. Thanks to pawpaws, the brief hunger scare was over. On September 23, the corps reached St. Louis; the great expedition had ended.[3]

⁂

In the 1930s, the Works Progress Administration (WPA) erected dozens of limestone structures at Fort Bellefontaine Park in north St. Louis. It was at this approximate location that the corps went ashore for one of many pawpaw-foraging excursions. The park was once a popular spot for picnicking and swimming, though its primary use today is as a residential youth facility called Missouri Hills Home. I've come here in mid-September — the same time of year the corps did more than two hundred years ago — to see if pawpaws are still growing, to see if I too can be "perfectly contented and . . . live very well on the pappaws." WPA structures still abound, including bridges, culverts, a large bathhouse and other "comfort stations," and an incredible, five-tiered Grand Staircase rising from the river's banks to the high bluff where the corps camped twice, once in 1804, and again in 1806, just before the expedition concluded. Now in disrepair — not unlike a few other

WPA structures and projects throughout the country — the stoneworks are encroached upon by the forest, lending the park a strange air of ruin, as if these buildings were built centuries ago, not mere decades, and are now being reclaimed by the landscape. Like the pawpaws I'm here to find, they're devalued if not forgotten — but all still exist, still beautiful, still inviting use.

I take the long hike to the Grand Staircase, walking first through the open prairie — a term the French gave to their meadows — mixed here with goldenrod, wild blue sage, milkweed, and flowers visited by orange and yellow butterflies. Unseen insects croak and chatter everywhere around me. It's ninety-eight degrees Fahrenheit, a sixty-five-year record high for St. Louis. Fields eventually give way to the forest edge and a trail along Coldwater Creek. An information kiosk shows an illustration of fossils of the giant beaver, twice the size of our modern *Castor canadensis*, which once lived here, and may have been one of the now-extinct mammals that ate pawpaws. A few ailanthus and mulberry trees have begun to colonize the grasses; dense honeysuckle vines crowd the understory. The woods are filled with sassafras, persimmon, redbud, black walnut, box elder, and oaks. But in other patches, Japanese honeysuckle is the only plant in the understory. Here, the forest — not just the limestone structures and manicured lawns — would be unrecognizable to Lewis and Clark, and to the Osage and the Kansas tribes they met near here.

I can hear Coldwater Creek through the dense stands of honeysuckle. Crouching below its vine-like branches, I inch toward the source. There's an odd abandoned building — perhaps a former comfort station or picnic shelter — its roof long gone. But around the limestone walls grow pawpaws. I shake the skinny trees and listen for dropping fruit. A tiny pawpaw falls onto a bed of leaves. I take it with me to the creek. The pulp is bright yellow. It has a good creamy texture but is a bit too bitter for my taste. I walk the creekbed, which is lined with steep, natural stone walls. Boulders create a path through the water. A belted kingfisher swoops and dives past me repeatedly, looking for a snack of its own.

I continue walking, alternating between the creekbed and the raised trail. Berry-flecked spicebush becomes abundant in the understory, and then so do pawpaws. They're everywhere. I'm drawn into a grove with at least a dozen trees, each more than thirty feet in height. I wonder if these were planted, or if this is the site of an old Indian orchard. And then I remember how much time has passed since these specific lands were occupied by Native Americans. Even the idea that this is a settler's orchard would be a stretch. Yet this grove is unique, almost savanna-like. I pick fruit off the ground; there might not be enough for an entire crew, but there's enough for me. Perhaps if I looked harder, and if my survival depended on it, I could find dozens more (and if my survival depended on this one fruit, I certainly wouldn't complain of bitterness). As I continue my walk, the path is lined with pawpaw, shagbark hickory, and vigorous grapevines. A lone squirrel darts ahead of me. Like the corps, I don't see much game. Though I'm not actively hunting, the squirrel is the only mammal I spot all day.

Following the creek leads me to the Missouri. It is massive, carrying rainfall from the Rockies and various Canadian streams. Within the river are islands of sediment and rock, fallen cottonwoods and piled sand. The Missouri was once forded by herds of bison, a life source to native peoples for at least twelve thousand years, and carried French and Spanish explorers, Lewis and Clark, and subsequent American settlers as a gateway to the West. During all that time pawpaws have thrived here.

A few yards from the riverbank is a bathhouse, now in ruins. The roof is gone but the structure is shaded still by the large-leafed canopy of more than a dozen pawpaw trees; they're everywhere, in fact, ascending the steep hillside.

Finally I arrive at the Grand Staircase. At the base, a shirtless man repeatedly lifts a large rock over his head. His dust-covered mountain bike leans against the limestone. He says he's just getting in his daily exercise. In a moment he tears down the trail, pedaling along the path from which I've just come. I climb the five tiers of the Grand Staircase, past empty pools and fallow planters, to the top of the bluff. The view of the river from here, befitting the staircase's title and size, is impressive. A few yards away, plaques mark the corps' two campsites here. Just down the path, teenagers are carrying furniture from a pickup truck into one of several dormitories on the grounds. I rest for a moment and eat one of the pawpaws I've collected. This one is not bitter, but sweet and watery. It's good. For all that has surely changed in this landscape, much has remained, not the least of which are the navigable waters of the Missouri itself, ahead of me in constant motion, and the sweet fruit of wild pawpaws, "of which this country abounds . . . which we find in great quantities on the Shores."

CHAPTER FOURTEEN

HISTORIC VIRGINIA

Thomas Jefferson's Monticello offers an unparalleled view of central Virginia: the Blue Ridge Mountains, the Piedmont, and nearby Charlottesville, home to Jefferson's other great architectural achievement, the University of Virginia. In between all of those sites, in the woods and along creeks and rivers, pawpaws abound.

Thomas Jefferson is rumored — as is frequently stated in news articles describing the fruit — to have believed that pawpaws had potential under cultivation. It's a feather in the cap of today's pawpaw's promoters: Jefferson's involvement validates their own claims of its merit.

Lewis and Clark's story of subsisting on pawpaws alone for three days may have been of interest to Jefferson, but it's unlikely that it would have been his first introduction to the fruit. The country of Jefferson's youth was filled with wild pawpaws. Later in life, records he kept (and he was meticulous, even obsessive about keeping records) show *Asimina triloba* as having been planted on his estate. Jefferson also sent pawpaw seeds to associates in Europe, as it was considered an exceptional and unique American biological discovery.

In early September 2012, I take a tour of Monticello, a national historic landmark and UNESCO World Heritage Site, hoping to find a pawpaw planting. I begin my search at the re-created kitchen garden, which is full of okra, its hibiscus flowers in full bloom, and beans, squash, and tomatoes, neatly arranged in rows on a high terrace behind Jefferson's home. Next, I search his "Fruitery," which includes a South Orchard of four hundred fruit trees, two vineyards, and "berry squares" of currants, gooseberries, and raspberries. I check Mulberry Row, the site of slave quarters just three hundred feet from Jefferson's home, named for the fruit-bearing tree that provided both shade and berries, and I search among his peach and apple plantings, and along submural beds of fig trees. But nowhere in the fruitery is there a trace of pawpaws.

I had read on the Monticello website that Jefferson's fruit production reflected the two schools of fruit growing that occurred in eighteenth-century Virginia. The first was "Field" or "Farm" orchards that produced fruit for cider, brandy, or livestock feed. "There is some truth to one historian's tongue-in-cheek remark that it was a significant event when Americans began eating their fruit rather than drinking it," the website remarks.[1] These trees were usually grown from seed, with unpredictable results. But Jefferson's was also an Old World orchard, with other plantings of grafted European cultivars, from Spanish almonds to French apricots. European pomologists guided the care of these trees. "The Fruitery at Monticello, however, was unique because it was both an Old World Fruit Garden and a colonial Virginia 'Farm Orchard,'" according to the website. "Like Jefferson himself, it represented the best of the European heritage combined with a distinctive New World vitality and personality."[2] I can think of no better candidate for such an orchard than the pawpaw: a hefty, custard-filled tree fruit with American roots.

During a group tour of the home I ask our guide if he knows anything about Jefferson's work with pawpaws, and whether there are any planted here. He checks with another expert and confers, but concludes rather definitively that, no, there weren't any pawpaws here, and that Jefferson didn't cultivate pawpaws in his day.

At the conclusion of the tour, we exit the home and enter the formal gardens. Walking along the west lawn, I admire the small fishpond, and the hedges and trees planted generations ago. And then, just beyond the more formal plantings, I spot it: a pawpaw tree, one of the largest I have ever seen. Even from a distance I can positively identify the leaves. For a brief moment I think maybe I've been duped by the similar-looking cucumber magnolia, but the tree is bearing its unmistakable fruit. A few pieces lie in the grass, while others still cling to branches. The tree has grown in the classic pyramidal pawpaw shape, with one lower branch large enough to climb on — a feat I have rarely encountered anywhere. Although it hasn't produced fruit in abundance, the tree is so large that there's enough for me to gather quite a few. The pawpaws are on average four or five inches long, larger than most wild fruit. I eat one on the spot: Not excessively seedy, it's sweet but does leave a bitter aftertaste. Nothing too exceptional, but it's here at Monticello, and that seems significant enough.

I can wish, but I don't imagine that this tree, large as it is, was planted by Thomas Jefferson. Pawpaw patches, however, as a single organism, can be incredibly long-lived. Considering this, the large pawpaw tree in front of me could be a clonal offspring, a seedling even, sprouted from dropped fruit of a tree that Thomas Jefferson planted in the early 1800s.

Either way, it's a discovery, since no staff I spoke with earlier had any knowledge of its existence. I show it to a Monticello Gardens tour leader. "Far out," he says. "You found that here?" More than twenty-seven million people have visited Monticello; on this day, hundreds if not thousands toured the site. Every walking tour of the home ends here, near this tree, and yet it remains unknown. Even here, pawpaw grows in anonymity.

❧

At the age of twenty-one, George Washington was the first English colonist to venture over the Appalachian Mountains on official order. His military career constantly sent him into the wilderness, where he confronted not only gunfire and cannon blast, but also difficult terrain and inclement weather. Still, it would be misleading to call the woods entirely hostile, as they were abundant with wild fruit, greens, and game. If Washington wasn't already acquainted with pawpaws as a boy in Virginia, he certainly would have discovered the fruit on campaigns in the mountains of that state, as well as in Pennsylvania. Everywhere he went was — and remains — pawpaw country. Like Lewis and Clark, the many settlers to follow, and the native peoples before him, Washington and his armies would have found this rich fruit a welcome blessing when provisions were low. And in the bottoms of the Potomac River, which his plantation overlooked, among the sycamores and hickories, were also pawpaws.

Today pawpaws are absent from the formal gardens, but they abound in the wild places surrounding Mount Vernon. They're behind the plantation's tobacco barn, where a small stream drains into the Potomac. Along with the pink blooms of swamp rose mallow (and lingering bits of litter) are a scattering of pawpaw trees. Another patch of wild pawpaws grows behind the replica of a small slave cabin. This section of Mount Vernon, called

Dogue Run Farm, was home to the hundreds of slaves Washington owned in his lifetime. Pawpaws would have been gathered from these woods and eaten by the nation's first president and his slaves alike.

Near Washington's tomb, just above one of the walking paths, a patch of several large pawpaw trees grows among dark, towering evergreens. Thousands of visitors walk this path every year, with ripe pawpaws growing close enough to fall on someone's head. When I examine the patch I am rewarded with a single, large piece of fruit.

One of the best and most often-repeated pawpaw myths says that chilled pawpaw was one of Washington's favorite desserts. I have so far been unable to find any evidence to substantiate this claim, but perhaps this is fitting, that the nation's first president, of whom there are so many legends — the chopping of the cherry tree; the wooden teeth that weren't — ought also to have some connection with America's largest, most impressive native fruit.

But let's say the story is true. Did he gather pawpaws while out on a fox hunt, or a walk around his estate? How would Washington's pawpaw have been presented to him? Would his enslaved chef, Hercules, have kept pieces of whole fruit in the ice cellar? And was it wild, or fruit picked from his garden? Perhaps Washington enjoyed slicing the fruit, twisting it open, and eating it with a spoon. He might have sucked on pawpaw seeds for every bit of the sweet pulp. Perhaps Hercules scooped it for him, presented it as a pudding in a bowl, seated in ice. Yes, maybe Washington did eat pawpaw by the chilled bowlful each September.

✦

The Charlottesville Farmers Market is a Saturday-morning happening. A massive parking lot that on another day would be a waste of downtown real estate is filled with booths, vendors selling fruits and vegetables, prepared foods, tacos, and more.

Daniel Perry, who owns and operates Jam According to Daniel, is experienced with all sorts of ripe fruit — from fig, peach, and strawberry, to apple, blueberry, and raspberry. His jams are displayed in mason jars at the market, all wrapped in black-and-white labels. One pound of local fruit in every jar, no pectin added.

A friend of Perry's, experimenting at home, made a pawpaw jam using Daniel's technique. It was a vibrant yellow, "fabulous, passionfruit-y, pineapple-y, sort of vanilla-y . . . tropical ensemble," he said. Intrigued, Perry then went to a local wild patch and gathered between twenty and thirty pounds of fruit. After several hours, he processed just a few pounds. So he called it a day, and planned to resume the task the following morning. That's when he encountered the notorious scent of ripening pawpaws. "It smells like if a perfume factory were an animal, and that animal was roadkill," Perry says. "It's just this sweet, sickly sort of smell."

Pawpaws typically last three to five days at room temperature before, as Daniel observed, they're unusable and far too overripe. His description may be sensational — and to some it's a pleasant aroma — but as ripening turns to fermentation, the scent can certainly be overwhelming. Of the ones Daniel gathered in the wild, many were picked up from the ground — as the song instructs — and were likely bruised, and well on their way to being too far gone before he'd even brought them home. His olfactory senses were doomed from the beginning.

This perishability, the pawpaw's short shelf life, is also often cited as the reason why pawpaws haven't been brought under commercial cultivation. There are ways to address this challenge, and many pawpaw growers are succeeding; nonetheless, it's true — and if George Washington really did enjoy a chilled pawpaw, we know that the lesson had already been learned in the eighteenth century — do not wait to get your pawpaw on ice.

⚬⚭⚬

The distance between historic Colonial Williamsburg and Yorktown is thirteen miles via the Colonial Parkway, a scenic roadway and part of the National Park Service. At least ten of those miles are lined with a dense and vibrant understory of pawpaws, with trees standing shoulder-to-shoulder the entire way. Of course I have to stop and go in to find fruit. As I load my hatchback with the first batch of picked-up pawpaws, gathered from the woods there, I am visibly shaking with excitement. It is the largest expanse of fruit-bearing pawpaws I've ever walked through. In the residential neighborhoods adjacent to the parkway, pawpaws grow like weeds, popping up in hedges and along unkempt property edges.

We drive farther, toward Yorktown, but I have to pull over a second time for an even larger patch. I fill a small bag and follow a deer trail back to the road. Exiting the woods I pass a giant southern magnolia — its own glossy leaves seeming all the more tropical in this forest of fragrant fruit — only to find a park ranger parked behind my car. "Just picking up pawpaws!" I call out, hoping I'm not breaking any ordinances. I hold up the bag as proof. Thankfully he gives me a wave and lowers himself back into the car, then drives on. I must look like a feverish madman, shaggy-haired, way too wide-eyed and excited, holding a bag of mushy green orbs. But he's a ranger here; maybe he's seen this before. Pickin' up pawpaws.

Later in the evening, at a motel in Williamsburg, I pull one of several dozen pawpaws from the room's jam-packed mini fridge. The fruit tastes wild, for sure, but not bitter, the texture slightly grainy; fruity and sweet. And chilled, as Washington would have had it.

CHAPTER FIFTEEN

NORTH CAROLINA

I

CAROLINA'S NEW FRUIT

Milton Parker is fired up. I approach him at the end of the fourth annual North Carolina Paw Paw Festival, which, though considerably smaller than Ohio's, has been a resounding success. The turnout has doubled each year, with today's attendance estimated at around five hundred. In part, its suc-cess is a testament to the fact that people still read local publications — two write-ups in local North Carolina magazines built considerable interest in the fruit leading up to the event. Parker has sold out of everything: forty pounds of fruit, forty trees, and ten pounds of puree. In fact, Parker and other vendors grossly underestimated demand, and there's been nowhere near enough pawpaw products to go around. Because of this excitement — Parker gives me a high-five and is beaming — his full head of white hair seems today more a youthful blond. He wears a black T-shirt with LOVE ALWAYS WINS written in bold white, jean shorts, and sandals. Seated in the bed of his truck he is framed by two stickers on the rear windshield, one praising Jesus, the other, a rather serious declaration: I'D RATHER BE PAW-PAW HUNTING. It's not at all an exaggeration.

"I think what's been accomplished between the article in our state magazine and this event today, we've created a huge tsunami of interest in the pawpaw," Parker says. "I'm excited. I'm really excited. Not from the standpoint that I was successful in selling the trees, the fruit, and puree, but the amount of interest now. People found out." Parker's excitement makes sense in context. You could ask, What is forty pounds of fruit compared with the thousands of fruit sold at the Ohio Pawpaw Festival? But here in North Carolina, particu-larly the eastern portion of the state, there is a significant learning curve.

Derek Morris, a Forsyth County extension agent, created the festival in 2008. Almost twenty years earlier, he tasted his first pawpaw off a landscape tree in Old Salem, North Carolina. "I knew what it was, but I'd never seen it in person before, so I brought it home and tasted it," Morris says. "I could not believe how good that fruit was, and it was just lying there wasting on the ground." When he learned about the success of the Ohio Pawpaw Festival, Morris decided North Carolina needed one of its own.

"It's amazing how many people don't know about it," Morris says. "I had a lot of people [at today's festival] say they'd never heard of one. Even the old people. And I don't remember my grandparents — my grandparents were from Virginia, just across the state line — I don't remember any of them talking about pawpaws." Unlike, say, southern Ohio, West Virginia, or eastern Kentucky, for example, where anyone with a touch of gray hair is more often than not entirely familiar with pawpaws. "I think a lot of it depends on exactly where you were raised," Morris says. "If you had a creek or river or stream on your land, or had neighbors who did, and they were growing there, you knew about them. If you didn't, you didn't." Parker too is clearly encouraged. "I think we've got some opportunities in North Carolina," he says.

KSU's Kirk Pomper has said that North Carolina, Kentucky, Ohio, and Maryland make up the current range of the commercial pawpaw industry. In Ohio and Kentucky, growers are seated in cultures that are familiar with pawpaws. In North Carolina, the presence of pawpaws is not because of the fruit's long-standing role in folk culture; it's because of a few individuals, including Morris and Parker, and just a few dedicated farmers. Its revival has taken decades of work, but it appears to now be paying off.

✦

I traveled to North Carolina with my friend Jon Yahalom. Jon had yet to explore much of the Southeast, but was no stranger to fruit hunting. His father, in fact, is a fruit nut himself, and was not shy about picking falling fruit from other people's yards in their home state of California. He once loaded the backseat of a car, to the top of Jon's head, with avocados. It was good then that Jon came prepared: There can be no shame in pawpaw hunting.

Our first night on the road, we camped at a site along the New River, a onetime boomtown turned ghost town: Brooklyn, West Virginia. It was dark and late when we crossed the New River Gorge Bridge — the largest steel single-span arch bridge in this hemisphere, standing 876 feet above the New River below. But we saw none of the river that night, just fog and mountains, and the droning hum of tires on bridge. We took the exit for Fayetteville and passed a few other even smaller towns until we reached the national park entrance, making a left turn onto a tree-canopied road and a small bridge over Coal Run. A tense series of switchbacks carried us out of the mountains and down into the bottoms of the New River.

In the morning, I explored our surroundings, which included the ruins of a stone building. Growing within and around it were dozens of young pawpaw trees, though none bore any fruit. As the heavy fog cover receded from the river, the forested slopes of the gorge were unveiled, though the mountain-tops stayed covered. We were deep in the bottomland pawpaw habitat.

As we drove into eastern North Carolina — our eyes scanning for roadside pawpaws — the Appalachian terrain eased into the Piedmont. The solitary peak of Pilot Mountain — a remnant of the ancient Sauratown Mountains — was a punctuation mark between landscapes. The Cheraw Indians (also known variously as Saura or Saraw) called the formation Jomeokee, or "great guide."[1] In *A New Voyage to Carolina* (1711), John Lawson included the Cheraw with the Esaw Indians, "a very large nation containing many thousand People," in whose country he reported killing and eating "scarlet ey'd duck . . . very good to eat."[2] Lawson also ate pawpaws in the Carolinas, where "rare Puddings of this Fruit," were once made.[3] I recalled this history as we drove farther east, past tobacco fields whose frumpy crops were splayed out in orderly rows. On occasion, I wandered into woodlots behind gas stations and restaurants, but found no pawpaw trees.

I stopped at a large roadside produce market to see if any pawpaws were on the shelves. I purchased sorghum syrup and a few peaches, but found no pawpaws. However, there were other region-specific native fruits, including Scuppernong grapes, the large, local muscadines named for the river that runs through the state's coastal plain. The Scuppernong, like the pawpaw, is wild and native to the Southeast, though it was taken under cultivation at least four hundred years ago.[4] Although many advocates say pawpaw belongs in orchards, right alongside apples, peaches, and pears, it should at least be cultivated in the small-scale manner of Scuppernongs: Where people once ate them wild, they're still offered for sale at select roadside stands, farmers markets, and the like. Which is the point of this weekend's pawpaw festival: to raise the fruit's profile.

❦

Milton Parker earned a master's degree in horticulture from North Carolina State and spent his entire working life in agricultural extension. Toward the end of his career, he was introduced to pawpaws, and he and his colleagues encouraged several local farmers to grow the fruit. For the past six years he has been promoting and selling fresh pawpaws at the Columbus County Farmers Market. And since he can't be there today, his wife is pushing pawpaws in his place. Like many pawpaw enthusiasts, partners tend to get drawn in, willingly or not. "When I retired I just got, *pshew*, I mean it was like it came off the wall and hit me," Parker says. "And I said, 'Yeah, let's go with it.' So I have. And I just, I've fallen in love with the pawpaw."

A few weeks ago I called several growers in eastern North Carolina in the hope that I could meet them and tour their farms. I eventually got their blessing, but also got a call from Parker, as the farmers had first contacted him. "I'm the pawpaw man in North Carolina," he said in a voice mail. And indeed he is. Parker, through encouragement, persuasion, and often relentless insistence, has worked to bring pawpaws into commercial cultivation on at least three separate farms in North Carolina, four including his own small home orchard near Whiteville.

As much as Parker wants to help develop a pawpaw market, he envisions a future that's centered on small and part-time farmers, not large agribusiness. The agribusiness model, Parker believes, would advocate for the use of a single pawpaw cultivar. Rather than narrowing the field, though, Parker advocates for, and celebrates, the current diversity of pawpaw genetics. "We need to protect the germplasm collection at Kentucky State University," he says. "We don't need to burn our bridges behind us. We need to have stuff that we can fall back on. I think we've got a good thing here, but we don't want to ruin a good thing."

Parker recalls the southern corn leaf blight, which, beginning in 1969, threatened to destroy the monoculture of hybrid crops from Florida to Minnesota. "If we had not had the corn germplasm down in Atlanta we would have lost our corn," Parker says. "Historically, man has had a history of use and abuse. And when you have something that's native, that's been designed by God, we have a tendency to put our hands on it and ruin it. We don't want to have the corporate boys stepping in. This is a fruit that has an ideal niche for the small farmer, the part-time farmer. For people that want to do something on a small scale."

Ken Drabik, biologist and annual Peterson Pawpaws vendor, agrees. "I'm very concerned about any type of monoculture emerging," he says. "I know that's 'good business.' I know that agribusiness generally likes a limited number of products. They want Coke and Pepsi. There may wind up being a lowest-common-denominator pawpaw that will emerge that will be not terribly interesting, but it will be a pawpaw."

Until that day comes, though — if agribusiness does ever reduce pawpaw to a plain and uniform fruit — it's still just small growers producing paw-paws in North Carolina, and their crop remains varied.

⚬⚭⚬

Lesley Sanderson has been farming his entire life, in addition to a career at the glass plant in Scotland County, from which he retired. I visit Sanderson at his home two days before the festival. We arrive early in the morning but the day's picking is already complete. Sanderson gets help from a few local high school boys and his granddaughters down the road. Pulling into Sanderson's driveway, it's clear that we have the right address. Beyond a sprawling southern magnolia, pawpaw trees appear, sprouting through-out the lawn: on the side of the carport, on either side of a large wooden swing — all the comfortable places where a pawpaw was eaten, and where spat seeds had sprouted.

Sanderson speaks with the rapid-fire delivery of a country-fair auction-eer, and although in his late seventies, he has the enthusiasm and energy of a much younger man. It's a good thing too, because he's busy. In addition to the upkeep of his farm and on-site sales, he'll even deliver. When we arrive midmorning, he's got several large bags of collards on his porch, and after a short while he drives them to a customer's home. As we talk, Sanderson insists on standing. "I'm still a young man," he says.

Sanderson gives us the pickup truck tour of his orchard, which includes eighty pawpaw trees, then lets us wander around. The trees are about seventeen years old (Parker had suggested on the phone that they're in decline). It's late August, and nearly all of the fruit has been picked, and then sold by Parker at the Columbus County Farmers Market. In a good year, Sanderson says a large tree will produce up to fifty pounds of fruit. But this has not been a good year: A late frost wiped out 85 percent of the crop, temperatures dropping below freezing just as blossoms were coming on. Weeds are high in the rows; insects hover and bore into overripe figs. The pawpaw trees, though perhaps in decline, are still striking: pyramidal in shape, with deep-green foliage. A few suckers rise below the main tree's bottom branches, each vying for supremacy. The earth here is sandy, not the rich, deep alluvial soil pawpaws tend to thrive in.

"I don't grow soybeans," Sanderson says, "I grow vegetables." In addition to the orchard, Sanderson raises collards year-round, mustard and turnip greens, butter beans, peas, and corn. And as for the fruit, it all started with strawberries. The county's agricultural agents had been hoping to diversify the crops grown by the state's many part-time and small-scale farmers, and they approached Sanderson and his late wife, Marie, about trying the fruit. The couple discussed the idea and later agreed to plant four acres in strawberries. Then came more fruit, this time blueberries and figs. And then, in 1999, a sixty-five-hundred-dollar grant was awarded to Sanderson — thanks to the work and urging of Parker, Charles Lowery, and Martin Brewington — to grow pawpaws and Asian persimmons on his farm in Robeson County.

In 2000, Sanderson became the first commercial pawpaw grower in North Carolina, 337 years after the first successful English colony was established here. After more than three centuries of commercial agriculture, pawpaws were finally brought into the mainstream.

❧

Sanderson was raised in Robeson County, one of six children, and grew up on his family's farm, where his father grew tobacco, cotton, and corn. Sanderson went to school at Old Prospect — two miles from his home — the same school where Marie would later teach. Like Lesley, his brothers and sisters got jobs in the local factories and cotton mills.

Robeson County is home to the Lumbee Indian tribe, a state-recognized tribe of fifty-five thousand enrolled members. Sanderson, a Lumbee himself, says his people knew nothing of pawpaws before he began this orchard. "This was new to all of us here in this county," he says, "this fruit, this was completely new."

It's true: For the average eastern North Carolinian, regardless of ethnicity, pawpaw is as unfamiliar as nispero, ylang-ylang, and yangmei. But it wasn't always the case in this region; pawpaw was once an important food source in the Carolinas. Native Americans, including Muskhogean-, Siouan-, Algonquian-, and Iroquoian-speaking groups, were eating the fruit when Europeans arrived — beginning, briefly, with the French in 1562, and later with permanent English settlements. Native American villages and individual homesites were surrounded by large fields planted in beans, corn, and squash — which, when you think about it, isn't too different from Sanderson's homestead.[5] Additionally, they were also growing many other now largely forgotten food crops of the Eastern Agricultural Complex — likely including little barley, goosefoot, erect knotweed, maygrass, sumpweed, and sunflower — quite unlike homesteads today. Nearer to the coast, the hearts of cabbage palms were harvested and, along with Indian hemp, used for food as well as fiber. From the forest they gathered and cultivated chestnuts, hickory nuts, and acorns; the roots of greenbrier, arrowhead, and Jerusalem artichoke; and fruits likes crab apples, blackberries, blueberries, persimmons, and pawpaws.[6] With the arrival of Europeans, the Indians soon added orchards of figs, apples, and peaches — fruits themselves not native to Europe, but rather Asia and the Middle East.[7] The continental merging of orchards began right away.

But European diseases soon devastated those tribes, and coupled with displacement, American Indian populations were drastically reduced in the Carolinas. One tribe, the Catawba, had gone from an estimated population of forty-six hundred in 1682 to merely four hundred souls at the time of American independence.[8] Lost were not only individual lives but also culture and foodways — and often the foods themselves. Marsh elder and maygrass were gone, replaced by vast fields of tobacco, indigo, and corn.

Although the Lumbee were among the earliest tribes to adopt European-style agriculture, they continued to know and depend on wild foods — as most rural Americans did — for meat, nuts, berries, and greens. So when Sanderson tells me that the Lumbee in North Carolina had no clue of the pawpaw's existence, it strikes me as surprising and a little sad. The idea that a Native American tribe in an eastern American state — one that survived both displacement and disease — would as a whole be unfamiliar with this most unique of native American fruit spoke to the fall of fruit, and of how many other foodways may have been lost. But perhaps I had romanticized the fruit too much. Here in eastern North Carolina, where the plains were once covered in vast longleaf pine savanna (and then clear-cut in subsequent centuries for tobacco, cotton, and other crops), perhaps it's as simple as what Derek Morris says: If they grew on your property, you knew about them. If they didn't, you didn't. And it happened that where the Lumbee settled — in the swamps of Robeson County — they were without pawpaws.

Sanderson believes that when he stops growing pawpaws, that will be their end in Robeson County. "The Indian people is not used to this fruit, so they will never go into that fruit." And though he would like to see a few young farmers pick up the crop, he says there aren't really any young farmers in the area. "Now the blueberry, back over here now" — Sanderson points toward his plump bushes — "that's a good mover in Robeson County. And it's well known in Robeson County from years ago, 'cause we used to pick a lot of them in the woods."

But what Sanderson doesn't know — or doesn't let on — is that pawpaws are enjoying a revival, and are being grown by young and first-time farmers elsewhere, even in North Carolina. Even in his skepticism, he admits folks are tracking him down for his pawpaws. "You'll have folks in the city that pick me up on that Internet, and they'll come by and maybe get a pound. They want to get two or three and try them in their yards." Despite what he will admit, for more than a decade Sanderson has helped spread pawpaws throughout the state — the offspring of his fruit thrive throughout the Carolinas.

I want to give Sanderson an idea of pawpaw's popularity in Ohio, particularly through Chmiel and the Ohio Pawpaw Festival, as well as the success Jim Davis has had with shipping direct to high-end chefs in New York City. He's stunned when I tell him the festival's attendance regularly exceeds eight thousand people over three days. I tell him about the wild patches filled with fruiting trees. I tell him the fruit's frozen pulp sells for as much as twelve dollars a pound. Sanderson lets out a shout, and says, "Boys, let me get my pickup!"

Sanderson excuses himself to deliver his final twenty-five pounds of pawpaw fruit to Milton Parker. Though he won't be there to see it, his fruit will cause a stir; there won't be enough to go around, the seeds will be saved and planted.

℀

At their 150-acre farm in Columbus County, Gary and Terrie Tyree grow organic vegetables, organic pawpaws, and organic tobacco. Though Gary grew up on this same farm, he chose a different profession, enjoying a career as a welder at a nuclear substation. Gary's wife, Terrie, grew up across the street (their son lives in her childhood home). Their families have farmed on these two-hundred-plus acres since the late 1800s.

Terrie welcomes us in from the rain into their home, which is shaded by a giant pecan tree, while hydrangea, pomegranate, and sago palms border the house. In the kitchen, Terrie pulls a few plump pawpaws from the refrigerator and Jon and I each eat one — cut in half, with a spoon. Mine is creamy, mild, and sweet. I came to North Carolina to learn about the state's emerging pawpaw culture and to find traces of its history, but if I must be honest, also for the promise of several orchards' worth of fruit. It's good.

The first pawpaws Gary grew came bare-root. They were planted and mulched; drip irrigation was installed. But it was a hot year, and every single tree, several thousand dollars' worth, died. Still, thanks to the persistence of Milton Parker, who connected Gary with a source for Peterson Pawpaws, that wasn't the end. Gary ordered a few dozen more, fertilized them, and they've since taken off. The Tyrees are now in their third year of heavy production.

As an organic grower, Gary was interested in the pawpaw's lack of pests, and indeed they haven't had any serious insect problems. And although he uses organic fertilizers, including feather meal, the orchard is located on a former cow and horse pasture atop at least seventy-five years' composted manure. The land here is rich.

They're growing organic fruit and vegetables — everything from okra to tomatoes, ice potatoes, Asian persimmons, and blackberries — but Gary says heirloom crops, never mind something like pawpaws, aren't in high demand locally. Even the organic tobacco is not produced for domestic consumers, but rather European markets. Still, that is beginning to change, even if slowly. The Cherokee Purple tomato for one, he says, is gaining in popularity. "The people don't hardly turn around for the difference in this part of the country," Gary says. "But those are starting to catch on pretty big." Unless he's prepared to create an elaborate shipping and storage infrastructure similar to Deep Run Orchard's, however, he will need to find a reliable, local outlet for those pawpaws.

As we tour his orchard, Gary tells me about Eastern Carolina Organics (ECO), a farmer-owned LLC that markets and distributes wholesale organic produce to retailers, restaurants, and buying clubs. It's the type of local business that farmers like the Tyrees and Sanderson — anyone with a niche crop — could definitely use in building a consumer base for obscure items, from lacinato kale and muscadine jelly to butterhead lettuce and fresh pawpaws. If the folks in Columbus County aren't willing to pay four dollars a pound for pawpaws, ECO will find consumers in metropolitan areas from Charlotte and Winston-Salem to Chapel Hill and Greensboro. But the Tyrees haven't yet brought their pawpaws to ECO; there's a demand throughout the state that so far the producers aren't meeting.

This year, Tyree's crop is sold by his friend Milton Parker at the Columbus County Farmers Market. He will sell them at the Columbus County market, and even if they go for a little less than at they might at, say, the Durham Farmers Market, Parker's salesmanship will make sure they find a home.

Gary believes pawpaws will eventually make their way into stores like Whole Foods, and into the mainstream — likely through frozen purees, or as an ingredient in ice creams and juices. But for all the importance of marketing, there's no way around the hard work, and extreme patience, farming demands. "We got to get growing them if you're going to do that," he says. "People's going to want them, and if there ain't no supply of them they'll ask, 'Why are you turning me on to something this good and can't support the habit?'"

II

THE PIEDMONT

Pawpaw season takes Wynn Dinnsen back to his youth, to summers spent handpicking tobacco. It was backbreaking work, and the scent of the crop burned your nostrils while your hands, too, were steeped in the odor. Tobacco was then taken for curing to barns — dark, musty spaces whose sole purpose was getting the crop ready for buyers. Today at Wynn's home orchard, there is no single-purpose room for the storage of pawpaws, so the smell of ripe fruit is everywhere. Wynn doesn't notice the pawpaw perfume coating his home during the day; it strikes him in the morning, when he wakes but is still in bed, a reminder that downstairs are ever-ripening paw-paws, fruits that need to be analyzed, pulped, and stored. And then there's the orchard, where he'll need to pick nearly a ton of fruit before it drops and the ants get them, if raccoons, opossums, and squirrels haven't already feasted in the night.

On his kitchen counter, plastic cups are filled with shiny black pawpaw seeds. Each cup is labeled with a number — 222, 227, 158, and so on — corresponding with a tree in his orchard. They're seeds from exceptional fruit, nuggets of genetic information he'd like to save, pass on, continue to propagate, and sell. Thumbing through his large spiral notebook Dinnsen records notes on the wide and varied characteristics of outstanding fruit. "I'm just glad it's got so much diversity," he says, echoing the sentiments of Milton Parker. "That's what's fun about it, is having the different flavors."

Each of his fruits is also labeled with a small white sticker corresponding to its tree. Dinnsen tries to label each pawpaw while it's still firmly attached to the peduncle, but it's difficult to keep up. Despite all the time he puts into his pawpaw experiment, he still manages a full-time nursery business as well. As for nearly every other pawpaw grower today, his crop remains a cottage industry at best, a labor- and time-intensive gamble.

Dinnsen started an organic farm in the 1970s but says the market wasn't yet established, so he switched careers. In the 2000s, he started a landscaping business, but then North Carolina's real estate bubble burst and business dried up. "I got into organic farming too early, and residential landscaping too late," he says. It takes about eight years for a pawpaw tree to begin bearing fruit. With his orchard maturing and producing more than two thousand pounds a year, he might have finally gotten his timing right, especially if the demand for pawpaws continues to grow.

Wynn did not come to pawpaws through Milton Parker. An acquaintance, a solar panel installer, told Wynn about the fruit and let him try one. But that's as far as he would go. The man would not divulge where the wild patch he had gathered from was located; like Italian truffles, these were guarded treasures. Wynn found a source for seed, and then waited eight years — the time it took to raise his seedlings to the production of their first fruit — to taste pawpaws again. For nearly a decade he raised trees for the promise of fruit, a fleeting flavor he'd experienced only once.

Now he's awash in fruit. For the past two years almost all of Wynn's paw-paws have gone to a single buyer: Durham's Fullsteam Brewery. Jon and I have plans to visit the brewery later this evening. Wynn thinks its beer is terrific, and would go with us into Durham if he didn't have so much work today. The pawpaw festival is tomorrow, and he has to prepare.

≈

Durham is not the tobacco city it once was. Many of the brick structures once serving as tobacco warehouses have been converted into a hub of the local food scene — restaurants, breweries, bakeries, all celebrating the local terroir. And a prominent member of that scene is Fullsteam Brewery. A "plow-to-pint" brewery, Fullsteam offers "distinctly Southern beer" that, according to its website, "celebrates the culinary and agricultural traditions of the South." There are brews made with summer basil and sweet potatoes; I've even heard talk of kudzu beer. The company also has a forager series in which it turns folks' abundance of figs, persimmons, and even chestnuts into quality beer. I'm enthusiastic about those beers and eager to try them, but I've come to Durham for one reason: pawpaw beer. And as luck would have it, they've pulled a keg out from the reserves and I've arrived just as it's being tapped.

The draft list is written on a chalkboard menu. Underneath the Summer Basil Farmhouse Ale and One Hope Rye, there it is. A Belgian style, 9 percent alcohol by volume Paw Paw beer. "Bright, tropical — wine-like," the description reads. It's a four-ounce pour, the beer sweet yet balanced. It doesn't taste like overripe, too-sweet, too-caramel fruit. It's great. We hang at the bar and listen as Fullsteam's customers ask the various bartenders where they got their pawpaws, and how they can get some for themselves. The fruit is having its moment.

III

THE NORTH CAROLINA PAW PAW FESTIVAL

The pawpaw fest opens with a buffet line of pawpaw snacks: dips, salsas, sliced fresh fruit, and ice cream. There are a few presentations and several question-and-answer sessions. The fruit is new, and folks want to learn as much as they can. Milton Parker quickly sells out of fruit and trees, as does Wynn Dinnsen. Because of the large turnout, there's not enough fruit to go around, not even to sample. I improvise, and recall that there's a bag of fruit in my car Wynn gave me the day before. I borrow a knife and set up a tasting station to offer free samples. In a few minutes, I look around and notice that the line is wrapped around the pavilion. I slice fruit for more than an hour – offering samples to nearly everyone in attendance. My tape recorder is placed on the table, and I ask folks to give me their impressions:

- "Oh, it's kind of soft. Oh, it's good. It tastes like – it is kind of like pudding."
- "It's good. Better than I thought it would be."
- "Better than persimmons. Oh yeah [laughing]."
- "I just thought it was a diddley we sang in school, you know? Pickin up pawpaws, puttin' 'em in your pocket! I didn't know they were for real [laughing]."
- A woman: "This is delicious! Nutritionally, it's high in potassium, right?" Man: "Yeah, all the essential amino acids. And more niacin than a banana. Not potassium, but more niacin."
- "Kinda like a ripe banana, ain't it?"
- "Oh, it's sweet!"
- "Smells good."
- "I've heard that song all my life. [laughs] First time [eating the fruit]. I went to school up in the mountains. Caldwell County. And my grandma used to sing it to me."
- "I have a neighbor who has a tree. But it was an old-timey tree you got in the wild somewhere, and we did not eat it until the entire surface looked like that."
- "Where I work down at the southern end of the next county, we've got a lot of wild ones growing along the creek, and we've gone down there in August and grab up a big shirt full of them."

IV

RIDGE AND VALLEY

We leave North Carolina and head for the mountains. After a quick dinner in Roanoke, Virginia, and a requisite drive along the Blue Ridge Parkway, we find our evening's campsite. Not far from where we stay tonight is the homeland of the Monacan Tribe of Virginia. It's where Professor Jay Vest grew up. Vest is professor of American Indian studies at the University of North Carolina, Pembroke, near Lesley Sanderson's home in Robeson County. Founded in 1887 as the Croatan Normal School, it was for the exclusive enrollment of American Indians in Robeson County. Though pawpaws are largely unknown among the Lumbee, Vest remembers eating them as a child in Virginia. When I spoke with him, he recalled childhood walks, with his father and siblings, into the woods each fall to harvest nuts, persimmons, and pawpaws. Like Morris said, if they grew on your property, you knew about them.

In the morning, we stop for breakfast in Lewisburg, West Virginia. The café is nestled amid a bicycle shop, an Irish pub, and, at the edge of town, Carnegie Hall. Running lengthwise through the café is a large communal dining table. We sit near a mother and her daughter. We've still got a few of Wynn and Derek's pawpaws (I managed to reserve a few for the road), and we're eager to share. The mother is delighted by the surprise. She grew up with them in the southwest corner of the state, but doesn't know where to look for them around Lewisburg. She's been describing them to an acquaintance and can finally let him try one. I hand one to each of them. Today happens to be her daughter's birthday, and she's eating her first pawpaw. "Tastes like an avocado!" she says.

I've ordered a peanut butter and banana sandwich. Yesterday we sampled several cultivars at Derek Morris's house. One particular variety, he said, was so banana-like, firm and chewy, it might be good on a sandwich. I slice open a large pawpaw and spread half of it alongside the banana and peanut butter. Tastes pretty good.

Driving north on US 219, we stop at several roadside markets. At one, an old man with a beard down to his chest is, with his son, selling tomatoes, peppers, and other homegrown produce. I ask about pawpaws. "Pawpaws!" says the son, gray-haired himself. "We used to have a couple pawpaw trees, till Daddy mowed them over! Haven't had pawpaws in years and would like some myself."

Farther on, near Elkins, a man wearing a baseball cap, jeans, and a white T-shirt stands holding a sign. He's staring into each passing car. His sign reads, RAMPS FOR SALE. But it's late summer, not ramp season. The man has been digging in the forest, rooting for ramp bulbs. "A lot of people don't like what I'm doing," he says. "They yell at me and tell me it's wrong." But he pays his state foraging fees, he says; he is legitimate. I'm unsure of the ecological repercussions but I've pulled over and already listened to his story, so I purchase a massive plastic bag of ramps for just five bucks.

Later, back in Pittsburgh, I plant those bulbs on the hillside above my community farm, and the following spring they sprout. That same spring, as the ramps are in full foliage, I also plant three pawpaw trees at the farm, the beginning of my own modest experiment. We could plant more, but few at the farm have ever heard of pawpaws, much less tasted one. What if no one likes it? I don't think I can convince them to give up space allotted for garlic, blueberries, and tomatoes for the dozen pawpaws I envision. Not yet. As in Robeson County, most residents of Pittsburgh, and much of southwestern Pennsylvania, aren't familiar with the fruit. But I'm confident my co-farmers will fall for it. I'm sure that in six years, they'll be asking why we didn't plant dozens of them. Or perhaps next year I should just take a page from Milton Parker's playbook, and insist that we do.

– CHAPTER SIXTEEN –

DOWN SOUTH

"Do not buy tobacco of pawpaw color (motley color); it is called 'fool-catcher.'"

— *KENTUCKY SUPERSTITIONS* (1920)[1]

It's late August and I have arrived at the Kentucky State Fair. After navigating my way through a sea of parked cars, I approach the convention center. I've come here because somewhere inside, beyond the fried dough, pickled okra, and buttermilk piecrusts, is a pawpaw exhibit. It's a competition that dates back as far as any officials can remember. "I'm not even sure who could tell you how long it's been going on," I was told. The first incarnation of the fair was held in 1816, and at some point in the past two hundred years pawpaws became part of it — they are tradition. More than half a million guests will attend the festival over a period of ten days, and while most come to support grandmothers in apple pie competitions, or to see headlining musical acts, a few of us do it for the pawpaws.

On my way to the agricultural wing, I wander past quilt displays, children's drawings, Kentucky-made furniture and sculptures, jars-upon-jars of put-up fruits and vegetables, tables filled with sorghum syrup and sorghum pops — a seemingly unending array of cultural products. In the livestock wing, massive cows parade like camels in an ancient bazaar; there are pigeons with unusual feathers jutting from their feet, showy like Elizabethan ruffs; rabbits the size of dogs; chickens, roosters, guinea hens, a cacophony of shrieking poultry.

Finally, I approach the wing with vegetables, melons, fruits, and nuts. A massive pumpkin the size of a doghouse rests in a wagon. Tobacco is hung upside down, growing in five-gallon buckets, arranged in piles. On display are nearly a hundred types of beans; heirloom tomatoes with names like Chocolate Stripes, Moonglow, and Green Copa; plates of black walnut, hickory, pecan; pears, apples, American persimmons, and, on a small section of table all to themselves, pawpaws. Pawpaws shouldn't be ripe yet in the Ohio River Valley. But here, now, I can smell that familiar fragrance, the sweet tropical aroma that from a single fruit can fill a room. These are *ripe*.

Kentucky's, like all state fairs, celebrates the best: quilts, cows, pies, most ridiculous-looking pigeon, and so on. These pawpaws are no exception: skin unblemished, smooth and round, large, and colored a bright lime green. Their shade is nearly uniform: green, but with an undercurrent of pale yellow. If you're accustomed to wild pawpaws, you might mistake these for something else altogether. Yet these are the same pawpaws eaten by the region's Shawnee, Cherokee, Yuchi, and Chickasaw, by Daniel Boone and the frontier's earliest settlers. Only, again, these are the best. In fact, when Brett Callaway planted the first orchard at Kentucky State University, he did it with seeds from the previous year's state-fair exhibit.

There's a clear blue-ribbon winner, not for taste, but for size: a submission by Jim Busch of his PA-Golden cultivar. Busch's entry consists of five fruits arranged on a paper plate; the largest is at least the size of an oblong softball. I want to sample a bit — to chomp into the big one — but that would certainly be frowned upon. Still, I'm willing to bet it would not be the first time someone had to leave the fair for eating an entry.

Many of the fairgoers I speak with are familiar with pawpaws, but others see the fruit for the first time and ask, "So that's a pawpaw?" For as long as they've appeared at the state fair — and for as long as people have eaten pawpaws in Kentucky — they're still a novelty.

Outside, I walk around the food court, where trucks and carts are lined up along a parklet and sidewalks. I stop for homemade ice cream and ask if the vendor has ever made a batch with pawpaws. I'm in Kentucky, after all — maybe I'll get lucky. "What's in it?" the woman asks. "Pawpaws!" replies a younger woman. The two are mother and daughter. They know the fruit, but have never made ice cream with it. So instead, I purchase a single scoop of peach ice cream. It's good, as have been all the peaches I've enjoyed this summer. But as the season is soon to change, I'm interested in something different, a tropical flavor that marks the end of summer in the Ohio Valley.

Despite the size of the fruit's native range — encompassing parts of twenty-six eastern states — only in Kentucky will you find a state-fair exhibit devoted to pawpaws. But despite the lack of official events elsewhere, there must be other places they are celebrated, eaten, and known. On this particular trip, I'm on a journey to find pawpaws, and pawpaw culture, in the Lower Mississippi Valley, Louisiana, and the Ozarks. It's a wide region, and I have just over a week to cover it.

There are exceptions in places, but in general the lower states of the pawpaw's native range have seen less of the growing renaissance taking place in the mid-Atlantic and midwestern states. But that doesn't mean their pawpaw cultures aren't just as rich. I'm curious to know if the fruit is still known, if its ripening is still relished by folks who remember pickin' up pawpaws on the banks of the Buffalo, the Red, the Tennessee. There are enthusiasts, pawpaw people, in just about every corner of the region who contribute to the fruit's renaissance. Among these players, I have two orchards and one nursery on my schedule, as well as a paddling excursion on the Mississippi River. For a fruit that's heavily associated with rivers, there is little reference to fruit growing, or fruit gathering, along this iconic American river. But surely it's out there. Neal Peterson has named his best fruit selections for the Indian names for our rivers — Susquehanna, Shenandoah, Rappahannock, Wabash, and so on. As a similar tribute, I'm heading south to find my own Mississippi pawpaw.

જજ

I leave Louisville and head for Mammoth Cave National Park where I'll camp for the night. But first, I make a stop in Hardin County. When Neal Peterson initially released his cultivars, John Brittain was one of just three nurserymen licensed to sell those grafted varieties. With a full beard and thin face, Brittain bears a certain resemblance to Abraham Lincoln, and at the age of sixty-five he is lean and tan from decades of outdoor work. Before we tour his property along the Nolin River, which empties into the Green River at the national park, we douse ourselves in organic, all-natural bug spray. Brittain says the tick population has exploded in recent years, and points to bites on his own ankles. As we apply the pleasantly scented oil, we both wonder about its effectiveness, knowing it's less toxic than DEET. Brittain is still getting bitten, after all. Perhaps with a little more work, an infusion of Annonaceous acetogenins could render an all-natural concoction a bit more potent. In the meantime, we spray ourselves and walk on.

Brittain's scion wood bank is a collection of grafted trees growing in a field. From these trees' branches he takes cuttings that are then grafted onto rootstock, which is grown from seed in the bottomland just down the hill. This is where pawpaw culture is kept alive and propagated, in a small patch near Upton, Kentucky. There's no laboratory, no cryogenic freezer, no test tubes. It's the work of human hands, and at the mercy of Mother Nature — a force that can often be quite punishing.

In 2011, when the Mississippi River threatened to flood Baton Rouge and New Orleans, after record floods had already taken lives and caused severe damage in several states upriver, rural farmland in Louisiana's Morganza and Atchafalaya floodways was inundated. But effects were also felt as far away as central Kentucky, and for several weeks the Nolin River kept Brittain's nursery under water. The majority of his young trees died. Since then, the past several years have been a process of recovery and rebuilding a diminished nursery stock.

While flooding isn't a constant threat to nurserymen, there are other natural threats to young trees. We say that pawpaw has no pests, and that for this reason it's attractive to organic growers. But that doesn't mean insects ignore pawpaws altogether. "There *are* pests," Cliff England once said. "Don't let anybody kid you." Among minor pests there is, of course, the zebra swallowtail butterfly, which feeds on leaves but doesn't do serious damage. The tulip-tree beauty (*Epimecis hortaria*), a moth, is less well known, but it also consumes *Asimina* leaves. Slugs, as well, will indiscriminately eat the leaves of young trees, especially in moist nursery conditions. And the larvae of the pawpaw sphinx (*Dolba hyloeus*) also feed on pawpaw leaves. Unfortunately for Brittain, pawpaw webworms (*Omphalocera munroei*) have taken up residence in his trees and could potentially denude all of the pawpaws in his scion bank if left unchecked. "It's about the only bad pest," he says. "You can see where they've been chewing, they get so big they'll even eat the stems." So Brittain carefully removes the affected leaves and squashes as many webworms as he can find. This deliberate yet low-tech task should be sufficient to ensure that his scion bank thrives. "It's easy to control as long as you pay attention to it," he says.

We climb into Brittain's small pickup truck and head down the hill along a winding, canopied road to tour his seedling patch, just a few yards from the Nolin River. We emerge from the forest and come upon a grove of knee-high pawpaws. "They're in there thick, there's at least a thousand. They won't all come up," Brittain says, then just as quickly adds: "Most of them will."

Brittain plants corn amid yet-to-germinate pawpaw seedlings. When the treelings emerge after months of developing taproots, the much-quicker-growing cornstalks offer the shade pawpaws will want at this young age. When it's time to graft in a year or so, the cornstalks are long gone and what's left is a lush grove of strong, young pawpaws, ready for digging and shipment. Generally, transplanting of pawpaws is not recommended – the plant's long taproot makes the job nearly impossible. Attempting to thin a patch is even less effective. In a colony, the majority of trees are actually suckers, which have a dramatically lower success rate than field-grown seedlings (suckers do not possess the developed, fibrous root system of a seedling). But Brittain uses a backhoe and digs very deep. His pawpaws overwhelmingly survive and establish successfully in their new homes, however many states away.

Brittain says growing seedling pawpaws with corn has been a good discovery, and other growers have devised similar innovations. At his farm in southern Ohio, Ron Powell places five-gallon buckets – with the bottoms cut out – over young trees. With the buckets in place, Ron's pawpaws are protected not only from the sun's rays but also from errant tractor mowing.

Brittain plans to retire soon and scale back his production of grafted nut trees: black walnut, butternut, hican, and so on. "It's a hard business," he says. "It's hard to graft little nut trees." Meanwhile, in addition to enjoying pawpaws as a native fruit that's relatively pest-free, he also finds them less difficult. "Everything about them is easier," he says. "After we're done doing nut trees we'll probably still be doing pawpaws."

⚬↛⚬

After leaving the nursery, I have a quick dinner and arrive at my campsite in the park. In the morning I pack up my tent and prepare to tour the largest cave system in the world. But with time to kill before the first tour, I'm afforded a chance at a little pawpaw hunting. Inside the park, patches of roadside pawpaws form dense colonies, as tightly packed as any thickets I've seen. I check among the trees but there's no fruit, ripe or unripe, to be found. While I'm hunting pawpaws, other plants catch my eye. A maypop vine climbs a nearby tree, its passionflower in full bloom. The flower is wide, as delicate as loosely woven silk; a tapestry in progress. I pick one of its green fruits, hanging singly from the vine. Like pawpaw, the maypop, or *Passiflora incarnata*, was eaten by Native Americans, and by early settlers and pioneers in the South. Wondering if it is ripe, I open it — *pop!* — but I am too early; the inside is dry and underdeveloped. I've eaten maypop only once before. The pulp is quite similar to its tropical relative, passion fruit, though a bit more tart. It is yet another component of the eastern forest that blurs the lines between tropical and temperate, a connection to the ancient past.

I descend a trail into a shaded hollow. The bank is lined with pawpaw trees, older and taller here, but again, I find no fruit. It's August in Kentucky, yet under this canopy it's a good ten degrees cooler. There's a light rain falling, but the leaves above catch most of the drops. Walking this trail, I'm reminded of great Indian roads: the Seneca Trail, the Great Minquas Path, the Catawba Trail, among others. Centuries ago, on trails like this one, Native Americans traveled great distances for trade, hunting, and war. And on those journeys they knew where the hunting of deer, buffalo, and turkey was good, and where, when, and what berries and greens were ripe for picking (including the appropriate time to open the maypops). In this month, travelers would have begun to shake the many pawpaw trees. They would have known where high-yielding or good-tasting patches were located; the experience would have been less a hopeful rambling — like my current exploration — than a visit to a familiar orchard.

When the visitors center opens, I buy a ticket for the tour. Waiting for the bus that will drive us to the cave, I speak with a couple who live nearby. The man was born and raised in Kentucky, but has lived all over the country, including Florida, where he worked on a shrimp boat and slept on beaches. The woman, a self-described military brat, spent her school years in Memphis. They've both heard of pawpaws, but it's been years since the man has eaten one. And while the woman has never tried pawpaw, she is no stranger to foraging, or to the woods. In fact, she's a ginseng hunter.

While pawpaws may hold the *promise* of value to orchardists and wild pickers, ginseng is already big business. According to West Virginia University, dried wild ginseng can sell for up to $350 a pound, and both wild and cultivated crops account for $70 million in exports annually.[2] But it's not the money that attracts my fellow tourgoer, nor is it strictly ginseng, as she has also dug redroot and yellow root, among other forest crops. "It's just an excuse to get out and hunt," she says.

Pawpaws might seem tricky to grow at first — with seed stratification, transplant challenges, and shade requirements — but compared with wild ginseng and ramps, they're in fact quite easily domesticated. The latter two plants not only favor shade, but require it, so they must be grown in the woods or under artificial conditions that mimic nature. Because ginseng and ramps are often simply wildcrafted — taken from the wild — biologists have warned that their demand could lead to their extirpation, since both are typically harvested as whole plants. Pawpaw, which is coveted primarily for its fruit, is less likely to be harmed by such fads. There might occasionally be a rush to taste pawpaws, but rarely because consumption will cure what ails the eater's health. But even with Nature's Sunshine's Paw Paw Cell-Reg, which is derived from the tree's twig bark, the process is as harmful as pruning a tree, which is to say, not very. And in time, if a population — whether in Kentucky or in South Korea — wants a more reliable and abundant source of pawpaw (for fruit or medicine), they can just plant an orchard — whereas ginseng and ramps have been less successful under large-scale cultivation, and continue to be harvested from the wild or in carefully maintained landscapes.

Finally, I tour the Mammoth Caves. As pawpaws evolved, traveling from the tropics to temperate Kentucky over millennia, these caves were forming too. Geologists have estimated that the oldest parts began forming around ten million years ago. And while that's certainly ancient, I recall that pawpaws are even more so.

The caves are impressive, as is their human story. Various Native American groups used them for shelter for thousands of years. Archaeologists have determined that among the arts practiced by the local prehistoric cave dwellers, textile manufacturing was the most highly developed.[3] At archaeological digs of similar dwelling sites in Kentucky, the most common fiber recovered was the inner bark of pawpaw — used in both textiles and cordage, varying greatly in its degree of coarseness.[4] In 1936 archaeologist Volney Jones documented remains of *Asimina triloba* fibers in nearby Salts Cave — within Mammoth Cave National Park — and elsewhere throughout Kentucky. Along with Indian hemp, linden, canary grass, cattail, leatherwood, and rattlesnake master, pawpaw bark was a common fiber in the prehistoric textiles uncovered, including sandals, slippers, belts, baskets, mats, blankets, cordage, and loincloths.[5] Pawpaws were eaten whenever available by those same prehistoric peoples, but those artisans may have prized the tree more for its fibers than for its fruit.

✺

Kentucky State University has a listing of pawpaw nurseries on its website, and since it's alphabetical by state, Alabamian Dale Brooks's is listed first. I emailed Dale ahead of my visit, and if I'd had any doubts of his commitment to the fruit, I was reassured by his email handle: pawpawman.

Dale was raised on a farm on Brindley Mountain, in north Alabama, a few miles south of the Tennessee River. Years after Dale had moved away, an old neighbor told him there were pawpaws in a holler there, but Dale didn't know them as a kid. He lives now in Decatur and says, "They're all over the place down here." Nearby, at the Wheeler National Wildlife Refuge, pawpaw spread through the bottomlands of the Tennessee, with suckers increasing in size like a staircase, smaller close to the river but larger as you approach their various mother trees.

As we tour his garden — eight acres of rare fruits and ornamentals — Dale makes a confession. "I got tired of planting the same thing everybody else had," he says, "and I started getting off in the fringes." He laughs, as though growing pawpaws — and Pakistan mulberry and mayhaws and rare bamboos — is a kind of counter-horticulture. In many ways it is; many folks in the area either don't know pawpaws or, in a familiar story, have lost touch with the fruit over the decades. But through the years, Dale and his wife, Reda, have done their best, to borrow a phrase, to bring pawpaws to the people.

"Have I ever told you how I got started in pawpaws?" Dale asks. "Back over on the other side of our yard there is a bunch of wild, native pawpaws. My wife got a tree book one year, and got to looking through it and identified it." This particular thicket — a clonal patch — wasn't producing fruit. By coincidence, though, it wasn't long until the Brooks were able to taste some. "My eldest son, one day he brought this fruit home [from school]," Dale says. "One of his teachers had a friend up in Ohio, came down and brought a sack and gave all of them one." Dale's son, rather than eating the pawpaw in class, brought it home to share with the family. "Good thing he did," Dale says with a laugh, knowing now the turning point that this single fruit was. "We got the cutting board out that night and sliced it up. And we all liked it. So I set out on trying to find me a source."

Dale ordered grafted trees, ordered seed. "I started making me a collection of it," he says, "and the trees got big enough, started having fruit on them." He protected the fruit from local critters by wrapping the clusters in chicken wire. "It was on a Friday, and I said [to the pawpaw], 'I'll see you tomorrow morning, mister.'" But as anyone tending a small patch of pawpaws could have predicted, something else beat him to it, despite his elaborate efforts. "Went out there, looked the next morning, and it wasn't there," Dale says. "It was about twelve foot over there, and about half of it was left." Wondering what I might do in that situation, I ask — since it was the first pawpaw he'd grown himself — if, despite the critter that had chewed on it and discarded it so callously, he ate it anyway. "Oh, yeah, oh sure," he says. "That don't slow you up."

Dale was soon growing so many pawpaws he didn't know what to do with them. He went to the Decatur Farmers Market and gave pawpaws to customers and vendors. Still, there was just so much. So, in 2003, the Brookses organized their first Pawpaw Day. Despite the fact that Dale does not enjoy public speaking, he invited hundreds of strangers to his home. *Alabama Living* magazine even advertised the event. The Brookses offered samples and had fresh fruit and trees for sale. More than a hundred people showed up. Four years later, they held another event, and two hundred people came. That year, Reda made ice cream. "My wife saw one woman go through the line three times," Dale says.

Dale's pawpaws are planted in a low site that is prone to flooding. After a heavy rain, water will stand for five or six hours before receding. A few years ago, his trees began to show signs of stress. Soon more than three hundred succumbed to oak root fungus, transforming a formerly lush grove into permanent winter. Pawpaws were thought to be resistant to the fungus, which rots the tree's root system, but it's hard to argue with dead trees. We're standing under one such skeleton, a lifeless twenty-five-foot ghost of a tree. "That was my best tree last year," Dale says, "and it's just dead. Graveyard dead."

If he plants again, Dale will hill the pawpaws higher. I spoke with an Ohio grower who has also suffered losses due to flood-prone sites, and he plans to dig swales and mounds in order to direct and capture water away from the surviving pawpaws. But for Dale to have gone from three hundred to a couple dozen trees is an incredible loss and, given the time it takes for pawpaws to reach mature fruiting age, a considerable investment of time and resources. I ask whether or not Dale plans to replant his orchard. "I've got to do one thing or another," he says. "I got to change my listing on the website if I'm not going to." And perhaps his email handle too.

Fruit typically begins ripening in Dale's orchard around the tenth of August. But this summer has been exceptionally cool, and although it's late August only one or two pawpaws have dropped. There does happen to be one waiting for us in the kitchen, however. It's an Overleese, "one of my favorite flavors," Dale says. Like he usually does when a visitor comes to taste pawpaws, he cuts it in half and eats the first spoonful. "I don't want the first pawpaw that you eat not to be good," he says. "Only thing that would make it better would be Dairy Queen vanilla. Pretty decent." I'm given the green light. I take a bite, my first of the season. I hate to disagree with Dale in his own home, but I think it's just fine on its own.

⟳

Earlier in the day I visited Old Decatur, admired its bungalows and live oaks, and drove into downtown. While sitting on a bench, eating a red pepper and onion burger (a local specialty), I noticed a sign for the Decatur Farmers Market, which happened to be today. I followed the signs to the railroad tracks where it's held every Saturday and arrived at the tail end of the 2013 Watermelon Festival; three vendors remained.

Although Anna Hallmark was born and raised in northern Russia — "near the Arctic Circle" — she's now an expert grower of heat-loving crops:

Piled on her table were fresh golden figs, fig preserves, and star-and-moon heirloom watermelons. Anna had heard of pawpaws, read about them on the Internet, but never seen or grown one. I'd hoped to have pawpaws to share at all of my impromptu stops — a Johnny Appleseed–inspired dishing of pawpaws — but since I hadn't found any ripe fruit in Kentucky, I had none to share with Anna. Instead I loaded up on fruit for myself.

Figs, like pawpaws, are delicate. Consider the following description from the California Rare Fruit Growers: "Figs must be allowed to ripen fully on the tree before they are picked. They will not ripen if picked when immature . . . Fresh figs do not keep well and can be stored in the refrigerator for only 2–3 days . . . Because of losses in transport and short shelf life, figs are a high-value fruit of limited demand."[6] Sound familiar? Yet despite these demands, figs represent a significant commercial crop. In a given year, the state of California alone produces more than thirty-eight thousand tons of figs, 90 percent of which are dried, cooked, or otherwise processed.[7] So why should transportation and shelf life be any more of a barrier to pawpaws? As an industrial crop, pawpaws — which do not lend themselves to drying — could find a similar niche in the form of frozen pulp. A second model for figs is to sell them at local markets, as Anna Hallmark does in Decatur, Alabama. Pawpaw growers like Milton Parker and Derek Morris in North Carolina, Ilze Sillers in Kentucky, and Stanton Gill in Maryland are already doing the same with pawpaws — their fruit is sold at farmers markets, and in some cases local food co-ops and grocery stores. And then there is a third, less business-oriented model for pawpaws and figs: home consumption. Figs are grown and eaten, in the South and elsewhere, as a backyard fruit with no design on sales: They're meant to be eaten, and eaten shortly after being picked, perhaps right under the tree. Or they're cooked into a jam or cake, wrapped in prosciutto, placed on a cracker and eaten with cheese — however the individual likes it. And it's not unlikely that from backyards, perhaps right under the tree, will always be the most common way Americans eat their pawpaws. But that, of course, still requires more people discovering that they can.

❧

Although Dale Brooks spends a considerable amount of time describing pawpaws to his fellow Alabamians, pawpaws were once better known in the state. Indeed, they were once thought to remedy teething pain and even, by at least one individual, to cure gonorrhea. Published in 1958, Ray B. Brown's collection of folklore and superstitions, *Popular Beliefs and Practices from Alabama*, contains two pawpaw-derived remedies. Both came from Lamar County, in northwest Alabama. The first was told to Brown by Mrs. Ora Jordan, a housewife from the town of Vernon: "For teething get nine papa seeds, string them and let the child wear them around the neck." According to Brown's notes, Mrs. Jordan had either used the remedy on her own child, or had been treated with it as a girl.

The second practice was recorded at a barbershop in Millport, where Brown collected a score of folk beliefs, attributed collectively to the "farmers and townspeople, mostly white . . . a cross section of Lamar County." He was told, "If you will drink papaw-root [sic] tea, you will cure gonorrhea."[8] It is the only remedy given for the infection in the book, a collection of more than forty-three hundred practices and beliefs.

According to the USDA's plant map, pawpaws are still present and vouched for in Lamar County. In fact, much of Alabama reports a wild or naturalized population of pawpaws. Whether the plant is still used medicinally, I cannot say.

There is much and diverse folklore associated with pawpaws. In 1946, Vance Randolph wrote that many Ozark farmers "say that it is a good idea to bury a bit of a cow's afterbirth under a pawpaw tree, as this will cause her to bring forth female calves thereafter."[9] Also in the Ozarks, "The relatives of a murdered man sometimes throw pawpaw seeds into the grave, on top of the coffin. It is said that this ensures the murderer will be punished."[10] In eastern Kentucky, strings of knotted pawpaw bark tied to stumps were once thought to bring good luck.[11] And at least one Kentucky ghost story involves pawpaws stolen from a graveyard. In east Tennessee, pawpaws were part of an herbal mix used to cure syphilis. The following text is quoted from Bill Henry's 1981 profile of Alex Stewart of Hancock County, Tennessee:

> *Alex can make apple butter, molasses, lye soap, hero medicine, and good corn whiskey. He can card, spin, weave, or tie a broom. In his time he has rafted logs down the Clinch River, made and hunted with a cross-bow, gathered tanbark and tanned hides (including his kids'). He has dug wells, worked as a cook and a butcher, made musical*

instruments, and rived shingles. Alex has owned and operated three sawmills, invented the mussel box, an aid in finding Tennessee pearls, and with his foot-powered spring-pole lathe, he has turned out count-less chairs, spinning wheels, and rolling pins.

Alex Stewart was a capable and prolific craftsman, self-reliant and hard-working. His "grandpap," Boyd Stewart, emigrated to the United States from Ireland before the Civil War, and the family had lived at Newman's Ridge ever since. Before long — among many arts — they learned to practice herbal medicine. And one such concoction, used to treat syphilis, included pawpaw root:

> *[Alex] believes the drugs now used to treat venereal disease merely arrest the condition; his medicine destroys the germ completely. For those who may want or need this medicine, the formula is: Poke root, Black root, Alum root, Paw paw root (get the fine ones which have small nodules or blisters on them), Rat's bane (Pipsissewa), Black haw, Hemlock, Goldenseal, Bittersweet, Yellow root, Red dogwood bark, and Yellow dogwood bark. Combine these herbs (I don't know the proper amounts) in three gallons of water. Steam, do not boil, until down to one gallon. The entire gallon must be taken to effect the cure.*[12]

The Stewarts had been in the United States for three generations and had adapted to the region's agriculture, manufactured the tools they needed and the instruments they wanted, and learned not only the names of the plants that surrounded them, but how to use them as medicine (the scope of Alex Stewart's herbal remedies went beyond the recipe provided above). But I often wonder how many generations it takes to lose these skills, and the knowledge of these plants. How long did it take to forget what to do with a pawpaw?

༄

Leaving Decatur I drive through Muscle Shoals and into downtown Florence to see the Florence Indian Mound, at forty-three feet the largest of these ancient earthen structures along the Tennessee River. It's a blip of green in an industrial zone. I sit on my rear bumper and eat a dinner that consists of a peanut butter sandwich with a side of Anna's golden figs and fresh peaches. Although I've recently visited two pawpaw growers, I have little fruit. In addition to the one Dale and I ate, he was able to give me two more ripe ones, but I intend to share these with my river guides in the Delta.

I've long wanted to see the Natchez Trace, so I drive toward Tishomingo State Park, just over the border in Mississippi. In order to cover a lot of ground on this short trip, I've been driving until late into the night, and setting up my tent in the dark. So usually when I wake up I have little idea of what it looks like wherever I am. This morning, based on how my shoulder feels, I know the ground is rocky. I step out of the tent and it's confirmed: sand and rocks. I'm at the southwest extremity of the Appalachian plateau. In 1832, Robert Baird wrote a guide to Mississippi for eastern emigrants. "As a whole, Mississippi possesses a great quantity of excellent lands," he said. "It was covered with a vast forest of oak, hickory, magnolia, sweet gum, ash, maple, yellow poplar, cypress in the swampy alluvial Mississippi bottoms, pine, holley, &c. &c. with a great variety of underwood, grape vines, paw-paw, spice wood &c."[13] Thirty years later, a geological survey of Big Bluff Creek in southeast Mississippi reported a "small fruited variety of the Pawpaw, together with Dogwood," in the undergrowth of longleaf pine forests.[14] Presently, according to the USDA's plant map, naturalized pawpaws are vouched for in Tishomingo County, as well as the dwarf paw-paw, *Asimina parviflora*. But I won't find any during my travels in eastern Mississippi. The trees are somewhere, but, as the Appalachians roll into the Mississippi hill country, they're evidently harder to find.

At nearby Bear Creek Mound, artifacts from paleo-Indians date back to 7000 BC. The park is named for Chickasaw chief Tishomingo. The Chickasaw, whose language belongs to the Muskogean family, likely called pawpaw *orko*, just as the Muscogee, or Creek, had.

For decades, Mississippi was considered frontier. The Natchez Trace — now a historic scenic route that extends from Natchez, Mississippi, to Nashville, Tennessee — began as a series of interconnected Native American trails. Not long after the Revolutionary War, American settlers began inter-loping into Mississippi, and the trace became a well-known and well-used gateway. Yet in the early 1800s, the region was still Choctaw Territory. The new settlers raised corn, sweet potatoes, field peas, and enough cotton to clothe themselves.[15] But they also ate from the wild — as the Choctaw had and continued to do — including grapes, persimmons, chinquapin and hickory nuts, plums, pokeweed, and pawpaws.[16]

The Choctaw descended from the Hopewellian and Mississippian peoples who had built the region's mounds as far back as seventeen hundred years ago. And they had eaten pawpaws for just as many years — except, of course, they had an entirely different name for the fruit: *umbi*.[17] The word lives on, quietly, in the name of a creek in Holmes County, Mississippi: Bophumpa Creek, spelled Boghumpa on earlier maps. "The first element is from Choctaw *bok*, 'creek,' while the second element may be from Choctaw *umpa*, 'rain' or *umbi*, 'paw-paw.'"[18] With pawpaws growing so frequently along waterways, it wasn't uncommon for those rivers and streams to be named for the trees. Another example exists in Georgia, where the Ulco-fau-hatchee translates from the Creek to "pawpaw thicket river."[19] As they pushed west, American settlers renamed rivers and streams, sometimes using Anglicized versions of the Native American words. These names survive, famously, as the Mississippi, Suwanee, Atchafalaya, and so on, and in less celebrated streams like Bophumpa Creek. Other times, settlers gave entirely new names to waterways. Yet the settlers continued to name these rivers for their features, as their predecessors had. Thus the many Paw Paw Creeks and Rivers throughout the eastern United States were inspired by the same *umbi* and *ulco* that were celebrated by the Choctaw and Creek centuries before. The languages may have differed, but the naming traditions were alike.

North of Tupelo, I leave the trace and drive several hours to Oxford, Mississippi. I want to see the town, including William Faulkner's famed Rowan Oak. Although I'm playing tourist, I also wonder if Faulkner knew of pawpaws, and if they grew in Bailey's Woods, the ninety-some-acre forest surrounding his home. I know that other American authors were familiar with the fruit. Robert Penn Warren was born and raised in Guthrie, Kentucky — just north of the Cumberland River near the Tennessee state line. In his novel *Flood: A Romance of Our Time*, a filmmaker visits the fictional town of Fiddlersburg. A couple — creations of the filmmaker — frequent the town for "nutting and pawpaw expeditions," among other pastimes.[20] Walt Whitman also wrote of them, "I cross the hummock-land or through pleasant openings or dense forests . . . I see the papaw-tree and the blossoming titi,"[21] as did Ohioan Sherwood Anderson, in his memoir: "We went together into the corn fields . . . We followed the winding of Coon Creek. We were in a little valley between low wooded hills. Pawpaws grew there."[22] June Carter Cash wrote that her southwest Virginia childhood was a "world of pawpaws, chinka-pins, and huckleberries."[23] In Wilson Rawls's coming-of-age novel *Where the Red Fern Grows*, he sets the scene of eastern Oklahoma: "Behind our house one could see miles and miles of the mighty Ozarks. In the spring the aromatic scent of wild flowers, redbuds, papaws and dogwoods, drifting on the wind currents, spread over the valley and around our home."[24] A 1954 children's book, written and illustrated by Palmer Brown, was titled *Beyond the Pawpaw Trees*; and set (and published) in West Virginia was the children's book *Decker Deer: The Miracle of Paw Paw Island*. There are countless other references to pawpaws in poems, memoirs, and works of fiction.

It's a quiet Sunday morning when I arrive at Oxford. The crowds of returning students have yet to arrive at Ole Miss, and there's just one other car parked at Rowan Oak. I walk under the alley of cedars. The only sound comes from my feet on the pebble walkway. I hike a trail into the woods and see hickory, sweet gum, oak, magnolia, many other trees and shrubs. It would be fine pawpaw habitat, but they are not here.

Later, I research Faulkner's works. In the short story "Red Leaves," a Chickasaw chief named Issetibbeha has died, and at his funeral, baked dog, succotash, yams cooked in ashes, and barbecue are served. According to local customs, Issetibbeha is to be buried with his most prized possessions, including the black slave who had been with him since boyhood. Not wanting to die, the slave flees to the woods. "He had run thirty miles then, up the creek bottom, before doubling back; lying in a pawpaw thicket he saw the pursuit for the first time."[25] After some time, the slave and his pursuers return to the funeral, his cruel fate accepted.

This is the only mention of pawpaws I have found in Faulkner's works. According to the map he drew, "Red Leaves" took place in the Chickasaw region south of the Tallahatchie River, south of the fictional hunting camp of Yoknapatawpha County, inspired, no doubt, by his own camp.

Faulkner was not the first to imagine hiding out in a pawpaw thicket; in fact, there are many historical accounts of doing so. In the Ohio River Valley alone, there are numerous accounts of pawpaw shelters. In one story, a man was hunting south of Point Pleasant, West Virginia, when he was pursued by Indians and jumped over a cliff. "He fell in a clump of paw-paw bushes and grape vines, which broke his fall and saved breaking his neck."[26] A few years prior, also near Point Pleasant, members of the Virginia militia hid their wounded in "an obscure place" following a skirmish and "substained [sic] them nine days upon paw paws."[27] According to a history by Charles Alexander McMurry, in 1788, when a group of settlers landed at the mouth of the Miami near present-day Cincinnati, "they ascended the steep bank and cleared away the underbrush in the midst of a pawpaw thicket, where the women and children sat down. They next placed senti-nels at a short distance from the thicket, and having first united in a song of praise to Almighty God, upon their knees they offered thanks for the past and prayer for future protection."[28] In 1791, during a skirmish near Mingo Bottom, members of the Virginia militia were fired upon, and sev-eral killed. "The enemy were concealed in a ravine amidst a dense cluster of paw-paw bushes . . . The plan of the Indians was to permit the whites to advance in numbers along the line before firing upon them."[29] During the Civil War, two of Missouri's enrolled militias were collectively known as the Paw Paw Militia. The militias earned the nickname because they comprised many Confederate sympathizers and hid out in the dense pawpaw thickets in order to avoid contact with Union troops — and then, come fall, subsisted on the pawpaw crop.

༄

I leave the hill country and head for the Mississippi Delta. I'm spared the sweltering August weather that is typical — summer has been mild all across the United States, which is why Dale Brooks's fruit was only beginning to ripen at a trickle. I don't see any roadside pawpaw patches on US 61, the fa-mous blues highway. In fact, there are few stretches of woods at all; fields of cotton, soy, and corn stretch to the horizon in a flat, wide-open landscape. The sky is big and when the sun sets below a whirl of clouds, they become a pile of pinks, blues, and whites.

Never having paddled the Mississippi, I thought it would be helpful to find local guides on the water. So when I saw the word *pawpaw* on a par-ticular company's website, I knew I'd found the right people. It wasn't just a listing of the trees you might see on a river trip; rather, Quapaw Canoe

Company's website was filled with poetic descriptions of sections of the Mississippi: "Wild, a journey descending out of the Eastern Woodlands into the rich North American sub-tropical forest with scenes of Spanish Moss, Palmetto, Paw-paws, Yankopin, Fire Ants and Alligators!"[30]

I arrive in Clarksdale several hours after sundown. After dropping my things at the company's headquarters, where I'm given lodging, I go for a walk. Just across the railroad tracks is Red's Juke Joint. I find a seat and listen to slide guitar by a bluesman named for a fruit — Watermelon Slim. I take it as a good omen for tomorrow's hunt.

In the morning, I meet with Quapaw's founder, John "Driftwood" Ruskey, and with Mark "River" Peoples, who will be my guide. We look over maps of the Mississippi and various water trails and pick the course that's most likely to turn up pawpaws. John can't guarantee I'll find any along this stretch, but says it offers as good a chance as any, since pawpaws favor higher elevations. I want to correct him, but then remember that this isn't the Appalachians; elevation is relative. In the Mississippi Delta the high ground is at most about three hundred feet above sea level. And in a flood ecosystem, these bluffs are like islands, the only well-drained soil where a pawpaw might survive. Foraging here will be different.

Before we go out on the river, I want John and Mark to know what these pawpaws taste like. Maybe the flavor will give them an idea of why I'm going to such lengths — or it may just further confound them. I have three small pawpaws from Dale Brooks's orchard to share. Ellis, or Brother E, walks in as I'm slicing. He is the Quapaw's driver. None recall eating or seeing a pawpaw, but John remembers sitting on his mother's piano bench as a boy in Colorado as she sang the old folk song. John was one of eight children, and in each verse she'd place a different child *way down yonder*. Brother E, a gardener himself with a plot of Sunflower riverfront in okra, corn, tomatoes, and more, is the next to try some. He grew up out in the country, and liked to hunt and fish. "Always on the creek," he says, and thinks he might have seen them before. "I think my mother called them little small bananas." Brother E is quiet, and deliberately tastes every morsel. "Let me hit it one more time, I'ma tell you what exactly it tastes like." He takes another scoop. "It's between a banana and an orange. Got a little mango in it," he says, and chews, and thinks some more. "That's a good taste." He puts the spoon down, licks his fingers. After a moment he smiles.

"I'm going to be all up and down that river looking for some pawpaw," he laughs. "Me and the Quapaw, looking for pawpaw."

As we launch the boat, a red bat flutters about the edge of the water. Mark is the first to notice it, and takes it as a good omen, which brings the omen tally up to two. We paddle out of the Quapaw Chute and on toward Island 63. The river is wide, and the current strong, but it's serene and welcoming too — we're paddling the great American river like it's no big deal. In less than an hour we arrive. The island is draped with long, sandy beaches. Under the bright-blue sky, this could be the Florida Keys. Low water levels expose terraced slopes formed by receding water, steps we use to enter the island. We tread through poison ivy, Virginia creeper, and various thorny bushes. We see the river's ubiquitous cottonwoods, willows, patches of persimmon, and cottonmouths. Mark has an eye for snakes — he spots them before either of us approach them, or he lets me know after I've stepped over one. Like me with my eye for pawpaw, Mark has learned to see snakes and other critters. Frogs, the snakes' dinner, hop about before our feet, as do crickets and beetles. We see a solitary swamp rose mallow in full bloom, and I am fooled time and again by persimmon leaves, wanting for them to be pawpaw. But after a few miles we turn back to our boat and continue paddling down the Mississippi.

&

Mark Twain, like Daniel Boone and George Washington, is another iconic American figure whom pawpaw boosters like to say enjoyed pawpaws. He was certainly aware of them. Recollecting his youth, Twain wrote in his autobiography, "I know how the wild black-berries looked, and how they tasted, and the same with the paw-paws, the hazelnuts, and the persimmons."[31]

The Adventures of Huckleberry Finn, of course, took place on this river, and on the same banks Mark and I are now exploring. Early on, Huck and Jim had eaten berries and "borrowed" a chicken. "Mornings before daylight I slipped into corn-fields and borrowed a watermelon, or a muskmelon, or a punkin, or some new corn, or things of that kind," Huck said. And if pawpaws had been in season, he and Jim would have eaten those too. But Twain knew better than to write that all of the river's bounty was ripe at the same time. Huck and Jim picked crab apples and "p'simmons," but dropped them because "crabapples ain't ever good, and the p'simmons wouldn't be ripe for two or three months yet."[32] Nor the pawpaws.

While pawpaws are absent from his most famous work, the fruit does figure elsewhere in Twain's writing and life. According to Albert Bigelow Paine's biography, the buried treasure in *Tom Sawyer* was inspired by a real-life adventure of the young Samuel Clemens and friends. Once the site of the treasure was located, Twain's boyhood friend Tom Blankenship — the inspiration for Tom Sawyer — "sat down under the shade of a pawpaw-bush and gave orders," which amounted to digging all day long. There was no treasure to be found, but the next day Blankenship had a dream that the gold was under "the little pawpaw-tree" where he'd sat and slept most of the day away.[33] And in another of Twain's works, the short story "Which Was the Dream?," two characters hail from the fictional town of Pawpaw Corners, Kentucky.

During Twain's lifetime, rural Americans were as familiar with pawpaws as ever. In his book *Twain's Feast: Searching for America's Lost Foods in the Footsteps of Samuel Clemens*, Andrew Beahrs writes, "In Twain's day wild things were at the heart of American cooking; they took pride of place alongside garden tomatoes, apple cider, and fresh corn. But that would be true only until people turned their faces from the things they loved — until they had let them slip."[34]

ༀ

A long paddle brings us past several islands whose sandy banks are colored a faint pink. One of the islands looks like a willow savanna — flat and sandy, a wide bluff above the Mississippi. It will make a perfect campsite. But before we set up camp, we continue our pawpaw hunt. Throughout the island are depressions made from the river's rise and fall; it reminds me of a miniature ridge-and-valley landscape. In high water, the valleys are pools teeming with fish, snakes, turtles, and so on. Today, in the absence of water, the mud is dry and cracked. Baked alligator gar skeletons are caked in mud, and our feet sink an inch or two with each step. We see snakes, mulberry trees, cottonwood, even a wild squash in bloom, but no pawpaws.

We reach the end of the island and turn back, hugging the west bank this time: mulberry, willow, cottonwoods. The willows are adapted to the river with its seasonal if not daily rise and fall. In high water, when sediment piles up against the tree's trunk, burying its former collar, new adventitious roots can emerge. Unlike the willows, pawpaws would soon die if submerged in this much water—as they did in Dale Brooks's flooded orchard. Indeed, pawpaw is often found growing along rivers, not in them.

We make a small fire to ward off mosquitoes, and sit, watching the river go by. The sun sets over the fields of Arkansas. Barges pass with increasing regularity, to be filled at riverside grain elevators. Earlier, we saw trucks unload their soybeans, corn, and other products. And now in just a few minutes those crops will be carried on.

Before we left Clarksdale, John Ruskey told me about the wild edibles Quapaw often finds on river trips, such as Juneberries and mulberries. Tonight our food is domestic: turkey sandwiches, watermelon, and a tropical mangosteen. But wild food was once an abundant source of activity on the Mississippi. Fishermen trolled the rivers and sold to local townspeople, and fruit and vegetable ships went up and down the Ohio and the Mississippi. Farther upriver, in 1845, Captain Bill Rollins piloted a boat down the Mississippi, headed for New Orleans. "Cairo [Illinois] was nothing then but a pawpaw thicket, and there was but one house there, a little shanty on stilts away back where you couldd't [sic] see it from the river," he recalled. "When a boat landed there the natives would swarm down and offer for sale pawpaws like apples and such things might be offered now."[35] There were many people in and on the river then, but Mark and I saw no other people today, just steel vessels, barges, and trucks.

In the morning we head for Melwood Lake, the western oxbow of the river's former course. We paddle up the chute to the entrance of the lake, here and there dodging airborne Asian carp. As we approach the north bank of the island, on the Arkansas side, I notice a greater diversity of trees, including sycamores, representing a higher canopy above the willow growth of the mucky bank. We land and tie to a leaning tree. I hike ahead of Mark. The bluff is high, a good sign that it could support pawpaws. This is the highest elevation we've encountered and I'm excited. I wrestle through poison ivy and prickly brambles again, and spot it from afar: what I'm hopeful is a thirty-foot pawpaw tree. There's even a colony of what appear to be suckers beneath. I was fooled by wishful thinking yesterday, by persimmons and mulberries, so I run closer to be sure, not wanting to holler back to Mark just yet, crying wolf again. But as I approach it I'm sure: We have found our Mississippi pawpaws.

I shake a few trees, hoping for a cascade of ripe fruit, but the mild summer means nearly all of it is still rock-hard. A few unripe ones fall, casualties of an aggressive hunt. Animals have picked through some of the ones we find, but discarded them; raccoons and opossums also prefer ripe fruit. As we pick through our few fallen fruits, two or three of the fig-sized ones, when squeezed, give just the tiniest bit. In a few days these will ripen. We'll bring them home to Clarksdale for the Quapaw crew.

We paddle seven miles back to our take-out point. The heat has returned to the delta. There are few other boats out — just a man dropping fishing nets on the other side of the river, and a barge — but Mark says that's beginning to change. For several years now John has been working on the *Rivergator: Paddler's Guide to the Lower Mississippi River*, a mile-by-mile description of the Lower Mississippi. It has information on where to camp, where good sandbars are located and at what time of year; when the Juneberries are ripe; when to tie up at Helena, Arkansas, for the King Biscuit Time Blues Festival; and maybe now a revised edition will include where to find pawpaws. We reach the boat ramp, and Brother E greets us at the landing. He walks down, singing, "Pickin' up pawpaws, put 'em in a basket . . ."

౪౭

A short distance above Vicksburg, Mississippi is an island called Paw Paw. I forget how I first learned of its existence, but I immediately wondered if it was covered in wall-to-wall pawpaws, how long ago it was named, and by whom. Paul Hartfield, of the US Fish and Wildlife Service, has graciously offered to take me out in his boat to see the island. An invertebrate biologist, Hartfield has worked to save several Mississippi River species from extinction, including the interior least tern and the pallid sturgeon. He knows a thing or two about pawpaws as well.

Compared with the Quapaw canoe, we're traveling at light speed. We stop to check on a population of least terns nesting on a sandbank, and then quickly cruise to our destination. Paw Paw Island is as lush as any of the islands I've seen this trip — and its elevation is just right for the trees. As I suspected, there are a lot of them — tall solitary trees, and dozens of thick patches. Paul then takes me farther up the Paw Paw Chute, which is much narrower than the broad Mississippi, with willows, cottonwoods, and other hardwoods hanging over the water. "You could be in the jungles of Belize," Paul says over the roar of the engine. We see a number of alligators on sandbars, diving underwater as we encroach on their comfort zones; a five-foot timber rattler glides on the water's surface; herons and cranes launch from the shore.

Paul wants to show me something unique. We hike up a small bluff, and there are a number of large pawpaw trees throughout the hilltop. But Paul is disappointed. Land managers have recently brush-hogged the property. "This was a dense, solid corridor of pawpaws," he says. "I thought I was about to knock your socks off. Could have taken you in the woods down yonder and found this many." Now and then landowners do consider pawpaw a weed tree, and as late as the 1980s various government agencies recommended eliminating the tree by any means at the manager's disposal.[36] Still, this pawpaw savanna is an impressive showing, and the trees they've left behind are quite large, several more than twenty feet tall. If they survive future brush hoggings, the cleared canopy might even give these pawpaw trees an advantage.

We find some fruit, all of which is rock-hard. We wanted badly to find ripe fruit. I warn Paul that underripe fruit can make you sick and then proceed to break one open anyway. There's a bit of soft white pulp in the center. We both taste it, careful not to consume too much, scraping the hard pulp like a cup of frozen gelato.

The island, it turns out, has been known as Paw Paw Island since at least 1835. During and after the Civil War, Paw Paw Island held camps of freed slaves,[37] and at least one Union soldier died of wounds here in 1863.[38] That same year, the Union bought a gunboat, then stationed in St. Louis, which was renamed the *Paw Paw*. It's unclear whether the ship was named for the island, for someone's hometown (Paw Paw, Illinois, Michigan, or Kansas?), or for the fruit itself.

A few weeks after our trip, Paul returned to this same spot along with John Ruskey and the Quapaw Canoes crew, to lead a wildlife expedition. He wrote to me in an email: "Paw paws were ripe on Paw Paw Island this weekend. Introduced about 50 people to the taste of this neat fruit! Thanks for getting me to pay attention . . . I am now a confirmed pawpaw nutcase."

I rejoin the trace just outside Natchez, where at the edge of the city I find an indoor farmers market. Inside, tables are piled high with watermelon, sun melon, okra, and tomatoes, and coolers stocked with cowpeas, field peas, butter beans, and more. While I'm browsing, a young woman in a tie-dyed T-shirt brings in several bags of muscadines. Ella Henderson, who is running the market today, remembers just one man who sold pawpaws back when the market was located downtown, but that was long ago. I eat one of her homemade sweet potato cakes and then drive through town.

Natchez, Mississippi, is a beautiful city with a collection of Spanish, French, English, and American architecture; it's situated on a bluff that overlooks the Mississippi. In *Domestic Manners of the Americans*, Frances Milton Trollope's 1832 travelogue, she described the scene: "The town of Natchez is beautifully situated on one of those high spots. The contrast that its bright green hill forms with the dismal line of black forest that stretches on every side, the abundant growth of the paw-paw, palmetto, and orange, the copious variety of sweet-scented flowers that flourish here, all make it appear like an oasis in the desert."[39]

Though the view is impressive, I don't spot any pawpaws, and in my travels in and around Natchez there appears to be a dearth of folks familiar with them. I've stopped frequently to ask about the fruit, but there have been no leads at various gas stations and restaurants, not even at the Tomato Place, a colorful produce-stand-meets-roadside-attraction featuring smoothies, fresh produce, a deli menu, even potted fruit trees for sale. I can imagine that in just a few years pawpaws could be sold here, in smoothies, or maybe even the trees themselves, but not yet. And maybe deeper in the country, near Bophumpa Creek, there's an old woman or a young boy, eating pawpaws right now. But a stranger like myself would never know.

❦

Almost one hundred miles away on the other side of the river, I meet Jerry Dedon at Louisiana State University's Ag Center. Though retired, he is busier than most, tending a large vegetable garden and a several-hundred-tree orchard, and managing several acres of a neighbor's land — which largely consists of attempting to control the feral hog population. Although Jerry had heard the word *pawpaw* all his life, he'd never tasted one until coming here for a tasting hosted by the Southern Fruit Fellowship. "When

I first tasted the pawpaw, I fell in love with it," he says. "It was just like eating egg custard."

Jerry soon after ordered more than three hundred dollars' worth of grafted pawpaws. The trees arrived bare-root, and each of them promptly died. So he planted seeds and started grafting his own. He continues to raise hundreds of seedlings each year, donating them to his friend's nursery in Walker, Louisiana. "I just want everybody to have a pawpaw tree, so I give them to him, and he sells to people who want them," he says. "I used to give a lot of pawpaw trees away, but I find that people aren't really as enthusiastic as I am about it. I've given many a pawpaw tree away and two years later, they say, 'Oh, it died in the pot before I could plant it.'" Jerry is undestandably more selective now. He has sent seed to interested growers in nearly every state, and as far away as England and Hungary.

While other amateur growers dabble in controlled crosses, looking for the next best cultivar, Jerry says, "My research is strictly off the tongue." He supports others who are breeding for bigger fruit with few seeds. "But my objective?" he says. "If it'll make it from the tree to the refrigerator, then I'm happy."

LSU, on the other hand, once partnered with Neal Peterson's Pawpaw Regional Variety Trials (RVT), whereby Neal sent out seed and budwood for the experiment to learn how his advanced selections (among other cultivars) would fare in southern Louisiana. We're now standing in the orchard, and even though it's just nine in the morning, the recent cool weather is long gone and the Louisiana heat and sun are beating down on us. The condition of the orchard has worsened dramatically since Jerry's first visit, and it clearly breaks his heart. Hurricanes, we will later learn, have done the most damage to the trees, which are unable to withstand harsh winds in an open orchard setting.

When Charles Johnson, an LSU fruit crops specialist, joins us, I ask if creating a buffer would help to protect pawpaws in a commercial orchard. "I think you would have to have something for a little bit of a windbreak," he says, "and they would do better if they've got a little bit of shade in the afternoon. Like if I plant pecan trees, I might plant them every other row in there, just to give you some shade and wind protection."

Tags are still affixed to the trees, labeling each variety — MD-14, Ark-21, 7-10-34, Taytoo, Wabash, Rappahannock, and others. Despite the battering of the trees, there are positive lessons to be learned. Other than mowing, the trees receive very little attention, and they're still producing excellent fruit. Jerry and I eat the ones we find — they're big and great. Again, other than the ones that have been jostled and made crooked by high winds, they're perfectly healthy. LSU has never sprayed for pests, never had any reason to do so.

Before the RVT it was unclear to researchers how pawpaws would perform in an orchard this far south. But Johnson says that chilling hours — the minimum number of cold hours a fruit tree needs to blossom — have not been a factor. Previous reports had indicated pawpaws need eight hundred to a thousand chilling hours. "Some years, in mild winters, we may get 250 here — but it has not affected the fruiting," he says.

Unfortunately for the pawpaw (and for Jerry), the fruit is no longer an official mission of the university. The USDA has approximately twenty trees planted at a research plot in Poplarville, Mississippi, which shares a similar climate and challenges to those found here in Baton Rouge. The researchers are not, however, doing any cultivar research; they're simply watching to see if they grow, and how long it takes until fruit production. Johnson says there has been interest in Louisiana, growers looking to plant a few in their yards, and a few more ambitious growers like Jerry. But in the years since the orchard was planted in Baton Rouge no commercial growers have followed suit. "It's an interesting crop," he says, "I think we could grow it. I'd like to see some growers just trying it, and they can be more innovative than I have been here. They can put them in different places in their orchards and on their farms, and find these niche places for them to grow." The pawpaw market in Louisiana is wide open.

♈

Pawpaws do seem to be a forgotten fruit in Louisiana. "I ask the so-called woodsmen, the people that are always in the woods," Johnson says, "and they say, 'I've never seen it, I wouldn't know a pawpaw if I saw it.' And they don't recognize the tree." Jerry agrees. People he knows in their eighties and nineties, who have "lived their life in the woods fox hunting, coon hunting, and raising cows," have never heard of them. "And they're in the woods by the thousands, along that Tickfaw River, but they'd never heard of them," he says. Many of Jerry's neighbors also say they wouldn't know one if they saw it — even though he's seen them growing on their property!

Jerry has one theory: that August is just too hot. Even the most avid hunters tend to avoid the woods this time of year, when the mosquitoes seem to bite more often and with more vigor, when the sun is high and baking. But in Louisiana, that's when the pawpaws are ripe. So from east Texas to the Florida panhandle the fruit goes largely unnoticed. Indeed, pawpaws are absent from much of the lower South's food writing. Paul Prudhomme didn't include them in any of his Cajun tomes; neither, at the turn of the century, did *The Picayune's Creole Cook Book*, which included everything from "compote of pigeon and frogs a la Creole" to blue plum jelly and banana sherbet.[40] Mississippi native Craig Claiborne, food editor and restaurant critic for the *New York Times*, forwent pawpaw in his *Southern Cooking* (though he did include a recipe for persimmon ice cream), and in *The Taste of Country Cooking,* Edna Lewis's seminal work on rural southern foodways, there's no mention of pawpaws, though wonderful recipes for wild foods are well represented, including dandelion blossom wine, persimmon pudding, hickory nut cookies, and watercress salad. But according to Jerry's theory, all of these omissions might make sense. Dandelions and watercress can be harvested in spring; persimmons and hickory nuts later into the fall. And August is not only hot, but also a busy time on the farm. When crops needed harvesting, there is simply no time for pawpaw hunting.

Another theory suggests that the lack of pawpaw culture here might also have to do with language. Once Europeans and Africans settled in Louisiana, a lingua franca — known as Mobilian Jargon — developed between speakers of Old World languages and the many Native American languages. And so the Louisiana Indians, who had previously known pawpaw by a variety of names, came to refer to pawpaw as *açmine*. Linguist Emanuel Drechsel observed that this word was often mistaken for jasmine, and the tree *açminier* for jasminier (the word *açmine* was taken into Mobilian Jargon either from the Illinois *rassimina* or the Virginia Algonquian or Powhatan *assimin*).[41]

Açminier first entered Louisiana French either through the Mobilian Jargon, or through the Acadians (Cajuns), who were exiled from Canada. As early as 1744, French explorers in Canada wrote of "l'Acimine" and continued to encounter the fruit in the North and throughout the Mississippi Valley. In Louisiana French, pawpaw was also frequently referred to as jasminier, or jasmine, as opposed to *jasmin*, which, confusingly, is Louisiana

French for jasmine. English speakers may have trouble with the pawpaw/ papaw/papaya confusion, but Francophones have it no easier. All of this is to say that in much of Louisiana, pawpaw may — literally — have not been part of the vocabulary.

And yet another thought is that in southern Louisiana, at least, there's never been a need for the poor man's banana. This far south, you could grow the real thing.

❧

But of course, folks do know pawpaw, even if they're fewer in number. At the Vermilionville living history village, in Lafayette, I meet Steve Chandler, who is taking a break from playing fiddle. I hold out a ripe pawpaw and ask what he knows about them. Without any hesitation he takes the pawpaw from my hand, tears it in half, and squeezes out a mouthful of pulp. "I know they taste good," he says. He wipes the pulp from his fingers and we shake hands. Although pawpaw trees might be thought of as rare in the Louisiana prairie of today, they were once known. They're included in Vermilionville's handout on wild foods and medicinal plants: *Assiminier*, its name in Louisiana French, was once used as a laxative.

In a curious scene from an 1874 Louisiana adventure novel by Thomas Mayne Reid titled *Bruin; Or, The Grand Bear Hunt*, a large group is preparing for a barbecue in the swamps. "[A] party of negroes had been busy in the woods, searching out the tall slender saplings of the pawpaw (*asimina triloba*), and now returned, bringing their spoil with them. The saplings were laid across the top of the pit, thus extemporizing over it a huge gridiron. The ox, which was to form the staple of the day's feast, had been killed and dressed; and having been split in halves after the fashion of the barbecue was laid upon the bars to roast . . . it is well known that the sap which exudes from the pawpaw, when thus exposed to fire, adds a new relish to whatever is cooked upon it."[42] This is the only reference I have ever seen extolling the virtues of pawpaw wood in culinary applications, barbecue or otherwise. Which is curious, because although the excerpt is from a work of fiction, there must be some truth in it. Reid was so specific about the species that he included its scientific name — either because he was sure of its culinary virtues and wanted to be clear in his instructions, or perhaps to avoid any confusion with *Carica papaya*. Until it can be proven otherwise, the prevalence of pawpaw-smoked barbecue is yet another unknown in the fruit's history.

✎

Jerry and I load my car with pawpaws until it is packed to the gills. As Dale Brooks once told *Southern Living* magazine, "Some people say they get a giddy feeling from the odor . . . I can't attest to that, but I do know that when I have them lying around the house, I'm extremely happy."[43] With that much fruit, the fragrance overpowers my little hatchback, and stays with me for the next thousand miles.

I drive first to a coffee shop that also happens to be a bakery specializing in cake balls. I wonder, since pawpaw flavor is preserved best when uncooked, if perhaps their cake balls would work. The basic recipe calls for combining fully cooked cake batter with a wet batter (such as pawpaw puree) that is then rolled and drizzled with icing. It seems perfect. I hope the friendly baristas and cooks will be willing to experiment with this new fruit. They try it but are not blown away, perhaps even holding back a little disgust at the texture. Still, they indulge me and my strange bag of fruit, with one employee saying it tastes like a mango. I keep waiting for them to *get* it, to fall in love with the fruit, but I eventually realize that no cake balls will be made today. Instead, I leave three pieces of fruit with a note for the manager, but I'm not optimistic that they won't end up in the trash.

Pawpaw detractors are nothing new. In 1902, the *Topeka Daily Capital* reported: "The pawpaw crop is light this year. This would be important if pawpaws were good to eat."[44] In his 1905 treatise on pawpaws, James A. Little addressed the anti-pawpaw contingent. "There are a few persons who do not relish the pawpaw and they give as a reason that they do not eat things a hog won't eat," he wrote. "They consider that a stunner. I tell them I don't eat everything a hog eats."[45]

But Jerry Dedon, of course, is not one of those people. Because of a late frost that killed many blossoms, the pawpaw trees in his orchard didn't produce much fruit. After I have returned to Pittsburgh, he sends me an email. "A friend and I went on the river today to check out his paw-paw trees and we came back with about a dozen nice ones he shook loose." Jerry won't be without pawpaws this year.

❧

In the woods of northern Louisiana, flatlands stretch to the horizon. Dense columns of pine form unbroken ranks, straight and tall. I stare into these woods and recall that just east of here, in the mid-1800s, Henry Bibb escaped from enslavement, if only briefly. Bibb was born into slavery in 1815, in Shelby County, Kentucky, approximately thirty miles from the Ohio River. The distance to that river was all that separated Bibb from freedom. He would overcome it more than once, and eventually became a leading abolitionist of his day. After his first escape, Bibb returned to rescue his wife, Malinda, and their child. The attempt failed, and the family was sold to a ruthless plantation owner in Claiborne, Louisiana. When it was discovered that Bibb — a deeply religious man — had attended a prayer meeting without permission and would be flogged and sold apart from Malinda, the family fled to the wilderness, slogging through the Red River swamps, "among the buzzing insects and wild beasts of the forest." While on the run, Bibb wrote that "Our food was parched corn, with wild fruits such as pawpaws, percimmons, grapes, &c. We did at one time chance to find a sweet potato patch . . . but most of the time while we were out we were lost."[46] They were eventually apprehended; Bibb was lashed, and sold away from Malinda. Though the family would never be reunited, Bibb did finally escape to freedom.

The terrain I see today seems sparsely populated, but I know its history of habitation is ancient. The Piney Woods, more than a poetic description of the landscape, is an official eco-region that includes east Texas, southern Arkansas, western Louisiana, and a bit of southeastern Oklahoma. The woods also represent the southwestern limit of *Asimina triloba*. According to *A Field Guide to Texas Trees*, pawpaw trees occur in several eco-regions in the Lone Star State: "the deep, rich soils of the bottomlands of the Pineywoods, Gulf Prairies and Marshes, and Post Oak Savannah." The book's authors state that in years past, "there were large drifts and thickets of Pawpaw, but now it is found as single, isolated understory trees, or in small groves."[47] Located in Harrison County, Texas, is Paw Paw Bayou — named, certainly, for the trees that once grew in abundance there.

In northeast Texas there is a geologic formation that dates back to the Early Cretaceous, known as the Paw Paw Formation. The pawpaw shales, or clays, were named for nearby Pawpaw Creek. In 1992, the skeletal remains of a large, prehistoric creature were discovered in this area, a creature now known as the *Pawpawsaurus*. An herbivore, the *Pawpawsaurus* likely ate fruits. Perhaps even a proto-*Asimina* was part of the armored giant's diet.[48]

But today, as you travel west into Texas, pawpaws are indeed fewer in number. The Sabine River, which divides Texas and Louisiana, marks the transition from pawpaw country to persimmon country. According to Caddo legend, an old Indian chief who lived on the banks of the Sabine told his two sons it was time they found their own land. "The chief told one to face east, the other west, and then walk in the directions they faced from sunup of one day until sundown of the next. Where each found himself at that time was the place for his tribe. The one walking east found the fruit of the pawpaw tree, and his people were called Natchitoches, 'pawpaw eaters.' The one walking west found persimmon trees, and members of his family were called Nacogdoches, 'persimmon eaters.'"[49] The city of Natchitoches, Louisiana, established by Louis Juchereau de St. Denis in 1714, was named for the tribe. I was unable to visit it on this trip, however, and cannot say whether any of its residents are still pawpaw eaters.

❧

I am driving north on US 167. It's twilight, and the setting sun casts a warm glow on the grasses and shrubs below the pine forest. I'm far from Cajun country, but there's a food truck in the tiny town of Bernice, Louisiana: the Rockin' Cajun Tamale. Bright bulbs advertise gator meat and crawfish pies. I make a U-turn and head for the window.

"Be right with you, cher," the proprietress calls out. I order a combination of boudin balls and crawfish pies. "Everything made from scratch, cher," she says. Mindy is from southern Louisiana and has been cooking Cajun food since she was a girl. She's talkative and friendly, and so I bring up pawpaws. She's unfamiliar with them, and calls her husband, Mike, to come and look.

"Yeah, I know pawpaw," he says, a little taken aback. "But I thought I was coming out here to see a *pawpaw*," he says, by which he means he thought there would be a grandfather standing here, not a piece of fruit. "I used to get them here, right up the road, several years ago," he continues. "You won't find them just anywhere." Mike then asks if I'm familiar with possum grapes, and takes me around back of the property to show me his own wild bounty. "They're little bitty, and they're loaded," he says. "Look up there, look how many. I'm fixin' to pick them and see if I can make me a wine." I ask if I should eat the seed inside. "Just chew it and spit it out, kind of like a huckleberry. We got huckleberries this time of year too. Huckleberries are real, real good for your liver. So the Indians say." The possum grapes are indeed tiny, and mostly consist of seed, but the little bit of flesh packs a large punch, like wild SweeTarts. Mike gives me a bunch to take on the road, and they're a nice follow-up to Mindy's rich, delicious crawfish pies. Meanwhile Mindy has been thinking on the pawpaw. "I think we call it for something else," she says. "We have nickname for the little bits of everything, so I just can't put finger for this." *Assiminier*, perhaps?

Later, I finally cross into Arkansas, and in El Dorado I stop for frozen yogurt at a gas station. It's around midnight, and I'm the only person in the store. I take the yogurt to a small bistro table out front and mix a medium-sized pawpaw into the cup. The fruit is a little overripe, with strong caramel notes. And while it's not Dale Brooks's preferred Dairy Queen vanilla, at this moment the combination is just right.

❧

The Ozarks are the oldest mountains in the US. When their peaks were at their highest, before they eroded to the hills they are today, pawpaws were present. When ground sloths and giant beavers and even mastodons wound their ways through the Ozark bottomlands, pawpaws were on the menu. And as they did elsewhere, the Native Americans who eventually settled in these hills ate pawpaws, and used the tree's fibers in textiles. In Missouri, carbonized pawpaw seeds date back to at least 1650 BC.[50] The fruit was eaten in bottomland camps, or taken back to caves and rock shelters where groups ate or cooked using large amounts of pawpaws. In one such dwelling, the dry cave conditions encouraged mummification. In one of the most elaborate burials yet discovered, a person was buried with a bundle of pawpaw bark and a woven bag "containing a brush and a bone awl."[51]

Settlers of European descent also ate pawpaws, of course, and although much time has passed since those frontier days, some culinary traditions haven't changed much since the 1800s. Fred Pfister, former publisher of *The Ozarks Mountaineer*, once wrote: "Ozarkers, culinary-wise, could be divided into two types. The first is the basic meat and potatoes type, with a mind closed to outside influences. The other type follows the philosophy if it grows and God made it, it can be eaten. This type's table would be graced with scrambled eggs and squirrels' brains, barbecued 'coon, woodchuck ragout, venison, pawpaw and persimmon bread, fruit pies and cobblers, and jams and jellies from the cornucopia of local plants such as blackberry, poke-berry, mulberry, raspberry, gooseberry, wild grape, plum, and elderberry. In short, anything that could be picked and prepared."[52] Further research shows that, historically, pawpaws were ubiquitous and widely eaten. The Paw Paw Militia earned its nickname in nearby Missouri, simultaneously snacking on the fruit and hiding in its thickets. So did the Paw-paw French, French colonists who settled around the Ozark community of Old Mines in the late 1700s. According to one descendant, the "funloving insult" referred to poor folks "who had to live on paw-paw in the summer and possums in the winter."[53] The name stuck, as did their language, and for centuries a unique dialect known as Paw-paw French was spoken in that corner of the Ozarks. Its speakers are now rare, but the language is still spoken.

Winding through the back hills, I find a family farm offering sorghum syrup, mayhaw jelly, and fresh eggs arranged on tables and carts in their front yard; and at a grocery store, muscadine grape juice. Elsewhere, at a gas station, a handwritten flyer advertises fresh milk for sale and includes a number to call for more information. Among these lingering food traditions, I'm hoping to find pawpaws.

I drive to Mountain View, home of the Ozark Folk Center. I stop for lunch at a local restaurant, and just outside my window is a lone, four-foot pawpaw tree. It has broad, long, beautiful leaves. Lunch is ham and beans, corn bread, black-eyed pea salad, and fried okra. I brought a pawpaw in with me, and spread it on the corn bread. Although my pawpaw is not dried, as the historical citations state, I imagine it tastes similar to what the Iroquois, among others, would have eaten.

At the Village Apothecary, Linda Ottum makes lye soap. "I grew up in northeast Arkansas, the flatlands, and there were pawpaw trees there as well," she tells me. "So it's not just an Ozark thing." I ask, but she doesn't know of any local trees where I might find some fruit. "You know, people, if they find their little mushroom patch, they will share mushrooms with you, but they're not going to tell you where they got them," she says. "And it's much the same with pawpaw. And in fact the only time that I remember having them, my dad, he'd been out hunting and he brought one home." Evidently Ottum's father was aligned with Pfister's second category of Ozark eaters: those of wild game and wild fruit.

Pawpaws and hunting often go hand in hand. For centuries, nocturnal hunters have sought out pawpaw and persimmon trees because raccoons, opossum, and other animals can be found here eating their fill of the fruits. Author Jesse Stuart wrote, "I knew where the pawpaw patches were. I went to those places for opossums."[54] In 1883, an article titled "An Arkansas 'Possum Hunt" stated, "We started up the creek bottom into the paw-paw and persimmon thickets, and soon the dogs opened."[55] And a 1908 article declared "the Piedmont Region the natural paradise of the nocturnal hunts-man" thanks to the spring and summer fruits, including "the toothsome paw-paw," adding that the "fat and greasy opossum is the prime object of the night-time hunter."[56] But even in daylight, the two can be paired. As a hunter in southwest Virginia once told me, while squirrel hunting in a massive pawpaw patch, "The squirrels would come in to eat pawpaws, and I'd eat pawpaw, and get my limit of squirrels, and sit there and eat pawpaws all day."

⤳

I continue to explore the village and enter Doris Panicci's leathercraft shop. From behind the counter, Doris sees what I'm carrying and cries out: "Pawpaw!" I'm encouraged and ask what she knows. "I know they used to make my mama sick every time she ate them, but she ate them anyway. Where I lived in Indiana, it's called Hoosier bananas. Live in Arkansas, call it Arkansas bananas. So, you know, they're just a banana anywhere you go." Doris lives nearby in Sugar Hill, "back in the boonies, five mile off the blacktop," where she and her husband settled after a few decades of travel-ing in rodeos. She left home at sixteen to be a trick rider, and picked up leatherworking on the road. "If somebody wanted some leatherwork done there wasn't anybody handy to do it, so I just started doing it myself."

She continues, "Pawpaws, it's, I don't know, maybe an acquired taste for some people. I'm not a big fan — my mother just, she knew where they was at and how to get them and everything." Doris was raised in Brown County, Indiana, in the hill country south of Indianapolis. "She had gallbladder problems — I discovered many years later — and I think that's why it upset her, because it'd make her sicker than a dog. But she'd eat it anyway. She'd just crave it. 'Oh, it's time for pawpaws!' She was just obsessed with them."

Doris's mother never cooked with pawpaws. "There was always so many people around that ate them and used them that I don't think there was any saved to can or anything like that," Doris says. "In fact I guess that they probably are a little delicate as far as canning." She's right, as far as my experience goes. It's rare that a canned pawpaw product — jam, jelly, or otherwise — retains the positive attributes of the fresh fruit. "But persimmon pudding," Doris says, "I'm about like that what mom was with the pawpaws — I make persimmon pudding every year for the holidays, and I'm the only one that eats it."

While I'm talking to Doris, several other visitors arrive. The first is Scott, the village blacksmith. "Hey, Scott, what do you know about pawpaws?" Doris asks. "They taste good," he says. I ask if he knows of any trees nearby. "Not anymore," he says. "All the ones I grew up eating as a kid have been bush hogged, cut out."

The second visitor is a tourist from Baton Rouge. "I heard of pawpaw but never ate it," she says. I tell her I've got ripe fruit to share, from, of all places, the experimental orchard in her hometown. "Oh, good for you," she says. "I mean, I don't eat just anything that hangs on a tree. No nutria, no pawpaw, no alligator." She laughs, good-naturedly I think, at both her joke and me and my pawpaws. "I hope you enjoy it," she says. I figure she would fall into Pfister's meat-and-potatoes category.

❧

The Ozark folklore surrounding pawpaws is the most colorful on record. Vance Randolph's wonderful collection *Ozark Folklore and Magic*, published in 1946, captures this:

> *Catfish and men, it is said, are the only living creatures known to eat pawpaws; dogs and even swine turn from them in disgust. However, though it is almost proverbial that catfish are "plumb gluttons for pawpaws," I have never seen a hillman use them as bait. "Fish that's a-feedin' on them things," an old man told me, "aint fit to eat nohow." It seems very odd that these fellows eat pawpaws themselves with every sign of relish but regard fish that have fed upon pawpaws as unwhole-*

some. Personally, I do not believe that catfish have any particular fondness for pawpaws . . . But the catfish-pawpaw legend is heard the length and breadth of the Ozark country, and is repeated even by second-growth hillbillies in the cities.[57]

In the Ozarks, as elsewhere, pawpaws were used medicinally. In her book *Ozark Pioneers*, Missourian Vickie Layton Cobb writes, "Pawpaw leaves were bruised to make a poultice to treat bee stings and snake bites. Doctors were scarce in the early days so the early settlers had only Mother Earth and prayer to turn to when there was sickness in the family."[58] And even into the late nineteenth century, pawpaw was still used by Ozarkians as cordage. An 1897 feature article, published in St. Louis, profiled local fishing techniques and described a handcrafted gig: "The gig consisted of a yellow pine shaft twelve feet long with a three- or four-pronged barbed fork, or metal gig, on one end and a leather or paw paw bark loop for the hand on the other. This weapon was hurled like a spear at the fish."[59] The 1917 *Journal of Heredity* article that announced the winner of the national pawpaw contest also wrote of the tree's versatility to Arkansans: "Dendrologists invariably describe it as weak, soft, and worthless, but W. T. Coleman, of Bono, Ark., writes that he knows of a house in which all of the rafters and joists are made of papaw, and that in earlier times it was much used for barn logs."[60]

Pawpaws were also associated with darker purposes. "The pawpaw tree is well known to be connected with witchcraft and devil worship, and even a gray-and-black butterfly (*Papilio ajax*) is looked upon as 'strange' because it is so often seen fluttering about pawpaw trees," Vance Randolph wrote. "People near Goodman, Missouri, tell me that there is some direct connection between pawpaw trees and malaria, but just what this relation is I do not know. Pawpaws are becoming rare in many sections where they were formerly abundant; this is regarded by the old-timers as a bad omen, perhaps a sign that the end of the world is at hand."[61]

Randolph wrote of many witch conjures practiced in the Ozarks. "Out in the woods at midnight [a witch master] bores a hole in the fork of a pawpaw tree, and drives a wooden peg into the hole. Once, despite the protests of a superstitious hillman who was with me, I pulled out one of these pegs and examined it. The end was covered with beeswax, in which several long hairs were imbedded. There was a circle of what appeared to be dried blood

higher up on the peg, and the auger hole contained a quantity of fine sand."
Randolph wrote of a similar "conjure" used by "cuckold husbands . . . primarily intended to deal with women who 'talk the Devil's language.'" There
were other, more direct ways of detecting a witch, including adding "a bit
of pawpaw bark to her tobacco." A witch would grow deadly sick, while "an
innocent woman is not affected."[62]

Ozark pawpaw lore was quite voluminous. Randolph reported that if
a person was dying, Ozark temperance workers recommended placing a
pawpaw in their hand: "If a drunkard, not knowing of the 'cunjure,' can
be persuaded to eat this pawpaw, he will quit drinking in spite of himself."
Randolph knew of one woman, who upon learning she was dying, called
for a pawpaw. "She held the fruit for a moment, then asked that it be
fed to her youngest son after her death. This was done, but the boy was
still a booze fighter the last I heard of him." In Jasper County, Missouri,
Randolph knew two sisters who went deep into the woods and bent several
pawpaw twigs, "tying them fast in the bent position with twisted locks of
their own hair. Relatives of these girls told me that this had to do with an
unsatisfactory love affair in which both girls were involved." Randolph also
reported that if the dead "can't rest in their graves, are somehow inclined
to loiter about redbuds, pawpaw trees, and haw bushes — though why they
should be attracted to these particular plants nobody seems to know."[63]

In addition to conjures and superstitions, pawpaws were also featured in
song. "Way Down Yonder in the Paw Paw Patch" is the best-known pawpaw
tune — and more famous than the fruit itself. But it's not the only one. "Way
Down Yonder" is sung by schoolteachers and young children, with an accompanying game. "Sweet Rose Marie," on the other hand — collected in
the Ozarks by Vance Randolph — is for adults only.

SWEET ROSE MARIE

In a pawpaw patch when the pawpaws were ripe,
I was loving sweet Rose Marie,
When she said, If you have a hot pawpaw
I'll let you tickle me.

I laid her down in the cool, cool shade
Beneath a pawpaw tree,

I tickled her once and I tickled her twice,
And she said, Let's make it three.

She grunted and giggled, she twisted and wiggled,
She said, Oh my, oh me!
I thought she was going to toss me up
To the top of the pawpaw tree.

Of all the sweet girls that I have loved
There was none so dear to me,
There was none could tickle me half so well
As darling Rose Marie.

The years have come and the years have gone,
Father Time has played hell with me,
'Twould do no good to meet Rose again
Beneath the pawpaw tree.[64]

The song was collected by Randolph in 1948 and published in his book *Blow the Candle Out: "Unprintable" Ozark Folksongs and Folklore*. It came from a manuscript copy belonging to Mr. J. C. Edwards. Randolph notes, "Almost certainly a private poetic effusion, not traditional, it has not been collected elsewhere." But how different the pawpaw's reputation would be if it were more associated with the tickling of Sweet Rose Marie than the game of lost little Susie.

❧

I leave Mountain View and head for the Buffalo National River. I exit the highway, and en route to my campsite I pass the ruins of Rush, a former zinc-mining town. Its residents would have picked and eaten pawpaws, and at the general store, where mail was collected, marriages were performed, and goods bought and sold, for a month each year pawpaws would have been available.

A park ranger visits the site, and we make small talk. He has never eaten a pawpaw — "I'm not from the South," he says — but he has noticed the trees throughout the area. I give him one to take home.

Before the sun sets, I go for a swim in the Buffalo River and gather hickory nuts from the woods. Not far from here, in 1916, a man named J. V. Waters camped on the banks of the Buffalo at Roughedge Hollow. "We stretched a wagon sheet over a pile of pawpaw limbs to sleep on," he wrote. "I fished with a cane pole and a live minnow."[65] Tonight I'll sleep atop a sleeping bag on the ground, which isn't much padding but sounds more comfortable than a pile of pawpaw limbs. This will be my last night on the road, and I want to eat a final pawpaw. I've been on the verge of proclaiming *Enough is enough, I've had one too many pawpaws this year*, but this latest one tastes like melon and is all-around great.

A sliced pawpaw reveals vibrant-yellow pulp.

Pawpaws are the largest edible fruit native to the United States. *Photo by Scott Bauer, USDA*

Pollinated by flies and beetles, pawpaw flowers smell yeasty or fermented, like rising bread dough and red wine. *Courtesy of Sue Ann Herald*

R Neal Peterson — aka Johnny Pawpawseed, the fruit's longtime champion — with a large cluster of fruit in his experimental orchard. *Courtesy of Neal Peterson*

Asimina is the only larval host of the zebra swallowtail butterfly.
Photo by Bob Peterson

A comparison of wild and cultivated fruit.

Jim Davis harvesting pawpaws at his Deep Run Orchard.

"French custard, ready for serving, hung from the trees." Walter Havighurst, 1946. *Courtesy of Dennis Hager*

Jon looks for fruit in a grove of pawpaws in eastern Kentucky, a few miles from the state-line village of Paw Paw.

Schooner, of Paw Paw, West Virginia, holds a record for most apples picked in a single day. His family is familiar with and fond of pawpaw apples — their term for the fruit.

Ron Powell leads a grafting workshop at the Ohio Pawpaw Growers Association's annual member meeting.

Pawpaw cultivars are propagated by grafting. Pictured here are demonstrations of the whip-and-tongue (left) and chip bud (right) methods. *Courtesy of Ron Powell*

Jerry Lehman inspects persimmons in his Terre Haute orchard.

Paddling a chute of the Mississippi River in August with Mark "River" Peoples of Quapaw Canoe Company, hunting pawpaws.

Paw Paw, Illinois, was originally the site of a Potawatomi village called Assiminehkon, or Pawpaw Grove.

Zingerman's Paw Paw Gelato in Ann Arbor, Michigan.

Pawpaw skin is thin and bruises easily, often darkening to black in just three days. The pulp, however, remains edible. *Special Collections, National Agricultural Library*

CHAPTER SEVENTEEN

APPALACHIA

I came to Pikeville, Kentucky, to see pawpaws for sale at the county farmers market. Although I arrived this morning just after nine, the fruit is gone. Denver Newsome has sold out. Luckily, it turns out they've not gone far, just ten feet over to the cab of a pickup loaded down with cushaws. The truck, and now the pawpaws, belongs to Bill Hughes. "He's the pawpaw man," Denver says.

Bill, who is wearing a broad straw hat, offers to show me how to eat one. "Just get the inside out of there, and eat 'em," he says, breaking it in half. "That there's a ripe one." He gives me the other half and we squeeze out the pulp. "A lot of people, they call it a Kentucky banana!" he says with a hearty laugh. "That's the first one I've had in two years. They're hard to find. They grow out in the hills, wild, and the bigger timber smothers them out." Bill was raised out toward the Virginia line. "Growing up, that was a delicacy," he says. "Of course, there used to be a whole lot more out in the hills than what there are now, because it's cleared out. But they're good for you."

Bill asks if I've ever heard of cushaws, and I respond with how I once read an essay by Fred Sauceman about Appalachian growers preferring cushaws to other squash because of their crooked necks. Loyal Jones, retired director of the Berea College Appalachian Center, told Sauceman: "If you were growing those big old pumpkins on one of these hillside cornfields, it might come loose and roll down and kill somebody, but those cushaws, they won't roll. They'll hook around a cornstalk or something and stay in the field."[1] Bill says they simply taste great. But as much as he loves cushaws, it's apparent they don't elicit in him the same level of excitement as the wild pawpaw; the former he has mastered in cultivation, the latter remains elusive.

Before I arrived, Denver, a former schoolteacher, had picked a bag's worth, about six pieces of medium-sized fruit, and sold them to Bill for just a dollar. In parts of eastern Kentucky, the price of pawpaws has increased very little in the past century. Denver also grows and sells several varieties of apples, Asian pears, and the beloved half-runner beans. For the next few weeks he will continue to pick and sell pawpaws; a second vendor will offer pawpaws the following week, picked from the woods behind her house, and so there will be two pawpaw vendors at the Pike County Farmers Market.

Pikeville-based food historian Mark F. Sohn included a few pawpaw recipes in his 1996 book, *Mountain Country Cooking: A Gathering of the Best Recipes from the Smokies to the Blue Ridge*. Of the pawpaw bread, Sohn writes, "Farmhouse cooks living in the [Shenandoah Valley] made a banana bread like this for generations, and cooks living farther south and in the damp valleys of the Ohio River make the bread with pawpaws."[2] In *A Taste of Kentucky* (1986) — a collection of folklore and foodways — Letcher County resident Molly Banks is credited for her pawpaw pie recipe. However, the author notes, "Paw paws are most commonly eaten raw and plain rather than cooked."[3] In eastern Kentucky, pawpaws are not just a roadside, river-bottom tree — they're often planted prominently in front yards, ornamentation in the edible landscape. Denver himself long ago saved seeds from a pawpaw and raised the tree in his yard — the one that produced today's bag of fruit.

Denver brought the pawpaws today because a woman had requested them. "Now I'm the pawpaw woman," she told him, "And you bring me them pawpaws as soon as you get them." Last year, Denver brought her a bushel's worth. This year she has competition. Denver hid this morning's pawpaws behind a basket, but Bill spotted them, and, well, "Finders keepers," he says.

"I know where a patch has been producing pawpaws now for forty years," Denver says, adding that he and his father used to hunt them. "I would stroll for miles to find a pawpaw patch." And once someone located a quality patch, they weren't likely to divulge its whereabouts. "Now, just like that man over yonder" — Denver points to Bill — "he would just about hold you up with a pistol if you got pawpaw!" Right on time, Bill strolls over and calls out, in character: "You ain't getting my pawpaws! Who do you think you are?" And so again, Denver allows: "He's a pawpaw man."

Bill complains about not finding as many pawpaws as they used to. Both men cite the expanding tree canopy as detrimental, but perhaps it's just that those in the know aren't sharing. "Have you heard of a morel mushroom?" Denver asks. "How many people will share their information, or knowledge, of where those are? If somebody lives a hundred miles away and just visits every now and then, Bill would share with them — he's more goodhearted than I am," Denver jokes. "But I don't believe I would take all my next-door neighbors to my secret pawpaw patch."

As a teacher, Denver taught his students to sing "Way Down Yonder." I ask if the children knew about the fruit in the song. "Oh, Lord, yes — they knew what a pawpaw was!"

&

The night before, my travel companion Jon and I stopped in Charleston, West Virginia. Through the heart of downtown runs Capitol Street, a pedestrian-friendly avenue lined with trees, strings of hanging lights, and welcoming Victorian storefronts, one of which belongs to Ellen's Homemade Ice Cream. For the past several years, Ellen's has offered pawpaw ice cream, made from the front-yard fruit of Charlestonian Aileen Wren. And it's one reason why I believe Charleston is ripe to follow in the footsteps of Athens, Ohio. Like Athens, Charleston is surrounded by millions of pawpaws. Bars and craft breweries already brew and sell unique regional beers — a pawpaw ale or saison would fit right in. And at the café in Taylor Books, where regional history and writers are celebrated, and whose live music acts are often rooted in Appalachian traditions, an item such as pawpaw crème brûlée, say, would not be out of place. Charleston even has a pawpaw legacy — in the early 1900s, Charleston grower L. Swartz had an orchard of one hundred trees,[4] and fruit was sold at the former Patrick Street market district as late as the 1940s.[5] And at new city farmers markets, pawpaws are still occasionally sold.

Charleston lacks a commercial pawpaw grower, with the nearest orchards currently in production at least three hours away in Kentucky and Ohio. But that might be okay for the Kanawha Valley — if local tastes are already acquainted with it, perhaps backyard selections, and growers, will do just fine. However it goes, whether the grower niche is waiting to be filled or not, there is already a pawpaw hero in Charleston: writer Colleen

Anderson. "One of the pawpaw's charms is the company it keeps," she once wrote. "Like the fruit, they tend to be slightly off the round."[6]

Anderson, you'll remember, is close friends with Neal Peterson and learned of the fruit from him. Neal convinced Anderson to join the PawPaw Foundation, and for some years she served on its board. Once, she and Neal drove a carload of fruit from Maryland to Chicago's Midwest Food and Wine Show, and in the late 1990s Anderson began reading a series of pawpaw tales on West Virginia Public Radio. When another Charleston writer and playwright, Arla Ralston — a defiant pawpaw detractor — grew tired of these reports, she demanded equal airtime for non-pawpaw praises, and a friendly battle ensued. Anderson argued that pawpaw was an aphrodisiac, linking the fruit to Bill Clinton, while Ralston formed a Pawpaw Prevention League in objection to the "third-rate fruit." Finally, as Zack Harold of the *Charleston Daily Mail* reported, Anderson and Ralston agreed to allow the success or failure of Ellen's pawpaw ice cream to settle the debate, and, "Sixteen years later, the pawpaw has emerged victorious."[7]

❧

After Pikeville we continue down the highway, deeper into the rugged mountains, heading straight for a mass of rain clouds. Broad-leafed umbrella magnolias line the roads, luxuriating in humid, subtropical forests. As we exit the highway and descend into the first of many hollers, the storm comes fast and hard. Winds shake the trees violently; brown and yellow leaves litter the slick asphalt. The leaf-fall is a reminder of the coming change of seasons, a transition marked not just by foliage but also by the ripening of pawpaws. The full transition is still a month or two away, though, and when the rain comes to a stop, the heat, humidity, and sunlight return.

The Lucky Penny General Store heralds our arrival in Phyllis. Inside, stacked on shelves above the hardwood floor, are sodas and snacks, tobacco, and fresh produce (onions, potatoes, peppers). There's also a full menu of cooked-to-order food from which we order sandwiches. Noting the produce, I ask the man behind the counter — Bryan — if he ever sells pawpaws. "No, but I know where there are some," he says. I tell him I'm doing general research on the fruit. "Well, let me go get you some," he says, and in a matter of seconds he goes out into the rain (which had started again), gets in his truck, and is off to fetch some pawpaws. When he returns, he pulls several pawpaws from a paper bag. A tree at Bryan's parents' place — just around the corner — is now producing. I wasn't expecting the pawpaws to be so large, so I'm impressed to see such round, plump fruit. We eat them and they're good. "I'm sure I'm going to be eating pawpaw pie or something," Bryan says. "My mom's going to make something out of them." Pawpaws aren't the only wild foods on the dinner table; in spring, his parents especially enjoy poke salad and morels, or "dry land fish," as they're locally known.

A young man of thirty, Bryan has lived his whole life in eastern Kentucky, though many of his peers have moved out of the region for work. He admits that there aren't many opportunities for those who stay, and that he occasionally offers store credit to those who need it. "It's hard, but we make it," he says. "Everybody just makes it." In lean times, previous generations supplemented their diets with wild foods. They're eaten less commonly today, but poke, pawpaws, and morels, and the people who love them, are part of what appeals to Bryan about the region. "I enjoy being here," he says, "There's something about the culture around here — we try to help people." He doesn't charge us for the sandwiches or the pawpaws, confident we'll pay it forward.

ch

The folks I speak with in Pikeville, Phyllis, Charleston, and elsewhere are familiar with and often fond of pawpaws. Although pawpaws are native to twenty-six eastern states — more than half the country — pawpaw culture appears stronger in Appalachia than anywhere else.

Long before European Americans settled in the mountains, American Indians cultivated many crops — including well-known items like corn, beans, squash, and tobacco — and combined those foodstuffs with items procured through hunting, gathering, and fishing. While this could describe any number of American Indian groups and subsequent pioneers, in a region where arable land was less abundant, the wild harvest may have held even greater importance. As historian H. Tyler Blethen writes, "European and African newcomers often took over the very fields that Indians had farmed and adapted Indian methods of slash-and-burn and of planting beans and squash among irregular rows of corn . . . in the backcountry [they] learned from the Indians how to dress, track, and decoy game and live off the land while hunting."[8] Living off the land meant that the morels and the ramps, the pawpaws and persimmons, the hickory nuts and the chestnuts were of greater importance in these mountains.

In rural Appalachia, the wilderness lingered where elsewhere it was cut down, plowed, or paved. "As late as the mid-nineteenth century [farmers] continued to leave four-fifths to three-quarters of their land unimproved, primarily in forest," Blethen writes.[9] Among other things, more woods meant more pawpaws — in the fall, when hogs were run through the woods, a farming family had a bounty of fruits and nuts to gather. This wild bounty was often so great that during this same period forest crops like ginseng and snakeroot, in addition to the various fruits and nuts, were brought to market for cash.

But with the onset of the Civil War, Appalachia entered a devastating period of economic decline. During this period rural Appalachians increasingly turned to the woods for supplemental foods. And later, by the 1920s, when many farm families elsewhere in the States were creating modern, homogenized, industrial-sized farms, Appalachia's families were not. "Appalachia comprises only 3 percent of the land area of the United States, but the 1930 census found one third of America's 'self-sufficing' farms tucked away there," writes historian Paul Salstrom. "The Census defined self-sufficing farms as 'where the value of the [home] farm products used by the family was 50 percent or more of the total value of all products of the farm.' In Appalachia in 1930, about a million farm dwellers lived that way, far more than any other region of the United States."[10] Self-sufficing not only meant raising a vegetable garden, but might also have included growing enough cotton for clothing, raising and butchering hogs, canning and drying foods, bartering, and curing sweet tooths with wild fruits. "Many of Appalachia's self-sufficing farm families brought in cash incomes of less than $100 a year (equivalent to about $1,000 today)," but many families were so "successfully self-sufficing that the Depression barely affected them."[11] In fact, for those who were accustomed to this way of life — as anyone who enjoys cured pork, chestnuts, pawpaws, and ramps can attest — they probably ate quite well. And so the old-timers we meet, who grew up in the Depression, remember eating pawpaws out of necessity, sure, but it was also a normal and joyful thing to do. And it's a tradition they passed on to their children and grandchildren.

✧

Paw Paw, Kentucky, is not easy to find. It's not even easy to define where Paw Paw *is*. We drive over two mountains, along several creeks, and make at least one wrong turn. "The road is just crooky, curvy, gnarly, either way you go," we were told. But the closer (we think) we get, the more pawpaws we see. A little lost, we ask a man about finding Paw Paw, who says it's just a little place, a few homes, over the mountain. We follow the road to the next community. Inside a country store — a plain cinder-block building — we ask the woman behind the counter if this, finally, is Paw Paw, Kentucky. "This whole area is Paw Paw," she replies. "Paw Paw, Virginia, and Paw Paw, Kentucky." Paw Paw . . . Virginia? Apparently, it works like this: We're actually now in Paw Paw, Virginia, but if we go back a few feet, we'll be in Paw Paw, Kentucky. And if we keep going, we're back in Virginia, and then we're back in Kentucky — or at least I think that's how it works. Two states, one Paw Paw.

Lisa, the store owner, heats a sandwich for Bobby May, who's been out hiking with his grandson Buddy. Bobby hasn't ever eaten a pawpaw but was just the other day saying there ought to be some planted prominently in town. Thanks to Bryan from the Lucky Penny, I have some fruit (and seed) to share. "I remember my dad always said you don't eat them until the frost hits them," he says. I think they're good to go now, but will let Bobby make up his own mind.

"I tell you one thing that had to do with pawpaw trees, too, now," Bobby says. "In the late '20s, W. Ritter Lumber — man, they cleared this country, and they got rid of a lot of trees. They cut the scrub, and stuff like pawpaws, they probably decimated." It's true. Nearly every tree we see on this trip is second-, third-growth forest — an eighty-year-old specimen would be an outlying elder. In fact, although modern environmental ravages seem more devastating than ever, it's true that around the turn of the century many sections of the country — Appalachia included — were grossly denuded, clear-cut to the point that great vistas became smoking, stump-filled wastelands. But the trees — various combinations of natives and exotics — came back. Whether there were once more or fewer pawpaws growing here, I don't know, but apparently at some point there were enough in this corner of Appalachia to inspire multiple town names. "There's another Paw Paw on the other side of

Buchanan County," Bobby says. Later, I have trouble finding it on any maps, but like the Paw Paw, Kentucky/Virginia, I'm sure it's there.

Before we go, Bobby tells us to look out for moonshine around Panther. Once, he even witnessed a politician giving out gallons of it from the back of a pickup. I'm not sure if he's telling us this because he thinks we'd like to hear it, or if this is truly his most vivid memory of Panther. Either way, I'm intrigued.

I'm not the first person to cross the country in search of Paw Paw towns. Raymond Jones was born in Kansas in 1920, to a father who adored pawpaws. At forty-two, Jones moved to California, "where pawpaws were nearly as scarce as hen's teeth," and he longed for them like few others before or since. In 1991 he launched *The Pawpaw Tracker*, an organization and newsletter whose goal was to collect the correspondence and knowledge of the nation's far-flung pawpaw lovers. Jones grew his own trees in Santa Clara, but still had a longing. So when he learned of Neal Peterson's efforts in Maryland, Jones (at the age of seventy-two) drove cross-country to the Maryland orchard. And as if the trip weren't long enough, he took detours to Paw Paw, Illinois, Michigan, West Virginia, Oklahoma, and into the hollers of eastern Kentucky where he found himself, as we just have, at the state-line village of Paw Paw. "Where, oh where is Paw Paw?" Jones wrote. He even photographed a woman, Ms. Media Ested, seventy-six, standing by her dooryard pawpaw tree. Ms. Ested said she had "had lived there all her life and had always called it Paw Paw."[12]

As we go back through Paw Paw, Kentucky (and then Virginia, and then Kentucky again — I think), we come to the former Paw Paw Groceries building, which is now a gym. Our new friend Bobby used to own the grocery, in fact. If the sign ever changes to reflect the new business inside, it will be one less reminder of where you are. Maybe Bobby will sprout the seeds I've given him, plant a tree, and someone in town will ask the building's owner to keep the sign.

☙

After a short drive we arrive at the Panther Wildlife Management Area, where we'll camp for the night. It's been a long day of talking pawpaws, and I wish we had come across a bottle of moonshine; instead, we settle for a six-pack. And while I never expected to stumble across a bootleg still, I'm aware that West Virginia does have a storied past with moonshine. Historically, the most popular moonshine was a white corn liquor, but it wasn't the only fermented drink made by Mountaineers. In 1962, Roy Lee Harmon reminisced in the *Raleigh Register* of one particular spirit: "Now paw paw brandy was a drink without a peer. You could take a few snifters of it and feel like you were float-ing on a pink cloud eating ice cream and viewing some beautiful scenery . . . Kids used to be paid to gather them for brandy making . . . You got very little paw paw brandy. It was rare stuff and caused some rare reactions. I knew a fellow who got a snoot full of the stuff one winter night and didn't show up until next day. He claimed he slept in a snowdrift and dreamed of little angels all night. He swore he kept nice and warm."[13]

Almost a century earlier pawpaw beer had a reputation for packing a punch in eastern Kentucky. "The paw-paw is ripe and the mountain man is in his glory brewing paw-paw beer," the *Courier-Journal* reported in 1896. "It is a combination that leaves terror in its wake . . . A fellow from over in Powell county was in town yesterday with a barrel of the stuff, but most of the boys fought shy of it, remembering their experience of last year."[14]

છુંજી

Before cooking dinner, we take a short hike up a hillside. The forest floor is damp, dotted with ferns and an understory of rhododendron and pawpaws. Midway up the hill I begin to see Fraser magnolia, its leaf differentiated from the other American species by a pair of lobes at its base. I've only read about these trees — which are also known as mountain magnolia — before seeing them now on this hike. Trees in the Magnolia family are among the most ancient, with several species dating back more than ninety-five mil-lion years, but Annonaceae is not too far behind. In fact, the *Magnolia* and *Asimina* genera likely weathered ice ages together in the Florida panhandle.

Today there are many unique plant species found in parts of Florida's panhandle that are otherwise rare in the Deep South. Many of these trees and flowers — from the bigleaf magnolia and pawpaw, to trout lilies and trilliums — are more common in the Appalachians, a thousand miles away. "During the Ice-Ages, as glaciers pushed northern vegetation southward, these plants remained in the sheltered ravines when the glaciers retreated," writes the Northwest Florida Environmental Conservancy. This is likely how a proto-pawpaw, or *Asimina triloba* itself, came to Florida. From here, the species evolved into its unique Floridian forms and spread southward.

Meanwhile, as the glacial coverings receded, *A. triloba* went north, back home to Pikeville, to Panther.[15]

᪐

Like Ray Jones, I have also visited other Paw Paw towns. The banks of the Potomac are home to Paw Paw, West Virginia. The region was once home to a thriving apple industry, and among the town's principal employers was a tannery. The roads and riverbanks that wind to and from the town are lined with unending pawpaw groves, and throughout the town — population approximately five hundred — trees are cultivated, including a pair in front of the post office.

Walking in town, I met a man named Schooner, seated by the sidewalk with a crate of pears. A former apple picker, Schooner set a record for most apples picked in a day, and remembers when the town was bustling. Schooner and his family — wife, daughter, and grandchildren — are all fond of their town's namesake fruit. "Down in Magnolia — probably six, seven miles if you take the road," his daughter told me, "down there they have a lot of pawpaw apple trees, it's just a whole field, and it's called the pawpaw patch."

Pawpaw *apples*? Perhaps because the region was such a large producer of apples, and Paw Paw itself a large packing and distribution center, they added the clarifying name of apple. And this was what the entire family called the fruit: pawpaw apples.

At another home in Paw Paw, a few men and women were gathered on a porch. I approached them and asked about pawpaws. "I love them," one of the men said. "I didn't know about them till maybe twenty years ago, somebody took me down along the Potomac and showed me what they looked like. There's hundreds of them right along the railroad, and even a walking trail where everybody goes down and gets them. There's a road goes down to the river — that's all pawpaws — you're walking under a couple hundred of them."

Just outside Paw Paw, West Virginia, is the Paw Paw Tunnel, a former railroad tunnel on the C&O Canal. The tunnel is now part of a bicycle trail from Pittsburgh, Pennsylvania, to Washington, DC. The woods on either side abound with pawpaw trees, and large sections of the 335-mile bicycle trail run under a pawpaw canopy.

❧

In the morning, we take a light breakfast at the Friendly Mart, near Panther. A few older men stroll in, pour themselves coffee, and sit at a table. I ask the eldest man, Mr. Bailey, about pawpaws. "Sometimes, just passing by, I might pick one up," he says. "They're dying out, though. Unless you transplant them and take care of them, they're going to be gone."

Many people I've met during my travels have told me that pawpaws are dying out. Denver and Bill said as much back in Pikeville. I heard similar reports in southern Ohio. Maybe it seems that way because the people in these hollers are eating them less and less; thus, the assumption is that they're dying out. Or maybe there's some truth to it. At the Lucky Penny, I was told there used to be a patch along the creek across from the store. But when I'd gone to look, the bank was thick with Japanese knotweed. Invasive exotics compete with and often replace pawpaws in the understory. With mountaintop removal, pawpaws are often buried in the rubble and blast of fallen peaks. When strip jobs are "reclaimed," they're not often on the list of replacement/restoration trees. When roads are widened, and roadsides sprayed with herbicides, pawpaws lose out.

Farther east, on the Coal Heritage Highway, US 52, is Kimball, West Virginia. Outside the town's only restaurant — Ya'sou Restaurant and West Virginia Grocery — Sylvester Edwards sells heirloom tomatoes, zucchini, and other vegetables. Edwards is a retired stonemason, but has farmed his entire life and now does it full-time. He was born and raised in western North Carolina and grew up eating pawpaws. He'd just recently moved to McDowell County, West Virginia, and in addition to the farm stand gives away produce at schools. "When I first moved here, I went looking for pawpaws and didn't find many," he says. "They'd been eradicated pretty much, and it used to be a staple here." In this county, the small kudzu-choked towns are struggling as coal production declines. Edwards and his fellow farmers want to demonstrate the possibilities of agriculture. "There's three small farms here now," he says, "and we're producing a lot of food."

In the 1920s, J. Russell Smith published *Tree Crops: A Permanent Agriculture.* His work, and his phrase, would later inspire the term *permaculture,* and his writings promoted terracing and tree crops as a sustainable way to farm without accelerating erosion and environmental degradation.

"Smith's ideas may well have represented — and may still today represent — the only sustainable way to practice agriculture on the hillsides of the Appalachian Plateau," writes Paul Salstrom.[16] Of the pawpaw, Smith wrote, "This is a native American tree of great beauty . . . [and has] the great advantage of having foliage that seems to be abhorred by all animals."[17] In *Farming Appalachia*, another of Smith's publications, he wrote that the pawpaw and other tree crops have "demonstrated themselves as being good yielders, hardy, and capable of growing without the plow," concluding that an "agriculture that is adjusted to both the market and the producing environment is bound to bring prosperity."[18]

Later this fall, Sylvester Edwards is putting in five hundred trees at his Creekside Farm. "We want to put at least twenty trees of pawpaw around the fringes of the orchard," he says. In Panther, Mr. Bailey warned that if folks don't look after the pawpaw tree, it's going to be gone. Here in Kimball, Edwards is doing his part.

❧

The Hatfield and McCoy feud is probably the best-known bit of history associated with the West Virginia–Kentucky border. Beginning around 1865, the two families conducted revenge killings of each other's clans for nearly thirty years on either side of the Big Sandy and Tug Fork Rivers. And it just so happens that three McCoy brothers were tied to several pawpaw trees and shot to death by the Hatfield clan. The event has come to be known as the Pawpaw Tree Incident, and a Commonwealth of Kentucky historical plaque marks the site.

We visit the marker, near Buskirk, Kentucky, just over the river from Matewan, West Virginia. A number of pawpaw trees still grow in a thicket by the river. Tourists drive the Hatfield and McCoy Trails, stopping here to read the plaque and imagine the execution. Some may know, but many others likely wonder — what's a pawpaw?

❧

On July 8, 1755, during the French and Indian War, a group of Shawnees attacked the Draper's Meadows settlement near present-day Blacksburg, Virginia, killing at least five. Five more settlers were taken captive, including a pregnant Mary Ingles and her two sons. The Shawnee and their prisoners marched for a month back to their village at the banks of the Scioto and Ohio Rivers. On the third day, Ingles gave birth to a child. As a prisoner, Ingles was put to work sewing "check shirts" and making salt. It is one of the most notorious incidents of kidnapping on the early Appalachian frontier.

In October, Ingles made her escape. Along with an "elderly Dutch woman" she walked through more than eight hundred miles of wilderness. Their journey began near the mouth of Big Bone Creek — approximately fifty miles below Cincinnati — along the Ohio, Kanawha, and New Rivers. As she later told her son, Ingles and the Dutch woman subsisted on walnuts, hickory nuts, wild grapes, and pawpaws. Ingles was eventually reunited with her husband, and had four more children. She would live sixty more years, until she died at Ingles Ferry, Virginia — which she and William founded in 1762 — at the age of eighty-three. The New River along which Ingles Ferry was established, the same river Mary Ingles followed to her freedom, would have been lined with pawpaw trees, as would the floodplain, cleared for the new town and for planting corn. It's unknown whether Ingles ever again enjoyed pawpaws, walnuts, hickory nuts, or even grapes. For Ingles, they would have been the food of freedom, or a reminder of captivity.[19]

We drive across West Virginia on US 60, the Midland Trail. Much of the route follows the course Mary Ingles took as she and the old Dutch woman fled their Indian captors in Ohio. In Cedar Grove, in a lawn across the street from the historic Little Brick Church, an enormous pawpaw tree — forty feet or more — is dropping large ripe fruit. They're rolling down the hill, so I feel okay gathering several for the road. The pawpaws Mary Ingles found may have been just as good — but they were likely hard to enjoy.

Just after Kanawha Falls, we cross over a bridge and come upon a parklet and a roadside waterfall maybe twenty stories high. There isn't a tremendous flow of water, but the geology here is stunning — a near-perfect semi-circle has been cut from the hillside; it looks like a massive outdoor shower. To make the scene even better, pawpaw trees are growing in the woods. As we're walking out, I spot bright-orange fungi on a log in the water. It's chicken-of-the-woods (*Laetiporus sulphureus*), the one mushroom I'm able to positively identify — and the one mushroom I repeatedly come across while hunting pawpaws. Each year, when pawpaws are ripe, the chicken-of-the-woods is out. I add it to the late-summer list — pawpaw, goldenrod, and chicken-of-the-woods.

At camp, we cook up the mushroom with a little beer. We eat grilled cheese and avocado sandwiches (items we "foraged" at a grocery store on the Midland Trail). And for dessert we eat one of the best pawpaws we've had all year. I realize plant breeders name fruit with a bit more discretion, but we'll go ahead and call ours the Cedar Grove.

❧

In the morning, I speak with a roadside produce vendor near Summersville. He says there aren't pawpaws on this side of the mountain, but near Tioga, where he's from, they are plentiful: He ate so many as a kid he doesn't care for them anymore. But he still has fond pawpaw memories. "Now, my mom made a pawpaw pie back in the '80s — the best pie I ever ate in my life," he says. A niece had been visiting from Detroit, and while they were out riding four-wheelers, the pawpaws were out and ripe. "My mom made that pie — it had something else in it, I don't know whether she put lime in it — but that was the best pie I ever ate in my life."

He continues, "Now, down on the Elk River, they're a nuisance. But in this part of the country, they don't grow." Which is fine. Because Braxton County, to the Elk River — where my grandparents were raised — is where we're headed.

It's humid and overcast as we follow the Little Birch River toward Sutton. A billboard asks, DO YOU DIG GINSENG? From the interstate there were no signs of pawpaws, but on this narrow two-lane road the landscape returns to the tropical-looking composition we saw in southern West Virginia: namely, umbrella magnolia and pawpaw. It feels as though we've once again entered a dark, Appalachian rain forest.

We park on the brick-paved Main Street and go for a walk. A few people are outside doing yard work, and some folks are seated outside at the Cafe Cimino eating a late breakfast. There's a former Gothic Revival church that's been converted to an art studio. Other storefronts house a quilting shop, a co-working space, and in one window, a collection of sculptures. Courthouse Square honors Revolutionary War soldiers buried in Sutton as well as locals who served in World War I. The Elk Hotel — once owned by my father's cousin Willard — is quiet, though through the window I can see a drum set. The Draft House, at the corner of the hotel, is quiet as well. Three men are seated in a vacant lot, talking.

A few years ago, when I asked my grandmother, who was born and raised in Sutton, about pawpaws, she didn't recall eating them, but she quickly broke into *"Pickin' up pawpaws . . ."* At eighty-two there were many things that were hard for her to remember, things I wish I had thought to ask earlier.

My uncle Barney, however, can vividly recall one particular encounter with mountain food in West Virginia. Uncle Barney has spent most of his life in a wheelchair. So when, as a boy, his uncle asked him if he liked ramps, it seemed like a strange question. Of course he likes ramps, they're very helpful for getting in and out of buildings. The next morning, his uncle fixed him a plate of scrambled eggs and ramps — with a generous extra helping of the pungent wild leeks, on account of Uncle Barney's enthusiasm for ramps the night before. Barney ate the entire plate, but has never willingly eaten another ramp since.

Continuing to explore Sutton, we drive down Old Woman Run, which parallels the road's namesake body of water. Houses line the holler between the road and the creek, and the hills rise steep on either side of us. There is little light here. All of a sudden, at the Sutton welcome sign, pawpaws appear in the understory. Excited — these are the first I've seen in Sutton — we are checking the fruit for ripeness when a man calls out from his driveway, "I've been watching them there, they ain't quite ripe yet." The man was born near Sutton, he tells us, but moved to Centralia, West Virginia, when he was young. He remembers pawpaws growing in amazing abundance in the river bottom there. "My gosh, there was a whole grove of them, they was just standing there — pretty nice trees," he says. "We used to go down there when they get ripe and eat them things till our belly ache." He spent many years "working away." When he came back to Sutton years later, he says it had changed, many of the old-timers gone. In high school, he delivered groceries. "I knew everyone on Main Street." He still eats pawpaws, as he did when he was younger. I ask him about the Moores — he remembers Willard, and his daughter Susie, who now lives elsewhere.

My grandparents moved away from Sutton in the 1950s. My grandfather joined the army and was stationed in Germany (where my father was born), in Taiwan (where another son was born), and elsewhere. They'd return to West Virginia to visit for brief stretches, but would not live here again for any solid length of time. They'd left the Pawpaw Belt behind.

At Flatwoods, just outside Sutton, there's an Amish bulk foods store and an adjacent farmers market. The market has been getting calls for pawpaws, but has no one to bring them in. One man working here says he knew of pawpaws growing up in Clay County, "all along the riverbank, all down there." One of his grandmothers would make pawpaw breads and such things. "No recipes," he says, "just a dollop of this, dollop of that."

Leaving Sutton, I've learned that pawpaws were once quite familiar, that people knew where to find and cook with them; some continue to watch for their ripening. Although I can't say for certain whether or not my family ate pawpaws, with Braxton County firmly seated in the Pawpaw Belt, I know the odds are good that they did.

CHAPTER EIGHTEEN

CHEROKEE

I came to Cherokee, North Carolina, to look for pawpaws in the Great Smoky Mountains, to speak with tribal members here, and to learn if anyone still goes pawpaw pickin'. Ahead of my trip, I received mixed signals: "Probably lots people in Cherokee still eat pawpaw," I was told, but just as often, "Well, pawpaws aren't a big thing around here." So to sort it out I drive south, get a motel room at the junction of US 441 and the Oconaluftee River, and spend several days on the pavement and in the woods.

I meet Jerry Wolfe, a well-known tribal elder and Beloved Man (an official, and rare distinction among the Easter Band of Cherokee Indians), at the Museum of the Cherokee Indian. He recalls seeing a pawpaw tree just once. "I never tasted it," he says, "but they used to tell me it's good to eat." This particular tree was in the national park, and his late wife had spotted it while out driving. They stopped the car and got out to inspect the tree, its leaves, and its curious fruit. For whatever reason, his wife knew it when she saw it and called out, "Oh, a pawpaw!" "It's been quite a number of years," Jerry says, "but I haven't seen it since. I've looked for it, whenever I'm passing or fishing up in there, but I think it died."

Similarly, at the Oconaluftee Indian Village, a man told me, "Our aunts and uncles always talked about them. When I was a kid, I remember eating them, and now there's none around here." And at the Cherokee Farmers Market, I met a grower who was well acquainted with wild foods, including black cherry and elderberry, and even recalled making chestnut bread, but who had little to no experience with pawpaws.

David Cozzo works for the Eastern Band of the Cherokee Indians' Extension Office's RTCAR program—the Revitalization of Traditional Cherokee Artisan Resources. The program works to preserve and cultivate the natural resources needed for traditional Cherokee basket making and pottery, but also wild foods, including cutleaf coneflower, licorice root, and ramps. According to Cozzo, RTCAR's ethnobotanist, the only wild pawpaws in the area grow near old homesteads. "I don't see them in the woods on a regular basis," he says. "But people move stuff around a lot. And pawpaw is definitely one of those plants. So if they're here, they've been put here."

The idea of moving plants is nothing new. Native Americans have done this for centuries. The Iroquois, for example, are thought to be responsible for the pawpaw's presence in Ontario, Canada, and western New York. In 1610, French explorer Pierre-François-Xavier de Charlevoix wrote that the Iroquois of New France obtained pawpaw from the "country of the Eriez," an Iroquoian group living south of Lake Erie.[1] Indeed, when you look at the map of the pawpaw's native (or naturalized) range, the US Department of Agriculture's illustration shows the fruit all but disappearing north of Allegheny County, Pennsylvania. But pawpaw is common throughout Ohio, even north of its supposed terminus in Pennsylvania. Pawpaw grows in two of Pennsylvania's Lake Erie counties, as well as Ontario, Canada, and into western New York, where it is found, except in isolated cases, only in the state's lakeside counties — the former core sites of the Five Nations. Pawpaw is not the only example. Earlier records also show a concentration of black walnut occurring at Iroquois/Five Nations sites — a tree, like pawpaw, with a more southerly range.[2]

What impact did Native American plantsmen have on the stock of wild pawpaws? The following is pure speculation, but consider: Some of the best-tasting and most prolific pawpaw patches today are found in southern Ohio, where the *Journal of Heredity*'s prizewinning Ketter fruit originated, as well as several other notable fruits from the same contest. This is the same region where Ohio's ancient mound-building cultures are known to have eaten great quantities of pawpaws, and where, more recently, the Shawnee celebrated the Pawpaw Moon: *a;si-mini-ki-sTwa* (*a? · ši mini-ki · šәwa*).

⁂

David Cozzo first tasted pawpaws in eastern Kentucky and quickly came to love the fruit; he now has a pair of trees planted at his West Asheville home. When he first moved to western North Carolina, he lived out in the country near the tribal boundary. Once, while out exploring, he found a pawpaw grove growing beside a wet cove. He also heard of another isolated pawpaw patch growing on top of a mountain. Both sites, Cozzo believes, exist because someone planted them.

In the 1950s, anthropologist John Witthoft came to western North Carolina and conducted an ethnobotanical survey within the tribe's Qualla Boundary. Although *Asimina triloba* was in fact rare, and an insignificant food product, the Cherokee did use a specific term for the plant: *disûnki*. The word was an opaque proper name that could not be translated. *Disûnki* meant only "pawpaw."[3] However rare it may have become in the modern Cherokee landscape, not long ago it was known by at least a few.

⚬⟞⟝⟝

Historically, of course, the Cherokee Nation was much larger, expanding far beyond the current boundaries and beyond North Carolina. In places as far north as Kentucky, early European colonists noted the Cherokee using nets and ropes made from the inner bark of pawpaw. Further, archaeological digs have indicated that pawpaw fibers were likely used in clothing and footwear, as well. I check at the museum, and across the road, at the Qualla Arts and Crafts Mutual, to see if I can find traditional crafts that utilize the pawpaw's inner bark. On display are beautiful, intricate baskets made from white oak and river cane. But nothing with pawpaw, which couldn't be used if it couldn't be found.

Eve Miranda, who works with Qualla Arts, has never made a pawpaw basket, but her family has used pawpaws medicinally for many years. "We mix it with autumn olive and make a punch out of the combo to fight prostate cancer," she wrote to me in an email. "Both ripen in our area relatively close together in time and so it makes it easier to gather, processing one and then gathering and processing the other, then combining." Miranda lives farther east, outside the Qualla Boundary.

I am not the first to wonder about pawpaw cordage. Doug Elliott — an author, storyteller, naturalist, and humorist in Union Mills, North Carolina — also read about the pawpaw nets and baskets. When he and his wife, Yanna, found a broken pawpaw tree, "she snatched that bark right out of my hands and she amazed me as she crocheted those natural inner bark fibers into a beautiful round doily-like thing," Elliott writes on his website.

"That same crocheted piece she made that day is now hanging on a wall in our house which overlooks a pawpaw patch on the banks of Chalk Creek in Rutherford County, NC."[4] Elliott himself has also made pawpaw rope and even a pawpaw whip.

❧

Pawpaws are less common in the southern Appalachians than they are in the mountains of eastern Kentucky and West Virginia. But they are here. The Foxfire magazine and book series — based out of Rabun Gap, Georgia, not considerably far from the Qualla Boundary — included a chapter on wild food plants in their third volume, with several recipes for pawpaws: baked pawpaws ("bake in skins; serve with cream"), pawpaw pie, pawpaw bread ("add pawpaw pulp to nut bread. It gives bread a lovely rose-red color"), and pawpaw flump, or float ("beat up pulp with egg white and sugar like an apple float"). "All the plants mentioned grow easily in, and are native to, our part of the mountains, and were used traditionally in the ways noted," the editors state. "Any recipes that turned up whose actual use we could not verify with our older contacts were simply left out of the chapter."[5] Farther north, the Appalachian American Indians of West Virginia published a cookbook with a recipe for pawpaw pones — a cornpone mixed with pawpaw pulp and other dried fruits. But pawpaws are absent in the cookbooks of Johnnie Sue Myers, a Cherokee food writer who lives in Cherokee. Which, again, drives home that there aren't many pawpaws within the Qualla Boundary. Baskets can't be woven, pies can't be baked, if the materials don't exist.

❧

I travel next to Bryson City, North Carolina, a small, vibrant, Main Street community just ten miles west of Cherokee on the Tuckasegee River. I walk into a bakery and ask the owner-baker about pawpaws. It just so happens that she recently made pawpaw bread. She grew up in the area but never heard of the fruits until recently, when the woman who babysits her son gave her a bucketful. "I think it's more of a country thing," she says. "Stuff that you don't get at the grocery store and you don't really eat if you live in town, if you don't grow it."

Western North Carolina, when it comes to pawpaws, is similar to the rest of the country. American Indians are likely to know pawpaws with the same frequency as other rural Americans — if they're growing on their property, or where they hunt and fish, then they're likely to come across them and know about them. If not, chances are they won't. "To me it certainly represents that unobtainable fruit," says ethnobotanist Steven Bond. "It's kind of this charismatic fruit that people have heard about, they've read about, they're in songs, they're in stories, but very few people have ever had one." In Oklahoma, where so many Native Americans were forced to relocate, pawpaws were found in the easternmost sections of the state. The farther west tribes were relocated, the less likely they were to have pawpaws around. According to Steven, in places like rural Oklahoma, the fruit is hardly forgotten, even if nobody talks about it. "In fact, it's quite the opposite," he says. "Where you don't tell people about where you harvest pawpaws, because there's so damn few of them you don't want to be in competition." It's in this context that David Cozzo offers to take me to the biggest, and perhaps only, pawpaw patch on Cherokee lands in North Carolina.

Kituwa is the ancient Cherokee mother town. On this site, an earthwork mound built more than a thousand years ago still stands. Within the past decade, the property passed out of Cherokee hands, but recently the tribe has reacquired Kituwa, and its approximately three hundred acres are now a Cherokee community farm. Here, along the Tuckasegee River, is likely the only pawpaw patch within the Qualla Boundary.

Cozzo gives me a tour, shows me the hay grown for cattle, fields of corn, the October beans, and some of the largest cushaws and healthiest squash plants I've ever seen. Kituwa's current groundskeeper, a young man named Johi, approaches us on a tractor. We tell him what we're looking for, and he says jokingly, "Ain't no pawpaws down there." He's well aware of what pawpaws are. "He's a country boy," Cozzo offers as explanation. Johi adds, "It's a staple of the people. . . the people that's in touch and who know what to eat." (He then shows Cozzo a cellphone picture of a wild berry, for help with identification. "I was going to make jelly out of it," he says.)

Cozzo leads us to the river. There's an old homesite, evidenced by a brick chimney: It's all that remains of the home. But according to Cozzo, the plants growing here are evidence enough of former habitation. We're standing in a large grove of pawpaws. The patch begins near the chimney and spreads to the river and down the bank at least a hundred yards. Because it's found nowhere else in the boundary, Cozzo believes the original tree was planted here by human hands, or grew from a discarded seed. "Another thing is the spicebush," he says. "You almost always see this by an old cabin site. Almost always. And it's called feverbush, too. So this was medicine you kept by your door," he says, pointing to the spicebush, "and this was food you kept by the door," pointing to the pawpaw.

We look in the grass and shake several trees for ripe fruit, but the harvest is at least a week away. "Don't worry," Cozzo says to Johi, "Andy won't be around when the pawpaws are ripe."

— CHAPTER NINETEEN —

NORTH AND MIDWEST

James A. Little claimed to have planted the nation's first "regularly laid" pawpaw orchard in Danville, Indiana, more than a hundred years ago. "The trees had been planted in hills similar to techniques for growing melons," Little wrote. "Five or six seeds were protected by barrels, which provided shade to young seedlings for two years."[1] His methods remain sound today. I've come to Danville on a Midwest Tour de Pawpaw. And while I was unable to locate Little's former orchard, I did find a pawpaw tree in one Danvillian's backyard. The tree's owner was outside, and so I stopped and asked her about it. She'd never even eaten from it. I encouraged her to try some, and offered to eat the first bite.

As I was leaving town I noticed a few pawpaws growing along a creek. I pulled into a Laundromat adjacent to the property and went to investigate. Hanging from a branch was one of the largest wild pawpaws I'd ever seen. It was thrilling. After several years of traveling to commercial orchards, of tasting the best pawpaws known to exist, I was still excited about wild fruit. And here they were — five of them, actually, uniformly large — just free for the taking. Or so I thought.

A man walked toward me, chewing a mouthful of food, sandwich in hand. I can't recall if he exited from the Laundromat, a parked vehicle, or somewhere else. A few feet away, a punctured archery target was affixed to a straw bale. "What are you doing?" the man asked. I told him the trees had caught my interest and that I was hoping to take a few photos. "Okay," he said, "you can take a picture." He finished chewing and continued. "We get a lot of weirdos around here, so when you see someone walking around your property, you have to ask."

I assured him I wasn't a weirdo, just curious about pawpaws. I then asked if I could pick any ripe ones. "Do not pick the fruit," he said. The pawpaws had been promised to someone else. He circled me, kept eye contact, and then repeated himself. "Do not pick the fruit."

Pawpaws are popular in Indiana. And of all the Insert-Your-Home-State-Here Banana appellations, Indiana's is the best because it rhymes. The state even has a second nickname for the fruit: the Hoosier banana. In his 1905 treatise, James A. Little also wrote, "To us of central Indiana it is as familiar as the apple."[2] I'm aiming to find out why this is true of Indiana to a larger degree than neighboring states. Were there more and better pawpaws here? Did the settlers depend on wild foods for a longer period? Or is it simply because *Indiana banana* sounds so good?

In Miami County, Indiana — which is named for the tribe and whose members (a number of whom still reside in the state) once ate pawpaws — is the ghost town of Paw Paw. The town was platted in 1847, but when a newly built railroad was built, it did not extend to Paw Paw and the town was deserted.[3] Although the village of Paw Paw no longer exists in Miami County, Paw Paw Township, in Wabash County, boasts more than fifteen hundred residents. Pawpaws were noted and celebrated in these northern counties, as well as in southern Indiana. In 1859, a judge in the city of Evansville, Indiana, remarked that the pawpaw, "indigenous to our bottom-lands, yields more spirit to the bushel than any other fruit," and that he had "contracted for one thousand bushels to distil [into pawpaw brandy] the coming season."[4]

"It was a dainty with many pioneers and the taste still lingers," one historian wrote in the 1950s.[5] President Benjamin Harrison, who hailed from Indianapolis, Indiana, was a famous pawpaw lover. When someone in the president's circle suggested the pawpaw was susceptible to great improvement, President Harrison was irked. "The news offended the President," the *New York Advertiser* reported, "because he thought it an insinuation that the paw-paw of his native State was not the most nearly perfect fruit in the world, which he knew it was."[6] There was also an old proverb, reported by the *Courier-Journal* in 1892, which I just nearly learned firsthand: "Deprive a Hoosier of his favorite fruit and he's your enemy for life."[7]

‹༄›

In 1942, the book *Songs of the Rivers of America* attributed "Pickin' Up Pawpaws" to Indiana's Wabash River. Any number of rivers might have laid claim to the tune; nevertheless, to the Wabash it went. Like other American rivers, the Wabash was once a great highway. Between its port towns plied steamboats, flatboats, various fishing vessels, and houseboats. In *The Wabash* (1940), William E. Wilson's literary portrait of the river, he described the steamboat traffic and the colorful salutations boatmen gave one another. "'Hello' . . . they called . . . 'Watcha loaded with?' Then the captain — no matter what his home port, his destination, or his cargo might be — would step to the rail of the texas and wave his arm in response. 'Fruit and lumber'" came one such response, "'pawpaws and hooppoles!'"[8] It's quite an image: steamboats loaded with pawpaws en route to Indianapolis, Danville, Lafayette, and elsewhere.

Yet the Wabash and pawpaws go back even farther. During the Late Woodland period, a Native American group known as the Vicennes culture emerged in the Wabash Valley of present-day Indiana and Illinois. Evidence from sites near Terre Haute demonstrates a society whose economy was based on agriculture and supplemented by hunting and gathering. These Native Americans ate maize and beans, but also groundnut, hazelnut, wild cherry, and pawpaw.[9] Surely, as I have discussed earlier, such skilled horticulturalists understood plant genetics in certain terms. But what Indianan Jerry Lehman is doing with pawpaws today — using nothing more than traditional plant-breeding techniques — is on a whole different level.

I've come to Terre Haute — the self-proclaimed capital of the Wabash Valley — to meet Jerry Lehman, an amateur plant breeder of the highest order. A former president of the Indiana Fruit and Nut Growers Association, Jerry is the world's preeminent breeder of American persimmons (having picked up the work of Jim Claypool) and has been working with pawpaw for the past twenty years.

As a boy growing up on a farm in Berne, Indiana, Jerry spent all of his free time fishing on the Wabash. And while he went on to a successful career in electronics, Jerry never left agriculture too far behind, planting fruit trees wherever his work took him. After he retired, Jerry started accumulating property around his home, and planting trees. "You can take the boy off the farm," he says "but you can't take the farm out of the boy."

Jerry didn't want a mere cornfield. "I wanted to get into breeding, and I was thinking of working with apples." he says. "But the problem with apples is every state has a university that has got an apple-breeding program. And you can't compete with that kind of thing." Through the Indiana Nut Growers Association, Jerry met Jim Claypool, who was looking for someone to continue his work. "And I said, 'Here's something that I can do, and possibly contribute.'" And contribute he has. Jerry's work with American persimmons has led to some of the largest, sweetest *Diospyros virginiana* anyone has ever seen.

Although his first love is clearly persimmons — the road he lives on was even renamed Persimmon Lane — Jerry became interested in pawpaws too, and around twenty years ago he began growing them.

When it comes to breeding, Jerry says it's a crapshoot. "Just like Mom and Dad get together, [and] none of the kids look like Mom and Dad." Except that with plants, he says, when you select two because you want to get the size of one and the sweetness of another, what you wind up getting is the smallness of one and the lack of sugar of the other. This may in fact usually be the case. But Jerry has had some great success. For each of the past three years a tree of his has won the contest for largest pawpaw at the Ohio Pawpaw Festival. And each year, the fruit has come from the same tree, a hand-crossed selection he has grown from seed. He shows me the latest fruit from that tree, which weighs in at 24.4 ounces. It's a monster pawpaw, truly the largest I've ever seen (this time it's absolutely true). I ask how he gets such large fruit. "Genetics," he says. "It's the tree.

"There was a gentleman in Owensboro, Kentucky, his name was Sam Norris. He was an electrical engineer, but he was a horticulturalist by hobby," Jerry explains, "and he wanted to develop a seedless pawpaw, which is a great goal. It'll never happen — but, nonetheless, it needs to be tried." Jerry collected material from Sam Norris's experiments. "Are they seedless? No. But offspring seem to produce larger fruit. Something genetically has happened there to cause those plants to be larger-fruited."

Jerry is an exceptional plant breeder, but he faces the same obstacles that most pawpaw growers do: raccoons, opossums, and other nocturnal marauders. To keep the critters out, and to keep fruit from falling, Lehman ties mesh onion bags over the largest pawpaws on important trees, especially the one that regularly produces his prizewinning fruits. It's a low-tech solution that works. Jerry also has a vision for an efficient pawpaw processor: washing machines. He describes to me how it would work, which involves repurposing and retrofitting a drum.

"I have used a hand-crank honey extractor," Jerry explains. "But the problem with the honey extractor, with the straight walls, as soon as you start to spin, the pulp and the seed spread up the wall and come out the top — where the washing machine has the lip on top to retain it. The extractor, the centrifuge, would sling that pulp out. And I think it would be a little bit more efficient than other machines."

I see the potential and offer that someone could use the basic design of a washing machine to build something new. Jerry, the practical midwestern farm boy, says sure, but sees no reason to reinvent the wheel. "Or they could, again, take the washing machine, because the tubs are perfect," Jerry says. "I believe it'll work."

♔

I leave Persimmon Lane and head toward the Illinois-Wisconsin border, where I will meet a grower pushing the northern limits of commercial pawpaw plantings. My view from the highway includes occasional woodlots and various crops, but most often just seemingly endless fields of corn. I remember, though, that this country was once as much a frontier as the storied peaks and hollows of Appalachia. In the early 1900s, poet Arthur Bryant described an early-spring morning, and the unspoiled Illinois country as encountered by early settlers:

> The pawpaw opens its dusky flowers;
>   On green savannahs spreading far,
> Shows the varied phlox its brilliant star.
> The crane's harsh note is heard on high
> As he floats like a speck in the azure sky . . . [10]

When I see the exit sign for Paw Paw, Illinois, I'm caught off guard. I knew it was here but failed to realize it was directly on my route. I take the exit, which deposits me into a sea of corn; coming off the highway, it feels like going below the ocean's waves. As the fields give way to the village, one of the first homes clearly has town pride: They've planted a pawpaw tree in the center of their yard, and a hand-painted wooden sign identifies the specimen: PAW PAW TREE. There's just the one, leaning against the power lines. I imagine the owners, tired of folks not knowing what a pawpaw tree was, planted it and painted the sign. "There, no more excuses." Farther down the road, the municipal Paw Paw welcome sign even features a graphic of a pawpaw cluster, with one piece of fruit split open. POPULATION 870, ESTABLISHED 1882.

The Pawpaw Tracker publisher Ray Jones also visited here on his own pawpaw road trip. Alice Zeman, a local historian, told him that "the paw-paw grove, from which the town received its name, was one of the largest in the area and included about 2,000 acres southeast of the present site of the village."[11] Paw Paw Grove, as it was once known, was located along the historic Chicago Road stagecoach line, which itself was created from trails the Potawatomi Indians had long used. Their route, no doubt, intentionally crossed through the pawpaw grove.

The area around present-day Paw Paw, Illinois, belonged to the Potawatomi and other Native American tribes as late as 1833. A village in the county was known as Assiminehkon, which translated to Pawpaw Grove (which would become the Paw Paw I have just visited).[12] Farther north, in DeKalb County, there is another Paw Paw Township.

As elsewhere in the Pawpaw Belt, the fruit was once popular and beloved in rural Illinois. At the turn of the last century, pawpaws were sold at local markets. A Bloomfield, Illinois, newspaper reported in 1902: "Some of the grocery stores have displayed basketful of pawpaws. They are green paw-paws, which are not supposed to be particularly palatable or wholesome."[13] Even readers of the *Chicago Daily Tribune* were concerned with pawpaws. "Other calamities might be borne with comparative equanimity," the *Tribune* reported in 1913, "but it is woefully depressing to learn that the pawpaw crop is almost a total failure this year."[14]

Pulitzer Prize–winning poet, and Illinois native, Carl Sandburg was also a pawpaw lover. In the 1930s, Sandburg made pleas for breeding "bigger and better pawpaws."[15] "American citizens are going to grow more pawpaws, eat them, and like it," read a 1937 bulletin from Berkeley, California. "This is the decision of Carl Sandburg, poet, who announces he has made it his life's mission. He insists he is going to make America pawpaw conscious."[16] Sandburg even became president of another North American Pawpaw

Growers Association, a group unrelated to the current NAPGA, and about which little is known.[17]

Near the southern Illinois village of Iuka, a particular pawpaw patch was for decades known as the best in the region. Neal Peterson once told me the story of an elderly man who recalled visiting that patch as a teenager in the early 1900s. It was a Saturday, and with chores finished, he and a friend decided to steal a neighbor's wagon and mule, and headed for the pawpaw patch with a jug of whiskey. They ate pawpaws all afternoon, got drunk, fell asleep, and lost the mule. The incident passed, but the patch continued to be regarded by many as the best in Illinois. In the 1980s, the late Illinois plantsmen Joe Hickman knew these pawpaws, and referred to them as Mitchel. Although many experts believe the cultivar Mitchel, as it exists in the current trade, was mixed up somewhere along the line (due to mislabeled or mishandled scion wood, perhaps) and is not the same fruit Hickman and the mule-riding farm boys of Illinois once knew, the idea of Mitchel originated, and perhaps even still lives, in a century-old pawpaw patch somewhere near Iuka.

❧

In Chicagoland, at farmers markets and fruit meet-ups, wineries and food expos, Oriana Kruszewski is known for her several varieties of candy-sweet Asian pears; they were her first love as a grower. But Oriana also likes mangoes. As a native of Hong Kong, tropical fruits were common in her childhood, and mangoes were and remain the top. So when someone, at a North American Fruit Explorers meeting, introduced her to pawpaws as a poor man's mango, she was not impressed. "Not good," she says. "I tasted it — it's okay." Still, Oriana and a friend, diligent fruit explorers, continued to hunt pawpaws in the woods of Indiana and Illinois. They gathered hundreds of pounds of fruit, grew out seedlings, and still, she wasn't impressed. Finally, on a gathering trip in Paw Paw, Michigan, it hit her. "We shook a tree and it dropped on my head and splashed all around," she recalls. "So I tasted it — really sweet, really good. Perfect."

Now, at her northern Illinois farm near the Wisconsin border, she grows several varieties of pawpaw along with Asian pears, black walnut, pine nuts, and American persimmons, selling them every October at the Green City Market in Chicago.

When I arrive at her farm, it feels unseasonably cold and windy. Fruit has been slow to ripen everywhere, especially this far north. It's not a new problem. To extend the ripening window, Oriana has constructed a high tunnel. Inside are about a dozen pawpaw trees. If the fruits freeze on the tree, they'll be ruined. In about a month, Oriana will find out if the high tunnel worked and her efforts have paid off.

This is where data, Ron Powell's efforts to document cultivar performance in diverse conditions, would help northern growers like Oriana determine which varieties to grow. Another northern Illinois grower has reported that Shenandoah ripened in mid-October and was finished by the end of the month; that Overleese came next; and that Sunflower began at the end of October and lasted until mid-November, just after a frost. Other reports have indicated that Summer Delight is timed well for the northern Midwest — in Kentucky, it ripens as early as late July. And NC-1, a controlled cross selected by Ontarian Doug Campbell and popular in many regions, is especially suited to the North. For growers in the Upper Midwest and New England, or other cool regions, finding the earliest-ripening varieties will be important.

The trees themselves — never mind the fruit for a moment — have proven incredibly hardy. Oriana's pawpaws have survived winters of negative thirty-nine degrees Fahrenheit. She has even named one particularly tough tree Hardy Wonder.

Some years Oriana's trees haven't borne well, again due to late ripening. Once, while her husband was working in Cincinnati, Oriana asked him to swing by Jerry Lehman's orchard in Terre Haute and purchase every bit of fruit he could carry. They went on to sell every piece, nearly five hundred pounds' worth, at the Chicago market.

✧

Pawpaws are the largest edible fruit native to the United States — but they are Canada's fruit as well. Their Canadian range is limited to the county's Carolinian forests in southern Ontario. Although many of those wild places have been lost to development, a few folks are working to protect existing patches, and reintroduce pawpaws throughout the province.

As program coordinator for the Naturalized Habitat Network of Essex County and Windsor (NHN), Dan Bissonnette leads Project Pawpaw, an initiative dedicated to raising the awareness of pawpaws and its benefits. "We totally missed the boat on it," Bissonnette told the website *Our Windsor* in 2012, adding that "forgetting it once grew here is cultural amnesia."[18] In 2012, the NHN published *The Pawpaw Grower's Guide for Ontario*. The organization works to restore the species in native ecosystems, but also envisions pawpaws becoming a sustainable "local food resource."

There are a few wild patches of established pawpaws in southwest Ontario, but they are guarded secrets. I've spoken with several Ontarian pawpaw fans, and none has successfully located these elusive stands. In Toronto, Forbes Wild Foods, a wild foods purveyor, sells pawpaws to restaurants and farmers markets, but its supply is limited and its sources, understandably so, are rarely divulged. Luckily for Canada's pawpaw folks, an Ontario nursery has long grown seedling pawpaws and grafted cultivars.

Niagara-on-the-Lake's Grimo Nut Nursery sells more than six hundred pawpaw trees a year. "Already demand has raised the possibility of a commercial industry in Ontario," wrote journalist Sarah Elton in 2009. "When a local fruit grower lost her contract with Del Monte, Linda Grimo told her that pawpaws were the future. And Torrie Warner, who cultivates 60 acres of peaches, pears and quinces in the Niagara region, has already followed Grimo's advice; when the local fruit-canning plant and grape-juicing facility both shut down, he replaced some of his pear trees with pawpaws. He plans to sell to the public in four years."[19]

In 2013, Toronto resident and pawpaw enthusiast Paul DeCampo nominated the Carolinian pawpaw to Slow Food Canada's Ark of Taste. A box of Grimo's pawpaws was shipped to Turin, Italy, for the induction, and according to DeCampo, the fruit "blew people's minds."

⁂

After visiting with Oriana, I stay the night in Chicago. The next day, rounding Lake Michigan, I leave the interstate to get a look at the Great Lake. I'm at a township park, and as I walk toward the shore I can hear its ocean-like roar. I walk down a set of wooden steps, which descend from a parking lot through a brief bit of woods and down to the lake. I can see the sand of the beach ahead. And to my right, a pawpaw tree. I don't know why it's still true, but I'm a bit surprised each time I see one. I knew they were reported to be native to this area, but I really hadn't expected to find a pawpaw on the banks of Lake Michigan. But I do. It's a small sprout, about two feet tall, growing under taller hickories and other shade trees. Maybe I shouldn't be surprised. After all, I'm only a few miles from Paw Paw, Michigan. One road leading to the town is Paw Paw Road, which passes Paw Paw Lake as it follows Paw Paw Creek.

Corwin Davis selected superior pawpaws from the wilds of Michigan in settings similar to this. In autumn, pawpaw leaves turn a striking bright yellow. Because the fruit ripens later in Michigan – and autumn comes sooner – fruit would still be on the trees when the change occurred, which made finding the trees, and then the fruit, easier for Davis.

Davis spent more than thirty years exploring the woods, propagating, disseminating material, and experimenting with growing pawpaws. By most accounts, he was a fun, eccentric pawpaw grower (I recall Colleen Anderson's "off the round" comment); I've been told he played the fiddle at least one NNGA meeting, and promoted, with humor and sincerity, the most unusual pollination techniques. I would have enjoyed meeting him.

Davis did most of his pawpaw exploring near Bellevue, Michigan, located at the northern edge of the tree's native range. He shipped plant material across the United States, including California ("These people will eat anything that will hold still long enough"), as well as France, Spain, Italy, Australia, and New Zealand.[20] And yet he was surprised, and perhaps a bit disappointed, that so few others were in the woods selecting pawpaws. "Inquires and orders for trees and seed come from the Paw Paw's best habitat," he wrote in 1983. "This is 100 miles south of here. Indiana, Illinois, Ohio, West Virginia, Kentucky and Tennessee have far more Paw Paws per square mile than Michigan. Yet orders from these states are more numerous than any other area. It makes one wonder if anyone is out looking for superior clones."[21] Of course, in those states pawpaw culture (and eaters) had persisted, so it makes sense that orders for grafted material and seed wood would be high. But Davis made a good point. His selections – cultivars including Davis, Prolific, Taylor, and Taytwo – as well as subsequent crosses and seedlings of his material, are still among the best. Considering they all originated in a limited geographic area, it means either that Michigan's wild pawpaws are for some reason superior to others, or that there are equally good pawpaws waiting to be discovered, and bred – in at least twenty-six states. "Let us put papaws on the table of everyone possible," Davis wrote.

"Us old folks can not stay around forever. If we are to progress in any endeavor, it is the young ones that will have to carry on."[22]

At Paw Paw Lake I find a small grove of trees, and even some fruit hanging from one tree. In Paw Paw itself, however, grapes are king. There are more than one hundred wineries in Michigan, and Paw Paw's St. Julian Winery is the state's oldest, having made wine in the town since 1936. But there is an overlap between pawpaws and grapes. Paul DeCampo has noticed that the range in which pawpaws thrive in Canada coincides with the province's grape-growing range. So at the fringe of the two plants' growing range, they must share space. Years ago, pawpaw rope was the preferred fiber for binding grapevines. "In the Pays du Vaux, straw is used for this purpose," observed German explorer Prince Maximilian of Wied-Neuwied in 1832, "on the Rhine, red osiers (*Sali purpurea*); in the gardens, the inner bark of the linden tree; [and] in North America, the inner bark of the pawpaw tree (*Annona triloba*), which, however, must first have been soaked in water, like flax."[23]

I don't find any pawpaw wine (made from *Asimina triloba*, that is), but I do see a few trees, including a pair of large ones at Paw Paw High School. It was one of these trees that dropped a perfect one on Oriana's head.

✥

Zingerman's Deli in Ann Arbor is a deli, sure, but it's also an artisanal food emporium, a showcase of locally made cheese, charcuterie, Michigan-raised fruits, vegetables, meats, and dairy. They make sandwiches and salads, but are also eager for visitors to try various types of imported and Michigan-made products. They even publish books on food and culture. It's a place, I've been told, where the employees feel like they're part of a family — a friend of mine worked there through college and still swoons at the mention of Zingerman's. They've got sister enterprises, including Zingerman's Roadhouse, a restaurant, and Zingerman's Creamery, a gelato company. So naturally, Michigan's most distinctive native fruit, the pawpaw, belongs here.

Around town, University of Michigan students don heavy boots and scarves, flannel shirts and knit caps. Whereas pawpaws are a late-summer fruit in the South, up north they're an autumn treat. Rhode Island's Rocky Point Farm even hosts an annual pawpaw event called Pumpkins and Pawpaws.

My host, a grad student at the University of Michigan, has rallied her friends to meet us at a local bar. We've brought pawpaws along – one of Jerry Lehman's largest (about the size of a grapefruit) and, for comparison, a wild one from Missouri. After a couple of rounds, at least a dozen friends have arrived. I place the pawpaws on the table as a centerpiece and attempt to give the fruit's condensed history. Then finally it's time to slice them open.

One friend, who is from Nigeria, is not impressed. "That's the smallest pawpaw I've ever seen!" he says. In Nigeria, the word *pawpaw* means one thing: papaya. I've brought Mr. Lehman's fruit tonight because it's one of the largest pawpaws anyone will likely ever encounter, only to have it mistaken for a tiny, sorry excuse for a papaya.

ↄⅉↄ

Marc Boone, a recently retired pipefitter, has for decades been growing the most unusual fruits hardy enough to survive Michigan's winters. In addition to apples – heirloom cultivars from the United States and Russia – he grows plums, pears, and other novel fruits. Marc discovered pawpaws by accident. At a point when he was reading lots of Brazilian literature, he read one novel in which two characters are fighting for the same lover. They are persuaded, however, to put aside their differences and share a jackfruit (which is the world's largest tree fruit, bigger than most watermelons, and is found in the tropics). The jackfruit indeed changes their minds. This reminded Boone of a temperate tree, the pawpaw, that he'd read was related to jackfruit. It's not true, but by the time he found out, he'd already added several hundred pawpaws to his orchard.

Boone eats most of the fruit he grows. He sells some occasionally – and his dogs leap into the trees to eat even more – but he's more of an experimenter than an entrepreneur. However, his aunt once urged him, repeatedly, to sell his pawpaws to Zingerman's Creamery. She called Zingerman's and told them the man growing them lived just a few miles away. His aunt saw the promise pawpaws held for both the buyer and seller, and eventually the two sides came together.

Boone sells his pawpaws whole to Zingerman's, whose staff originally processed the fruit by hand. Recently, Zingerman's has collaborated with Michigan State University's Dennis Fulbright, who developed an automated hopper for separating seeds from pulp (separating skins, however, is still done manually). The hopper was designed by an Italian firm that has developed similar machines for processing chestnuts, among other crops. Because of this machine, an informal co-op of pawpaw growers has coalesced around MSU. This infrastructure (and the organization of existing horticultural groups) has allowed pawpaws greater exposure and marketability: They've even been sold at Whole Foods stores in Michigan.

Since the folks at Zingerman's buy tons of fruit — nearly all of the Boone's harvest, and the fruit of other growers — they amass an impressive stockpile of pulp, and their Paw Paw Gelato is currently available all year. Ice cream shops in other states also make pawpaw ice cream — some have for nearly a decade — but only at Zingerman's is it available year-round. The feat is a pawpaw first. But it's one that could easily be repeated elsewhere. Boone has no helping hands on the farm. His trees — low-maintenance natives — require so little attention that he's able to produce several hundred pounds of fruit for a single buyer with ease.

Under each tree, in rows, Boone lays three to five feet of straw to cushion the pawpaws' fall. (A Kentucky grower also reported using hay — left over from her horses — in the pawpaw orchard. She took precautions a step farther and covered the hay with sheets. The fruit was neither bruised nor dirty). Boone has a hay field, so it doesn't cost him much. With many fruit trees, mulching this high can be a problem. Especially in winter, layers of straw invite voles, which are attracted by the warmth but then stay to eat the tree's bark. But Kentucky State University has observed that voles do not damage pawpaw trunks, and that it's likely thanks to the trees' acetogenin compounds.[24] As an added bonus, straws and other mulches build the organic matter of the orchard's soil.

In season, Marc walks the rows twice a day, dragging a large plastic bin by a long rope, picking up pawpaws from the straw beds. Since the fruit will ultimately be turned into ice cream, an occasional scratch or bruise is less of an issue than if their destination was a produce stand. Boone's fruit won't be mailed across the country, either, so it doesn't require the careful selection — for optimum ripeness — performed at Jim Davis's Deep Run Orchard. Other than delivering them to the Creamery, this is all the work that the pawpaws require once they've begun to drop.

I walk with Boone, picking pawpaws from the straw beds and checking the fruits in the trees, which are largely far from ripe. Then we come upon an enormous pawpaw, one that I swear rivals Jerry Lehman's entry. Marc remains cool but allows me to take it with me to the Ohio festival, and enter it in the contest.

In the morning, before leaving Ann Arbor en route to the festival, I need to fulfill my mission to grab a pint of Zingerman's Paw Paw Gelato. There is already a long line at the bakery, folks getting coffee, pastries, breakfast. The label is playful and, in my opinion, captures the spirit of pawpaw enthusiasts. Zingerman's had requested that Marc supply them with slightly riper pawpaws, preferring the stronger caramel flavor. The dark-hued gelato bears this out.

In a peculiar way, I feel let down. Not by the gelato itself, which is excellent, but from the experience. I'm not sure what I was expecting — more fanfare; neon lights pointing to the elusive, one-of-a-kind, only-at-Zingerman's Paw Paw Gelato; streamers and confetti dropping when I spotted it — but instead it's just a regular pint of pawpaw gelato alongside all the other flavors. Nothing out of the ordinary. But then I realize this is exactly what the fruit's ardent supporters have long envisioned: that pawpaws would become part of American agriculture, alongside apples, pears, squash, and tomatoes; that pawpaw gelato or ice cream would be no more exotic than peach or strawberry. After all, there were once Pawpaw Moon celebrations; we feasted on them on the frontier; we relied on them in lean times but more often ate them just because we loved them; we named rivers and islands, bayous, and coves for them, even towns from Virginia to Kansas. Shouldn't pawpaws be ordinary, too?

EPILOGUE

I end where I began: at the Ohio Pawpaw Festival. The weather, as I've come to expect, is great. I enter Marc Boone's fruit in the largest-pawpaw contest, but it does not take first place. Jerry Lehman has won again.

In the few years since I first learned about pawpaws, they've made huge strides. More and more cookbooks and gardening books include the fruit and tree; they can be found at more and more farmers markets, from New York City's Union Square to Big Stone Gap, Virginia. A Louisville-based chef plans to include pawpaw flan in his upcoming cookbook; and at the 2014 International Biscuit Festival, in Knoxville, Tennessee, a pawpaw pecan buttermilk biscuit (topped with Tennessee whiskey and sorghum caramel!) was a runner-up for the People's Choice Award. If a fruit can be hip, pawpaws are. Pawpaws are included in municipal tree sales and giveaways — from New York to Missouri — for habitat restoration and improving urban tree canopies. Festivals now occur not only in Ohio but also Rhode Island, Maryland, Virginia, and Delaware. And the North Carolina Paw Paw Festival has grown to an annual attendance of well over a thousand. In Iowa, the recently planted Quad City Food Forest included numerous pawpaws among its ninety fruit and nut trees, and at my home in Pittsburgh, young trees can be found in several community gardens and on restaurant menus. Each season, several breweries announce the release of their first-ever pawpaw beer, from the Paw Paw Berliner Weisse of Full Pint Brewing (Pennsylvania) to the Paw Paw French Saison of the Missouri Ozarks' Piney River Brewing. Durham's Fullsteam Brewery has returned to the fruit, this time with a hoppy pawpaw ale. Pawpaw gelato and ice cream remain fixtures at Zingerman's and Ellen's Homemade, but has also appeared at The Bent Spoon in Princeton, New Jersey, and elsewhere. Jeni Britton Bauer (of Columbus, Ohio's Jeni's Spendid Ice Creams) even made a batch of pawpaw ice cream for a recent Slow Food Columbus farm dinner.

We've seen this attention before — recall the *Journal of Heredity*'s contest; the efforts and ingenuity of horticulturalists throughout the last century; even past presidents and countless poets who have sung the pawpaw's praises, to no avail. The national media has turned its attention to pawpaw off and on for decades — from *ABC World News* to the *Washington Post* and *NPR* — often predicting that pawpaws could be the next big thing. And during that same time period, the fruit's biggest promoters — Neal Peterson and Kirk Pomper, Jerry Lehman and Ron Powell, to name just a few — have been waiting, and working, wondering when it might actually happen.

With the rise of the local food movement, the awareness of the importance of native plants, the search for a return to authentic, regional cuisines, and the desire for organic, sustainable agriculture, the current cultural climate might finally be the one in which pawpaw breaks through. Still, for there to be a national awakening to pawpaws, we're going to need a lot more fruit.

Wild pawpaws are abundant. But in an urbanized nation, most Americans don't have access to the fruit. Which puts me in danger of making the same wishful proclamation that James A. Little made in 1905. But since it's still true, here I go: If Americans want pawpaws, folks will need to start setting them out in orchards, and growing them like any other commercial fruit.

Then again, what if the current excitement over pawpaws is a bubble? What if all this attention leads to large investments, and eventually a bust? It would surely mean heartbreak to some. But for many folks — whose families who have eaten pawpaws for generations — a pawpaw bust won't mean too much. The annual tradition of pawpaw pickin' will continue.

Or what if all this attention is a negative thing? Neal Peterson says, "We aren't there yet, but the bandwagon effect is ultimately a destructive influence. My vision is for something that's very sustained and is absolutely as solidly a part of what we grow and eat as apples and pears. Not that it'll ever be that level, and it doesn't have to be." Something sustained, something solid. "Are we going to see them at Walmart, fresh?" asks ethnobotanist Steven Bond. "Probably not. And if they ever do find their way to Walmart, fresh, they probably won't be any good, just like any of the other damn fruit there."

Will pawpaw become the niche crop that replaces tobacco? Maybe. Maybe not. As a staple for small growers tobacco still appears to be on its way out, but hemp is already making a comeback in states like Kentucky. If hemp turns out to be a winning cash crop for small farmers, it will likely limit the extent to which they add pawpaw trees as a high-earning, niche crop. But perhaps the emerging farmscape will look even different, with no one single crop replacing tobacco. Perhaps a diversified farmscape would be more beneficial — for the environment, for the market, and for consumers — one in which corn and hemp, apples and sorghum, goats and pawpaws, all share space.

Regardless, there's still a lot of education to be done. The state of Ohio's 2014 official travel guide — a magazine available at every rest stop on Ohio's turnpike and interstates — includes a list of the state's symbols: the state tree, flower, wildflower, bird, and so on, and of course, Ohio's official state native fruit, the pawpaw, with a color image accompanying each symbol. But for the pawpaw, they printed a cut papaya.

The state of Ohio is in good company. Ahead of Thanksgiving, 2014, the *New York Times* created a wonderful online feature listing a dish that evoked each of the fifty states. For West Virginia, the *Times* chose a pawpaw pudding. The feature included wonderful, original illustrations accompanying each dish. For the pawpaw pudding, however, the illustration included was, again, that of a papaya, not a pawpaw. The *Times* issued a correction, and even a new illustration, but it fell a little short.

On April 2, 2014, First Lady Michelle Obama planted a pawpaw tree at the White House. Working with the founders of FoodCorps and students from DC-area elementary schools, Ms. Obama planted "fruits and vegetables, including collard greens, rhubarb, onions, strawberries, raspberries, and a new addition, a paw paw tree."[1] But just one. Hopefully there are plans for an additional pawpaw tree, because without it, the lone tree is unlikely to bear fruit.

⁂

In 2012, Kirk Pomper became associate research director at KSU. He maintains a 25 percent research appointment working with pawpaws, but the time he can devote to *Asimina triloba* has been greatly diminished. Much of KSU's pawpaw research is now directed through Sheri Crabtree. She is one of the world's foremost experts in pawpaw, but to put the development of an entire crop on one person's shoulders is an incredible weight. So Kirk and Sheri often partner with Ron Powell, Jerry Lehman, the Ohio Pawpaw Growers Association, and others. Meanwhile, the germplasm collection remains intact, and KSU's future cultivars continue to be observed, and await release.

In 2014, Neal Peterson did not attend the Ohio Pawpaw Festival. He doesn't always attend, but neither did Ken Drabik, Nate Orr, or Lance Beard. It's expensive to drive fresh pawpaws from Maryland to Ohio. It promotes pawpaws, which is great, but at this point people know. Still, it feels strange that none of Jim Davis's pawpaws were sold at the festival.

For some, that's fine. Chris Chmiel created the festival to celebrate southern Ohio's bounty of wild pawpaws, and he is clearly succeeding in that mission. But for others, improved pawpaws are essential to the fruit's future. And despite their growing popularity, there just aren't enough folks growing pawpaws. That is changing, but growing fruit trees, especially pawpaws, takes time.

❧

Neal Peterson never became a commercial pawpaw producer. He continues to speak and promote pawpaws, he works with nurseries and consults with farmers. And because of a growing demand and interest in pawpaws abroad, Neal is pursuing trademarks and patents for his cultivars to be introduced in Europe and Japan.

Although he does not produce fruit in an orchard, Neal's breeding work continues. For the past decade he has crossed *Asimina triloba* with several of the Florida pawpaws — including *A. obovata* and *reticulata* — as ornamental landscape plants. The Florida species have inferior fruit — small, seedy, and less sweet — but exceptional, large-lobed blooms. Peterson's hybrids are cold-hardy, shrub-like, with flowers ranging from maroon to white, and some with blended whirls. And a few of them produce fruit that's not too bad either. They're striking, novel plants. The hybrids Neal is now observing are third-generation, and may soon be released — but only if Neal finds a selection that holds up under propagation.

Meanwhile, a large organic farm has been working with Neal, exploring how to plant pawpaw cultivars for market production. The farm is located at the foothills of Virginia's Blue Ridge Mountains, and in the woods surrounding it pawpaws abound. In fact, the farm has sold these wild pawpaws at farmers markets for several years, earning up to twelve dollars a pound. Still, the farm sees potential in the cultivars, and last spring planted several hundred grafted trees. The pawpaws have struggled through their first summer, perhaps from the heat, direct sun, or a lack of water. The farm may seek further advice from Neal Peterson, from KSU, or from the various fruit growers associations familiar with pawpaws. But if they can survive these first few years, the pawpaws will likely thrive. After all, the trees have done a good job of it here for quite some time.

ACKNOWLEDGMENTS

I want to thank all of the friends and family who have encouraged and supported me during the research and writing of this book. I must especially
thank Erika, for believing in me and this project, and my parents, Barbara
and Charles. Thank you to those who took the time to read early versions of
the book and provide feedback, including Zach and Melissa; to Jill; and to
Ad, for feedback and coaching through the entire process. I am grateful to
every person who spent time talking pawpaws with me, including everyone
quoted in this book and the many who are not, but especially Derek Morris,
Ron and Terry Powell, Kirk Pomper, Sheri Crabtree, Jerry McLaughlin, Jim
and Donna Davis, Colleen Anderson, Dale Brooks, Jerry Dedon, Oriana
Kruszewski, David Cozzo, Steven Bond, Steve Corso, Matthew Rowley,
Robert Brannan, Wynn Dinnsen, and Jerry Lehman. I want to thank the
many terrific librarians and staff at the Carnegie Library of Pittsburgh
(especially the Main and Allegheny branches, and the Interlibrary Loan
department); and Marta Ramey of the Briggs Lawrence County Public
Library in Ironton, Ohio. A big thanks to John Ruskey and Mark "River"
Peoples, and to Paul Hartfield, for piloting me down the Mississippi. Thank
you to Michael W. Twitty, for early encouragement and direction; to Neal
Peterson, who has been a patient teacher and guide; and to Lisa Roney and
the many professors, editors, and teachers I have learned from. I want to
thank Chelsea Green, and specifically Michael Metivier, for bringing this
project to fruition.

Thank you to Scott Bauer of the USDA, Sue Ann Herald, Neal Peterson,
Bob Peterson, Dennis Hager, and Ron Powell, for your outstanding photo
contributions; and to Lynn Stanko of the National Agricultural Library.

Thanks to all the friends who have joined me at the Ohio Pawpaw
Festival; to Jon, for accompanying me on several tours de pawpaw; to Isaac
Wiegman, for suggesting I check out some festival in Ohio; and to James,

Dom, Gina, Laura, Paul, Jessica, and the many other friends who gave me shelter during my travels.

I would also like to thank all 137 backers of my 2012 Kickstarter campaign for their support that sent me way down yonder, with special thanks to Tori Becker, Gus Lehnerer, Jim Doyle, Justin Geibel, Ed Fore, Claudia Quartana, Sooze Bloom deLeon Grossman, Dwight Bishop, and Mom; to Erika, for shooting the video; to Tim, for website assitance; and to Nina, for lending her expert video-editing skills to the effort.

Finally, thanks to all the pawpaw pickers, growers, writers, and pontificators who have made this unique fruit a compelling part of American culture. There were many pawpaw people before me, and there are many I have yet to meet.

— APPENDIX 1 —

PAWPAW ICE CREAM

Vanilla, walnuts, and other flavors and ingredients work well with pawpaw. But if this is your first batch, I would encourage you to try it plain and to let the pawpaw stand on its own. The following is my basic pawpaw ice cream recipe:

2 cups pawpaw pulp (or more, if you have it)
1 cup sugar
2 cups cream
2 cups milk

Combine the pawpaw and sugar. Stir in the cream and milk. Pour the mixture into an ice cream maker and freeze according to the manufacturer's directions.

— APPENDIX 2 —

A SELECTION OF PAWPAW NURSERIES

This listing is not exhaustive, but should be a starting place for those looking to grow pawpaws.

ENGLAND'S ORCHARD AND NURSERY

2338 Highway 2004

McKee, KY 40447-9616

nuttrees@prtcnet.org

606-965-2228 or 606-493-8239

Cultivars: Davis, Overleese, Rebecca's Gold, Halvin's Sidewinder, Summer Delight, and others. Also sells pawpaw seed from Jerry Lehman's Indiana breeding orchard.

NOLIN RIVER
NUT TREE NURSERY

797 Port Wooden Road

Upton, KY 42784

john.brittain@windstream.net

www.nolinnursery.com

270-369-8551

Cultivars: Allegheny, Shenandoah, Susquehanna, Wabash, Rappahannock, Potomac, KSU-Atwood, NC-1, Overleese, Sunflower, Greenriver Belle, PA Golden 1, Sue, and others.

GRIMO NUT NURSERY
979 Lakeshore Rd, RR3
Niagara-on-the-Lake, Ontario, Canada ON L0S 1J0
nut.trees@grimonut.com
www.grimonut.com
905-934-6887
Grafted and seedling pawpaws.

EDIBLE LANDSCAPING
361 Spirit Ridge Lane
Afton, VA 22920
800-524-4156
info@ediblelandscaping.com
www.ediblelandscaping.com
Cultivars: Peterson Pawpaws, Mango, Sunflower, Prolific, NC-1, and others.

NASH NURSERIES
4975 Grand River Road
Owosso, MI 48867
info@nashnurseries.com
www.nashnurseries.com
517-651-5278
Cultivars: Peterson Pawpaws and others.

FORREST KEELING
88 Forrest Keeling Lane
Elsberry, MO 63343
info@fknursery.com
www.fknursery.com
573-898-5571
Cultivars: Peterson Pawpaws, Mango, NC-1, Overleese, PA-Golden, Sunflower, Wells, and others.

STARK BROS.
P.O. Box 1800
Louisiana, MO 63353

info@starkbros.com
www.starkbros.com
800-325-4180
Cultivars: Mango, NC-1, Prolific, SAA Overleese, Sunflower, and others.

ONE GREEN WORLD
PO Box 881
Mulino, OR 97042
www.onegreenworld.com
877-353-4028
Cultivars: KSU-Atwood, Sunflower, Overleese, Mango, Taylor, NC-1, Peterson Pawpaws, and others.

HIDDEN SPRINGS NURSERY
170 Hidden Springs Lane
Cookeville, TN 38501
hiddenspringsnursery@hotmail.com
hiddenspringsnursery.com
931-268-2592
Cultivars: KSU Atwood, Mango, Mary Foos Johnson, NC-1, Mitchell, Wells, Overleese, and others.

OIKOS
PO Box 19425
Kalamazoo, MI 49019-0425
www.oikostreecrops.com
Seedling pawpaws.

SHADOW NURSERY
254 Shadow Nursery Road
Winchester, TN 37398
shadownursery@aol.com
www.shadownursery.com
931-967-6059
Cultivars: Mango, Hilcrest, Prolific, Sunflower, Wells, Peterson Pawpaws, and others.

— APPENDIX 3 —

CULTIVAR PROFILES AND IMPRESSIONS

The following is not a comprehensive list of all pawpaw cultivars, but rather a collection of impressions and data from some of the country's leading pawpaw growers. The listed cultivars were chosen because they are considered exceptional, and for their availability in the trade. These profiles are provided to give the backyard grower and the future orchardist some guidance in selecting which pawpaws to grow. The information below has been gathered from personal conversations and correspondence with growers, as well as the websites of quoted nurserymen, and from the published research of Kentucky State University (KSU notes: "Fruit size categories of small, medium, and large are <100 g, 100 to 150 g, and >150 g, respectively").

Some cultivars are patented, trademarked, and sold only through licensed nurseries. Others are openly traded.

If you are currently growing pawpaw cultivars, consider joining and reporting your impressions and data to the North American Pawpaw Growers Association, or a corresponding state chapter. There are also a number of horticultural organizations that share and report on the culture of growing pawpaws, from the North American Fruit Explorers and the California Rare Fruit Growers, to the Northern Nut Growers Association and various state organizations.

ALLEGHENY
A Neal Peterson selection that is smaller than others, with fruits typically less than eight ounces. "Flavor sweet, rich, a hint of citrus," Peterson reports.

"Texture medium firm, smooth. Flesh color yellow." Fruit size is reported to benefit from thinning. Percent seed by weight is about 8 percent.

ARK-21

"It is just like a banana," says Jerry Dedon. "It is so sweet and so mild. And it's nothing but a seedling that LSU got from Petit Jean Mountain, Arkansas. Grew wild in the woods." Dedon says it was his favorite variety growing at LSU's Regional Variety Trials. Also a favorite of LSU's Charles Johnson.

DAVIS

A Corwin Davis selection, found growing in the wild in 1959. KSU reports "medium sized fruit, up to five inches long; green skin; yellow flesh; large seed; ripens first week of October in Michigan." Derek Morris says, "Good quality, medium to large, light-yellow-fleshed fruits that keep fairly well but fruits are not as large as Overleese or Sunflower. Not much yellowing on skin."

GREENRIVER BELLE

Original tree found growing in the wild near the Green River in Hart County, Kentucky, selected by Carol Friedman "for large and luscious fruits," reports Nolin River Nut Tree Nursery. "I think of it has having a very bright flavor, and I know several locals that this one is the hands-down favorite," says Derek Morris. "Fruits are almost identical to PA-Golden in size and shape though not quite as productive. Unfortunately, not very large-fruited, rather seedy, and fruits do not keep for long before losing quality." Ron Powell reports little to no *Phyllosticta*. "My favorite because of its firmer texture," he says. "Some have reported a cinnamon aftertaste."

HALVIN'S SIDEWINDER

A selection from the wild by Tyler and Danae Halvin in Iowa. Cliff England reports: "Fruit is eight to fourteen ounces. Great flavor (very sweet, no aftertaste), has a hint of pineapple flavor. Original tree was growing as an understory tree and was approximately forty feet tall. Stated to be the largest native pawpaw fruit to be found in southwestern Iowa, not far from Bedford."

KENTUCKY CHAMPION

Woody Walker describes the Kentucky Champion as "the Big Daddy" of the pawpaw forest. He discovered it in 2009 in Madison County. According to Cliff England, "It's a good candidate for climates that are challenged for growing-degree-days... The seed-to-pulp ratio is good (about 8.3 percent). The skin is attractive and durable; it resists dark spots, bruising, and other discoloration. The pulp is firm and golden-orange in color with a melon-orange flavor and pleasant lingering aftertaste. It's sweet with a subtle tartness that's been likened to pineapple or raspberry." This cultivar will have limited availability for the next several years.

KSU-ATWOOD

In 2009 KSU-Atwood became the first cultivar to be released from Kentucky State University's breeding program. It is large, round, and mango-flavored. Ron Powell describes it as an "excellent-tasting and clean fruit," with very little *Phyllosticta*. The fruit was selected at KSU's research farm as a seedling from Maryland. "The release is named for Rufus B. Atwood, who served as president of Kentucky State College (now university) from 1929 to 1962," KSU reports. "Fruit: greenish-blue skin, yellow-orange flesh, few seeds. Fruit size and flavor medium; averaging 120 g/fruit and 150 fruit per tree at KSU."

LYNN'S FAVORITE

"An excellent-producing tree that bears heavy every year," according to Ron Powell. "Thin, clean, smooth skin, not susceptible to *Phyllosticta*." Won Best Fruit at the Ohio Pawpaw Festival in 2014. Selected from the Corwin Davis orchard. KSU reports, "Yellow fleshed, large fruit; ripens 2nd week of October in [Michigan]."

MANGO

Mango was a wild tree growing in Tifton, Georgia, and selected by Major C. Collins in 1970. KSU reports vigorous growth. Derek Morris says, "Fast growing and large tree, very productive with medium to mostly large fruits. Seed to flesh ratio is good. I note leaves slightly smaller than most others." Jerry Dedon says, "It was real good . . . but that rascal will deteriorate fast. And I mean it will get just like a water balloon." Reports from North

Carolina indicated the same. However, these qualities may give Mango an advantage in processing: "Because of the rather large size, fewer seed[s] than many, and its softer flesh, [it] may be easier/quicker to pulp out," Morris reports. And some do report that it tastes like mango.

MARIA'S JOY

A cross of Davis x Prolific made by Jerry Lehman of Terre Haute, Indiana. Won Best Fruit at the Ohio Pawpaw Festival in 2012. "An excellent-tasting fruit but not yet available in the trade," says Ron Powell. Several cultivars from Jerry Lehman's breeding orchard await release, perhaps including the perennial Largest Fruit winner at the Ohio Pawpaw Festival.

MARY FOOS JOHNSON

This cultivar was selected from the wild in Kansas by Milo Gibson. The seedling was donated to North Willamette Experiment Station in Aurora, Oregon, by Mary Foos Johnson. KSU reports, "Large fruit; yellow skin; butter-color flesh; few seeds; ripens first week of October in [Michigan]."

NC-1 (OR CAMPBELL'S #1)

Perhaps the most ornamental pawpaw tree. Its large leaves are a dark, near-blue green. Derek Morris reports fruits that resemble Overleese in quality, "being mostly large and rounded with great seed to flesh ratio and they maintain quality longer than many others." However, it may not be as productive as other varieties.

NC-1 produces quality fruit in the South, but is especially suited to colder climates, ripening in September in Ontario — very early for the northern regions. Which is fitting: A hybrid seeding of Davis and Overleese, it was selected by R. Douglas Campbell in Ontario, Canada, in 1976. Grimo Nut Nursery recommends NC-1 to its growers in colder climates. "Fruit has few seeds; yellow skin and flesh; thin skin; early ripening" — around the middle of September in Ontario and early September in Kentucky, KSU reports. "Fruit size large; averaging 180 g/fruit and 45 fruit per tree at KSU."

Ron Powell notes, "Leaves can become infected with *Phyllosticta* but the fruit does not split."

NYOMI'S DELICIOUS

"Original trees grown in Berea, Kentucky and is a local favorite of the neighborhood," reports Cliff England. "Light yellow fruit with no after taste. Very heavy producer of 10 to 12 oz. pawpaw fruit that are 4 to 6 inches long. Hangs in cluster of 4's and 5's."

OVERLEESE

This cultivar, selected in the wild by W. B. Ward in Rushville, Indiana, in 1950, is a perennial favorite among backyard growers. "Oval to round, few seeds, excellent flavor, excellent for shipping, excellent taste," Ron Powell reports, "[and] parent of many other improved cultivars," including Peterson's Shenandoah. Derek Morris says, "Exceptional quality medium to large fruits, early ripening. Medium productivity. Very good seed to flesh ratio and fruits maintain quality over a long time. This one is just as good, if not better, when skin turns dark . . . the flesh takes on a very rich butterscotch flavor and texture is divine — melts in the mouth." Other reports suggest a melon aftertaste. KSU reports middle September ripening in Kentucky and first week of October in Michigan, "Fruit size large, averaging over 170 g/fruit and 55 fruit per tree." Won Best Fruit at the Ohio Pawpaw Festival in 2011.

PA GOLDEN #1

Derek Morris reports, "Very productive variety, early ripening. Fruits are average to good but do not age very well and somewhat seedy. Small to medium sized, can display lots of skin yellowing when ripe." Morris says PA Golden #1 is thought to be a great pollinating variety.

There are four other PA-Goldens, each selected and introduced by John Gordon of Amherst, New York. According to Ron Powell, PA Golden #1 "is the cultivar that is sold in the trade as PA-Golden. These are all small fruit but my tree has produced up to sixty-five pounds per year. The fruit may at times have a bitter taste but otherwise is acceptable. Of the four, PAG #3 is the best. It is slightly larger and the appearance is the best as it has more tolerance to *Phyllosticta*. Still quite popular since it is also quite winter-hardy." Jim Davis reports that this variety is an early producer at his Maryland orchard.

John Gordon was an active member of the Northern Nut Growers Association starting in the early 1960s and made a number of pawpaw selections whose ancestry can be traced back to George A. Zimmerman. Gordon grew and selected many seedlings from the trees of George L. Slate of Cornell University, who had gathered fruit and seed from Zimmerman's Fernwood estate in Pennsylvania.

POTOMAC

A Peterson Pawpaw selected as a seedling from the Blandy Experimental Farm. "Flavor sweet and rich," Peterson reports. "Texture firm, melting, smooth. Flesh color medium yellow." Ron Powell says that in the humid Ohio River Valley, Potomac is susceptible to splitting due to *Phyllosticta*. "Very large fruit," he adds; "produces fruit over a pound." KSU reports, "Extremely fleshy," and approximately 4 percent seed by weight. "Fruit size large; averaging 235 g/fruit and 45 fruit per tree at KSU. Problems with fruit cracking some years." Lee Brumley, of Indiana, reported growing a 28.64-ounce Potomac pawpaw (in the Spring 2011 *Pawpaw Pickin's* newsletter). According to Mario Mandujano, research technician at Michigan State University, Potomac produces extremely large fruit but ripens too late for Michigan.

PROLIFIC

Morris notes that Prolific "has a unique dense texture, it almost has a chewy feel compared to others. Productive, late-ripening, fast-growing variety. Fruits are medium to large and, at least to me, have a slight coconut undertone but fruits usually leave a slight bitter aftertaste. Because of this (I suppose), I have had people in taste tests say they pick up coffee notes in this one. Light yellow flesh." KSU reports: "Large fruit, yellow flesh; ripens first week of October in [Michigan]. Fruit size medium at KSU." Prolific was selected by Corwin Davis, near Bellevue, Michigan, in the mid-1980s.

QUAKER DELIGHT

Quaker Delight was found in the arboretum of Wilmington College by Dick Glaser, and won the Ohio Pawpaw Festival in 2003 for best flavor. According to Ron Powell, characteristics include: "creamy texture, light creamy color, medium size, fairly early — early September — and a light, mild flavor. It probably deserves to be propagated just as much as a number of older and even newer cultivars."

RAPPAHANNOCK

A Peterson Pawpaw selected as a seedling from the Blandy Experimental Farm. In cultivation, under full sun, Rappahannock's leaves grow upward, as opposed to the typical shingled downward habit of pawpaws in cultivation. KSU reports that this makes the fruit more visible under the canopy of leaves. Peterson reports firm flesh and sweet flavor, with only 3 percent seed by weight.

Although Ron Powell and others have reported poor performance in the Midwest, growers in North Carolina and Louisiana have favorable reviews. Morris says, "Great quality, medium to large fruits, very productive, traits as advertised — low seed count . . . Fruit keeps well." KSU reports, "This fruit typically exhibits a yellowish color break at picking stage . . . Fruit size small; averaging 95 g/fruit and 95 fruit per tree at KSU."

REBECCA'S GOLD

Although this variety is often cited as small, Ron Powell says, "The largest fruit from my planting in Butler County, Ohio, came off of Rebecca's Gold at over one pound. A good-tasting, very sweet, and soft fruit. When the fruit hits the ground, it usually is mush. Very thin skin. We attempt to pick the fruit before it hits the ground." Selected from Corwin Davis seed, in Bellevue, Michigan, by J. M. Riley in 1974. "Medium sized fruit; kidney-shaped; yellow flesh," reports KSU. "Fruit size medium at KSU."

SHENANDOAH

A Peterson Pawpaws selection and seedling of Overleese, Shenandoah has been described as a "beginner's pawpaw" for its mild flavor. Peterson says it was the clear favorite of customers at the farmers market in Washington, DC. "Smooth, custardy texture, with just the right balance of fragrance, sweet fruity flavor, and agreeable aftertaste," he notes. KSU reports, "Fruit with few seeds" — approximately 7 percent by weight. "Fruit has creamy yellow flesh. Ripens in September in Kentucky. Fruit size medium-large; averaging 150 g/fruit and 80 fruit per tree at KSU."

Mario Mandujano says Shenandoah is his favorite: "With that one not only can I eat one, I can eat five or six." And "Shenandoah is just incredible," echoes Deep Run Orchard's Jim Davis. Ron Powell says, "The best of Neal's selections to grow in the Ohio River Valley since it is only slightly susceptible to *Phyllosticta*."

SUE

A small to medium-sized fruit introduced by Don Munich from southern Indiana. "A very good-producing cultivar with very mild-tasting fruit," reports Ron Powell. "No *Phyllosticta* issues. The fruit is very soft and thin-skinned. For those who do not like a strong-tasting fruit, this is the one to let them taste."

SUMMER DELIGHT

According to Cliff England, Summer Delight is "just an average-sized pawpaw of eight to twelve ounces that absolutely tastes delicious, has a yellow-tinted skin that is thick, and ships and stores well. The remarkable thing about this pawpaw is that it ripens in the last week of July to the first week of August. Here in Kentucky, of all the cultivars we have, it is the first to ripen. It is not precocious and takes four to five years to come into production, but it is well worth the wait. In most years the fruit is on the ground long before you expect it to be. Summer Delight has a smooth-textured flesh, few seeds, and a melon aftertaste."

SUNFLOWER

Sunflower was discovered in 1970, in the wild, near Chanute, Kansas, by Milo Gibson, and is one of few pawpaws reported to be self-compatible. KSU reports, "Large fruit; yellow skin; butter-color flesh; few seeds; ripens early to mid-September in Kentucky and first week of October in MI. Fruit size large; averaging 155 g/fruit and 75 fruit per tree at KSU."

Derek Morris reports that Sunflower "tends to grow more wide than tall." Additionally, it produces the largest single fruit in Morris's orchard each year. He says that although the flavor of Sunflower is generally very good, he has noticed a slight bitter finish in some of its fruits. "One other feature of this variety is that it is among the latest ripening, so late that growers in far northern areas may not get ripe fruit."

Morris adds that Sunflower "is the favorite among many growers and a variety I would not want to be without. It always ranks high in taste tests. It also has nice thick flesh/texture and relatively few but large seed[s]. It has been noted that seedlings from Sunflower make especially strong rootstock for those who want to do their own grafting."

Sunflower won Best Fruit at the Ohio Pawpaw Festival in 2006 and 2010. "It is one that I always recommend to growers," says Ron Powell.

SUSQUEHANNA

A Peterson Pawpaws selection and seedling tree grown from the collection at the Blandy Experimental Farm. KSU reports, "Fruit has few seeds, very fleshy, medium yellow flesh; thickish skin; this variety is less fragile than most," with few seeds, approximately 4 percent by weight. "Ripens late September in Kentucky. Fruit size large; averaging 185 g/fruit and 40 fruit per tree at KSU." John Brittain reports, "Very large fruit, mid–late season ripening, moderate yields; very sweet rich flavor, firm buttery texture, few seeds."

"Those Susquehanna, they're about the best," says Alabama grower Dale Brooks. And Neal Peterson says, "Susquehanna is without a doubt my personal favorite — if I had to choose one."

SWEET ALICE

Selected from the wild in West Virginia by Homer Jacobs of the Holden Arboretum, in Mentor, Ohio, in 1934. One of the oldest pawpaw cultivars that remains in the trade. KSU reports medium fruit size.

TAYLOR

Selected from the wild in Eaton Rapids, Michigan, by Corwin Davis in 1968. "Fruit: green skin; yellow flesh; ripens in September in Kentucky and 1st week of October in [Michigan]," reports KSU. "Fruit size medium; averaging 110 g/fruit and 70 fruit per tree at KSU."

TAYTWO

Selected from the wild in Eaton Rapids, Michigan, by Corwin Davis in 1968, and sometimes spelled *Taytoo*. "Fruit: light-green skin; yellow flesh; ripens in September in Kentucky and 1st week of October in [Michigan]," KSU reports. "Fruit size medium; averaging 120 g/fruit and 75 fruit per tree at KSU." Also an early producer in Jim Davis's Maryland orchard.

WABASH

A Peterson Pawpaws selection; a seedling from the Blandy Experimental Farm. KSU reports: "Percent seed ~ 6% by weight. Texture medium firm, creamy, smooth. Flesh color yellow to orangish. Fruit size large; averaging 185 g/fruit and 65 fruit per tree at KSU. Problems with fruit cracking some years." Although Ron Powell says Wabash is his choice of the six Peterson introductions, "I have found that it is difficult to graft and grow. A very good-tasting fruit but the plant is slow to produce fruit."

SAA-ZIMMERMAN

"Selected as seedling from seed originating from G. A. Zimmerman collection by John Gordon, Amherst, NY, in 1982," reports KSU. "Large fruit; yellow skin and flesh; few seeds."

ZIMMERMAN

Selected in New York from George A. Zimmerman seed by George Slate. KSU reports medium-sized fruit.

NOTES

PROLOGUE

1. *Seed World* 10, no. 4 (August 19, 1921): 52. Seed Trade Reporting Bureau, Chicago, IL.

CHAPTER ONE

1. Euell Gibbons, *Stalking the Wild Asparagus* (New York: David McKay Company, 1962), 162.
2. American Genetics Association, "Where Are the Best Pawpaws?" *Journal of Heredity* 7, no. 7 (1916): 294.
3. Corwin Davis, "Update on Papaws," *Northern Nut Growers Association Annual Report* 70 (1979): 82.
4. Personal communication with Kirk Pomper, 2013.
5. George A. Zimmerman, "The Papaw," Northern Nut Growers Association (1938), 99–102.

CHAPTER TWO

1. R. Neal Peterson, "Pawpaw *(Asimina)*," *Acta Horticulture* 290 (1991): 567–600.
2. Connie Barlow, *The Ghosts of Evolution: Nonsensical Fruit, Missing Partners, and Other Ecological Anachronisms* (New York: Basic Books, 2000), 93.
3. Arthur Caswell Park, "Iroquois Uses of Maize and Other Food Plants," in *Parker on the Iroquois: Iroquois Uses of Maize and Other Food Plants, the Code of Handsome Lake, the Seneca Prophet, the Constitution of the Five Nations*, ed. William N. Fenton (Syracuse, NY: Syracuse University Press, 1968), 95.
4. Marjorie Harris, *Botanica North America: The Illustrated Guide to Our Native Plants, Their Botany, History, and the Way They Have Shaped Our World* (New York: HarperResource, 2003), 169.
5. Samuel Cole Williams, ed., *Adair's History of the American Indians* (New York: Promontory Press, 1986), 439.
6. Personal communication with Steven Bond.
7. William A. Read, *Louisiana Place Names of Indian Origin: A Collection of Words* (Tuscaloosa: University of Alabama Press, 2008), 45. https://books.google.com/books?id=MSbUOTHeSWoC&source=gbs_navlinks_s
8. William Bright, *Native American Placenames of the United States* (Norman: University of Oklahoma Press, 2004), 30.
9. Daniel E. Moerman, *Native American Ethnobotany* (Portland, OR: Timber Press, 1998), 110.

10. Harris, *Botanica North America: The Illustrated Guide to Our Native Plants, Their Botany, History, and the Way They Have Shaped Our World*, 169.

11. Luis Hernández de Biedma, Gonzalo Fernández de Oviedo y Valdés, and Rodrigo Ranjel, *Narratives of the Career of Hernando de Soto in the Conquest of Florida*, vol. 1, trans. Buckingham Smith, ed. Edward Gaylord Bourne (New York: A. S. Barnes and Company, 1904), 222. https://books.google.com/books?id=-_XQwYabIk8C& source=gbs_navlinks_s

12. Lawrence A. Clayton, Vernon James Knight Jr., and Edward C. Moore, eds., *The De Soto Chronicles: The Expedition of Hernando de Soto to North America in 1539–1543*, 2 vols. (Tuscaloosa: University of Alabama Press, 1993), 219 [note 332 in vol. 2].

13. John L. Cotter, *New Discoveries at Jamestown: Site of the First Successful English Settlement in America* (Washington, DC: National Park Service, US Department of the Interior, 1954), 74.

14. Ed Southern, ed., *The Jamestown Adventure: Accounts of the Virginia Colony, 1605–1614* (Winston-Salem: John F. Blair, Publisher, 2004), 31.

15. James M. Crawford, ed., *Studies in Southeastern Indian Languages* (Athens: University of Georgia Press, 1975), 365.

16. John Smith, *The Generall Historie of Virginia, New England & The Summer Isles*, vol. 1 (Glasgow: James MacLehose and Sons, 1907), 335. https://books.google.com/books?i d=Im0LAQAAIAAJ&source=gbs_navlinks_s

17. Daniel F. Austin, *Florida Ethnobotany* (Boca Raton: CRC Press, 2004), 122. Austin's writings on the *Asimina* genus is a tremendous resource compiling historic references and uses of pawpaw.

18. Stephen Lyn Bales, *Natural Histories: Stories from the Tennessee Valley* (Knoxville: University of Tennessee Press, 2007), 151.

19. John Lawson, *Lawson's History of North Carolina* (London, printed for W. Taylor and F. Baker, 1714).

20. Keith A. Baca, *Native American Place Names in Mississippi* (Jackson: University Press of Mississippi, 2007), 15–16.

21. Geoffrey D. Kimball, *Koasati Dictionary* (Lincoln: University of Nebraska Press, 1994), 345.

22. James Owen Dorsey and John R. Swanton, *A Dictionary of the Biloxi and Ofo Languages: Accompanied with Thirty-One Biloxi Texts and Numerous Biloxi Phrases* (Washington, DC: Government Printing Office, 1912), 323. https://books.google.com/ books?id=6vo_AQAAMAAJ&source=gbs_navlinks_s

23. Carolyn Quintero, *Osage Dictionary* (Norman: University of Oklahoma Press, 2009), 86. https://books.google.com/books?id=eHwCBQAAQBAJ&source=gbs_navlinks_s

24. Austin, *Florida Ethnobotany*, 122.

25. James M. Craford, *The Mobilian Trade Language* (Knoxville: University of Tennessee Press, 1978), 119 [note 28]. Crawford notes that Joliet may have been the first European to attempt to write the Algonquian word for "pawpaw," as *Assons*.

26. Emanuel J. Drechsel, *Mobilian Jargon: Linguistic and Sociohistorical Aspects of a Native American Pidgin* (Oxford, UK: Clarendon Press, 1997), 89, 95.

27. Pierre-François-Xavier de Charlevoix, *Histoire et description générale de la nouvelle France, avec le journal historique d'un voyage fait par odre du roi dans l'Amérique septentrionale* (Paris, 1774), 395. https://books.google.com/books?id=yCFK4dJCci0C &source=gbs_navlinks_s

28. Pierre-François-Xavier de Charlevoix [English translation], *Journal of a Voyage to North-America*, vol. 2 (Dublin: John Exshaw and James Potts, 1766), 167. https://books .google.com/books?id=taZCAQAAMAAJ&source=gbs_navlinks_s

29. Peter Kalm, *The America of 1750: Peter Kalm's Travels in North America*, vol. 2, ed. Adolph Burnett Benson (New York: Dover Publications, 1964), 533. https://books .google.com/books?id=2fkMAQAAMAAJ

30. Michel Adanson, *Familles des Plantes* (Paris, 1763), 521.

31. Daniel Boone, *Life and Adventures of Colonel Daniel Boon: The First White Settler of the State of Kentucky* (Brooklyn: C. Wilder, 1823), 12.

32. Timothy Flint, *Biographical Memoir of Daniel Boone, the First Settler of Kentucky, Interspersed with Incidents in the Early Annals of the Country* (Cincinnati: George Conclin, 1837), 108.

33. John Filson, *The Discovery, Settlement and Present State of Kentucke* (Westminster, MD: Heritage Books, 2009), 23–24. https://books.google.com/books?id=ZJoCn2qf7y4C& source=gbs_navlinks_s

34. William Sudduth, "A Sketch of the Life of William Sudduth," in *Daniel Boone and Others on the Kentucky Frontier: Autobiographies and Narratives, 1769–1795*, ed. Darren R. Reid (Jefferson, NC: McFarland & Company, 2009), 120–25.

35. Beckner, Lucien, trans., "Rev. John Dabney Shane's Interview with Mrs. Sarah Graham of Bath County," *Filson Club Historical Quarterly* 9 (1935), 222–41.

36. Ecocrop, "*Annona senegalensis*," http://ecocrop.fao.org/ecocrop/srv/en/ cropView?id=3243 (accessed February 28, 2015); National Research Council, *Lost Crops of Africa*, vol. 3: *Fruits* (Washington, DC: National Academies Press, 2008), 243. http://books.nap.edu/openbook.php?record_id=11879&page=243

37. Herbert C. Covey, *African American Slave Medicine: Herbal and Non-Herbal Treatments* (Lanham, MD: Lexington Books, 2007), 181.

38. John T. Schlotterbeck, *Daily Life in the Colonial South* (Santa Barbara: Greenwood Press, 2013), 236. William Dillon Piersen, *Black Yankees: The Development of an Afro-American Subculture in Eighteenth-Century New England* (Amherst: University of Massachusetts Press, 1988), 103. https://books.google.com/books?id=th01vkRw2d8 C&source=gbs_navlinks_s

39. John Uri Lloyd and Curtis Gates Lloyd, *Drugs and Medicines of North America*, vol. 2 (Cincinnati: Robert Clarke & Co, 1886–87), 51. https://books.google.com/books?id= 4h8TAAAAIAAJ&source=gbs_navlinks_s

40. Andrew F. Smith, *Starving the South: How the North Won the Civil War* (New York: St. Martin's Press, 2011), 203. https://books.google.com/books?id=wcAf7HzaShYC& source=gbs_navlinks_s

41. Bell Irvin Wiley, *The Life of Johnny Reb: The Common Soldier of the Confederacy* (Baton Rouge: Louisiana State University Press, 1978), 102.

42. Arthur W. Bergeron, ed., *The Civil War Reminiscences of Major Silas T. Grisamore, CSA* (Baton Rouge: Louisiana State University Press, 1993), 165.

43. John Randolph McBride, *History of the Thirty-Third Indiana Veteran Volunteer Infantry During the Four Years of Civil War* (Indianapolis: Wm. B. Burford, 1900), 54. https://books.google.com/books?id=44svAAAAYAAJ&source=gbs_navlinks_s

CHAPTER THREE

1. Thomas Farrington De Voe, *The Market Assistant* (New York: Hurd and Houghton, 1867), 384. https://books.google.com/books?id=2z4EAAAAYAAJ&source=gbs_navlinks_s

2. Lloyd and Lloyd, *Drugs and Medicines of North America*, 49–60. https://books.google.com/books?id=4h8TAAAAIAAJ&source=gbs_navlinks_s

3. *American Gardening*, vol. 11: *The American Garden: An Illustrated Journal of Horticulture*, ed. L. H. Bailey (New York: Rural Publishing Company, 1890), 714.

4. Harrisburgh, PA, *Evening News*, October 12, 1918.

5. Greenville, PA, *Record-Argus*, September 23, 1912.

6. W. H. Ragan, *Transactions of the American Horticultural Society for the Year 1888*, vol. 5: *Being a Report of the Eighth Annual Meeting, Held at San Jose, Cal.* (Indianapolis: Carlon & Hollenbeck, 1888), 161. https://books.google.com/books?id=CP5OAAAAIAAJ&source=gbs_navlinks_s

7. J. Horace McFarland, "Some American Trees," in *The Outlook*, vol. 76: *January–April, 1904* (New York: The Outlook Company, 1904), 817–27. https://books.google.com/books?id=J7gRAAAAYAAJ&source=gbs_navlinks_s

8. *The Country Gentleman*, vol. 70 (Albany: Luther Tucker & Son, 1905), 1198. https://books.google.com/books?id=1igiAQAAMAAJ&source=gbs_navlinks_s

9. James A. Little, *The Pawpaw (*Asimina triloba*), A Native Fruit of Great Excellence* (Clayton, IN: Orville G. Swindler, 1905).

CHAPTER FOUR

1. American Genetics Association, "Where Are the Best Pawpaws?": 291–96.

2. American Genetics Association, "The Best Papaws," *Journal of Heredity* 8, no. 1 (1917): 21–33.

3. Agricultural Marketing Resource Center, "Blueberries," http://www.agmrc.org/commodities__products/fruits/blueberries (accessed February 28, 2015).

4. J. Kim Kaplan, "Blueberry Growing Comes to the National Agricultural Library," *Agricultural Research* (May–June 2011): 14–16.

5. Kirk W. Pomper, Desmond R. Layne, R. Neal Peterson, and Dwight Wolfe, "The Pawpaw Regional Variety Trial: Background and Early Data," *HortTechnology* 13, no. 3 (July–September 2003).

6. Tom Burford, *Apples of North America: Exceptional Varieties for Gardeners, Growers, and Cooks* (Toronto: Timber Press, 2013), 13.

7. Henry T. Finck, "The Pawpaw — An American Fruit," *House and Garden* (March 1922): 38. https://books.google.com/books?id=oqdAAQAAMAAJ&source=gbs_navlinks_s

8. R. Neal Peterson, "Pawpaw (*Asimina*)."

9. Zimmerman, "The Papaw."

10. R. Neal Peterson, "Pawpaw Variety Development: A History and Future Prospects," *HortTechnology* 13 (2003): 449–54.

11. David Fairchild, *The World Grows Round My Door* (New York: Charles Scribner's Sons, 1947), 174.

CHAPTER FIVE

1. Peterson, "Pawpaw Variety Development."

2. Ibid.

3. W. S. Flory Jr., "Species and Hybrids of Asimina in the Northern Shenandoah Valley of Virginia," *Northern Nut Growers Association Annual Report* 49 (1958): 73–75.

4. Peterson, "Pawpaw Variety Development."

CHAPTER SIX

1. Federal Writers Project of the Works Progress Administration for the State of Kentucky, *Kentucky: A Guide to the Bluegrass State* (New York: Hasting House, 1954), 330.

2. John S. Kessler and Donald B. Ball, *North from the Mountains: A Folk History of the Carmel Melungeon Settlement, Highland County, Ohio* (Macon: Mercer University Press, 2001), 88. https://books.google.com/books?id=qX7gRuT1zyQC&source=gbs_navlinks_s

3. Walter Havighurst, *Land of Promise: The Story of the Northwest Territory* (New York: Macmillan Company, 1946), 43.

4. "Frank Ketter, Prominent Irontonian Passes Away," *Ironton (OH) Daily News*, January 16, 1943.

5. "Mrs. Frank Ketter Passes Peacefully to Eternity," *Ironton (OH) Evening Tribune*, May 14, 1939.

6. C. Hirschinger, Wisconsin State Horticultural Society, "Tree Fruits and Why Fall Apple Trees Have Been More Hardy than Winter Apple Trees," *Annual Report of the Wisconsin State Horticultural Society* 31 (1901): 42–47. https://books.google.com/books?id=rrNOAAAAMAAJ&source=gbs_navlinks_s

7. Michael Pollan, *Botany of Desire: A Plant's-Eye View of the World* (New York: Random House, 2001), 9.

8. Sharon M. Kouns, "Villages, Townships and Towns of Lawrence County, Ohio: How They Got Their Names," http://files.usgwarchives.net/oh/lawrence/history/names.txt (accessed February 28, 2015).

CHAPTER SEVEN

1. Hank Burchard, "The Pawpaw Chase," *Washington Post*, September 17, 1999, N.40.

2. Ibid.

CHAPTER EIGHT

1. Carrie Ann Knauer, "An Orchard Specializes in Pawpaws," *Christian Science Monitor*, September 23, 2009. http://www.csmonitor.com/The-Culture /Gardening/2009/0923/an-orchard-specializes-in-pawpaws

CHAPTER NINE

1. Crawford, ed., *Studies in Southeastern Indian Languages*, 365.

CHAPTER TEN

1. Colleen Anderson, "Hitting the Road on a Pawpaw Pilgrimage," *Charleston Gazette* [*Sunday Gazette-Mail*], October 4, 1992, 1E, 3E.
2. Ibid.
3. Richard Lund, "Paw Paw — From Discovery to Clinical Trials," YouTube, September 27, 2011, https://www.youtube.com/watch?v=hD6MGd0Dz5o (accessed June 3, 2015).
4. Lloyd and Lloyd, *Drugs and Medicines of North America*, 49–60. https://books.google .com/books?id=4h8TAAAAIAAJ&source=gbs_navlinks_s
5. Ibid.
6. Jerry L. McLaughlin, Gina B. Benson, Tad A. Turgeon, and James W. Forsythe, "Use of Standardized Mixtures of Paw Paw Extract (*Asimina triloba*) in Cancer Patients: Case Studies," in *Botanical Medicine: From Bench to Bedside*, ed. Raymond Copper and Fredi Kronenberg (New Rochelle, NY: Mary Ann Liebert, 2009), 139–53.
7. Stephen J. Cutler and Horace G. Cutler, *Biologically Active Natural Products: Pharmaceuticals* (Boca Raton: CRC Press, 1999). https://books.google.com/ books?id=yUY_iDQcD-AC&source=gbs_navlinks_s
8. R. N. Peterson, J. P. Cherry, and J. G. Simmons, "Composition of the Pawpaw (*Asimina triloba*) Fruit," *Annual Report of the Northern Nut Growers Association* 77 (1982): 97–107.
9. Robert Brannan, "Pawpaw Research, in Brief," *From the Pawpaw Patch* 20, no. 1 (2013): 3.
10. D. Caparros-Lefebvre and A. Elbaz, "Possible Relation of Atypical Parkinsonism in the French West Indies with Consumption of Tropical Plants: A Case-Control Study, Caribbean Parkinsonism Study Group," *Lancet* 354 (1999): 281–86.
11. Lisa F. Potts, Frederick A. Luzzio, Scott C. Smith, Michal Hetman, Pierre Champy, and Irene Litvan, "Annonacin in *Asimina triloba* Fruit: Implication for Neurotoxicity," *NeuroToxicology* 33 (2012): 53–58.
12. David L. Debertin, "Emerging Trends in Kentucky Agriculture and the Future of Rural Kentucky in the 21st Century," University of Kentucky, http://www.uky.edu /~deberti/exten.htm (acccessed March 7, 2015).
13. Julian J. N. Campbell, "Historical Evidence of Forest Composition in the Bluegrass Region of Kentucky," http://www.bluegrasswoodland.com/uploads/CH volume07page231.pdf (accessed March 7, 2015).
14. Marion, KY, *Crittenden Press*, June 4, 1903, 3.
15. *Stanford Interior Journal*, 1894.
16. Louisville, KY, *Courier-Journal*, September 12, 1896, 6.

17. Marc Stadler, "The 3rd International Papaw Conference," *Pawpaw Pickin's* (Ohio Pawpaw Growers Association) 11, no. 2 (2011), 6.

CHAPTER ELEVEN

1. "Natural Sciences and Engineering Research Council of Canada Approves Bevo Co-Sponsored Research Grant," CNW Telbec, February 15, 2012, http://www.newswire .ca/fr/story/922053/natural-sciences-and-engineering-research-council-of-canada -approves-bevo-co-sponsored-research-grant (accessed March 7, 2015).
2. Pomper, Layne, Peterson, and Wolfe, "Pawpaw Regional Variety Trial," 412–17.
3. Marissa Palin Stein, "The Rise of the Kiwifruit," California Agriculture Online, University of California Agriculture, http://californiaagriculture.ucanr.org/landing page.cfm?article=ca.v068n03p96&fulltext=yes (accessed March 7, 2015).
4. California Kiwifruit Commission, "History of Kiwifruit," California Kiwifruit Commission, http://www.kiwifruit.org/about/history.aspx (accessed March 7, 2015).
5. Julia Morton, "Soursop: *Annona muricata*," Purdue University, Horticulture, https://www.hort.purdue.edu/newcrop/morton/soursop.html (accessed March 7, 2015). "In each fertile segment there is a single oval, smooth, hard, black seed, 1/2 to 3/4 in (1.25–2 cm) long; and a large fruit may contain from a few dozen to 200 or more seeds."
6. Patrick O'Malley and Lester Wilson, "Enhancing Value and Marketing Options for Pawpaw by Developing Pulp Separation and Preservation Techniques," Leopold Center for Sustainable Agriculture, Iowa State University, Competitive Grant Report M2009-20, https://www.leopold.iastate.edu/sites/default/files/grants/M2009-20.pdf (accessed March 7, 2015).
7. François André Michaux and Thomas Nuttall, *The North American Sylva, Or, A Description of the Forest Trees of the United States, Canada and Nova Scotia*, trans. John Jay Smith, vol. 2 (Philadelphia: Robert P. Smith, 1855), 23. https://books.google.com /books?id=0VFHAAAAYAAJ&source=gbs_navlinks_s
8. John Beatty, *The Citizen-Soldier: The Memoirs of a Civil War Volunteer* (Lincoln: University of Nebraska Press, 1998), 272.
9. "Another Wet Blow," *Sandusky (OH) Star-Journal*, April 27, 1921.
10. American Genetics Association, "The Best Papaws."
11. *Annual Report on the Geological Survey of the State of Ohio* 1–2 (Columbus: Ames B. Gardiner, 1836), 268. https://books.google.com/books?id=9ai_AAAAIAAJ& source=gbs_navlinks_s

CHAPTER TWELVE

1. William P. C. Barton, *Vegetables Materia Medica of the United States* (Philadelphia: M. Carey & Son, 1818), 11. https://books.google.com/books?id=3cJcAAAAcAAJ&source =gbs_navlinks_s
2. Reuben Gold Thwaites, *Afloat on the Ohio: An Historical Pilgrimage of a Thousand Miles in a Skiff, from Redstone to Cairo* (Carbondale: Southern Illinois University Press, 1999), 215.

3. Harry Gordon, *The River Motor Boat Boys on the Amazon, Or, The Secret of Cloud Island* (New York: A. L. Burt Company, 1913), 93. https://books.google.com/books?id=P11 DAQAAMAAJ&source=gbs_navlinks_s

4. Steven J. Shotola et al., "Sugar Maple Invasion of an Old-Growth Oak-Hickory Forest in Southwestern Illinois," *American Midland Naturalist* 127, no. 1 (1992): 125–38.

5. Kirk W. Pomper, Jeremiah D. Lowe, Li Lu, Sheri B. Crabtree, and Lauren A. Collins, "Clonality of Pawpaw (*Asimina triloba*) Patches in Kentucky," *Journal of the Kentucky Academy of Sciences* 70, no. 1 (2009): 3–11.

6. Desmond R. Layne, "The Pawpaw [*Asimina triloba* (L.) Dunal]: A New Fruit Crop for Kentucky and the United States," *HortScience* (1996): 15–22.

7. Katherine Goodrich, "Does Your Pawpaw Smell Flowery or Fermented?" *Palmetto* 24, no. 4 (2007): 12–15.

8. Library of Congress, "What Is the Largest Flower in the World?" Everyday Mysteries: Fun Science Facts from the Library of Congress, http://www.loc.gov/rr/scitech /mysteries/flower.html (accessed March 7, 2015).

9. Pennsylvania State University, "Red Trillium," Virtual Nature Trail at Penn State New Kensington, http://www.psu.edu/dept/nkbiology/naturetrail/speciespages /red_trillium.html (accessed March 7, 2015).

10. Neal Peterson, "How to Hand-Pollinate Pawpaws," *California Rare Fruit Growers* (1997): 10–11. http://www.clemson.edu/hort/peach/pdfs/FG97.pdf (accessed March 7, 2015).

11. Ray Jones, "Germination at Home," *The Pawpaw Tracker* 92, no. 1 (1992): 8.

12. Layne, "The Pawpaw."

13. Barb Ernst, "Growing Paw Paws from Seed," *Pawpaw Pickin's* (Ohio Pawpaw Growers Association) 4, no. 1 (2005): 4.

14. Finck, "The Pawpaw — An American Fruit."

15. Davis, "Update on Papaws," 82–84.

CHAPTER THIRTEEN

1. Harry W. Fritz, *The Lewis and Clark Expedition* (Westport, CT: Greenwood Press, 2004), 63.

2. William Clark, Gary E. Moulton, and Thomas W. Dunlay, eds., *The Definitive Journals of Lewis & Clark: From the Ohio to the Vermillion*, vol. 2 of the Nebraska Edition (Lincoln: University of Nebraska Press, 1986), 510.

3. Meriwether Lewis, William Clark, Charles Floyd, and Joseph Whitehouse, *Original Journals of the Lewis and Clark Expedition, 1804–1806*, vol. 5 (New York: Dodd, Mead, 1905), 382–95. https://books.google.com/books?id=OvEtAAAAYAAJ&source= gbs_navlinks_s

CHAPTER FOURTEEN

1. "Overview of Fruits at Monticello," http://www.monticello.org/site/house-and -gardens/overview-fruits-monticello (accessed March 7, 2015).

2. Ibid.

CHAPTER FIFTEEN

1. "Pilot Mountain State Park, History," North Carolina State Parks, http://www .ncparks.gov/Visit/parks/pimo/history.php (accessed March 7, 2015).

2. Lawson, *Lawson's History of North Carolina.*

3. Ibid.

4. Catherine Kozak, "Mother of All Vines Gives Birth to New Wine," *Virginian Pilot,* July 14, 2008. http://hamptonroads.com/2008/07/mother-all-vines-gives-birth-new-wine (accessed March 7, 2015).

5. John J. Winberry and Roy S. Stine. "Settlement Geography of the Carolinas Before 1900," in *A Geography of the Carolinas,* ed. David Gordon Bennet and Jeffrey C. Patton (Boone, NC: Parkway Publishers, 2008), 53–94.

6. Ibid.

7. Ibid.

8. Ibid.

CHAPTER SIXTEEN

1. Daniel Lindsey Thomas and Lucy Blayney Thomas, *Kentucky Superstitions* (Princeton, NJ: Princeton University Press, 1920), 224.

2. John A. Scott Jr., Sam Rogers, and David Cooke, "Woods-Grown Ginseng," West Virginia University Extension Service, http://www.ntfpinfo.us/docs/other/Scott1995 -WoodsGrownGinseng.pdf (accessed June 3, 2015).

3. W. S. Webb and W. D. Funkhouser, "The McLeod Bluff Site in Hicman County, Kentucky," *Reports in Archaeology and Anthropology* 3, no. 1 (1933): 140.

4. Ibid.

5. Patty Jo Watson, *Archaeology of the Mammoth Cave Area* (New York: Academic Press, 1974), 35.

6. "Fig: Fruit Facts," California Rare Fruit Growers, http://www.crfg.org/pubs/ff /fig.html (accessed March 7, 2015).

7. "Figs," Agricultural Marketing Resource Center, http://www.agmrc.org/ commodities__products/fruits/figs (accessed March 7, 2015).

8. Ray B. Browne, *Popular Beliefs and Practices from Alabama* (Berkeley: University of California Press, 1958), 26, 69.

9. Vance Randolph, *Ozark Magic and Folklore* (1947; repr. New York: Dover Publications, 1965), 48.

10. Ibid., 316.

11. *Richmond (KY) Climax,* February 5, 1896, 3.

12. Bill Henry, "Alex Stewart: A Personal Reminiscence," *Tennessee Folklore Society Bulletin* 47, no. 2 (1981): 48–66.

13. Robert Baird, *View of the Valley of the Mississippi, Or, The Emigrant's and Traveller's Guide to the West* (Philadelphia: H. S. Tanner, 1834), 264–65. https://books.google.com /books?id=ypg1AQAAMAAJ&source=gbs_navlinks_s

14. E. W. Hiligrad, *Report on the Geology and Agriculture of the State of Mississippi* (Jackson: E. Barksdale, State Printer, 1860), 370. https://books.google.com/books?id=UfEtkwf Kad8C&source=gbs_navlinks_s

15. Chester Sullivan, *Sullivan's Hollow* (Jackson: University Press of Mississippi, 1978), 9. https://books.google.com/books?id=SOMWxZqd-dgC&source=gbs_navlinks_s

16. Ibid.

17. Baca, *Native American Place Names in Mississippi*, 16.

18. Ibid.

19. Bright, *Native American Placenames of the United States*, 30.

20. Robert Penn Warren, *Flood: A Romance of Our Time* (New York: Random House, 1964), 91.

21. Walt Whitman, "O Magnet-South," in *Leaves of Grass* (New York: Penguin, 1980), 362–63.

22. Ray Lewis White, ed., *Sherwood Anderson's Memoirs: A Critical Edition* (Chapel Hill: University of North Carolina Press, 1969), 50.

23. John Carter Cash, *Anchored in Love: An Intimate Portrait of June Carter Cash* (Nashville: Thomas Nelson, 2008), 17–18. https://books.google.com/ books?id=gyIttRsce-oC&source=gbs_navlinks_s

24. Wilson Rawls, *Where the Red Fern Grows* (New York: Dell Laurel-Leaf, 1989), 8–9.

25. William Faulkner, "Red Leaves," in *The Portable Faulkner* (New York: Penguin Books, 2003), 67.

26. John P. Hale, *Trans-Allegheny Pioneers (West Virginia and Ohio): Historical Sketches of the First White Settlers West of the Alleghenies, 1748 and After* (Westminster, MD: Heritage Books, 1988), 273. http://books.google.com/books?id=wSpGQcJPLp4C&source= gbs_navlinks_s

27. Neal O. Hammon and Richard Taylor, *Virginia's Western War: 1775–1786* (Mechanicsburg, PA: Stackpole Books, 2002), 46.

28. Charles McMurry, *Pioneer History Stories of the Mississippi Valley: For Fourth and Fifth Grades* (New York: Macmillan Company, 1903), 127. https://books.google.com /books?id=RI1BAAAAYAAJ&source=gbs_navlinks_s

29. Wills De Hass, *History of the Early Settlement and Indian Wars of Western Virginia: Embracing an Account of the Various Expeditions on the West, Previous to 1795* (Philadelphia: King & Baird, 1851), 320. https://books.google.com/books ?id=Z9pBcqE_U6AC&source=gbs_navlinks_s

30. Quapaw Canoe Company, "Expeditions — Extended Expeditions," http://www. island63.com/expeditions-extended_expeditions.cfm (accessed March 8, 2015).

31. Mark Twain, *The Autobiography of Mark Twain*, ed. Charles Neider (New York: HarperCollins Publishers, 2000), 16.

32. Mark Twain, *The Adventures of Huckleberry Finn* (New York: Modern Library, 1993), 100–01.

33. Albert Bigelow Paine, *Mark Twain: A Biography, The Personal and Literary Life of Samuel Langhorne Clemens*, vol. 1 (New York: Harper & Brothers Publishers, 1912), 62–63.

34. Andrew Beahrs, *Twain's Feast: Searching for America's Lost Foods in the Footsteps of Samuel Clemens* (New York: Penguin Press, 2010), 283.

35. *Paducah (KY) Evening Sun*, March 24, 1897, 3.

36. Ronald L. Powell, "Where, Oh, Where Is Pretty or Poor or Dear Little Nellie?" http://www.ohiopawpaw.com/PawpawHistory.pdf (accessed March 8, 2015).

37. Robin D. G. Kelley and Earl Lewis, eds., *To Make Our World Anew: A History of African Americans* (Oxford, UK: Oxford University Press, 2000), 264. https://books.google.com/books?id=xMlMAgAAQBAJ&source=gbs_navlinks_s

38. William Royal Oake, *On the Skirmish Line Behind a Friendly Tree: The Civil War Memoirs of William Royal Oake, 26th Iowa Volunteers*, ed. Stacy Dale Allen (Helena: Farcountry Press, 2006), 84. https://books.google.com/books?id=ut39BFr9ExEC&source=gbs_navlinks_s

39. Frances Trollope, *Domestic Manners of the Americans* (Mineola, NY: Dover Publications, 2003), 12.

40. *The Picayune Creole Cook Book* (New York: Dover Publications, 1971).

41. Emanuel J. Drechsel, *Mobilian Jargon: Linguistic and Sociohistorical Aspects of a Native American Pidgin* (Oxford, UK: Clarendon Press, 1997), 89, 95.

42. Captain Mayne Reid, *Bruin; Or, The Grand Bear Hunt* (London: Routledge, Warne, & Routledge), 299–301. https://books.google.com/books?id=wcQBAAAAQAAJ&source=gbs_navlinks_s

43. Steve Bender, "Giddy Over Pawpaws," *Southern Living* 33, no. 8 (1998): 30.

44. *Topeka Daily Capital*, September 26, 1902, "On Second Thought" [column].

45. Little, *The Pawpaw*.

46. Henry Bibb, "Narrative of the Life and Adventures of Henry Bibb, an American Slave," in *I Was Born a Slave: An Anthology of Slave Narratives*, vol. 2: *1849–1866*, ed. Yuval Taylor (Chicago: Lawrence Hill Books, 1999), 4–101.

47. Benny J. Simpson, *A Field Guide to Texas Trees* (Lanham, MD: Taylor Trade Publishing, 1999), 66. https://books.google.com/books?id=FcwVAAAAQBAJ&source=gbs_navlinks_s

48. North Texas Fossils, "Pawpaw Formation," http://www.northtexasfossils.com/pawpaw.htm (accessed March 8, 2015).

49. Cecil Elkins Carter, *Caddo Indians: Where We Come From* (Norman and London: University of Oklahoma Press, 1995), 101.

50. Frances B. King and James E. King, "Interdisciplinary Approaches to Environmental Reconstruction: An Example from the Ozark Highland," in *Case Studies in Environmental Archaeology*, ed. Elizabeth J. Reitz, Lee A. Newsom, and Sylvia J. Scudder (New York: Plenum Press, 1966), 71–86.

51. Writers' Program of the Works Progress Administration in the State of Arkansas, *Arkansas: A Guide to the State* (New York: Hastings House, 1941), 25.

52. Fred Pfister, *Insiders' Guide to Branson and the Ozark Mountains* (Guilford, CT: Morris Book Publishing, 2009), 60. https://books.google.com/books?id=5SpZmBLVnTQC&source=gbs_navlinks_s

53. Bill Vivrett, "Will the Circle Be Unbroken?" http://www.angelfire.com/tx3/viverette/missouri/tributeelmer.html (accessed March 8, 2015).

54. Jesse Stuart, "Beyond Dark Hills," in *Jesse Stuart on Education*, ed. J. R. LeMaster (Lexington: University of Kentucky Press, 1992), 31–52.

55. "An Arkansas 'Possum Hunt," *Wallace's Monthly* (July 1883): 420.

56. J. C. Stribling, "The Black Ghost of the Rocky Branch or the Slave-Time Possum Hunter," in *Pendleton Farmers' Society* (Atlanta: Foote & Davies, 1908), 100–05. https://books.google.com/books?id=YoFFAAAAYAAJ&source=gbs_navlinks_s

57. Randolph, *Ozark Magic and Folklore*, 251.

58. Vickie Layton Cobb, *Ozark Pioneers* (Chicago: Arcadia Publishing, 2001), 31. https://books.google.com/books?id=l7nlTnpwiPAC&source=gbs_navlinks_s

59. Lynn Morrow and Linda Myers-Phinney, *Shepherd of the Hills Country: Tourism Transforms the Ozarks, 1880s–1930s* (Fayetteville: University of Arkansas Press, 1999), 122. https://books.google.com/books?id=6D0-YmjQfdsC&source=gbs_navlinks_s

60. American Genetics Association, "The Best Papaws," 28.

61. Randolph, *Ozark Magic and Folklore*, 261.

62. Ibid., 281–82, 289.

63. Ibid., 151, 168, 237.

64. Vance Randolph, *Blow the Candle Out: "Unprintable" Ozark Folksongs and Folklore*, vol. 2: *Folk Rhymes and Other Lore*, ed. G. Legman (Fayetteville: University of Arkansas Press, 1992), 74. https://books.google.com/books?id=S93LdPw2KP0C&source=gbs_navlinks_s

65. Kenneth L. Smith, *Buffalo River Handbook* (Little Rock: Ozark Society Foundation), 197. https://books.google.com/books?id=0zdyADEqn_IC&source=gbs_navlinks_s

CHAPTER SEVENTEEN

1. Fred Sauceman, "Of Sorghum Syrup, Cushaws, Mountain Barbecue, Soup Beans, and Black Iron Skillets," in *Cornbread Nation 3: Foods of the Mountain South*, ed. Ronni Lundy (Chapel Hill: University of North Carolina Press, 2005), 216–25.

2. Mark F. Sohn, *Mountain Country Cooking: A Gathering of the Best Recipes from the Smokies to the Blue Ridge* (New York: St. Martin's Press, 1996), 242–45.

3. Janet Alm Anderson, *A Taste of Kentucky* (Lexington: University of Kentucky Press, 1986), 79. https://books.google.com/books?id=o8xnHLCMIyAC&source=gbs_navlinks_s

4. American Genetics Association, "The Best Papaws," 21–33.

5. Writers' Program of the Work Projects Administration in State of West Virginia, *West Virginia: A Guide to the Mountain State* (New York: Oxford University Press, 1941), 194–95.

6. Anderson, "Hitting the Road on a Pawpaw Pilgrimage."

7. Zach Harold, "Fans Say Pawpaws, a Forgotten American Fruit, Are Poised for Popularity," *Charleston Daily Mail*, September 9, 2014. http://www.charlestondailymail.com/article/20140909/DM06/140919993

8. H. Tyler Blethen, "Pioneer Settlement," in *High Mountains Rising: Appalachia in Time and Place*, ed. Richard A. Straw and H. Tyler Blethen (Urbana: University of Illinois Press, 2004), 17–29.

9. Ibid.

10. Paul Salstrom, "The Great Depression," in *High Mountains Rising: Appalachia in Time and Place*, ed. Richard A. Straw and H. Tyler Blethen (Urbana: University of Illinois Press, 2004), 74–87.

11. Ibid.

12. Ray Jones, "Greetings from Pawpaw, USA," *The Pawpaw Tracker* 3, no. 1 (1993): 7–10.

13. Roy Lee Harmon, "Did the Drys Destroy the Formula for Making Liquor, Huh Daddy?" *Raleigh Register*, July 31, 1963, 4.

14. Louisville, KY, *Courier-Journal*, September 12, 1896, 6.

15. "Steepheads," Northwest Florida Enviornmental Conservancy, http://www.nwflec.com /northwestfloridaenvironmentalconservancypart2/id12.html (accessed March 8, 2015).

16. Paul Salstrom, *Appalachia's Path to Dependency: Rethinking a Region's Economic History 1730–1940* (Lexington: University Press of Kentucky, 1994), 121. https://books. google.com/books?id=eKIeBgAAQBAJ&source=gbs_navlinks_s

17. J. Russell Smith, *Tree Crops: A Permanent Agriculture* (New York: Harcourt, Brace, 1929), 239.

18. J. Russell Smith, "Farming Appalachia," *American Review of Reviews* 53 (1916): 329–36.

19. John P. Hale, *Trans-Allegheny Pioneers (West Virginia and Ohio): Historical Sketches of the First White Settlers West of the Alleghenies, 1748 and After* (Westminster, MD: Heritage Books, 1988), 273. http://books.google.com/books?id=wSpGQcJPLp4C&source= gbs_navlinks_s

CHAPTER EIGHTEEN

1. Pierre-François-Xavier de Charlevoix, *History and General Description of New France*, vol. 2, trans. John Gilmary Shea (New York: John Gilmary Shea, 1870), 191. https://books.google.com/books?id=2eR5AAAAMAAJ&source=gbs_navlinks_s

2. William Engelbrecht, *Iroquoia: The Development of a Native World* (Syracuse, NY: Syracuse University Press, 2003), 28.

3. David N. Cozzo, "Ethnobotanical Classificiation System and Medical Ethnobotany of the Eastern Band of the Cherokee Indians" (PhD diss., University of Georgia, 2004), 55.

4. Doug Elliott, "Way Down Yonder," August 29, 2012, https://dougelliottstory. wordpress.com/2012/08/29/way-down-yonder (accessed March 8, 2015).

5. Eliot Wigginton and His Students, eds., *Foxfire 3: Animal Care, Banjos and Dulcimers, Hide Tanning, Summer and Fall Wild Plant Foods, Butter Churns, Ginseng and Still More Affairs of Plain Living* (New York: Anchor Books, 1975), 274, 299.

CHAPTER NINETEEN

1. Little, *The Pawpaw*.

2. Ibid.

3. Arthur Lawrence Bodurtha, *History of Miami County, Indiana: A Narrative Account of Its Historical Progress, Its People and Its Principal Interests*, vol. 1 (Chicago: Lewis Publishing, 1914), 197. http://books.google.com/books?id=gRgVAAAAYAAJ& source=gbs_navlinks_s

4. De Voe, *The Market Assistant*, 384.

5. Logan Esarey, *The Indiana Home* (Bloomington: Indiana University Press, 1953, 1976), 53–54. https://books.google.com/books?id=nMG0Pi_VGfEC&source=gbs _navlinks_s

6. "The Indiana Paw-Paw," Louisville, KY, *Courier-Journal*, July 10, 1892, 3.

7. Ibid.

8. William E. Wilson, *The Wabash* (New York: Farrar & Rinehart, 1940), 267–68.

9. Robert J. Barth, "The Vincennes Culture in the Lower Wabash Drainage," in *Cahokia and the Hinterlands: Middle Mississippian Cultures of the Midwest*, ed. Thomas E. Emerson and R. Barry Lewis (Urbana: University of Illinois Press, 1991), 257–63. https://books.google.com/books?id=55h7hrf-ET0C&source=gbs_navlinks_s

10. Arthur Bryant, quoted in *Transactions of the Illinois State Horticultural Society* 36 (1902): 134–35. https://books.google.com/books?id=tAQhAQAAMAAJ&source= gbs_navlinks_s

11. Jones, "Greetings from Pawpaw, USA."

12. Frederick Webb Hodge, ed., *Handbook of American Indians North of Mexico in Four Parts*, vol. 1: *A to G* [*Smithsonian Institution Bureau of American Ethnology Bulletin* 30] (Washington, DC: Government Printing Office, 1912), 101, 102. https://books .google.com/books?id=t9Y_AAAAYAAJ&source=gbs_navlinks_s

13. *Pantagraph*, September 20, 1902, 8.

14. *Chicago Daily Tribune*, August 10, 1913, 4.

15. "Carl Sandburg to Lecture Here," *Record-Argus*, February 19, 1937, 1.

16. "Champions Pawpaw," *Anniston Star*, January 19, 1937, 7.

17. George Ross, "In New York," *Anniston Star*, July 11, 1936, 4.

18. "PawPaw: Essex County's Next Superfruit?" *Our Windsor*, http://www.ourwindsor.ca /community-story/1322972-pawpaw-essex-county-s-next-superfruit-/ (accessed March 8, 2015).

19. Sarah Elton, "Everyone's Got Pawpaw Fever: A Mix of Guava and Banana, This Coveted Fruit Is, Oddly, Native to Ontario's Carolinian Forest," *Maclean's*, November 2, 2009. http://www.macleans.ca/culture/everyones-got-pawpaw-fever (accessed March 8, 2015).

20. Davis, "Update on Papaws," 82–84.

21. Ibid., 79–82.

22. Ibid., 82–84.

23. Stephen S. Witte and Marsha V. Gallagher, eds., *The North American Journals of Prince Maximilian of Wied*, vol. 1: *May 1832–April 1833*, trans. William J. Orr, Paul Schach, and Dieter Karch (Norman: University of Oklahoma Press, 2008), 306. https://books .google.com/books?id=CntWAwAAQBAJ&source=gbs_navlinks_s

24. Kirk W. Pomper, Sheri B. Crabtree, and Jeremy D. Lowe, "Organic Production of Pawpaw," Kentucky State University Cooperative Extension Program (2010), 5. http://www.pawpaw.kysu.edu/PDF/OrganicPawpawPBI-004.pdf

EPILOGUE

1. Freda Kahen-Kashi, "First Lady Michelle Obama Plants White House Garden," *ABC News*, April 2, 2014, http://abcnews.go.com/blogs/politics/2014/04/first-lady -michelle-obama-plants-white-house-kitchen-garden (accessed March 10, 2015).

INDEX

Bold page numbers refer to the color insert.

ACEnet (Appalachian Center for Economic Networks), 93–94, 101, 122

aciminier (acimine, açmine, açminier, les Aciminiers), 17, 191–92

Adair, James, 10

Adanson, Michel, 17

Adventures of Colonel Daniel Boon, The, 17

Adventures of Huckleberry Finn, The, 183–84

African Americans
  pawpaws sold at markets by, 23
  slaves, pawpaw use by, 19–20, 146, 194

African fruits, pawpaws related to, 19–20

agricultural crop, pawpaws as, 41–42.
  See also commercial pawpaw industry;
  orchards, pawpaw
  high-value crop, 41–42, 65, 120, 175
  monoculture, avoiding, 152–53
  for small farms, 119–20, 152–53,
    215–16
  tobacco, replacement for, 100, 109–11,
    120

agronomists, experimental, 24–25

Alabama, 12, 30, 45, 102, 172–78, 263

Ali Baba's food carts, 93–94

Allegheny pawpaw cultivar, 67, 75–76, 78, 88, 255–56

Allium triccocum. See ramps *(Allium triccocum)*

alluvial soil, 3

America, history of pawpaws in. *See* history of pawpaws, American

American Genetics Association contest, 29–30, 40–42, 52, 100, 125, 222. *See also* Ketter pawpaw cultivar

American Horticultural Society, 24

American pawpaw belt, xv–xvi, xviii, 85

amino acids, in pawpaw, 107

Anchutz, Jacob, 55

Anderson, Colleen, 39, 40, 46, 100, 207–8

Anderson, Sherwood, 180

animals, 26, 239
  Annonaceous acetogenins, repelled by,
    94–95
  pawpaw fruit eaten by, 19, 26, 198,
    230–31
  seed dispersal by, 9, 108, 131

Annonaceae, xv, 4–5, 19–20, 89, 130. *See also* medicinal uses, pawpaw and other Annonaceae plants

Annonaceous acetogenins, 103–5, 108–9
  animals and insects repelled by, 95,
    103–4, 168, 239
  as cancer-fighting substance, 7, 103–4
  forest composition, effect on, 133
  as toxins, 108–9

Annona spp.
  A. atemoya, 43
  A. cherimola, 106, 107, 121
  A. muricata, 105–7, 121
  A. reticulata, 106
  A. senegalensis, 19–20
  A. squamosa, 43, 106

antioxidants, 106

Appalachia, 41, 49, 205–20

Appalachian American Indians of West Virginia cookbook, 224

Appalachian Center for Economic Networks (ACEnet), 93–94, 101, 122

apple cultivars, 31, 54

apple orchards, 54–55

ARK-21, 256

Arkansas, 30, 43, 134, 196–203, 256

Ark of Taste, 79, 235

Asimina spp., 4–5. *See also* pawpaw

    A. incana, 43

    A. longifolia, 43

    A. obovata, 43, 244

    A. parviflora, 178

    A. reticulata, 43, 244

    A. triloba, derivation of botanical name, 14, 16–17

assiminier (asimines, assimin), 16–17, 191–92

Atwood, Rufus B., 257

Aubrey, Allison, 72

Audubon, John James, 6

Austin, Ruth and Ann, 51–52

Bailey, Kim, 95

Bailey, Mr., 214, 216

Baird, Robert, 178

Bales, Stephen Lyn, 15

"banana" names for pawpaw, 1, 25, 103, 198, 205, 228

bananas, 7, 97–98, 107, 121, 161

    pawpaw as replacement for, 97–98, 206

    in pawpaw flavor, 2, 182

    pawpaw resemblance to, 1, 24, 54, 162, 256

Banks, Molly, 206

Barber, M. A., 26

bare-root plants, 157, 189

bark fibers, use of pawpaw. *See* fibers, use of pawpaw

Barton, William P. C., 129

Bartram, William and John, 6

Bartram's Travels, 6

Beahrs, Andrew, 184

Beard, Lance, 83, 88–90, 244

Beatty, John, 124–25

beer, pawpaw, 27, 71, 91–92, 123–25, 160, 241

beetles, 4, 132, 2

Bergefurd, Brad, 119–20

beverages, pawpaw. *See also* beer, pawpaw; brandy, pawpaw

    soda, 91

    wine, 71, 111

Bevo Agro Inc., 115

Beyond the Pawpaw Trees, 180

Bibb, Henry, 194

Binneteau, Julien, 16

Biographical Memoir of Daniel Boone, The First Settler of Kentucky, 17–18

Birds of America, 6

Bissonnette, Dan, 99, 234–35

black walnut, 96

Blandy Experimental Farm, 44–46, 260, 261, 263, 264

Blankenship, Tom, 184

Blethen, H. Tyler, 209–10

Blow the Candle Out: "Unprintable" Ozark Folksongs and Folklore, 202

blueberry, 30–31, 33

Bond, Steven, 225, 242

Boone, Daniel, 17–18, 110

Boone, Marc, 122, 238–40

botanical name, derivation of, 14, 16–17

Botany of Desire, The, 55

brandy, pawpaw, 27, 124–25, 213

Brannan, Robert, 31, 38, 106–7, 115–16, 118, 121, 123

breeding, pawpaw, 29–33. *See also* American Genetics Association contest; genetic characteristics, pawpaw; Pawpaw Regional Variety Trials

    Davis, Corwin, by, 236

    Dinnsen, Wynn, by, 159

    Kentucky State University contest, 100

    Kentucky State University germplasm repository (*See* Kentucky State University)

    Lehman, Jerry, by, 229–31

    Little, James A., by, 26

    Peterson, Neal, by (*See* Peterson, Neal)

Brewington, Martin, 154

Brittain, John, 167–69, 263

Britton-Bauer, Jeni, 241

Brooks, Dale, 2, 131, 172–74, 263

Brooks, Reda, 172–73

Brown, Palmer, 180

Brown, Ray B., 176

Bruin; Or, The Grand Bear Hunt, 192

Brumley, Lee, 260

Bryant, Arthur, 231

Buckeye Brewing Company, 91

Buckman, Benjamin, 26, 42–44, 45

Buckman pawpaw cultivar, 44
Bud's at Silver Run, 71
Burbank, Luther, 31–32, 135
Burchard, Hank, 63, 65
Busch, Jim, 166
butter, pawpaw, 51

California, 128, 134, 236
California Rare Fruit Growers, 42, 175, 255
Callaway, Brett, 63, 100, 109, 111, 120, 166
Campbell, R. Douglas, 234, 258
Campbell's #1 (NC-1) pawpaw cultivar, 258
Canada, 114, 115, 234–35. *See also* Ontario, Canada
Cananga odorata (ylang ylang), 106
cancer-fighting compounds, 7, 103–6, 223
Cane Creek Farm, 95
caramel taste/fragrance, pawpaw, xiv, 2, 60, 90, 112, 196, 240
carbohydrates, in pawpaw, 107
Carica papaya (papaya), 14–15
Cash, June Carter, 180
Chandler, Steve, 192
Chaney's Dairy Barn, 92
Chapman, John ("Johnny Appleseed"), 55–56
Charlevoix, Pierre-François-Xavier de, 17, 222
Cherokee, 11, 221–26
Cherokee, North Carolina, 221–26
Cherokee Farmers Market, 221
Cherry, John, 106
chicken-of-the-woods mushroom, 217–18
chilling hours, 190
Chmiel, Chris, 85, 87–88, 91–96, 114, 122–23, 129, 156, 244
Choctaw, 16, 178–79
Civil War, 187
    Paw Paw Militia, 181, 197
    troops, pawpaws eaten by, 20–21, 124–25
Claiborne, Craig, 191
Claypool, Jim, 229–30
cleft grafting, 116–17
Cobb, Vickie Layton, 200
Coleman, W. T., 200
Collins, Major C., 257

color, pawpaw
    pulp (flesh), xiv, 30, 92, 113, 120, 141, 256–58, 260, 262, 264, **1**
    skin, 23, 61, 71, 77, 102, 117, 120, 166, 257, 261
Columbus County Farmers Market, 152, 158
commercial pawpaw industry, 24–33, 90, 120–23, 241–45. *See also* agricultural crop, pawpaws as; breeding, pawpaw; Deep Run Orchard; Kentucky State University Pawpaw Program; marketing pawpaw fruit and products; shipping of pawpaws
    blueberry development compared, 30–31, 33
    Chmiel, Chris, role of (*See* Chmiel, Chris)
    economic benefits of, 41–42, 65, 120, 175
    fig industry compared, 175
    genetic selection for, 29–30, 33, 115–16
    kiwi industry compared, 120
    medical uses, 103–6
    Ocean Spray cooperative and, 67
    Peterson, Neal, role of (*See* Peterson, Neal)
    states with, 150 (*See also specific states*)
contests. *See also* American Genetics Association contest; Ohio Pawpaw Festival
    Kentucky State Fair, 165–66
    Kentucky State University, 100
cookbooks. *See* food writing, pawpaws in
corn, interplanting with pawpaw of, 169
Cornell University, 73–74, 260
Corso, Steve, 127–30, 133–35
Country Gentleman, 25
Coville, Frank Vernon, 31, 33
Cox, Nelson, 54
Cox, Steward, 54
Cozzo, David, 221–23, 225–26
Crabtree, Sheri, 101, 102, 109, 112, 243–44
cultivars, pawpaw, 31–32, 73. *See also* PawPaw Regional Variety Trials
    Allegheny, 67, 75, 78, 88, 255–56
    ARK-21, 256
    for beer, 124

Buckman, 44
Buckman, Benjamin, collected by, 43
for commercial development, 115–16
  (*See also* genetic characteristics,
  pawpaw)
Davis, 236, 256
disappearance of, 42–44
Fairchild, 43, 44
Greenriver Belle, 256
Halvin's Sidewinder, 256
Hope's August, 43
hybrids, 43–44, 258
Kentucky Champion, 99, 257
Ketter, 32, 43–44, 47–60
KSU-Atwood, 101–2, 257
Long John, 43
Lynn's Favorite, 257
Mango, 257–58
Maria's Joy, 258
Martin, 44
Mary Foos Johnson, 258
Mason-WLW, 32
Middletown, 32
Mitchel, 233
naming, 66–67
NC-1 (Campbell's #1), 234, 258
Nyomi's Delicious, 259
Osborne, 43
Overleese (*See* Overleese pawpaw
  cultivar)
PA-Golden (*See* PA-Golden pawpaw
  cultivar)
Peterson, Neal, developed by, 38,
  61, 66–67, 244 (*See also* Peterson
  Pawpaws)
Potomac, 67, 260
profiles and impressions, 255–64
Prolific, 236, 260
Quaker Delight, 113–14, 260–61
Rappahannock (*See* Rappahannock
  pawpaw cultivar)
Rebecca's Gold, 261
SAA-Zimmerman, 264
Shenandoah (*See* Shenandoah pawpaw
  cultivar)
Sue, 262
Summer Delight, 234, 262

Sunflower, 118, 234, 262–63
Susquehanna (*See* Susquehanna
  pawpaw cultivar)
Sweet Alice, 32, 263
Taylor (*See* Taylor pawpaw cultivar)
Taytwo (*See* Taytwo pawpaw cultivar)
Uncle Tom, 26
Wabash, 67, 189, 264
Wells, 100
Zimmerman, 264
Zimmerman, George, propagated and
  collected by, 43, 260, 264
cultivated pawpaws, 1, 7, 31–32, 95, **3**.
  See also commercial pawpaw industry;
  orchards, pawpaw
    at Monticello, 143, 144
    by Native Americans, 10–12, 222
    organic, 7
    sales of, 32
cushaw squash, 205
custard apple family. *See* Annonaceae

Davis, Corwin, 4, 32–33, 42, 46, 236,
  256–57, 260–61, 263
Davis, Donna, 69–72, 74, 78–81, 83, 88
Davis, Jim, 69–81, 83, 88–90, 114, 156,
  244, 259, 261–63, **3**
Davis pawpaw cultivar, 236, 256
DeCampo, Paul, 235, 237
Decatur Farmers Market, 173–75
Decker Deer: The Miracle of Paw Paw Island,
  180
Dedon, Jerry, 2, 188–91, 193, 256, 257
Deep Run Orchard, 69–81, 88–90, 98, 114,
  259, 263, **3**
Delaware, 30, 97, 241
De Soto, Hernando, 11–13
De Soto Chronicles, The, 12
De Voe, Thomas Farrington, 23
Dinnsen, Wynn, 2, 158–61
*Discovery, Settlement and Present State of
  Kentucke, The,* 18
distributors, pawpaw, 70, 79, 235
Do It Yourself Shop, 91
domestication of pawpaw, move toward,
  23–28, 30–31. *See also* commercial
  pawpaw industry

Domestic Manners of the Americans, 188
Downing, Ernest, 32
Drabik, Ken, 88–90, 99, 153, 244
Drechsel, Emanuel, 191
dried pawpaw
    illness caused by, 10
    Native Americans, use by, 10
dropped fruit. *See* fallen fruit, handling of
Drugs and Medicines of North America,
    20, 23
Dupont Circle FreshFarm market, 64–66
dwarf pawpaw *(Asimina parviflora),* 178

Earthy Delights, 70, 79, 92
Eastern Carolina Organics, 158
Eckert, Dorothy, 82
economic benefits, pawpaw, 41–42, 65,
    120, 175
Edible Landscaping, 252
Edwards, Sylvester, 215–16
Eli Lilly Company, 105
Ellen's Homemade Ice Cream, 207,
    208, 241
Elliott, Doug and Yanna, 223–24
Elton, Sarah, 235
emetic, pawpaw as, 89, 105
Encee (NC) apple cultivar, 54
England, Cliff, 115, 168, 256, 259, 262
England's Orchard and Nursery, 251
Epimecis hortaria (tulip-tree beauty
    moth), 168
Ernst, Barb, 134
Ested, Media, 212
Europe, pawpaw interest in, 99, 115, 143,
    236, 244
European settlers, 5–6, 13–20, 52, 110,
    196–97, 216–17
evolution of pawpaw, 4–5
Experiments in Blueberry Culture, 31

Fairchild, David, 32–33, 46
Fairchild Botanical Garden, 63
Fairchild pawpaw cultivar, 43, 44
fallen fruit, handling of, 1, 71, 76, 80,
    95–96, 239
Farming Appalachia, 216
Farmingdale, Illinois, 42–43

farmstands. *See* markets and farmstands,
    pawpaws sold at
fat, in pawpaw, 107
Faulkner, William, 179–80
fencerows, pawpaws located in, 95
fermentation, pawpaw, 111, 124–25, 147.
    See also beer, pawpaw; brandy, pawpaw
Fernwood. *See* Zimmerman, George A.
fertilization, 76, 81, 95, 123, 157
festivals, 97, 241. *See also* North Carolina
    Pawpaw Festival; Ohio Pawpaw Festival
    Hot Dog Festival, 56
    International Biscuit Festival, 241
    Pawpaw Day, 173
    Pumpkins and Pawpaws, 237
fiber, in pawpaw pulp, 107, 196
fibers, use of pawpaw, 11, 172, 223–24, 237
Field Guide to Texas Trees, A, 194
figs, 175
Filson, John, 18
flavor (taste), pawpaw, 10, 12, 18, 19, 50,
    72, 90, 148, 4
    bitter, 74, 88, 122–23, 141
    Buckman farm, fruit from, 43
    contest, factor in, 29–30, 100
    cultivars, trait in, 255–57, 259–63
    Fernwood (Zimmerman estate), fruit
        from, 44
    frozen pulp, 92
    Kentucky State University pawpaws, 102
    Overleese cultivar, 174
    pawpaw beer, 124
    pawpaw ice cream and gelato, 112, 240
    Peterson, Neal, data collected by,
        61–63, 66
    selection for, 10, 46, 61–63
    uncooked pawpaw, preserved in, 193
    variations in, xiv, 2
flesh, pawpaw. *See* pulp, pawpaw
flies, 4, 132, 2
Flint, Timothy, 17–18
Flood: A Romance of Our Time, 179
flooding, pawpaws affected by, 168, 173–74
Florida, 5, 12, 99, 213
flowers, pawpaw, 4, 131–33, 2
folklore, pawpaws associated with, 176–77,
    199–202

food products, pawpaw, 27, 91–93, 101, 111, 199. *See also* beverages, pawpaw; ice cream, pawpaw
food writing, pawpaws in, 191, 206, 224, 241
foragers, pawpaws marketed by, 23, 27, 71, 91, 135
foraging, 39, 80, 171
Forbes Wild Foods, 235
Ford, Tom, 70
forest development, effect of pawpaws on, 127, 130–31, 133–34
Forrest Keeling nursery, 252
fossils, pawpaw seed, 7, 9
Foxfire magazine and book series, ix, 224
Fox Paw Farm, 114, 117–20
fragrance, pawpaw flower, 131–32, 2
fragrance, pawpaw fruit, 12, 19, 50, 193
    caramel, 2, 90
    ripeness indicated by, 75, 147, 158–59, 166
Friedman, Carol, 256
Fulbright, Dennis, 238
Fullsteam Brewery, 160
fungal problems, pawpaw tree, 26, 76, 77, 174. *See also Phyllosticta*

Gardner, Lorraine, 63
Geauga County Park District pawpaw study, 127, 130–31, 133–34
gelato, paw paw, 238–40, 241, 7
genetic characteristics, pawpaw, 29–30, 33, 66, 89, 115–16, 159. *See also* American Genetics Association contest; breeding, pawpaw
    diversity of, 102, 152–53
    Kentucky State University contest, 100
    seediness, controlling, 61
    USDA germplasm repository (*See* Kentucky State University)
Georgia, 5, 11, 12, 96–97, 179, 257
germination, pawpaw seeds, 134–35
Germplasm Repository, United States Department of Agriculture National Clonal. *See* Kentucky State University
Gibbons, Euell, 2, 39–40
Gibson, Milo, 33, 258, 262

Gilbert, Jim, 62–63, 66
Gill, Stanton, 71–72, 81
ginseng, 171
Glaser, Dick, 33, 113–14, 260
global market for pawpaws, 99, 115, 236
goats, 94–95
Good Foods Co-op, 111
Goodrich, Katherine, 132
Gordon, John, 259–60, 264
Goss, Benjamin, 27
Gotenbusch, Gary, 112
grafted pawpaw trees
    Brooks, Dale, nursery of, 173
    Chmiel, Chris, grown by, 95
    Corso, Steve, grown by, 128
    Davis, Corwin, grown by, 236
    Dedon, Jerry, grown by, 189
    Grimo Nut Nursery, 235
    Kentucky State University, 102, 111
    neglect, effect of, 45
    Nolin River Nut Tree Nursery, 167–69
    Peterson, Neal, grown by, 38, 62, 64, 111
    Powell, Ron, grown by, 114, 116
    Sillers, Ilze, grown by, 111
grafting methods, 113–14, 116–17, 5
Graham, Sarah, 19
grapes
    pawpaw northern range and, 237
    possum, 195–96
    Scuppernong, 151–52
graviola *(Annona muricata)*, 105–7, 121
Gray, Clarence "Catfish," 49
Green City Market, 233–34
Greenriver Belle pawpaw cultivar, 256
Grimo, Linda, 235
Grimo Nut Nursery, 235, 270
ground ivy, 95–96
growing conditions, 3
guanabana (Annona muricata), 105–7, 121

habitat restoration, 97, 241
Hale, George, 95
Hallmark, Anna, 174–75
Halvin, Tyler and Danae, 256
Halvin's Sidewinder pawpaw cultivar, 256
Hamilton, Robert, 99
Harmon, Roy Lee, 213

Harold, Zack, 208
Harpers Ferry, West Virginia, 37–38
Harrison, Benjamin, 228
Hartfield, Paul, 186–88
harvesting, 71, 75–81. *See also* fallen fruit, handling of
    fragility of fruit, 1, 7
    Kentucky, timing in, 126
    method of, 1, 75–76
    ripe fruit, identifying, 71, 75
    storage of harvested fruit (*See* storage, harvested pawpaws)
    time of harvest, regional differences in (*See* ripening of fruit)
Hatfield and McCoy feud, 216
Havighurst, Walter, 4
hay, 239
head lice control, 104, 106
heirloom pawpaws, grafting of, 114
hemp, 243
Henderson, Ella, 188
herbal remedies. *See* medicinal uses, pawpaw and other Annonaceae plants
Herbal Sage Tea Company, 91
herbicide sprays, 50, 52, 215
Heritage Foods, 70, 79
Hershey, John W., 32
Hickman, Jim, 233
Hidden Springs Nursery, 253
high tunnel, 234
Hirschinger, C., 54
history of pawpaws, American, 5–7, 9–21
    Civil War (*See* Civil War)
    De Soto expedition, 11–13
    domestication, move toward, 23–28
    European settlers (*See* European settlers)
    Lewis and Clark expedition, 6, 139–42
    at Monticello, 143–45
    Native Americans (*See* Native Americans)
    near Mount Vernon, 145–46
    prehistoric period, 7, 9
    slaves, use by, 19–20, 146, 194
Hoertt, Greg, 123–25
Holden Arboretum, 127–30, 133–34
home consumption, pawpaws, 175

Hope's August pawpaw cultivar, 43
Hughes, Bill, 205–7
Hummer, Kim, 100
hunting, pawpaw and, 19, 198
hybrid varieties, 43–44, 244

ice cream, pawpaw, 27, 92, 135, 173
    Goss, Benjamin, credited with invention of, 27
    Kentucky State University, served at, 112
    recipe for, 249
    restaurants, sold by, 71, 207, 208, 238–41, 7
Illinois, 185, 229, 231–34, 236
    American Genetics Association contest, participation in, 30
    Buckman, Benjamin, Farmingdale estate, 26, 42–43
    Kruszewski, Oriana, orchard, 233–34
    Paw Paw, town of, 6, 212, 231–32
    pawpaws, demand for, 72, 234
Illinois (Native Americans), 16, 191
illness, pawpaw as cause of, 10, 89, 105, 198–99
Indiana, 23, 65, 198, 227–31, 236, 260, 262, 6. *See also* Lehman, Jerry; Little, James A.
    American Genetics Association contest, participation in, 30
    Hale, George, farm, 96
    history of pawpaws in, 23, 139, 228–29
    Johnny Appleseed, nurseries planted by, 55
    Miami county, 228
    Paw Paw, town of, 6
    Pawpaw Regional Variety Trials, plantings for, 118
    plant material collected from, 43, 45, 102, 126, 259
Indiana Fruit and Nut Growers Association, 229–30
Indiana Horticultural Society, 25, 26
Ingles, Mary, 216–17
insect pests, 26, 77, 168–69, 190. *See also* zebra swallowtail butterfly (*Protographium marcellus*)
insect repellent, pawpaw plant chemical as, 56, 103–4, 168

Integration Acres Farm, 91–96, 114, 122–23
intercropping, 94–95, 169
International Biscuit Festival, 241
International Pawpaw Conference, 99, 111–12, 116
intestinal parasite removal, pawpaw product for, 104
invasive plants, 27, 134, 215
Iowa, 118, 241, 256
Iowa State University, 122
Iroquois, 10, 222
irrigation, 76, 135, 157

Jackie O's Pub & Brewery, 91, 92
Jacobs, Homer, 32, 263
Jamestown settlement (Virginia), 13–14
Japan, 244
jasmine (jasminer), as name for pawpaw, 191–92
Jefferson, Thomas, 6, 143–45
"Johnny Appleseed" (Chapman, John), 55–56
Johnson, Charles, 189–90, 256
Johnson, Mary Foos, 258
Joliet, Louis, 16
Jones, James G., 124–25
Jones, Loyal, 205
Jones, Raymond, 63, 134, 212, 232
Jones, Volney, 172
Jordan, Ora, 176
Journal of Heredity, 29, 40–42, 100, 125, 200, 222
Journal of Materia Medica, 105

Kalm, Pehr, 17
Kansas, 6, 10, 23, 25–26, 30, 141, 258, 262
Kansas Territory drought, pawpaw as food source during, 25
Kaplan, J. Kim, 31
Kentucky, 2, 51, 59, 150, 211–12, 236, 251, 4
    American Genetics Association contest, participation in, 30
    Appalachian region, 205–7, 209, 211–13
    folklore, 176
    Hardin County, 167–69
    Hart County, 256
    history of pawpaws in, 17–19, 21, 23, 110, 139, 194, 213, 216, 223
    Letcher County, 206
    Madison County, 257
    Mammoth Cave National Park, 167, 170–72
    nurseries located in, 251
    Paw Paw, town of, 6, 211–12
    Pawpaw Regional Variety Trials, plantings for, 118
    Pike County, 205–7
    price of pawpaw fruit in, 73
    ripening of fruit, timing of, 126, 234, 256–59, 262–63
    tobacco crop, pawpaw as replacement for, 100, 109–11, 242–43
    USDA germplasm repository, seeds collected for, 100, 102, 166
    Warren, Robert Penn, birthplace of, 179
    Woodford County, 109–11
Kentucky Champion pawpaw cultivar, 99, 257
Kentucky Nut Growers Association, 100
Kentucky State Fair, 100, 165–67
Kentucky State University Pawpaw Program, 64, 99–106, 109–12, 118, 126, 166, 239, 243–44, 255–64
    establishment of, 63, 100
    patch spread, study of, 131
    seed-sowing method, 134
    USDA Germplasm Repository, 63, 100–102, 111–12, 152
Ketter, Estella M. (Mrs. Frank), 30, 47, 53–54
Ketter, Frank, 53
Ketter pawpaw cultivar, 32, 43–44, 47–60
kiwi, 120
Kretzmann, Stevik, 63, 66
Kruszewski, Oriana, 72, 233–34
KSU-Atwood pawpaw cultivar, 101–2, 257

Lawson, John, 15, 20, 151
Layne, Desmond, 100, 109, 110, 111, 118, 131
Lee, Robert E., 20–21

Lehman, Jerry, 99, 229–31, 234, 238, 241, 244, 258, **6**
Lewis, Edna, 191
Lewis and Clark expedition, 6, 139–42
literature, pawpaw mentioned in, 179–80, 183–84, 192
Little, James A., 25–28, 42, 193, 227
local food, pawpaw as, 97–98
Long John pawpaw cultivar, 43
Louisiana, 11, 16, 21, 30, 102, 118, 168, 188–96, 261
Louisiana State University, 188–90, 256
Lowery, Charles, 154
Lynn's Favorite pawpaw cultivar, 257

Macbride & Gill Falcon Ridge Farm, 71–72
Mackintosh, Bill and Lori, 46, 73–74
Mackintosh Farms, 73
Mammoth Cave National Park, 167, 170–72
Mandujano, Mario, 260, 261
mango, 1, 7, 32, 97, 233
mango-flavored pawpaw, xiv, 2, 182, 193
Mango pawpaw cultivar, 257–58
Maria's Joy pawpaw cultivar, 258
Market Assistant, The, 23
marketers, pawpaw fruit, 70, 79, 235
marketing pawpaw fruit and products, 91–93, 114, 116, 158, 237–40. *See also* contests; festivals; markets and farmstands, pawpaws sold at; restaurants, pawpaw sales to
markets and farmstands, pawpaws sold at, 58–59, 128, 152, 158, 173–75, 205–7, 221, 233–35, 241. *See also* commercial pawpaw industry
    Deep Run Orchard, pawpaws from, 71–74
    demand for pawpaws at, 65–66, 72, 120, 234, 245
    Dupont Circle FreshFarm market, 64–66
    grocery store sales, 109, 111, 120, 158, 232
    wild pawpaws, sales of, 23, 51–52, 54, 72, 81–83, 244–45
Martin, S. C., 125

Martin pawpaw cultivar, 44
Mary Foos Johnson pawpaw cultivar, 258
Maryland, 19, 61–63, 97, 150, 241. *See also* Deep Run Orchard; University of Maryland
    American Genetics Association contest, participation in, 30
    Fairchild, David, home, 32, 46
    Pawpaw Regional Variety Trials, plantings for, 118
    plant material collected from, 45, 46, 257
Mason-WLW pawpaw cultivar, 32
Maximilian, Prince, 237
May, Bobby, 211–12
mayapple, 129
maypop *(Passiflora incarnata),* 170
McBride, John Randolph, 21
McFarland, J. Horace, 24–25
McLaughlin, Jerry, 103–6
McMurry, Charles Alexander, 181
Meadowcroft Rockshelter, 7
medicinal uses, pawpaw and other Annonaceae plants, 11, 20, 49, 103–6, 192
    cancer-fighting compounds, 7, 103–6, 171, 223
    head lice control, 104, 106
    intestinal parasites, removal of, 104
    Korean interest in, 115
    sexually transmitted diseases, 176–77
    teething pain, 176
Michaux, François André, 124
Michigan, 79, 103, 235–40, 261, 263. *See also* Davis, Corwin
    American Genetics Association contest, participation in, 30
    nurseries located in, 252, 253
    Paw Paw, town of, 6, 212, 233, 236–37
    Pawpaw Regional Variety Trials, plantings for, 118
    ripening of fruit, timing of, 126, 256–60, 262
Michigan State University, 238–39
Middletown pawpaw cultivar, 32
Midwest Food and Wine Show, 208
minerals, in pawpaw, 107
Miranda, Eve, 223
Mississippi, 30, 178–88, 190, **6**

Mississippi River
canoe trip, 181–87, **6**
explorations of, 11, 16–17, 190–91
flooding, 168
Missouri, 90, 97, 139–42, 241, 252–53
American Genetics Association contest,
participation in, 30
history of pawpaws in, 23
Ozark County, 90
Paw Paw Militia, 181
Mitchel pawpaw cultivar, 233
monoculture, avoiding pawpaw, 152–53
Monticello, 143–45
Morgan, Violet, 50–51
Morgantown Farmers Market, 81
Morris, Derek, 117, 150, 156, 256–63
*Mountain Country Cooking: A Gathering of
the Best Recipes from the Smokies to the Blue
Ridge,* 206
Mount Vernon, 145–46
mulches, 96, 239
Munich, Don, 262
Myers, Johnnie Sue, 224

name derivation, pawpaw. *See* pawpaw
*Narratives of the Career of Hernando de Soto
in the Conquest of Florida,* 12
Nash Nurseries, 252
Natchez Trace, 178, 188
Natchitoches, Louisiana, 11, 195
National Public Radio (NPR), 72
Native Americans, 5, 9–16, 18–19, 41,
216–17, 221–26
Alabama, 12
Arkansas, 196
Georgia, 11, 12, 179
Illinois, 232
Indiana, 229
Kansas, 10, 25, 141
Kentucky, 18–19, 170–72
Louisiana, 11, 16, 191, 195
Mississippi, 178–79
Missouri, 196
North Carolina, 15–16, 151,
155–56, 162
Ohio, 18, 86–87, 123–24

pawpaw, names for, 11, 16, 179, 191,
223, 232, **7**
pawpaw trees cultivated by, 10
prehistoric period, 7, 9, 171–72,
196, 222
South Carolina, 15–16
Virginia, 13–14
native plant, pawpaw as, 26, 29, 94
native range, pawpaw, xv, 194, 234, 236
Naturalized Habitat Network of Essex
County and Windsor, 234
Natural Sciences and Engineering Research
Council of Canada, 115
Nature's Sunshine, 104, 171
NC-1 (Campbell's #1) pawpaw cultivar,
234, 258
Nebraska, 10, 118
Newsome, Denver, 205–7
New Voyage to Carolina, A, 15–16, 151
New York, 10, 45, 79, 118, 222, 259, 264
*New York Farmer and Horticultural
Repository,* 24
niacin, 10, 107
niche, pawpaw, 3, 7, 158, 207, 242–43
nitrogen, 76
Nolin River Nut Tree Nursery, 167–68,
251, 256
Norris, Sam, 230
North American Fruit Explorers, 42,
233, 255
North American Pawpaw Growers
Association, 114, 232–33, 255
North Carolina, 15–16, 97, 117, 149–63,
221–26, 257–58, 261
American Genetics Association contest,
participation in, 30
Pawpaw Regional Variety Trials,
plantings for, 118
North Carolina Pawpaw Festival, 149–50,
156, 160–61, 241
Northern Nut Growers Association, 31, 42,
43, 100, 255, 260
Northwest Florida Environmental
Conservancy, 213
Northwoods Nursery, 111
nurseries, apple tree, 55

nurseries, pawpaw tree, 32, 62, 97, 99, 115, 189, 255
  Brooks, Dale, of, 172–74
  Dinnsen, Wynn, of, 159
  Grimo Nut Nursery, 235
  listing of, 172, 251–53
  Nolin River Nut Tree Nursery, 167–68, 251, 256
  Northwoods Nursery, 111
  Ohio Pawpaw Festival, sales at, 86
  Peterson PawPaws sold through, 38, 66, 81
  seeds, planting, 134
  in South Korea, 115
nutrients, pawpaw, 7, 10, 106–7
Nyomi's Delicious pawpaw cultivar, 259

oak root fungus, 174
Obama, Michelle, 243
Ocean Spray cooperative, 67
Ohio, 47–55, 59–60, 65, 102, 150, 222, 236, 260–63. *See also* Chmiel, Chris; Ohio Pawpaw Festival; Ohio Pawpaw Growers Association; Powell, Ron
  Adams County, 125
  American Genetics Association contest, participation in, 30, 125 (*See also* Ketter pawpaw cultivar)
  Athens County, 60, 85, 94, 101, 122
  Corso, Steven, orchard, 128–29, 135
  Gallia County, 52
  Geauga County, 127–31, 133–35
  history of pawpaws in, 18, 23, 32, 125, 180, 217, 222
  Holden Arboretum, 127–30, 133–34
  Lawrence County, 30, 47–56, 59–60
  papaya as official native fruit, 243
  Pawpaw Regional Variety Trials, plantings for, 118
  plant material collected from, 43
  tobacco crop, pawpaw as replacement for, 120
Ohio Pawpaw Festival, 83, 85–98, 117, 156, 244
  Best Pawpaw contest winners, 87, 114, 257, 259, 260, 263

  Largest Pawpaw contest winners, 230, 240, 241, 258
Ohio Pawpaw Growers Association, 86, 113–19, 244, 5
Ohio State University, 119–20, 123
Oikos nursery, 253
Oklahoma, 10, 212, 225
O'Malley, Patrick, 122
Omphalocera munroei (pawpaw webworm), 77, 168–69
One Green World nursery, 62, 253
Ontario, Canada, 10, 99, 102, 222, 234, 252, 258
orchards, pawpaw, 53–54, 242. *See also* Deep Run Orchard
  budwood, collection of, 81, 116, 168
  chilling hours for, 190
  fertilization, 76, 81, 95, 123, 157
  goats in, 94–95
  high tunnel, use of, 234
  Illinois, 109–11, 233–34
  Indiana, 25–26, 227
  irrigation, 76, 135, 157
  Kentucky State University, 100–102, 111–12, 118
  Little, James, developed by, 25–26, 227
  Maryland, 46, 61–64
  Michigan, 238–40
  mulch, walnut shells as, 96
  North Carolina, 153–60
  nutrient deficiencies, 76
  Ohio, 91–96, 114, 117–20, 122–23, 128, 134–35
  Peterson, Neal, developed by, 46, 61–64
  pollination, 81
  pruning, 75, 81
  ripening of fruit in, 71, 75–77
  shade for, 189
  thinning of fruit, 78
  walnut trees, intercropping of, 95
  West Virginia, 207
  wild pawpaw patches, cultivation of, 95
  windbreaks for, 189
Oregon, 118, 253, 258
organic cultivation of pawpaws, 7, 56, 157, 168, 244–45
Organic Gardening, 100

ornamental plant, pawpaw as, 24–25
Orr, Nate, 88–90, 244
Osborne pawpaw cultivar, 43
Ottum, Linda, 197–98
Overleese pawpaw cultivar, 116, 118, 126, 174, 234, 259
Ozark Folklore and Magic, 199–200
Ozark Pioneers, 200
Ozarks, 176, 196–202, 241

PA-Golden pawpaw cultivar, 75, 118, 166, 259–60
Paine, Albert Bigelow, 184
Panicci, Doris, 198–99
Panther Wildlife Management Area, 212
papaw dice game, 20
papaya *(Carica papaya),* 14–15, 238, 243
Parker, Milton, 149, 152–53, 154, 156–58, 160
Parkinson's disease, atypical, 107
patches, pawpaw
   clonal, 131, 145, 173
   spread of, 130–31
   transplanting pawpaws, success of, 169
Pauley, Finley, 58–59
pawpaw
   derivation of name, 14–17, 20
   other names for, 1, 16–17, 191–92 (*See also* "banana" names for pawpaw; Native Americans)
pawpaw, places named for, 6, 11, 179, 186–87, 194–95, 214, 236–37. *See also* Paw Paw, towns named
Paw Paw, towns named, 6, 211–12, 214, 228, 231–33, 236–37, **4–5, 7**
Pawpaw (Asimina triloba), *The, A Native Fruit of Great Excellence,* 25
Paw Paw Cell-Reg, 104, 171
pawpaw cultivars. *See* cultivars, pawpaw
pawpaw detractors, 193, 208
Pawpaw Extravaganza Dinner, 92
Paw Paw Formation, 194–95
PawPaw Foundation, 46, 63, 106, 118, 208
Paw-paw French, 197
Paw Paw Gelato, 238–41
Pawpaw Grower's Guide for Ontario, The, 235
Paw Paw Island, Mississippi, 186–88

Paw Paw Militia, 181, 197
Paw Paw Para-Cleanse, 104
PawPaw Regional Variety Trials, 64, 70, 118, 189–90, 256
Pawpawsaurus, 195
pawpaw sphinx *(Dolba hyloeus),* 168
pawpaw thickets, shelter in, 180–81
Pawpaw Tracker, The, 63, 212, 232
Pawpaw Tree Incident, 216
pawpaw trees. *See* trees, pawpaw
pawpaw webworm *(Omphalocera munroei),* 77, 168–69
Pennsylvania, 32, 222, 241
   American Genetics Association contest, participation in, 30
   author, pawpaws grown by, 126, 163
   history of pawpaws in, 17, 23
   Lancaster County, 131
   Red Barn Farm, 81–83
   Zimmerman, George A., estate, 32–33, 42–46, 260
Peoples, Mark "River," 182–86, **6**
Percy, George, 14
perishibility, pawpaw, 1, 7, 26, 29–30, 147. *See also* shipping of pawpaws
permaculture, 94–96, 215
Perry, Daniel, 146–47
Perry, Robert, 112
persimmons, breeding of, 229–30
pests, pawpaw, 26, 77, 157, 168–69, 190. *See also* animals; fungal problems, pawpaw tree; *Phyllosticta; zebra swallowtail butterfly (Protographium marcellus)*
Peterson, Neal, 37–46, 73, 111, 233, 242, 244–45, 263, **2.** *See also* PawPaw Foundation; Pawpaw Regional Variety Trials; Peterson Pawpaws
   Davis, Jim, and, 70, 79
   International Pawpaw Conference and, 99, 101
   Kentucky State University, collaboration with, 109
   nurseries, sales of budwood to, 81
   orchards developed by, 46, 61–64
   pawpaw nutrition study, 106–7
   pawpaws, breeding of, 37–46, 61–64, 66, 244

on pawpaws as banana replacement, 97
on pawpaw toxicity, 108
tissue culture propagation project, role
in, 116
Peterson Pawpaws, 67, 78, 88–90, 98, 102,
118, 157, 260–64
nurseries, sold through, 38, 66, 81
at Ohio Pawpaw Festival, 88
Pfister, Fred, 196–97
Phyllosticta, 77, 256, 257, 259, 260, 262
phytochemicals, in pawpaw, 107
"Pickin' Up Pawpaws," 1, 57, 161, 186, 201,
219, 229
pie, pawpaw, 27, 57, 218
Pike County Farmers Market, 205–7
Pina Colada pawpaw, 102
Piney Woods, 194
Pollan, Michael, 55
pollination, 3–4, 38, 81, 123, 132, 2
polyphenolic compounds, in pawpaw skin
and subdural layer, 74
Pomper, Kirk, 67, 99, 100–103, 108–9, 111,
122, 134, 150, 243
pones, pawpaw, 224
Popenoe, John, 63
*Popular Beliefs and Practices from
Alabama,* 176
possum grapes, 195–96
Potomac pawpaw cultivar, 67, 260
Powell, Ron, 101, 113–20, 122, 125–26,
169, 234, 244, 256–64, 5
Powell, Terry, 118–19, 122
Powhatans, 13–14
processing methods, pawpaw, 73–74,
92–93, 101, 121–23, 231, 238–39
procyanidins, 107
Project Pawpaw, 234–35
Prolific pawpaw cultivar, 236, 260
propagation, pawpaw trees, 116, 168.
See also grafted pawpaw trees; grafting
methods
protein, in pawpaw, 107
Protographium marcellus (zebra swallowtail
butterfly). *See* zebra swallowtail butterfly
(*Protographium marcellus*)
Prudhomme, Paul, 191
pruning, pawpaw trees, 75, 81

pudding, pawpaw, 243
pulp, pawpaw. *See also* seed-to-pulp ratio,
pawpaw fruit
color of (*See* color, pawpaw)
fiber in, 107, 196
frozen, 92–93, 123
texture (*See* texture, pawpaw)
Pumpkins and Pawpaws event, 237

Quad City Food Forest, 241
Quaker Delight pawpaw cultivar, 113–14,
260–61
Quapaw Canoe Company, 181–87, 6

Ralston, Arla, 208
Ramey, Marta, 54
ramps (*Allium triccocum*), 128, 134,
162–63, 171, 219
Randolph, Vance, 176, 199–202
Rappahannock pawpaw cultivar, 61, 67,
117, 189, 261
rassimina, 16, 191
Rawls, Wilson, 180
Rebecca's Gold pawpaw cultivar, 261
recipes, pawpaw, 249. *See also* food writing,
pawpaws in
Red Barn Farm, 81–83
Regional Variety Trials. *See* PawPaw
Regional Variety Trials
Reid, Thomas Mayne, 192
Remsbury, Geo., 26
restaurants, pawpaw sales to, 71, 111,
235, 241
Revitalization of Traditional Cherokee
Artisan Resources, 221–22
Rhode Island, 97, 237, 241
Riley, J. M., 261
Riley, James Whitcomb, 6
ripening of fruit, 75–77, 239–40, 8
after harvest of, 2
fragrance and (*See* fragrance, pawpaw
fruit)
regional differences in, 2, 126, 234,
256–63
roadside stands. *See* markets and
farmstands, pawpaws sold at
Rocky Point Farm, 237

Rollins, Bill, 185
Ruskey, John "Driftwood," 182, 185, 187

SAA-Zimmerman pawpaw cultivar, 264
St. Denis, Louis Juchereau de, 195
St. Louis, Missouri, 139–42
Salstrom, Paul, 210, 216
Sandburg, Carl, 232–33
Sanderson, Lesley, 153–56, 162
Sauceman, Fred, 205
scent, pawpaw. *See* fragrance, pawpaw
Schoepf, Johan David, 105
Schwartz, Harry, 46
Scuppernong grapes, 151–52
seed collection, 26, 46, 80, 100, 102, 128, 159, 166, 206
seedling depository, Blandy Experimental Farm, 45
seedlings, pawpaw tree, 32, 46, 61, 86, 128, 235. *See also* grafting methods
    corn interplanted with, 169
    first fruit, growth period to, 159
    genetically distinct, in patches, 131
    Ohio Pawpaw Growers Association, offered by, 117
    rootstock recommendations, 109
    shade for, 169, 189
    thinning, 169
seeds
    dispersal of, 9, 108, 131
    fossils of, 7, 196
    removing, 122–23 (*See also* processing methods, pawpaw)
    selling, 115, 120
    sowing and germination, 134–35
seed-to-pulp ratio, pawpaw fruit, 29, 61, 102, 120, 121
sexually transmitted diseases, pawpaw as remedy for, 176–77
shade, orchard, 169, 189, 227
Shadow Nursery, 253
Shenandoah pawpaw cultivar, 61, 66–67, 75, 78, 81, 88, 234, 261–62
shipping of pawpaws, 120
    breeding pawpaws for, 29–30
    by commercial orchard, 70, 78–79
Short, Charles Wilkins, 110

Sillers, Ilze, 109–11
Simcox, Joseph, 99
Simmons, Joseph, 106
size, pawpaw fruit, 255–64, **1**
    contest winners, 100, 166, 230, 240, 241, 258
    Deep Run Orchard, 76–78
    Kentucky State University, fruits bred by, 100, 102, 126
    Peterson, Neal, data collected by, 61
    wild fruit, 1
Slate, George L., 260, 264
slaves, pawpaw use by, 19–20, 146, 194
Slow Food Canada, 235
Slow Food USA, 79, 241
slugs, 168
Smith, J. Russell, 215–16
Smith, John, 15–16
Snowville Creamery, 92
soda, pawpaw, 91
Sohn, Mark F., 206
soil, 3, 76, 157
songs, pawpaw in, 201–2. *See also* "Pickin' Up Pawpaws"
Songs of the Rivers of America, 229
soursop (*Annona muricata*), 105–7, 121
South Carolina, 15–16, 20, 118
South Korea, 115
South Mountain Creamery, 71
Spender, Sean, 99
spicebush, 129, 226
Squaw Winter: A Love Story Based on the Indian Folklore of Highland County, 50–51
Stadler, Marc, 116–17
Stalking the Wild Asparagus, 39–40
Stark Bros. nursery, 252–53
State Arboretum of Virginia. *See* Blandy Experimental Farm
Stewart, Alex, 176–77
Stănică, Florin, 116
storage, harvested pawpaws, 78–81, 92–93, 102, 120, 123
Strachey, William, 14
Stuart, Jesse, 6, 198
suckers, 3, 44, 47, 116, 169, 172, 185
    of seedlings, 45
    suckering, study of, 131

Sudduth, William, 18
Sue pawpaw cultivar, 262
Suleimenov, Zhanibek, 63
Summer Delight pawpaw cultivar, 234, 262
Sunflower pawpaw cultivar, 118, 234, 262–63
Susquehanna pawpaw cultivar, 61, 67, 75, 78, 88, 263
Sutton, West Virginia, 218–20
Swartz, L., 207
Sweet Alice pawpaw cultivar, 32, 263

taste, pawpaw. *See* flavor (taste), pawpaw
Taste of Kentucky, A, 206
Taylor pawpaw cultivar, 43, 44, 236, 263.
Taytwo pawpaw cultivar, 77, 189, 236, 263
teething pain, pawpaw as remedy for, 176
Tennessee, 30, 45, 176–77, 236, 241, 253
Texas, 30, 194–95
texture, pawpaw, 14, 19, 120–21, 141, 148, 193
    cultivars, trait in, 113, 256, 259–64
    custard-like, xiv
    Peterson, Neal, data collected by, 61
thinning, pawpaw trees, 169
Thirsty Dog Brewing Co., 91
Thwaites, Reuben Gold, 129–30
tissue culture, 116
tobacco, 100, 109–11, 120, 242–43
Tom Sawyer, 184
Topeka Daily Capital, 193
toxicity, pawpaw, 107–9
transplanting, pawpaw trees, 169
Tree Crops: A Permanent Agriculture, 215–16
trees, pawpaw. *See also* seedlings, pawpaw tree
    bare-root, 157, 189
    bark fibers, use of (*See* fibers, use of pawpaw)
    global market for, 115
    hardiness of, 234
    pruning, 75, 81
    sales of, 86, 118 (*See also* nurseries, pawpaw tree)
    thickets, shelter in, 180–81
    thinning, 169
    transplanting, 169

twigs, medical use of, 104–5, 171
Trollope, Frances Milton, 188
tropical tree, pawpaw as, ix, xiii, xiv, 43, 97, 117, 129–30
    Africa, Annonaceae species native to, 19
    evolution of pawpaw and, 5
    explorers and, 12, 14
tulip-tree beauty moth *(Epimecis hortaria),* 168
Twain, Mark, 183–84
Twain's Feast: Searching for America's Lost Foods in the Footsteps of Samuel Clemens, 184
twigs, medical use of, 104–5, 171
Twitty, Michael W., 19
Tyree, Gary and Terrie, 156–58

Uncle Tom pawpaw cultivar, 26
understory, 3, 44–45, 194, 213
United States Department of Agriculture (USDA)
    National Clonal Germplasm Repository (*See* Kentucky State University)
    Poplarville, Mississippi, research plot, 190
United States Food and Drug Administration (FDA), 109
University of British Columbia, 115
University of Kentucky, 118
University of Louisville, 108
University of Maryland
    Western Maryland Research & Education Center, 62
    Wye Research and Education Center orchard, 46, 61–64

varieties, pawpaw. *See* cultivars, pawpaw
Vest, Jay, 161–62
Vicennes culture, 229
Virginia, 5, 42, 180, 211–12, 216–17, 244–45, 252. *See also* Blandy Experimental Farm
    history of pawpaws in, 13–14, 21, 143–48, 181, 191
    Mackintosh Farms, 46, 73–74
    Rappahannock County, 72
vitamin C, 106

Wabash pawpaw cultivar, 67, 189, 264
Walker, Woody, 99, 257
walnut, black, 96
Ward, W. B., 33, 126, 259
Warner, Torrie, 235
Warren, Robert Penn, 179
Washington, George, 6, 145–46
Washington Botanical Society, 97
Washington Post, 63, 65
"Way Down Yonder in the Paw Paw Patch."
  See "Pickin' Up Pawpaws"
Weasel Boy Brewing Company, 91
Wells pawpaw cultivar, 100
West Virginia, 3–4, 37–38, 41, 49, 55, 119,
  150–51, 162, 180, 212–16, 236, 243. *See
  also* Appalachia
    American Genetics Association contest,
      participation in, 30
    Braxton County, 218–20
    Charleston, 53, 207–8
    history of pawpaws in, 181
    Huntington, 56–60
    Paw Paw, town of, 6, 73, 5
    Pendleton County, 42, 63–64
    plant material collected from, 32, 43,
      102, 263
    Webster County, 41
West Virginia Public Radio, 208
West Virginia University Kerneysville Tree
  Fruit Research and Education Center, 46
Where the Red Fern Grows, 180
whip-and-tongue grafting, 113, 5
White, Elizabeth, 31
White, Orland, 44, 45
Whitman, Walt, 6, 179–80
wild custard apple *(Annona senegalensis),*
  19–20
wild edibles, 39–40, 184, 185, 191, 194,
  221. *See also* ramps *(Allium triccocum);*
  wild pawpaws
    blueberries, 31
    Native Americans and early settlers,
      eaten by, 12–20, 155, 229

wild pawpaws, 1, 89–91, 194, 227–28, 242, 3
  contests to collect genes of, 100 (*See
    also* American Genetics Association
    contest)
  crops from, 54
  cultivars selected from wild, 126,
    256–59, 262, 263
  cultivation of, 95
  decline in, 27–28, 50, 52, 134, 215
  genetic diversity of, 102
  growing conditions, 3
  limited fruit produced by, 3
  markets, sold at (*See* markets and
    farmstands, pawpaws sold at)
  Michigan, 236–37
  Ontario, 235
  pest resistance, 77, 94–95
  propagation methods, 3–4
Wildside Winery, 111
Williams, Jeanne and Llew, 81–83
Williams, Mary and Clyde, 49–50
windbreaks, 189
wines, pawpaw, 71, 111
Wisconsin State Historical Society, 30, 54
Witthoft, John, 223
Wolfe, Jerry, 221
wood, pawpaw
  barbecue fire using, 192–93
  as building material, 200
Wren, Aileen, 207

Yahalom, Jon, 150, 157, 160, 206, 4

zebra swallowtail butterfly *(Protographium
  marcellus),* 4, 168, 3
Zeman, Alice, 232
Zimmerman, George A., 5, 32–33, 43–46,
  260, 264
Zimmerman pawpaw cultivar, 264
Zingerman's Creamery, 237–40, 241, 7
Zuccherelli, Giuseppe, 116

ABOUT THE AUTHOR

JONATHAN YAHALOM

Andrew Moore grew up in Lake Wales, Florida, just south of the pawpaw's native range. A writer and gardener, he now lives in Pittsburgh, Pennsylvania. His stories have been published in the *Pittsburgh Post-Gazette*, *The Daily Yonder*, and the *Biscayne Times*. *Pawpaw* is his first book.

∽✲⌒

ABOUT THE FOREWORD AUTHOR

Michael W. Twitty is a dynamic culinary historian, historic interpreter, and food writer based in the Washington, DC, area and is interested in discovering and bringing to life the foods of his ancestors — enslaved African Americans in colonial and antebellum America. He blogs at Afroculinaria.com.

the politics and practice of sustainable living

CHELSEA GREEN PUBLISHING

Chelsea Green Publishing sees books as tools for effecting cultural change and seeks to empower citizens to participate in reclaiming our global commons and become its impassioned stewards. If you enjoyed *Pawpaw*, please consider these other great books related to food and culture.

CHEDDAR
A Journey to the Heart of America's Most Iconic Cheese
GORDON EDGAR
9781603585651
Hardcover • $25.00

TASTE, MEMORY
Forgotten Foods, Lost Flavors, and Why They Matter
DAVID BUCHANAN
9781603584401
Paperback • $17.95

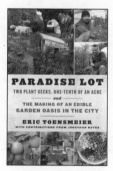

PARADISE LOT
Two Plant Geeks, One-Tenth of an Acre, and the Making of an Edible Garden Oasis in the City
ERIC TOENSMEIER with contributions from JONATHAN BATES
9781603583992
Paperback • $19.95

THE NEW BREAD BASKET
How the New Crop of Grain Growers, Plant Breeders, Millers, Maltsters, Bakers, Brewers, and Local Food Activists Are Redefining Our Daily Loaf
AMY HALLORAN
9781603585675
Paperback • $17.95

CHELSEA GREEN PUBLISHING
the politics and practice of sustainable living

For more information or to request a catalog, visit **www.chelseagreen.com** or call **(800) 639-4099**.

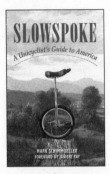
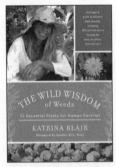
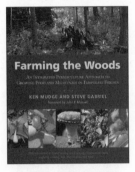

5-5-16